Middle Eastern and North African Societies in the Interwar Period

Social, Economic and Political Studies of the Middle East and Asia

FOUNDING EDITOR: C.A.O. VAN NIEUWENHUIJZE

Editor

Dale F. Eickelman

Advisory Board

Fariba Adelkhah (*SciencesPo/CERI, Paris*)
Ruth Mandel (*University College London*)
Roger Owen (*Harvard University*)
Armando Salvatore (*McGill University*)

VOLUME 120

The titles published in this series are listed at *brill.com/seps*

Middle Eastern and North African Societies in the Interwar Period

Edited by

Ebru Boyar
Kate Fleet

BRILL

LEIDEN | BOSTON

Cover illustration: Fıskiyeli Havuz ve Uybadin Köşkü (Fountain and the Uybadin Köşk), 1927, from Koç Üniversitesi – VEKAM Arşivi/Koç University – VEKAM Archives.

Library of Congress Cataloging-in-Publication Data

Names: Boyar, Ebru, editor. | Fleet, Kate, editor.
Title: Middle Eastern and North African societies in the interwar period / edited by Ebru Boyar, Kate Fleet.
Description: Leiden, The Netherlands : Boston : Brill, 2018. | Series: Social, economic and political studies of the Middle East and Asia ; volume 120 | Includes bibliographical references and index.
Identifiers: LCCN 2018024226 (print) | LCCN 2018028694 (ebook) | ISBN 9789004369498 (E-book) | ISBN 9789004367142 | ISBN (hardback :alk. paper) |
Subjects: LCSH: Middle East--Social conditions--20th century. | Africa, North--Social conditions--20th century.
Classification: LCC HN656.A8 (ebook) | LCC HN656.A8 M53 2018 (print) | DDC 306.0956--dc23
LC record available at https://lccn.loc.gov/2018024226

Typeface for the Latin, Greek, and Cyrillic scripts: "Brill". See and download: brill.com/brill-typeface.

ISSN 1385-3376
ISBN 978-90-04-36714-2 (hardback)
ISBN 978-90-04-36949-8 (e-book)

Copyright 2018 by Koninklijke Brill NV, Leiden, The Netherlands.
Koninklijke Brill NV incorporates the imprints Brill, Brill Hes & De Graaf, Brill Nijhoff, Brill Rodopi, Brill Sense and Hotei Publishing.
All rights reserved. No part of this publication may be reproduced, translated, stored in a retrieval system, or transmitted in any form or by any means, electronic, mechanical, photocopying, recording or otherwise, without prior written permission from the publisher.
Authorization to photocopy items for internal or personal use is granted by Koninklijke Brill NV provided that the appropriate fees are paid directly to The Copyright Clearance Center, 222 Rosewood Drive, Suite 910, Danvers, MA 01923, USA. Fees are subject to change.
Brill has made all reasonable efforts to trace all rights holders to any copyrighted material used in this work. In cases where these efforts have not been successful the publisher welcomes communications from copyright holders, so that the appropriate acknowledgements can be made in future editions, and to settle other permission matters.

This book is printed on acid-free paper and produced in a sustainable manner.

Contents

Acknowledgements VII
List of Figures VIII
Notes on Contributors IX

1 Approaching Societies in the Interwar Middle East and North Africa 1
   Ebru Boyar and Kate Fleet

2 State-Society Relations through the Lens of Urban Development 27
   Ulrike Freitag

3 Beirut's Musical Scene: A Narrative of Modernization and Identity Struggles under the French Mandate 54
   Diana Abbani

4 Tourism and Mobility in Italian Colonial Libya 78
   Brian L. McLaren

5 The Call of Communication: Mass Media and Reform in Interwar Morocco 97
   Emilio Spadola

6 Doctors Crossing Borders: The Formation of a Regional Profession in the Interwar Middle East 123
   Liat Kozma

7 There She is, Miss Universe: Keriman Halis Goes to Egypt, 1933 144
   Amit Bein

8 Taking Health to the Village: Early Turkish Republican Health Propaganda in the Countryside 164
   Ebru Boyar

9 The Provision of Water to Istanbul from Terkos: Continuities and Change from Empire to Republic 212
   Kate Fleet

10 Reforms or Restrictions? The Ottoman Muslim Family Law Code and Women's Marital Status in Mandate Palestine   239
   Elizabeth Brownson

11 Mapping Social Change through Matters of the Heart: Debates on Courtship, Marriage and Divorce in the Early Turkish Republican Era (1923–1950)   259
   Nazan Çiçek

Bibliography   291
Index   319

Acknowledgements

This volume began life as a conference, *Middle Eastern Societies (1918–1939): Challenges, Changes and Transitions*, which was organised by the Department of International Relations, Middle East Technical University, Ankara, in association with the Skilliter Centre for Ottoman Studies, Newnham College, Cambridge and was held at the Middle East Technical University, Ankara, in October 2015. We should like to thank Professor Hüseyin Bağcı, then Head of the Department of International Relations at METU, for his support, Büşra Barın and Gözde Emen for their help throughout the conference, and the Skilliter Centre for Ottoman Studies, Newnham College, Cambridge. We are also grateful to VEKAM, Koç University, and its Director Professor Filiz Yenişehirlioğlu for organising the exhibition, "Başkentli: Osmanlı'dan Cumhuriyet'e Ankara'da Sokak ve İnsan/ The Capital: Streets and People in Ankara from Ottoman Empire to Republic", which was held during the conference.

We should like to thank all those who participated in the conference and made it both a successful and a thoroughly enjoyable occasion; those who contributed chapters to this volume with whom it has been a pleasure to work, and, at Brill, Nicolette van der Hoek and Nienke Brienen-Moolenaar who make publishing a pleasure.

List of Figures

4.1	View of *raid automobilistico* of Rodolfo Graziani along the Mediterranean coast at Sirt, June 1931	82
4.2	Resettlement camp, Marsa Brega, ca. 1930	84
4.3	Mussolini motorcade at Tobruk during inauguration of *strada litoranea*, 1937	87
4.4	Muslim colonization village of Alba (al-Fager), Libya, 1939	89
4.5	View of Yifran Hotel and surroundings, from *Itinerario Tripoli-Gadames*, 1938	93
4.6	Tourists in the courtyard of 'Ain el-Fras Hotel, Ghadames, 1935	94
6.1	Medical students rushing to attend their seven o'clock morning class	132
6.2	A fifth-year student faithfully doing his daily work	133
8.1 A & B	Lice	181
8.2	Itch mite	190
8.3	Tapeworm	192
8.4	"The fly is the greatest enemy of your eye"	193
8.5	"Trachoma is quickly transmitted"	194
8.6	A young girl with smallpox boils	196
8.7	"This happened because I did not take care of my teeth"	198
8.8	A syphilitic in the third phase of his disease	200
8.9 A & B	A syphilitic man	201
8.10	"Trachoma, if not treated, blinds"	202
8.11	A group of blind children	205
8.12	A blind little girl	206
8.13 A & B	Babies	207
8.14 A & B	Boys with swollen bellies	208

Notes on Contributors

Diana Abbani
received her Ph.D. from the Sorbonne University in Arabic Studies. In her dissertation "Music and Society in Beirut in the Early 20th Century", she presents a historical rethinking of the cultural and intellectual history of Beirut, by looking at the relation between music, technology and society.

Amit Bein
is Associate Professor of Modern Middle East History at Clemson University. His research focuses on political, diplomatic, and social changes in Turkey and the Middle East during the closing years of the Ottoman empire and the early decades of the post-Ottoman Middle East. His publications include *Ottoman Ulema, Turkish Republic: Agents of Change and Guardians of Tradition* (Stanford, 2011), and *Kemalist Turkey and the Middle East: International Relations in the Interwar Period* (Cambridge, 2017).

Ebru Boyar
is Professor in the Department of International Relations, Middle East Technical University, Ankara, where she teaches Ottoman, Turkish and modern Middle Eastern history. She is also Academic Advisor at the Skilliter Centre for Ottoman Studies, Newnham College, University of Cambridge. Her research focuses on Ottoman and Turkish social, intellectual and diplomatic history. Her publications include *Ottomans, Turks, and the Balkans: Empire Lost, Relations Altered* (London, 2007), *A Social History of Ottoman Istanbul* (Cambridge, 2010), co-authored with Kate Fleet and *Ottoman Women in Public Space* (Leiden, 2016), co-edited with Kate Fleet.

Elizabeth Brownson
is Assistant Professor of History at the University of Wisconsin-Parkside and the author of two articles in the *Journal of Palestine Studies*. Her research focuses on Palestinian women's status in Muslim Family Law since the British Mandate period. Brownson received a Fulbright-Hays fellowship to complete her dissertation, which she is revising for publication.

Nazan Çiçek
(Ph.D., School of Oriental and African Studies, University of London, 2006) is the author of *The Young Ottomans: Turkish Critics of the Eastern Question in the Late Nineteenth Century* (London, 2010). She currently teaches at Ankara

University in the Faculty of Political Sciences. She has published articles on the political, social and intellectual history of the Ottoman empire and Turkish republic in several edited books and journals.

Kate Fleet
is the Director of the Skilliter Centre for Ottoman Studies, Newnham College, University of Cambridge. Her books include *European and Islamic Trade in the Early Ottoman State: the Merchants of Genoa and Turkey* (Cambridge, 1999), *A Social History of Ottoman Istanbul* (Cambridge, 2010), together with Ebru Boyar, *Ottoman Economic Practices in Periods of Transformation: the Cases of Crete and Bulgaria* (Ankara, 2014), together with Svetla Ianeva, and *Ottoman Women in Public Space* (Leiden, 2016), edited with Ebru Boyar. She is the editor of *The Cambridge History of Turkey: Byzantium-Turkey, 1071–1453* (Cambridge, 2009) and, together with Suraiya N. Faroqhi, of volume II, *The Ottoman Empire as a World Power, 1453–1603* (Cambridge, 2012). She is Editor-in-Chief of *Turkish Historical Review* and an Executive Editor of the *Encyclopaedia of Islam Three*.

Ulrike Freitag
is a historian of the modern Middle East and the Director of Leibniz-Zentrum Moderner Orient in Berlin in conjunction with a professorship at Freie Universität Berlin. She received her Ph.D. in 1991 at the Albert-Ludwigs-Universität in Freiburg with a thesis on Syrian historiography in the twentieth century and taught at SOAS, London. In 2002 she completed her state doctorate on "Indian Ocean Migrants and State Formation in Hadhramaut" (Leiden, 2003) at Rheinische Friedrich-Wilhelms-Universität in Bonn. She has published on modern Arab and Indian Ocean history. Among her recent publications are the co-edited volumes *Urban Violence in the Middle East. Changing Cityscapes in the Transition from Empire to Nation State* (New York and Oxford, 2015), *Understanding the City through its Margins* (Abingdon, 2018), and the articles "A twentieth-century merchant network centered on Jeddah: the correspondence of Muhammad b. Ahmad Bin Himd", *Journal of Northeast African Studies*, 17/1 (2017) and "Scholarly exchange and trade: Muhammad Husayn Nasif and his letters to Christiaan Snouck Hurgronje", in *The Piety of Learning*, ed. Michael Kemper and Ralf Elger (Leiden, 2017).

Liat Kozma
is Associate Professor at the Department of Islamic and Middle East Studies at the Hebrew University, Jerusalem. She is the author of *Policing Egyptian Women: Sex, Law and Medicine in Khedival Egypt* (Syracuse, 2011); and of *Global Women, Colonial Ports: Prostitution in the Interwar Middle East* (Albany, 2017).

Beginning from September 2017, she directs the ERC-funded research group "A Regional History of Medicine in the Middle East, 1830–1960".

Brian L. McLaren
is Associate Professor and Chair at the Architecture Faculty, the College of Built Environments, University of Washington, Seattle. His research focuses on the relationship between architecture and politics during the Fascist period in Italy. His publications include *Architecture and Tourism in Italian Colonial Libya: An Ambivalent Modernism* (Seattle, 2006).

Emilio Spadola
(Ph.D., Columbia University, 2007), is Associate Professor of Anthropology and Middle East and Islamic Studies at Colgate University, Visiting Associate Professor of Anthropology at Tufts University, and President of the Middle East Section of the American Anthropological Association. His work examines intersections of religion, media, security, and modernity in Morocco and the Muslim World. His book, *The Calls of Islam: Sufis, Islamists, and Mass Mediation in Urban Morocco* (Indiana, 2014), was awarded Honorable Mention for both the 2014 Clifford Geertz Book Prize, by the Society for the Anthropology of Religion, and the 2015 L. Carl Brown Book Prize, by the American Institute of Maghrib Studies.

CHAPTER 1

Approaching Societies in the Interwar Middle East and North Africa

Ebru Boyar and Kate Fleet

The interwar period in the Middle East and North Africa, from the collapse after the First World War to the outbreak of the Second World War in 1939, is usually examined from the point of view of nation state building and the creation of national identity. As Cyrus Schayegh has noted, most historians "have reflexively chosen the new, single politics of the post-Ottoman Levant as their framework of analysis",[1] an approach which has tended to overplay state frontiers and underplay regional networks. It also overplays the power of the state mechanism and underplays the extent to which in reality states, rather than being able to impose measures, found themselves forced to negotiate with society or to follow the path of persuasion, as was the case, for example, with the health policies pursued by the government of the new Turkish republic.[2] Rather than state, it was often trans-regionalism, where factors such as mass communication, music and the spread of ideas were important, and microregionalism that shaped society. Viewing the region from within state borders also obfuscates an understanding of identity in this period, for identities were not necessarily linked to states but were often more related to a transnational or microregional sense of belonging. This in part stemmed from the legacy of an Ottoman past which stamped the early post-war years, even if it was often denied or denigrated in the re-writing of history which occurred as part of the national identity building process. While much official rhetoric presented a picture of total rupture between an Ottoman past and the present, the continuities were evident in many spheres of social life. Rather than official rhetoric or state-centric visions, it is with the social realities of the region that the chapters in this volume are concerned. The book seeks to examine what sort of

---

1 Schayegh, Cyrus, "The many worlds of 'Abud Yasin: or what narcotics trafficking in the interwar Middle East can tell us about territorialization", *The American Historical Review*, 116/2 (2011), pp. 274–5.
2 See Ebru Boyar's chapter, "Taking health to the village: early Turkish republican health propaganda in the countryside", in this volume.

'new world' emerged in terms of social connections, urban-rural relations and transnational contacts, and how the peoples of the region positioned themselves both within the region and more globally, and in relation to the often invented past.

While the new political map of the Middle East and North Africa emerged, its new state borders drawn up by the pencils and rulers of the victorious powers,[3] such political entities did not match neatly onto the social realities of the region. Tribes moved regardless of frontiers, populations, such as those in southern Turkey, northern Iraq and northern Syria, were tied together without any regard for the new political boundaries. Quite apart from failing to cut what were now transnational social relations, the borders also failed to unite the populations within them, and urban-rural divides resulted often in an urban elite which felt itself closer to the urban elite in another state in the region than it did to the people in its own state. Well-to-do inhabitants of Istanbul, for example, had more in common with a similar social stratum in Beirut or Cairo than they did with the population of central Anatolia. For the Istanbulite hero of Yakup Kadri Karaosmanoğlu's 1932 novel *Yaban*, his time in an Anatolian village was *gurbet*, an exile in a foreign land.[4] Other members of the new Turkish state preferred life under colonial, non-Muslim rule in Syria rather than submission to the political ideology of the new state which required them to remove their fezzes, for them a quintessential religious symbol.

Social divisions within the new states were further exacerbated by colonial policy as French or British administrations chose certain elements of society as 'collaborators' in order to secure loyalty and ease or sustain colonial control. As Elizabeth Thompson points out, "the French, like the Ottomans, awarded benefits in the self-interest of the state. Also like the Ottomans, the French used social policy to construct a loyal social hierarchy".[5] In Iraq, British officials disagreed among themselves about how to view, and thus how to rule, the population, some officials seeing Iraqi society in terms of the tribe, and thus arguing that Iraq should be ruled according to what they took to be the existing

---

3   Harold Nicolson described Georges Benjamin Clemenceau, Lloyd George and Woodrow Wilson with their armchairs drawn up crouching low over a large map on the floor as they carve up territory. His description is accompanied by the phrase "bubble, bubble, toil and trouble", Nicolson, Harold, *Peacemaking 1919* (London: Constable & Co. Ltd., 1933), p. 274, diary entry dated 13 May 1919.
4   Karaosmanoğlu, Yakup Kadri, *Bütün Eserleri I: Yaban* (originally published in 1932) (Istanbul: İletişim Yayınları, 2005), p. 21.
5   Thompson, Elizabeth, *Colonial Citizens, Republican Rights, Paternal Privilege, and Gender in French Syria and Lebanon* (New York: Columbia University Press, 2000), p. 77.

tribal system, tribal shaikhs becoming "loyal feudatories of British imagining",[6] while others perceived it rather in terms of individuals.[7] Regardless of any clashes in perceptions, the British moved ahead with "the creation of a class of individuals whom it may be harsh, but is nevertheless convenient, to call 'collaborators'", a creation which was "one of the fundamentals of British policy in Iraq".[8] Rural-urban divides deepened, as was the case in Morocco under the French or in Iraq where, Noga Efrati argues, "the urban-rural dichotomy was at the centre of the British conception of Iraq",[9] and urban areas were developed with the aim of creating spaces for metropolitan populations set apart from indigenous peoples, the case, for example, in Tripoli under Italian colonial rule in Libya.[10] The British also dipped a toe into religious waters, using the fortuitous timing of the opening of the colonial exhibition in London in 1924 which coincided with Mustafa Kemal's abolition of the Caliphate. The West African "walled city", part of the exhibition, "advertised George V as the leader of the world's largest Muslim population living inside the territories of the British Empire" and signalled the "advantages possessed by the British Empire over the world of independent Islam".[11]

Social response to the changed post-war world was inextricably bound up with the colonial context, with support for or the struggle against colonial administrations, and with the creation of new concepts of cohesion and loyalty. Colonial exhibitions in London in 1924–1925 and Paris in 1931, set out the colonial vision of the world, couched in colonial language. The exhibition in London displayed "the British Empire in miniature", in the words of the first Labour Party Prime Minister Ramsay MacDonald, a British empire presented "not as a warlike institution, but as a mighty instrument in the peace and

---

6 Dodge, Toby, *Inventing Iraq. The Failure of Nation Building and a History Denied* (London: Hurst and Co., 2003), p. 61.

7 Noga, Efrati, "Colonial gender discourse in Iraq. Constructing noncitizens", in *The Routledge Handbook of the History of the Middle East*, ed. Cyrus Schayegh and Andrew Arsan (London and New York: Routledge, 2015), p. 160.

8 Sluggett, Peter, "Les mandats/the mandates: some reflections on the nature of the British presence in Iraq (1914–1932) and the French presence in Syria", in *The British and French Mandates in Comparative Perspectives/ Les Mandats français et anglais dans une perspective comparative*, ed. Nadine Méouchy and Peter Suglett (Leiden and Boston: Brill, 2004), p. 122.

9 Efrati, "Colonial gender discourse in Iraq", p. 162.

10 See Brian L. McLaren's chapter, "Tourism and mobility in Italian colonial Libya", in this volume.

11 Stephen, Daniel Mark, "'The white man's grave': British West Africa and the British Empire Exhibition of 1924–1925", *Journal of British Studies*, 48/1 (2009), p. 110.

economy of the world".[12] According to *The Times*, it spread before the British people "the wondrous reality of Britain's might and magnitude".[13] For Marcel Olivier, the delegate general of the colonial exhibition in Paris, the exhibition there demonstrated that "colonization is legitimate. It is beneficial. These are the truths that are inscribed on the walls of the pavilions at the Bois de Vincennes".[14]

Much of the drive behind such exhibitions was economic and consumerism played a fundamental role in colonial administrations. The power of consumerism as a method of tying the population into the colonial system was described by Esther Wissa, the prominent Egyptian feminist and co-founder of the Egyptian Feminist Union, who argued in a letter dated December 1924 that "confined and captive" Egyptians consumed and so produced what the colonisers wanted, consumers.[15] "The force-feeding of bound colonial economies with metropolitan products and culture, and the eventual longing for these objects that gradually developed, emphasized the intimate and embodied reach of the colonial market and the consumerist politics mobilized in response to it".[16] Consumerism, in the words of an Egyptian poem published in the magazine *Ruz al-Yusuf* in 1932 offered Egyptians "a glass of poison mixed with honey".[17]

Not only did the local populations consume but they were in turn 'consumed'. The tourist trade in the Italian colony of Libya required, as Brian McLaren argues in his chapter in this volume, that the Libyans be "tied ... to the land and to their history according to an unchanging vision of their cultural past".[18] Tourists required an 'authentic' experience of indigenous culture, provided for them by, for example, the Arab Café of the Suq al-Mushir in Tripoli. Faced with a lack of local musicians and dancers, the Italian authorities established an Arab music school to produce them in order to ensure that the western tourists were provided with the interpretation of Libyan culture that they

---

12   "A world's parliament", *The Times*, 8 April 1924, p. 19.
13   "British Empire Exhibition", *The Times*, 23 April 1924, p. i.
14   Olivier, Marcel, "Avant-Propos", *Le Livre d'Or de l'Exposition Coloniale Internationale de Paris, 1931* (Paris: Librairie Ancienne Honoré Champion, 1931), p. 11, referred to in Morton, Patricia A., "National and colonial: the Musée des colonies at the Colonial Exposition, Paris, 1931", *The Art Bulletin*, 80/2 (1998), p. 357.
15   Esther F. Wissa, letter date 20 December 1924, Cairo, TNA, FO 141/511/5/14083, in Reynolds, Nancy Y., *A City Consumed. Urban Commerce, the Cairo Fire, and the Politics of Decolonization in Egypt* (Stanford: Stanford University Press, 2012), p. 80.
16   Reynolds, *A City Consumed*, p. 80.
17   Reynolds, *A City Consumed*, p. 95, referring to *Ruz al-Yusuf*, no. 221, 9 May 1932.
18   McLaren, "Tourism and mobility in Italian colonial Libya", p. 80.

wished to see.[19] The result of Italian policy was "carefully curated indigenous spaces – where the Libyans and their culture were put on display".[20]

Colonial input did not mean a colonial outcome, however. As Afsaneh Najmabadi has argued, while it has often been pointed out that the modern meaning of *vatan* was "informed by the French notion of *la patrie* ... this was not simply a process of transplanting an exotic alien plant into an enemy soil" but was more akin to a grafting operation. "The point is", for Najmabadi here, "not to deny the intertextuality of Iranian modernist discourse with Europe" but rather "to bring out the inventiveness of cultural grafting, the originality of the copy".[21] Local society, in other words, could not be ignored. While Ahmet Hamdi Tanpınar's comment that "everything crossing the customs became Muslim"[22] might be something of an exaggeration when applied to the post-war world of the Middle East and North Africa, absorption and adaption were nevertheless part and parcel of society construction in this new world, the author of an article in the Iranian newspaper *Ettela'at* from April 1931 noting (with disapproval) that "everything new that has gained a foothold in our country has immediately taken up our peculiar appearance".[23] At the same time, impetus for social change was seen at least by some as being homegrown. One of the basic assumptions behind the original plan for the Egyptian Association for Social Studies, established in 1937, was that "any change, in order to be effective, must spring from within and be in the direction of people's own desires. If these desires do not exist, they should be created".[24]

The result was often a mélange of colonial and new nationalist elements. The architectural identity of Beirut, for example, as argued by Robert Saliba, represented a dualistic interplay of Ottoman and French colonial politics, the growing economic importance of Beirut as "la Porte de l'Orient", and its medieval architectural hertitage. "These factors would determine the extent of

---

19   McLaren, "Tourism and mobility in Italian colonial Libya", pp. 92–3.
20   McLaren, "Tourism and mobility in Italian colonial Libya", p. 95.
21   Najmabadi, Afsaneh, *Women with Mustaches and Men without Beards. Gender and Sexual Anxieties of Iranian Modernity* (Berkeley, Los Angeles and London: University of California Press, 2005), p. 100.
22   Tanpınar, Ahmet Hamdi, *Beş Şehir*, ed. M. Fatih Andı (Istanbul: Yapı Kredi Yayınları, 2001), p. 157.
23   Devos, Bianca, "Engineering a modern society? Adoptions of new technologies in early Pahlavi Iran", in *Culture and Cultural Politics under Reza Shah. The Pahlavi State, New Bourgeoisie and the Creation of a Modern Society in Iran*, ed. Bianca Devos and Christoph Werner (Abingdon, Oxon, and New York: Routledge, 2014), p. 273.
24   Johnson, Amy J., *Reconstructing Rural Egypt. Ahmed Hussein and the History of Egyptian Development* (New York: Syracuse Univesity Press, 2004), p. 36.

Beirut's receptivity and inner permeability to Western stylistic influence".[25] Such influences were also evident in the new Beiruti musical scene, as Diana Abbani's chapter in this volume shows.[26] Consumerism, too, exhibited a similar dualism. The Turkish newspaper *Akşam* ran adverts in August 1929 for both "Krem Mouson", the cream to use "if you want to be immediately recognised in high society and gain a connection to such circles", and for "Safa Sürmesi" (kohl of delight), a product which "had been famous in the East and particularly in Egypt for 30 years" and was now being produced in Turkey. The advert, which gave the name of the kohl in both Turkish and Arabic, was accompanied by a picture of a woman holding a bottle of the kohl with, behind her, Kız Kulesi (in Istanbul) and the pyramids.[27]

Not all of this was new – the French had been in North Africa since 1830, the British in Egypt since 1882 – but what was new was the speed of communication: ideas, and people, now travelled faster and further. While the development of infrastructure had begun in the late Ottoman empire, with the telegraph, steamships and railways, it was only after the First World War that such developments boomed. Such expansion in communications was now to offer a new tool for social development. As Emilio Spadola argues in this volume, "for nationalists in Morocco and elsewhere in the MENA, the interwar expansion of global communications meant that communication and its effects required conscientious social adaptation and political domestication; in short, reformists saw both personal and social awareness of communication as the condition for weaving individual bodies into the social body".[28] New technologies and means of communications, road and rail networks, the press, radio and cinema, now linked the region, internally and externally, physically and intellectually.

Anxious to leave behind "the age of the oxcart" and to see trains speeding over sturdy tracks and automobiles surging along secure highways,[29] the early Turkish republican leaders listened with interest to the proposals put forward

---

25 Saliba, Robert, "Looking East, looking West: provincial eccleticism and cultural dualism in the architecture of French Mandate Beirut", in *The British and French Mandates in Comparative Perspectives/ Les Mandats français et anglais dans une perspective comparative*, ed. Nadine Méouchy and Peter Suglett (Leiden and Boston: Brill, 2004), p. 207.
26 See Diana Abbani's chapter, "Beirut's musical scene: a narrative of modernization and identity struggles under the French Mandate", in this volume.
27 *Akşam*, 2 August 1929, pp. 11 and 12.
28 Spadola, Emilio, "The call of communication: mass media and reform in interwar Morocco", in this volume, p. 99.
29 Ökçün, A. Gündüz, *Türkiye İktisat Kongresi 1923 İzmir. Haberler – Belgeler – Yorumlar* (Ankara: Ankara Üniversitesi Siyasal Bilgiler Fakültesi Yayınları, 1968), no. 31, p. 83.

by Fiat in August 1922 to set up a transportation network over one or more routes running from Samsun to Mardin via Sivas, from Samsun to Ankara, and from İnebolu to Ankara. A contract would also be negotiated for postal transportation and the transporting of state goods. The economy ministry viewed Fiat's approach favourably for it regarded the expansion of transportation networks as of great importance for the economic development of the country and for the stimulating of commercial activity.[30] In 1933, the tenth anniversary of the founding of the republic, the government boasted that in the short space of ten years it had created "an important railway network".[31] Setting out with the mentality that the young Turkish republic "cannot be a country without roads", the Ministry of Public Works created "great innovations in travel", investing heavily in road and bridge construction, and building roads across the country, including one running 610 kilometres from Trabzon to the Iranian border where it joined with the road to Tabriz.[32] In Iran, the automobile was regarded as a good thing, being one of "these devices, which civilization has created and which assure the fortune of mankind".[33] Iranian drivers, however, did not fall into the same category, most drivers not bothering to check the roadworthiness of their vehicles and regarding smoking, drinking alcohol and sleeping as perfectly ok activities when behind the wheel.[34] For the Italians in Libya, communications networks were of crucial importance and there was under Badoglio, who was appointed governor of the regions of Tripolitania and Cyrenaica in January 1929, a "deep ideological investment of the Italian colonial administration ... in the principle of mobility",[35] a mobility that did not, however, apply to the Libyans. In Morocco, too, the colonial rulers developed an extensive transportation infrastructure and by the mid-1930s the main regions were linked by a road and rail network.[36]

One major tool for the rapid dissemination of ideas was the press. Newspapers could be published in one state, distributed in others and carry information from throughout the region; they could spread outside the region, Turkish papers being published in Greece and in Bulgaria, to the annoyance of the authorities in both countries which accused them of spreading Turkish

30   Başbakanlık Cumhuriyet Arşivi, Ankara, 30 10 154 87 3, Ağustos 1338 [1922].
31   T.C. Nafia Vekaleti, *On Senede Türkiye Nafiası 1923–1933* [Ten Years of Public Works in Turkey], 3 vols. (Istanbul: Matbaacılık ve Neşriyat Türk Anonim Şirketi, 1933), vol. I, p. 24.
32   T.C. Nafia Vekaleti, *On Senede Türkiye Nafiası 1923–1933*, II, pp. 40 and 46.
33   Devos, "Engineering a modern society", p. 274, quoting from *Ettela'at*, 4 September 1934.
34   Devos, "Engineering a modern society", p. 274.
35   McLaren, "Tourism and mobility in Italian colonial Libya", p. 83.
36   Hunter, F. Robert, "Promoting empire: the Hachette tourist in French Morocco, 1919–36", *Middle Eastern Studies*, 43/4 (2007), p. 580.

propaganda;[37] and foreign papers could enter the region, Arabic-language papers from Buenos Aires and São Paulo circulating in Algeria, for example.[38] During the interwar period, material from Lebanon and Egypt dominated the Iraqi print market,[39] Egyptian women's magazines, such as *Fatat al-sharq* (Girl of the East) and *Majallat al-sayyidat wa al-rijal* (Ladies' and Men's Review) were distributed in the Levant in the 1920s and 1930s,[40] and *al 'Arus* (The Bride) featured stories about "Egyptian women's nationalist demonstrations as models for Syrian women".[41] *Al-Minhaj* (The Path), which was set up in Egypt by the Algerian Ibrahim Atfiyyash "as the voice of the Salafi Ibadi diaspora in the Mashriq",[42] and appeared between 1924 and 1927, circulated in North Africa and East Africa, publishing news on Algeria, the Arab world, Kemalism and the abolition of the Caliphate.[43] The transnational nature of the press is perhaps best summed up by the description of *al-Umma*, founded by the Algerian Abu al-Yaqzan in 1933 and closed down by the French in 1938, which was described as "the echo of the East and of Islam in the Arab Magrib, having the roar of Palestine, the rise of Syria, the awakening of Egypt, the life of the Hijaz, the ambition of Iraq, the wailing of Tripoli, the cry of Tunisia, and the pleas of Morocco".[44]

Radio and cinema, too, spoke to a transnational audience and were perceived as propaganda tools by governments across the region. The Cumhuriyet Halk Partisi (The Republican People's Party), the ruling party in Turkey, announced at its party congress in May 1935 that "the Party considers the *radio* to be one of the most valuable instruments for the political and cultural education of the nation. We shall erect powerful broadcasting stations, and shall

---

37   Boyar, Ebru and Kate Fleet, "'Mak[ing] Turkey and the Turkish revolution known to foreign nations without any expense': propaganda films in the early Turkish Republic", *Oriente Moderno*, 24/1 (2005), p. 120; see also Boyar, Ebru and Kate Fleet, "A dangerous axis: the 'Bulgarian Müftü', the Turkish opposition and the Ankara government, 1928–1936", *Middle Eastern Studies*, 44/5 (2008), 775–89.

38   McDougall, James, *History and the Culture of Nationalism in Algeria* (Cambridge: Cambridge University Press, 2009), p. 57.

39   Bashkin, Orit, "Representations of women in the writings of the intelligentsia in Hashemite Iraq, 1921–1958", *Journal of Middle East Women's Studies*, 4/1 (2008), p. 54.

40   Thompson, *Colonial Citizens*, p. 216.

41   Thompson, *Colonial Citizens*, p. 214.

42   Ghazal, Amal N., "The other frontiers of Arab nationalism: Ibadis, Berbers, and the Arabist-Salafi press in the interwar period", *International Journal of Middle East Studies*, 42/1 (2010), p. 111.

43   Ghazal, "The other frontiers", p. 110.

44   Ghazal, "The other frontiers", p. 112.

provide for the easy purchase of cheap receiving sets. We shall consider it our task to render *moving pictures* in the country useful to the nation".[45] The cinema, a "locus of modern middle-class activity" in interwar Syria,[46] was regarded as a 'must-have' sign of modernity. According Lilo Linke, the people of Gökçeli in the province of Adana in Turkey "would rather watch mosquitoes on the screen than remain forever behind the times".[47] Both the production of films and their contents were transnational, linking the region together through those who made and played in the films and through the subjects covered. The first Turkish talkie, *İstanbul Sokaklarında* (In the Streets of Istanbul), produced in 1931, was directed by the leading Turkish theatre and film director of the 1920s and 1930s, Muhsin Ertuğrul, the director of photography, Nikolas Farkas, was Hungarian, and those in the film included the Greek actor Gavrilides and the very famous Egyptian actress Aziza Amir.[48] The film, location scenes of which were shot in Greece, Egypt and Turkey while the sound filming was done in Paris, was shown in various Balkan countries, including Greece, Poland and Egypt, as well as in Turkey.[49] The visit of Reza Shah to Turkey in 1934 provided a most useful propaganda opportunity for both countries. It was exhaustively covered by the Turkish press which described its "neighbour and brother" Iran as "a close friend of and admirer of the new and powerful Turkey",[50] and an Iranian propaganda film was made about the Shah's journey and shown throughout Iran.[51]

Just as ideas moved through the region, transported in print or on the screen, so too did people move. Keriman Halis, the Turkish Miss Universe, went to Egypt in 1933, staying three months amid streams of acclamation in the Egyptian press, a visit, which Amit Bein argues in this volume, calls into question the generally accepted picture of a split between Turkey and the other states of the region in the aftermath of the Ottoman collapse and instead indicates that "there were many more nuances to Turkish-Egyptian relations than

---

45 Linke, Lilo, *Allah Dethroned. A Journey through Modern Turkey* (London: Constable and Co., 1937), p. 332.
46 Watenpaugh, Keith D., "Middle-class modernity and the persistence of the politics of notables in inter-war Syria", *International Journal of Middle East Studies*, 35/2 (2003), p. 264.
47 Linke, *Allah Dethroned. A Journey through Modern Turkey*, p. 255.
48 Scognamillo, Giovanni, *Türk Sinema Tarihi* [The History of Turkish Cinema] (Istanbul: Kabalcı Yayınevi, 2003), p. 52.
49 Onaran, Alim Şerif, *Muhsin Ertuğrul'un Sineması* [Muhsin Ertuğrul's Cinema] (Ankara: Kültür Bakanlığı Yayınları, 1981), pp. 187–94.
50 "Türk-İran Dostluğu" [Turkish-Iranian Friendship], *Cumhuriyet*, 4 June 1934.
51 Devos, "Engineering a modern society?", p. 270.

has often been reflected in the historiography of the period".[52] Women were constantly on the move, attending conferences and congresses on the position of women throughout the region. Lebanese activist Nur Hamada aimed to set up branches of her Women's Arabic Assembly in every Arab country and to have an annual Arab women's conference in different Arab countries.[53] Turkish and Iranian delegates as well as women from Iraq, Afghanistan, Syria, Lebanon and the Hijaz attended the first Eastern Women's Congress in Damascus in 1930,[54] Lebanese and Turkish delegates were at the Tehran Eastern Women's Conference in 1932,[55] and Syrian, Lebanese and Iraqi women attended the Eastern Women's Conference for the Defence of Palestine in Cairo in 1938.[56]

Such transnational connections were also evident in the sphere of medicine. The networks and interconnections between medical doctors, evidenced by the transnational medical congresses, resulted, according to Liat Kozma, in the "the formation of a transnational professional identity".[57] From 1931, the Egyptian Medical Association held its annual conference, usually in another Arab country in alternate years, in Beirut in 1931, in Jerusalem in 1933, in Damascus in 1935 and in Baghdad in 1938, attracting participants from across the region, from Egypt, Syria, Lebanon and Palestine predominantly but also from Jordan, Iraq, Sudan and Saudi Arabia. "Through these encounters, in lecture halls, by the pyramids or on steamship or train rides, connections between doctors working throughout the region were created or reinforced. Thematic discussion on shared concerns, be it malaria or rural hygiene, further strengthened the exchange of ideas and a sense of shared destiny and shared mission".[58] Such interconnections were developed also through education,

---

52 Bein, Amit, "There she is, Miss Universe: Keriman Halis goes to Egypt, 1933", in this volume, p. 146.

53 Efrati, Noga, "The other 'awakening' in Iraq; the women's movement in the first half of the twentieth century", *British Journal of Middle Eastern Studies*, 31/2 (2004), p. 172.

54 Amin, Cameron Michael, "Globalizing Iranian feminism, 1910–1950", *Journal of Middle East Women's Studies*, 4/1 (2008), p. 19; van Os, Nicole A.N.M., "Ottoman Muslim and Turkish women in an international context", *European Review*, 13/3 (2005), p. 467; Fleischmann, Ellen L., *The Nation and its "New" Women. The Palestinian Women's Movement 1920–1948* (Berkeley, Los Angeles and London: University of California Press, 2003), p. 180.

55 Thompson, *Colonial Citizens*, p. 138; van Os, "Ottoman Muslim and Turkish women in an international context", p. 467.

56 Thompson, *Colonial Citizens*, p. 148.

57 Kozma, Liat, "Doctors crossing borders: the formation of a regional profession in the interwar Middle East", in this volume, p. 123.

58 Kozma, "Doctors crossing borders: the formation of a regional profession in the interwar Middle East", p. 139.

medical schools drawing students from the Arab states and Turkey, and scientific and medical journals published in Cairo, Beirut and Damascus but circulating "between these urban centers and beyond".[59] Medical knowledge was exchanged throughout the region, a treatment for trachoma used in Algeria, for example, being trialled in Gaziantep in south-eastern Turkey in the 1930s. In the same period, medicine for trachoma was also sent from Italy to Gaziantep to be tried out there.[60]

Despite the construction of new state boundaries, the Middle East and North Africa can be said to have been as interconnected as ever, indeed more so. It was also more internationally connected. In the case of Turkey, international connections were not something the British wished to see. In late December 1919 the Foreign Office in London informed the League of Nations of concerns about Turkish nationalists.

> It is rumoured that the Nationalists are calling together delegates from the different Islamic countries who are to make some pronouncement regarding the solidarity of Turkey and Islam. These delegates propose to represent Azerbaijan, Afghanistan and Arabia and at least one Indian agitator is reported to be on his way to the Conference. Admiral de Robeck suggests that King Hussein should be asked to issue a statement to the effect that no Arab representative has been deputed to attend the Conference.[61]

Gertrude Bell was not keen on Turkey's connections to the north. In a letter to her stepmother in January 1920, she referred to "the Turks to the north of us, exasperated and embracing Bolshevik propaganda, destructive Bolshevism which is all the Turks are capable of".[62] International connections, however, were the order of the day and it was in this environment that the post-war generation developed their political outlook and challenged the existing order. Young Moroccan nationalists who opposed French rule were thus "conditioned by salafi reformism, Wilsonian ideals of self-determination, the military success of Ataturk and 'Abd al-Karim al-Khattabi, the rise of the Pan-Islamic

---

59 Kozma, "Doctors crossing borders: the formation of a regional profession in the interwar Middle East", p. 143.
60 Ayberk, Dr. Nuri, *Türkiyede Trahom Mücadelesi* (Istanbul: Kader Basımevi, 1936), pp. 22–5.
61 League of Nations Archives, Geneva (hereafter LON), R564/11/2557/2557, 23 December 1919.
62 Gertrude Bell to her stepmother, 12 January 1920, Gertrude Bell Archive, Newcastle University, http://www.gerty.ncl.ac.uk/letter_details.php?letter_id=370, accessed 12 April 2017.

movement, and the stirrings of nationalism in the Middle East and the Indian subcontinent".[63]

The press played an important part in such global connections. The Egyptian press followed the Indian boycott movement and reported on the strategy of economic boycott, a tactic imitated by Egyptian activists, and profiles of Indian women appeared frequently in the Egyptian women's press. Gandhi's stop over at the Suez Canal on his way to London in September 1931 was extensively covered and "by the middle 1930s Egyptian satarists used images of Gandhi and homespun cloth to denounce local elites and government officials as tools of imperialism".[64] Gandhi was much admired by many. For Fatima Sharifa al-'Abed, daughter of Syria's first president Muhammad 'Ali al-'Abed, he was "the greatest man now living on earth". In an interview she gave to *The Bombay Chronicle* in 1932, she stated that "he who does not appreciate Gandhi is a person who denies truth, an enemy of truth".[65]

International conferences and congresses also served to connect the region to the world beyond. The first international congress of tropical medicine held after World War I took place in Cairo in December 1928.[66] The women's movement of the region, which formed part of a "broader global phenomenon in almost all parts of the world, including India, the United States, Europe, Latin America, and parts of Africa and Asia",[67] had a global reach. Women travelled from the Middle East and North Africa to attend conferences outside the region, prominent Egyptian women, for example, attending the International Alliance for Women for Suffrage and Equal Citizenship conference in Rome in 1923,[68] and Turkish delegates attending the International Women Suffrage Alliance in Geneva in 1920, an international congress in Lyon on the position of women in Turkey, the congress of International Organisation of Female Doctors in London and a Women's International League for Peace and Freedom

---

63 Wyrtzen, Jonathan, "Colonial state-building and the negotiation of Arab and Berber identity in Protectorate Morocco", *International Journal of Middle East Studies*, special issue, *Relocating Arab Nationalism*, 43/2 (2011), p. 231.
64 Reynolds, *A City Consumed*, p. 84.
65 "Arab Lady's Impressions of India", *The Bombay Chronicle*, 30 April 1932, p. 1.
66 Abugideiri, Hibba, "The scientisation of culture: colonial medicine's construction of Egyptian womanhood, 1893–1929", *Gender and History*, 16/1 (2004), p. 93.
67 Fleischmann, Ellen, "The other 'awakening': the emergence of women's movements in the modern Middle East, 1900–1940", in *Social History of Women and Gender in the Modern Middle East*, ed. Margaret L. Meriwether and Judith E. Tucker (Boulder, Colo.: Westview Press, 1999), p. 97.
68 Weber, Charlotte, "Between nationalism and feminism: the Eastern Women's Congresses of 1930 and 1932", *Journal of Middle East Women's Studies*, 4/1 (2008), p. 84.

meeting in Washington, all in 1924,[69] and the International Alliance of Women meetings in Marseilles in 1933.[70] Nationalist struggles elicited intra-regional support, Iraqi women sending letters of support to Syrian women and telegrams of protest to the League of Nations and the French Foreign Ministry. They also raised money for women in Palestine.[71] Feminist leaders from Afghanistan, Australia, China, India, Japan and Java were invited to attend the first Eastern Women's Congress in Damascus in 1930[72] and representatives from Afghanistan, Australia, China, India, Japan and Java attended the 1932 conference in Tehran.[73] The 12th International Alliance of Women's Congress was held in Istanbul in 1935, after which delegates went to Ankara and were received by Atatürk.[74] Delegates were reported in the Turkish newspaper *Tan* to have said that they had not been able fully to appreciate "new Turkey" in Istanbul but that now, having seen Ankara and met the man who had founded new Turkey, they were able to grasp the full significance of the new state.[75] According to *The Times*,

> Mrs Corbett Ashby and Lady Astor, the British members of the party, with whom the President of the Republic talked at some length, said afterwards that they had been greatly impressed by the new Angora, and expressed warm admiration of the head of the State. Kamal Atatürk told the delegates that just as the women and men of Turkey had joined forces to create the new Turkey, so must the women and men of all nations work together to preserve the peace of the world.[76]

Many of the women's movements in the region took Turkey as the "gold standard"[77] in matters of female emancipation. Nur Hamada, president of the second Eastern Women's Congress held in Tehran in 1932, described the women of Turkey as having "the highest degree" of progress.[78] On the issue of veiling,

---

69 van Os, "Ottoman Muslim and Turkish women in an international context", p. 466.
70 Libal, Kathryn R., "Staging Turkish women's emancipation: Istanbul, 1935", *Journal of Middle East Women's Studies*, 4/1 (2008), p. 36.
71 Efrati, "The other 'awakening' in Iraq", p. 171.
72 Weber, "Between nationalism and feminism: the Eastern Women's Congresses of 1930 and 1932", p. 87.
73 Weber, "Between nationalism and feminism: the Eastern Women's Congresses of 1930 and 1932", p. 91.
74 Libal, "Staging Turkish women's emancipation: Istanbul, 1935", pp. 36–7.
75 "Atatürk Kadın Delegeleri Kabul Etti", *Tan*, 27 April 1935, p. 1.
76 "Women Visitors to Angora", *The Times*, 27 April 1935, p. 11.
77 Amin, "Globalizing Iranian feminism, 1910–1950", pp. 22–3.
78 Amin, "Globalizing Iranian feminism, 1910–1950", p. 21.

Turkey was held up by some as a contrast to Arab backwardness. Articles in *al-Mar'a* (Woman), published in Damascus between 1930 and 1932, totally rejected veiling "as the totem of Arabs' backwardness in contrast to the Turks".[79] Turkey was taken as a model by Iraqi intellectuals, who in "defining the functions of women in modern Muslim societies ... sought inspiration in the writings of Egyptian and Turkish writers".[80] The journal *al-Hadith* (The Modern), founded by Edmond Rabbath and Sami al-Kayyali and described by Keith Watenpaugh as "Aleppo's *Esquire*", "championed Arab women's rights and franchise" and "showed a fascination with Republican Turkey and Kemalism".[81] News from Turkey was said to have been influential among Iraqi women in the early 1920s.[82]

Education was seen by some as a factor in the success of Turkish women. One article which appeared in *al-'Arus*, the journal published in Damascus by Mary 'Ajami, argued that the unveiling of women in Turkey was due to their higher level of education, while another ascribed it to their having taken part in the war with Greece and to the economic crisis which had propelled them into the workforce.[83] The success was also ascribed to the role of Mustafa Kemal Atatürk. In an interview with a reporter for the Turkish newspaper *Cumhuriyet*, the Egyptian Huda al-Sha'rawi, one of the delegates received by Atatürk after the Women's Congress held in Istanbul in 1935, described how much Egyptians admired the Turkish leader. "We regard it as an honour to follow the way that he has opened" she declared. "You call him Atatürk [father of the Turks] but we call him Ataşark [father of the East] because he is the father and leader of not only Turkey but also of all the East and especially of brother [kardeş] Egypt. We follow with envy the development which has been obtained by Turkish women thanks to Atatürk".[84] Fatima Sharifa al-'Abed was also an admirer for she claimed that "responding to Kemal Pasha's one word 'forward', the women of Turkey had advanced to the level of their European sisters, enjoying equal rights with men in business, public administration, everywhere".[85] One deputy in a debate in the Lebanese Representative Council in 1923, where it was noted that women had joined the Turkish delegation at the Lausanne peace talks, stated that he agreed with Mustafa Kemal that "the chief cause that led to our failure in social organization is our neglect of the women's issue and her low

---

79 Thompson, *Colonial Citizens*, p. 137.
80 Bashkin, "Representations of women in the writings of the intelligentsia in Hashemite Iraq, 1921–1958", p. 53.
81 Watenpaugh, "Middle class modernity", p. 261.
82 Efrati, "The other 'awakening' in Iraq", p. 161.
83 Thompson, *Colonial Citizens*, pp. 129–30.
84 "Mısır Kadınları ve Atatürk: 'Siz Büyük Şefinize Atatürk Diyorsunuz. Biz Onu Ataşark Diye Anarız!'", *Cumhuriyet*, 28 April 1935, pp. 1, 6.
85 "Arab Lady's Impressions of India", p. 1.

status ... the happiness of the country rests on women's sharing with men in public affairs".[86] Articles appearing in *al-Mar'a al-jadida* (The New Woman), the journal published in Beirut by Julia Dimashqiya, greatly praised Mustafa Kemal for his support for women's reforms and predicted that Turkey would "vanquish 'reactionaries'". The journal also published "photographs of unveiled Turkish women activists posing with sympathetic Turkish (male) officials".[87] For Fatimih Sayyah, one of the leaders of the Women's Party in Iran, it was the numbers of educated women that made the difference; "if we want to individually compare learned and enlightened Turkish women with enlightened and educated Iranian women, we shall find no difference with respect to their level of progress or capability or enlightenment or excellence. However, it is worth noting that the number of educated and learned Turkish women is greater than that of educated Iranian women".[88] This image of enlightened female emancipation was one Turkey was keen to promote. Turkish postcards depicting unveiled Turkish women out and about with male companions were sold in Damascus in 1922 and were, according to the American consul, much sought after in "local feminine circles".[89]

It should be pointed out, however, that not all were enthralled by the 'new women'. Gertrude Bell, who was honorary secretary of the British Anti-Suffrage League, was no fan of suffrage for women in Iraq "feeling that women presently occupied with domestic concerns, did not deserve the right to vote".[90] In Turkey female suffrage, civil liberties and rights to hold political office were perceived as threatening by some sectors of society. "Feminists were caricatured as 'tyrants' and their male family members were portrayed as being so oppressed by their incessant demands that they were driven to form men's rights organizations".[91]

The Ottoman Legacy

The societies of the new Middle East and North Africa which emerged from the destruction of the First World War required an element essential to all social units: history. This history was to be a new construction. But it was also a

---

86   Thompson, *Colonial Citizens*, p. 122.
87   Thompson, *Colonial Citizens*, p. 129.
88   Amin, "Globalizing Iranian feminism, 1910–1950", pp. 22–3.
89   Thompson, *Colonial Citizens*, p. 129.
90   Bashkin, "Representations of women in the writings of the intelligentsia in Hashemite Iraq, 1921–1958", p. 56.
91   Libal, "Staging Turkish women's emancipation: Istanbul, 1935", pp. 43–4.

lived legacy. For those states which were created out of the rubble of the Ottoman empire, these two representations of the past at times contradicted each other, the generations which passed from Ottoman rule to new nation state being recipients of an official rhetoric which presented them with a re-written past, and new present, which did not necessarily reflect their lived experience. Identities for many were fluid rather than national, the Ottoman past was not in reality anathema to all, and modern Turkey was not the shunned neighbour, shut off from the Arab world, which much official rhetoric depicted it as.

"The past", as Eric Hobsbawm has noted, "is an essential element, perhaps *the* essential element" in the ideologies of nationalism. "If there is no suitable past, it can always be invented".[92] For all the political entities of the region, be they Mandate powers, colonial rulers, monarchs, presidents or nationalist forces, a suitable history was required, a history appropriate for the new nation or, in the case of colonial and Mandate powers, one that would construct a state they could understand and which would legitimise their presence. The French in Algeria used history as an essential tool in their construction of the colonial state[93] while in Morocco they used history and ethnography to create colonial knowledge which presented them with a Morocco they could understand and provided a "veneer of legitimacy" which helped justify their rule.[94] It was through history, therefore, that people were to come to know and love their country. As Rashid Yasami, an Iranian scholar active in the interwar period, put it, "Why do we love Iran? Because we know it. How do we know it? Through history".[95] The reality of such history was largely irrelevant, for nationalist history is, in the words of Mark Mazower, "all about false continuities and convenient silences, the fictions necessary to tell the story of the rendez-vous of a chosen people with the land marked out for them by destiny".[96]

For many of the new states, the backdrop against which their new histories were written was the Ottoman past, which was either written out altogether, the history writing process requiring "the erasure of Ottoman presence and

---

92 Hobsbawm, Eric, *On History* (London: Abacus, 1997), p. 6.
93 Hannoum, Abdelmajid, "The historiographic state: how Algeria once became French", *History and Anthropology*, 19/2 (2008), p. 94.
94 Wyrtzen, "Colonial state-building and the negotiation of Arab and Berber identity in Protectorate Morocco", p. 230.
95 Vejdani, Farzin, *Making History in Iran: Education, Nationalism, and Print Culture* (Stanford: Stanford University Press, 2014), p. 69.
96 Mazower, Mark, *Salonica City of Ghosts, Christians, Muslims and Jews 1430–1950* (London and New York: Harper Perennial, 2005), p. 474.

contribution to the history of the region",[97] or used as a foil against which to display progress or account for lack of it. Both colonial and nationalist historiography re-wrote the history of the post-First World War period, removing the Ottoman component and instead producing "uncomplicated narratives of national struggle and awakening", even if this was not necessarily how those who lived through the period experienced it.[98] The Ottoman past provided common ground for both the colonial rulers and local intellectuals, resulting in a "hybridized national synthesis" in the case of Iraq where educators produced a "romantic national history and a romanticised vision of Iraq's tribes".[99] When not erased, the Ottomans were all bad, both colonial powers and nationalists reviling them.[100] Such condemnation of the Ottomans spread over to condemnation of the Turks. The abolition of the Caliphate, a suicidal act for Abdullah, ruler of Transjordan,[101] prompted his father King Hussein to comment that the Turks had "made war upon religion as though it were a secularised State. The French made a revolution and a Republic, but they do not war upon religion, and French Ministers themselves attend church. Now nobody can say the Turks are Moslems".[102] For the Turks themselves condemnation of the Ottoman past also formed part of their presentation of their own recent past, and the government of the new Turkish republic made great play of the contrast between the Ottoman empire and the Turkish state presenting the Turkish present, and future, as much better in every way than the Ottoman past.

For the Mandate governments, too, there was a stark contrast between conditions under British or French rule and that of the previous Ottoman administration. The British, whose perception of the Ottoman past "profoundly shaped" how they dealt with Iraqi society and how they constructed their rule, set out to give credibility to their Mandate by separating the corrupt Ottoman government from the subject Arab population. "The past role of the 'bad'

---

97 Watenpaugh, Heghnar Zeitlian, "An uneasy historiography: the legacy of Ottoman architecture in the former Arab provinces", *Muqarnas, History and Ideology: Architectural Heritage of the "Lands of Rum"*, 24 (2007), p. 33.
98 Provence, Michael, "Ottoman modernity, colonialism, and insurgency in the interwar Arab East", *International Journal of Middle East Studies*, 43/2 (2011), p. 207.
99 Bashkin, Orit, "'When Mu'awiya entered the curriculum' – some comments on the Iraqi education system in the interwar period", *Comparative Education Review*, special issue *Islam and Education – Myths and Truths*, guest editors Wadad Kadi and Victor Billeh, 50/3 (2006), p. 353.
100 Watenpaugh, "An uneasy historiography: the legacy of Ottoman architecture in the former Arab provinces", p. 37.
101 "Hussein The New Khalif", *The Manchester Guardian*, 13 March 1924, p. 9.
102 "Hussein The New Khalif", p. 9.

Ottoman Empire could then unambiguously be contrasted with the present and future role of the 'good' British one".[103] The Ottomans were often represented as backward and their reforms meaningless. Robert de Caix, Secretary-General of the French High Commissioner in Syria, and from 1925 to 1938 the French representative of the Mandates Commission at Geneva, described the reforms undertaken by the Ottomans as mere "window-dressing", and "a Western varnish which was lacking in substance".[104] For de Caix "for a long time, Turkey had been an army, a predominant nation and religion, camped in the middle of an empire".[105] The French administrators thus often presented their own reforms against the backdrop of Ottoman backwardness. In public health, for example, the French, when talking of their investment in this area, claimed that "hygiene wasn't practiced at all under the Turks".[106] If such reforms were slow to take root, or entirely lacking in some cases, such failure could be put down to the difficulties which the Mandate administrators found themselves faced with as a result of the inadequacies of the previous Ottoman regime.

While backwardness could be presented as something overcome or combatted by the new administrations, Mandate governments on occasion found it useful to hide behind an assumed concern for local traditions, and thus for the Ottoman past. When it came to the position of women, failure to improve their status was explained away by the need to show concern for local customs and to avoid offence, something that did not concern colonial administrators in areas in which they wished to change the status quo. In the case of inheritance law which disadvantaged women, for example, Robert de Caix maintained during a detailed discussion in 1933 before the Permanent Mandatory Commission of a petition concerning inheritance presented by Marguerite Sagiati from Aleppo,[107] that while "from the Western point of view, that law might be regarded as an anachronism" it was a matter of custom.[108]

Such attitudes were not, however, necessarily supported by the League of Nations. The Permanent Mandatory Commission expressed concern over the maintenance in force of laws "contrary to the explicit provisions of the

---

103   Dodge, *Inventing Iraq*, p. 44.
104   LON, C.406.M.209.1933.VI. Permanent Mandates Commission, Minutes of the Twenty-Third Session, 19 June–1 July 1933, p. 136.
105   LON, C.489.M.214.1934.VI. Permanent Mandates Commission, Minutes of the Twenty-Six Session, 29 October–12 November 1934, p. 158.
106   Thompson, *Colonial Citizens*, p. 77.
107   For details of the case see LON, C.406.M.209.1933.VI. Permanent Mandates Commission, Minutes of Twenty-Third Session, 19 June–1 July 1933, pp. 128–30, 132–3, 144, 157–9, 174–6.
108   LON, C.406.M.209.1933.VI. Permanent Mandates Commission, Minutes of Twenty-Third Session, 19 June–1 July 1933, p. 128.

Mandate",[109] a concern also expressed by the Aleppo court which noted in the 1931 ruling in the Sagiati case that the Turkish republic had rejected such laws which were still in force in Syria.[110] Marquis Theodoli, the Chairman of the Commission, noted that "in countries like Palestine and Turkey it had been thought advisable to rescind legislation of that kind, and that consequently it might be considered surprising that this had not been done earlier in Syria",[111] a point he put directly to Robert de Caix during the discussion of the Sagiati petition when he asked "why, in Syria, a country as advanced as Palestine or Turkey, it had not been possible to bring the law more into line with modern ideas, whereas in Palestine and Turkey the laws had been adapted to the progress of the human conscience". De Caix, described by Gertrude Bell as "the wily de Caix",[112] replied that Palestine was a very different case, its aim being "to a large extent … to settle a foreign population" and that Turkey was very different because "there had been a process of imperative transformation that could not have been expected from a Mandatory". He continued

> indeed, it must not be forgotten that this was a very delicate matter, and that, whatever modern Western ideas with regard to equality of the sexes might be, the system of succession to which the country had been accustomed for years could only be influenced from outside gradually and with prudence.[113]

Pressed by Rappard, a member of the Commission, de Caix maintained that a reform of the law of succession would be "impossible to enforce", an assertion to which Rappard retorted that "nevertheless the Ghazi [Atatürk] had done so". De Caix pointed out that "the Ghazi could take liberties with Moslem institutions which a Mandatory Power could not have taken, and which could have been denounced as an attack on the rights of the majority population".[114]

---

109   LON, C.406.M.209.1933.VI. Permanent Mandates Commission, Minutes of Twenty-Third Session, 19 June–1 July 1933, p. 128.
110   LON, C.406.M.209.1933.VI. Permanent Mandates Commission, Minutes of Twenty-Third Session, 19 June–1 July 1933, p. 130.
111   LON, C.406.M.209.1933.VI. Permanent Mandates Commission, Minutes of Twenty-Third Session, 19 June–1 July 1933, p. 133.
112   Gertrude Bell letter to father, 3 March 1926, http://www.gerty.ncl.ac.uk/letter_details.php?letter_id=887, accessed 12 April 2017.
113   LON, C.406.M.209.1933.VI. Permanent Mandates Commission, Minutes of Twenty-Third Session, 19 June–1 July 1933, p. 144.
114   LON, C.406.M.209.1933.VI. Permanent Mandates Commission, Minutes of Twenty-Third Session, 19 June–1 July 1933, p. 130.

De Caix's insistence on the impossibility of change when it came to the position of women was evident in the discussion of another petition sent to the League in September 1933 concerning the imprisonment of a 16-year-old girl by her husband. In response to a question by Mlle Dannevig, a member of the Commission, about the possibility of the girl having been married against her will, or without her knowledge, de Caix replied that "in Moslem life, the position as regards the girl's consent to the marriage was not the same as in Western countries at the present time". Mlle Dannevig asked whether it was "normal for such practices to continue under the mandatory regime", to which de Caix responded that "it was impossible for the authorities to ensure otherwise than by gradual stages a degree of emancipation for Moslem women which would place them on the same footing as European women. The social evolution was proceeding gradually".[115] The basic stance was, therefore, that when it came to the position of women, the Mandate powers were happy to maintain the situation that had existed in the Ottoman past as this smoothed their relations with the local powerholders at no cost, since the position of women was not an issue of major concern for the colonial administrators. Here there was no condemnation of the Ottomans, or a drive to change what was seen as backward, but an acceptance that custom was custom and should not be challenged.

Quite apart from any appeal to the sanctity of custom, the mandatory authorities found Ottoman legislation to their liking when it enabled them to ensure the controls they required. This was the case, for example, when it came to labour unions. To ensure that workers did not organise themselves, the French relied on a 1912 Ottoman law that prohibited employee unions and strikes.[116]

In some instances, the administration of the Mandate governments lagged significantly behind the position that had existed under the Ottomans, and behind that adopted by other coutries in the region. When Lord Lugard, a member of the Commission, "expressed his satisfaction" in 1934 at a meeting of the Permanent Mandates Commission discussing the 1933 annual report on Palestine and Transjordan, that the minimum marriage age for girls had been increased to 14,[117] he overlooked the fact that under the Ottoman Law of Family Rights (*Hukuk-ı Aile Kararnamesi*) of 1917, as Elizabeth Brownson points out in this volume, the minimum female marriage age was 17, although a girl younger

---

115   LON, C.619.M.292.1933.VI. Permanent Mandates Commission, Minutes of Twenty-Fourth Session, 23 October–4 November 1933, p. 67. See also pp. 121–2.
116   Thompson, *Colonial Citizens*, p. 83.
117   LON, C.259.M.108.1934.VI. Permanent Mandates Commission, Minutes of Twenty-Fifth Session, 30 May–12 June 1934, p. 31.

than 17 could marry provided that she had reached physical maturity and the consent of the court had been obtained for the marriage by her parents.[118] The Ottoman law, abolished in Turkey in 1926, remained in place in Syria until 1949 and in Jordan until 1951.[119]

At the same time, Mandate powers could be taken to task for their failures by comparing the situation with that under the Ottomans, a negative representation which the Mandate powers inevitably rejected. Thus, for example, in the discussion of the 1933 annual report on Palestine and Transjordan at the meeting of the Permanent Mandates Commission in 1934, J.H. Hall, Chief Secretary to the Government of Palestine, rejected the criticism of Palacios, a member of the Commission, that "the rights conferred by the new Municipal Corporation Ordinance were more restricted than those which had existed under the Turkish regime".[120] In the same discussions concerns were expressed about the new legislation relating to the press, under which the Mandate government had the power to "suspend the publication of a paper if it contained any matter likely to endanger the public peace". Lord Lugard commented that he thought "the Ordinance went further than was usual", regarding the Ordinance as "rather drastic". Hall replied that he "believed that a similar provision had existed prior to the new Ordinance, and that similar regulations existed elsewhere".[121]

In a discussion about the Holy Places during the examination of the 1932 annual report on Palestine and Transjordan, the Chairman, Marquis Theodoli, commented that he "thought it rather strange that when the Holy Places were in the hands of the Turks, who were Moslem, they took steps to maintain respect for the *status quo*, whereas at the present time the mandatory Power did not appear to attach sufficient importance to these questions". M.A. Young, the Chief Secretary of the Government of Palestine, who was not happy with these remarks, replied that "the Government of Palestine set the greatest store by keeping order in the Holy Places" and that he thought "it probable that, in the time of Turkish rule, much more serious incidents had arisen than the one under consideration".[122]

---

118   See Elizabeth Brownson's chapter, "Reforms or restrictions? The Ottoman Muslim Family Law Code and women's marital status in Mandate Palestine", in this volume, p. 246.
119   Tucker, Judith, "Revisiting reform: women and the Ottoman Law of Family Rights, 1917", *The Arab Studies Journal*, 4/2 (1996), p. 4.
120   LON, C.259.M.108.1934.VI. Permanent Mandates Commission, Minutes of Twenty-Fifth Session, 30 May–12 June 1934, p. 22.
121   LON, C.259.M.108.1934.VI. Permanent Mandates Commission, Minutes of Twenty-Fifth Session, 30 May–12 June 1934, pp. 23–4.
122   LON, C.406.M.209.1933.VI. Permanent Mandates Commission, Minutes of Twenty-Third Session, 19 June–1 July 1933, p. 109.

The Ottoman past was thus something of a moveable feast. Used persistently as a mirror by the Turkish government in order to display the great advances of the new Turkish state, vilified or ignored by much Arab historiography, Mandate authorities adopted a policy of pick and choose, condemning Ottoman backwardness in some instances and boasting of progress but in others choosing to preserve Ottoman legislation either to bolster control or because to do so brought benefit without any loss, as was the case with women's rights.

Regardless of any rhetoric, however, the post-war era did not in fact represent such a stark contrast with what had gone before. As James Gelvin has pointed out, "in terms of cultural and social history, the era of the Mandates does not reveal ... a significant break from earlier times", and social structures and conceptions about the ordering of society come from the beginning of the second half of the nineteenth century.[123] Arabist Salafi nationalism "had its roots in late 19th-century intellectual and theological developments that were redefining the concept of the *umma*" and the correlation between Islam and national identity in the interwar period "developed in the Ottoman context and continued in the post-Ottoman order".[124] National celebrations in the new Arab states relied on the "symbolic precedent" of the Ottoman empire[125] and the organisation of urban space and urban development showed an Ottoman imprint, having often begun in the late days of the Ottoman empire. Middle Eastern cities could in fact build on a long tradition of civic spirit, as Ulrike Freitag argues in her chapter in this volume.[126] Debates, such as those in Egypt about hygiene, cleanliness and household management, had their roots in the nineteenth century, though they were now "marked by new theories of scientific management and household efficiency that had begun in the early twentieth century to dominate the practice of domestic management in the West".[127] As Nazan Çiçek points out in her chapter in this volume, "despite the insistence of the republican regime on the so-called ontological rupture

---

123   Gelvin, James L, "Was there a Mandate period?" in *The Routledge Handbook of the History of the Middle East*, ed. Cyrus Schayegh and Andrew Arsan (London and New York: Routledge, 2015), p. 420.
124   Ghazal, "The other frontiers", p. 106.
125   Podeh, Elie, *The Politics of National Celebrations in the Arab Middle East* (Cambridge: Cambridge University Press, 2011), p. 45.
126   See Ulrike Freitag's chapter, "State-society relations through the lens of urban development", in this volume.
127   Joubin, Rebecca, "Creating the modern professional housewife: scientifically based advice extended to middle- and upper-class Egyptian women, 1920s–1930s", *The Arab Studies Journal*, 4/2 (1996), p. 40.

between itself and its predecessor, as far as the debate on marriage is concerned the continuum between the late Ottoman times and the early years of Turkish nation state is unmistakable".[128] The same can be said for the Turkish views of Ottoman neglect of concepts of public good and public benefit,[129] or of the health and welfare of the population,[130] for, despite the rhetoric of the new republic about Ottoman failure and republican success, much of what was done was not so much a total innovation as an, often more successful, pursuit of the same goals.

That the early years of the interwar Middle East and North Afrca should have been strongly marked by continuity with the past should hardly be a surprise given the fact that many of the intelligentsia and political leaders of the states of the region had received their education in the Ottoman capital, Istanbul. Orit Bashkin notes that in Iraq "the Sunni male elites of the 1920s and 30s, mostly graduates of the Ottoman education system, were conversant in the writings of Turkish and Egyptian intellectuals".[131] The influential Iraqi educator Sati' al-Husri's mother tongue was Turkish and his "vast knowledge of philosophy and political thought was a product of an Ottoman cosmopolitan milieu".[132] In her memoirs, Saniha Amin Zaki, born in Iraq in 1920, describes her father's study where he had three immense book cases, one for books in Arabic, one for books in Turkish and one for English, French and German books.[133] He had studied at the Haydarpaşa Military College in Istanbul from where he graduated as a army officer[134] and he became the director of education in Mosul. The name selected for Saniha Amin Zaki's younger brother was Khalluk (Haluk), which pleased her mother and her cousin "because it is the name of the son of a famous Turkish poet, Tawfiq [Tevfik] Fikret".[135] This 'Turkish' connection was described by Gertrude Bell in letter to her father in May 1921:

---

128 Çiçek, Nazan, "Mapping social change through matters of the heart: debates on courtship, marriage and divorce in the early Turkish republican era (1923–1950)", in this volume, p. 260.
129 See Kate Fleet's chapter, "The provision of water to Istanbul from Terkos: continuities and change from empire to republic", in this volume.
130 See Boyar, "Taking health to the village: early Turkish republican health propaganda in the countryside", in this volume.
131 Bashkin "Representations of women in the writings of the intelligentsia in Hashemite Iraq, 1921–1958", p. 54.
132 Bashkin, "'When Mu'awiya entered the curriculum'", p. 349.
133 Amin Zaki, Saniha, *Memoirs of a Female Iraqi Doctor* (n.p.: n.p., 2014), p. 19.
134 Amin Zaki, *Memoirs of a Female Iraqi Doctor*, p. vi.
135 Amin Zaki, *Memoirs of a Female Iraqi Doctor*, p. 3.

I considered that it wasn't odd that there should be so much pro-Turkish sympathy here with all the Turkish blood. Many of the official classes ... are of Turkish stock; still more, they have married Turkish women when they were in C'ple or elsewhere. Even among strong Nationalists it's rather a feather in your cap to have a Turkish wife – they are held to be better educated than the Arab women, and indeed up to a point they usually are. The links are strong and the Arab state ought to be in close friendship with Turkey, at any rate during this generation which got most of its schooling in C'ple. I notice among our Ministers a marked tendency to revert to Turkish practice, even when it wasn't at all good. It's what they knew.[136]

The Ottoman past therefore suffused much of the social relations and outlook of the inhabitants of the new states, while at the same time, the political dimension of the new world, with the Mandate states and the rise of Arab nationalism, resulted in an often rather complex role for Turkey in the new geopolitical map. The relationship between Turkey and the Arab world has tended to be presented in rather stark terms as one of rupture and growing hostility. The reality, as evidenced by Keriman Halis's stay in Egypt, was, however, much more subtle and nuanced as societies across the region remained entangled in a shared past and common cultural heritage. In the popular image Turkey was viewed, at least on occassion, as a progressive, modern state to be emulated. Turkey also owed its positive image in the Arab world, or at least its initial positive image, to the success of the Turkish defiance of the colonial powers and its emergence as an independent state. Ramadan Shallash, who was educated in the military academy in Istanbul, fought in the Ottoman army during the First World War and was said to have been "on the payroll of the Arab government in Damascus" in 1919, channeled funds, including those he received from the Damascene government, to Mustafa Kemal in Anatolia for use in his struggle against the British. In 1925, when inciting Syrian villages against France, he,

---

[136] Gertrude Bell to her father, 15 May 1921, http://www.gerty.ncl.ac.uk/letter_details.php?letter_id=473, accessed 12 April 2017. See also Bell's letter to her father in June 1926 "I then came home, breakfasted and did an hour's work after which I set out again on visits, First the Naqib, then the Ministers, then selected notables and finally the Queen and 'Ali and his family. I found Faisal with 'Ali and we all went together to see the old grandmother who being 90 or so is moribund from the effects of her motor journey from 'Amman. She was lying on a mattress on the floor, almost incapable of speech, poor thing. 'Ali's wife is a nice woman but as she was brought up in C'ple [Istanbul (Constantinople)] she scarcely talks any Arabic", 23 June 1926, http://www.gerty.ncl.ac.uk/letter_details.php?letter_id=917, accessed 12 April 2017.

according to French intelligence, "rode into Christian hamlets in the anti-Lebanon mountains, admonishing the villagers to 'make your village like Ankara in 1920 with Ghazi Mustafa Kemal!'".[137] Postcards of Mustafa Kemal and other heroes from the Turkish nationalist forces were produced and circulated in Algeria into the late 1930s.[138]

With the passing of time, however, the ties of a shared world became weakened, as new generations grew up in a nation state-dominated landscape and without any imbedded connection to the Ottoman world. Turks became Turks, unrelated to the Ottomans who were confined to a distant past. Saniha Amin Zaki, who certainly knew about the Turks who were viewed positively, described how when she was eight she came across a book in her father's study on the Ottomans. "I knew vaguely that the Ottomans had once been in Iraq, but I had no idea why they came or why they left. Nothing about them was explained in school or at home, but people always spoke of them with awe as great people who were part of our heritage". She asked her father about the book "and for some reason he said that there really was no reason to take the book seriously; I ought to stick to school books. I could see that he didn't want to talk about the Ottoman times at all".[139]

Conclusion

In the popular perception, the Middle East and North Africa in the interwar period is often seen as the era of Mandates, one in which the region was 'modernized' and societies rendered better thanks to the introduction of innovations and improvements ushered in by western governments who, under the benign gaze of the League of Nations, improved the lot of those who had been downtrodden by the inept or simply bad government of the Ottomans. Perhaps seduced by the simplicity of this vista, many modern historians of the Middle East and North Africa, adopting the cartographical example of the British and French administrators who took their pencils and rulers to a region largely unknown to them, have tended to see the region in terms of dichotomies and clear-cut divisions, and with a clarity that it does not warrant. All this leads to a dangerous simplicity of perception and overlooks the fact, for example, that events were seen as both positive and negative at the same time

---

137   Provence, "Ottoman modernity, colonialism, and insurgency in the interwar Arab East", p. 220.
138   McDougall, *History and Culture of Nationalism in Algeria*, pp. 58–9.
139   Amin Zaki, *Memoirs of a Female Iraqi Doctor*, pp. 19–20.

by different groups in the same region or the same society, as was the case with the removal of the Caliphate. Ottoman influence was not all bad, Turkey was not totally isolated from the rest of the region, with its face looking only westwards, identities were not instantly realigned to fit within the borders of the newly created states. The period was instead one of flux, marked by mobility, both physical and mental, a reordering of belonging and a rearrangement of political allegiance and alliances. It is this complexity that makes it an era so difficult to conceptualise but one the comprehension of which is essential to a fundamental grasp of the history to follow.

CHAPTER 2

State-Society Relations through the Lens of Urban Development

Ulrike Freitag

This chapter aims at highlighting major themes in post-Ottoman urban history in the interwar period. It does so from a comparative and hence mostly literature-based perspective, but includes issues stemming from the author's own research on Ottoman and post-Ottoman Jeddah. While this town of 20,000 to 30,000 inhabitants might seem a somewhat peripheral choice, both in terms of size and location, I hope to show that many of the issues addressed in this chapter were actually relevant in such a smallish location. In some ways, it can thus be seen as typical for former provincial centres beyond the urban metropoles of Istanbul, İzmir, Beirut, Alexandria or Cairo. While a number of actual developments in cities are specific to the respective urban sites, I argue that many reflect wider changes in the relationship between states and their populations, so that many developments in cities can be considered as indicative of wider socio-political changes.[1] The example of Jeddah also helps to illustrate that modernization was an aspiration shared between governments and local elites, and that local elites tried to push for and support government intervention in this field. The comparison will be limited to Middle Eastern cities, but it needs to be kept in mind that a number of overall developments in urbanism reflect even larger global trends.

Speaking specifically of the interwar period, it needs to be mentioned explicitly that many of the urban developments described here were set in motion already in late Ottoman times and often only bore fruit after the period ended.[2] Furthermore, in the post-Ottoman period, the notion of 'state' varied

---

1 Thompson makes this argument for Syria, see Thompson, Elizabeth, *Colonial Citizens: Republican Rights, Paternal Privilege, and Gender in French Syria and Lebanon* (New York: Columbia University Press, 1999), p. 5.
2 Fawaz, Leila and Robert Ilbert, "Political relations between city and state in the colonial period", in *The Urban Social History of the Middle East, 1750–1950*, ed. Peter Sluglett (Syracuse: Syracuse University Press, 2011), pp. 141–53; Gül, Murat, *The Emergence of Modern Istanbul: Transformation and Modernisation of a City* (London and New York: Tauris Academic Studies, 2009), pp. 7–71.

quite considerably between different territories – from the newly emergent nation states of Turkey and Egypt to the bulk of the Arab East where a Mandate system was imposed and hence French and British models loomed large and societies rebelled against new systems. On the Arabian Peninsula, only a protracted political and military process resulted in the establishment of the modern states of Saudi Arabia and the Republic of Yemen. These processes not only impacted on the actual power of state elites to implement urban planning, they also shaped different societal claims and expectations. In conjunction with different economic trajectories, they also resulted in quite distinct micro-periodisations which will not be reflected in this survey. Even the world economic crisis of 1929 affected different economies, and hence states and societies, in different ways. In a number of cases, such as Turkey and Egypt, it triggered state investment to bolster the effects of the crisis such as unemployment, and hence increased state intervention. This was quite impossible for the newly founded Saudi state which was fighting bankruptcy at the time. Other underlying developments in the period, such as the massive rural to urban migration, also impacted significantly on urban development. Two examples may suffice: a particularly dramatic case is that of Beirut which grew from 90,000 to 237,000 inhabitants between 1920 and 1943, accommodating at the end of the process one quarter of the Lebanese population and tripling the urban surface.[3] Haifa's population grew from 20,000 in 1918 to 100,000 in 1939 partly due to internal migration, but also as a result of Jewish immigration.[4] In many cases, this development had already started during the Ottoman period, in others such as Jeddah, migration only became a significant factor after World War II. Consequently, while common traits will dominate in the following narrative, which is seeking to generalise, there are many differences in detail which cannot be engaged with but which need to be kept in mind.

There was a major common thread in the different emerging political entities, namely a sustained effort by governments to develop their states

---

3 Eddé, Carla, "La municipalité de Beyrouth (1920–1943): un difficile équilibre entre héritage ottoman et contraintes mandataires", in *Municipalités méditerranéennes: Les réformes urbaines ottomanes au miroir d'une histoire comparée*, ed. Nora Lafi (Berlin: Klaus Schwarz Verlag, 2005), pp. 255–6.

4 Seikaly, May, *Haifa: Transformation of a Palestinian Arab Society, 1918–1939* (London and New York: I.B. Tauris, 1995), p. 47. The rapid growth of cities was a global phenomenon in the nineteenth and early twentieth century, c.f. Osterhammel, Jürgen, *Die Verwandlung der Welt: Eine Geschichte des 19. Jahrhunderts* (Munich: Beck, 2009), pp. 366–81; and, for a number of Western metropoles, Dennis, Richard, *Cities in Modernity: Representations and Productions of Metropolitan Space, 1840–1930* (Cambridge and New York: Cambridge University Press, 2008), pp. 22–3.

economically and politically, irrespective of the political system. While cities were a prime target of this developmental impetus, which often took the shape of unabated modernization, as will be shown, there were also concerted efforts to shape a societal sense of identity for the new political entities. This occurred often in conjunction with attempts to downplay internal problems or secondary contradictions such as economic disparities, class or gender inequalities. As Avcı and Lemire have argued for Jerusalem, this urge to forge new identities, probably in conjunction with the memory of the war and famine, led to a very negative image of the recent Ottoman past. This can certainly be observed in the former Arab provinces. In combination with a European urge to emphasise modernity as a distinctly Western import, notably in the mandatory states, this has led to the overwhelming impression of rupture in the historiography.[5] Of course, urban modernity could also take a nationalist tinge: Falih Rıfkı Atay, when he was the Honorary Chairman of the Ankara Master Planning Commission in the early Turkish republic, distanced himself from the Ottoman past by arguing that the "Ottomans built monuments, the Turks are the builders of cities".[6]

However, while cities were to some extent laboratories for governmental experiments and intervention, they also became important stages for societal reactions to political, economic and social change. While there were rural uprisings and revolts, it was urban movements and actions that received more attention, be it protests by urban workers, political and confessional clashes or the emergence of new political and social movements.[7] This runs of course

---

5 Avcı, Yasemin and Vincent Lemire, "De la modernité administrative à la modernisation urbaine: une réévaluation de la municipalité ottomane de Jérusalem (1867–1917)", in *Municipalités méditerranéennes: Les réformes urbaines ottomanes au miroir d'une histoire comparée*, ed. Nora Lafi (Berlin: Klaus Schwarz Verlag, 2005), pp. 73–5.

6 Çınar, Alev, "The imagined community as urban reality: the making of Ankara", in *Urban Imaginaries: Locating the Modern City*, ed. Alev Çınar and Thomas Bender (Minneapolis: University of Minnesota Press, 2007), p. 153.

7 Beinin, Joel, *Workers and Peasants in the Modern Middle East* (Cambridge and New York: Cambridge University Press, 2001), pp. 71–98; Mazza, Roberto, "Transforming the Holy City: from communal clashes to urban violence, the Nebi Musa riots in 1920", in *Urban Violence in the Middle East: Changing Cityscapes in the Transformation from Empire to Nation State*, ed. Ulrike Freitag, Nelida Fuccaro, Claudia Ghrawi and Nora Lafi (New York and Oxford: Berghahn Books, 2015), pp. 179–96; Fuccaro, Nelida, "Reading oil as urban violence: Kirkuk and its oil conurbation, 1927–58", in *Urban Violence in the Middle East: Changing Cityscapes in the Transformation from Empire to Nation State*, ed. Ulrike Freitag, Nelida Fuccaro, Claudia Ghrawi and Nora Lafi (New York and Oxford: Berghahn Books, 2015), pp. 222–42; Baron, Beth, *Egypt as a Woman: Nationalism, Gender, and Politics* (Berkeley: University of California Press, 2005), *passim*.

counter to the often-stated view that the confessional, tribal and/or clannish nature of Middle Eastern ("Islamic", "Arab" or "Ottoman") cities prevented the emergence of an urban society showing civic spirit and having its own identity.[8] This chapter takes a critical view of this paradigm and will highlight society as an agent in urban change where appropriate. The state-society alliance with regard to the modernizing agenda that emerges quite strongly for Jeddah, but also for some other cities, should not only and idealistically be understood as the expression of a civic spirit. It also reflects certain mechanisms adopted by a state with few resources of its own which enabled it to pressurise the urban elites into contributing substantially to a development which both sides agreed was necessary, even if views on who was supposed to lead and finance changes might have differed considerably.

How to Describe the Urban Transformation?

Much of the literature on the urban transformations discussed in this chapter describes these in terms of modernization or modernity; the former is often applied to concrete infrastructural measures, the latter conceived as a more overarching, at times holistic conceptual transformation resulting in specific political and administrative arrangements as well as in spatial ruptures.[9]

Given the often scathing criticism of modernization theory which assumed a one-directional path to development along the Western model, well expressed in Lerner's classical title "Mecca or Modernization", as well as the dismissal of the equally problematic concept of 'modernity', for example by Cooper, this very frequent use of the term is somewhat irritating.[10] It probably reflects the materials with which authors have been working on historical Middle Eastern

---

8   Fawaz and Ilbert, "Political relations", p. 142; Avcı and Lemire, "De la modernité", p. 86.
9   On this with regard to Western metropoles see Dennis, *Cities in Modernity*, pp. 53–79. For the (former) Ottoman lens see Souami, Taoufik, "Émergences des professionnels locaux de l'urbanisme", in *Concevoir et gérer les villes: milieux d'urbanistes du sud de la Méditerranée*, ed. Taoufik Souami and Éric Verdeil (Paris: Économica/Anthropos, 2006), p. 19; Parusheva, Dobrinka, "Europe imagined and performed: the impact of Western Europe's modernity on Southeast European urban space", in *Städte im europäischen Raum: Verkehr, Kommunikation und Urbanität im 19. und 20. Jahrhundert*, ed. Ralf Roth (Stuttgart: Steiner, 2009), p. 191. The more intellectual and holistic aspect of "modernity" comes across well in Habermas, Jürgen, *Die Moderne, ein unvollendetes Projekt: Philosophisch-politische Aufsätze, 1977–1990*, 1st ed. (Leipzig: Reclam, 1990), p. 39.
10 Lerner, Daniel, *The Passing of Traditional Society: Modernizing the Middle East*, 5th ed. (New York: Free Press, 1964), pp. 113–49 with further literature pp. 274–88.

urbanism in the late nineteenth and first half of the twentieth century. Thus, Çınar has argued that in Turkey

> the concepts of modernity, modernness, modernization, and modernism have been at the center of political discourse since the early nineteenth century and have come to constitute the basis of the founding ideology when the new Turkish state was established in 1923. As the Turkish case illustrates, regardless of how it is defined, the idea of modernity can have an immense transformative and constitutive power in the ongoing formation of a social-political order, the constitution of the public sphere, and the shaping and transformation of urban life.[11]

Cooper would agree with such a statement, notably as Çınar emphasises the need to study the "specific conceptualization of modernity" which in Turkey resulted in a specific "nation-building project which was implemented through the creation of a new capital city".[12] Incidentally, holistic notions of urban planning were themselves a fairly new, 'modern' notion at the time, developed in Europe only from the 1920s onwards.[13] This was likely linked to a new attention to notions of community and society, which the new architecture was meant to serve, and which thus also fit very well with the idea of building a new, wholly transformed nation.[14] In the Turkish imagination, such urbanism was also very explicitly linked to Western style developmentalism.

The outspoken Westernization was reflected in the employment of German, Austrian and Swiss planners and architects in the construction of Ankara.[15] In Bilad al-Sham (Greater Syria), European models were also of paramount importance, but the local actors had less influence over their choice and/or adaptation as it was often mandatory officials deciding such matters.[16]

---

11 Çınar, "The imagined community", p. 152.
12 Çınar, "The imagined community", p. 152; c.f. Özervarlı, M. Sait, "Intellectual foundations and transformations in an imperial city: Istanbul from the late Ottoman to the early republican periods", *The Muslim World*, 103 (2013), 518–34.
13 Souami, Taoufik and Éric Verdeil, "Introduction", in *Concevoir et gérer les villes: milieux d'urbanistes du sud de la Méditerranée*, ed. Taoufik Souami and Éric Verdeil (Paris: Économica/Anthropos, 2006), pp. 1–12; c.f. Dennis, *Cities in Modernity* with regard to a number of Western metropoles.
14 Heynickx, Rajesh and Tom Avermaete, "Community as a prism", in *Making a New World: Architecture and Communities in Interwar Europe*, ed. Rajesh Heynickx and Tom Avermaete (Leuven: Leuven University Press, 2012), pp. 9–26.
15 Gül, *Emergence*, pp. 86–7.
16 Ghorayeb, Marlène, *Beyrouth sous mandat français: construction d'une ville moderne* (Paris: Éditions Karthala, 2014).

This notwithstanding, it is important to remember that similar – albeit less comprehensive – notions of urban development can be traced to late Ottoman times, and even then were the result of global connections and the circulation of knowledge and technologies. This earlier phenomenon is often underestimated by postcolonial writers such as Appadurai.[17] Regardless of its origins, a "developmentalist ethos" certainly prevailed in the interwar period.[18] Development was the tool through which modernity was to be achieved, and hence 'developmentalism' will be used in this article to refer to concrete measures aimed at that very goal, regardless of whether they formed a coherent entity or whether they were put forward in a more piecemeal fashion.

In many Middle Eastern cities, among them Jeddah, there is little evidence of the existence of a comprehensive vision of institutional and urban development. Rather, one gets the impression of at times uncoordinated attempts to make particular matters work. Implicitly or explicitly, this was often based on either Ottoman or Western models of urban transformation, the former being very much associated with the latter in places such as the Yemen or the Hijaz where the Ottomans were almost regarded as Westerners due to cultural differences.

Finally, it needs to be explicitly mentioned that not only states, or state institutions like municipalities or governors tried to modernise. Members of the public often complained about the lack of – usually specific – services and shared the desire to improve roads, drainage and other facilities.[19] In Jeddah, water and education were the sectors in which local notables pressed the government for action, and contributed significantly in financial as well as organisational terms since Ottoman times. Of course, this should also be understood in terms of the 'politics of notables' who could accrue social capital by investing in public infrastructure. This can be illustrated using the example of water supply: Jeddah relied on rainwater from cisterns outside of the city, which were privately owned. There had been an intermittent supply of water from sources outside the city by aqueducts which subsequent rulers had built and maintained. Besides the usual wear and tear, as well as destruction from Bedouins at times of conflict, there are repeated reports about the obstruction of public waterworks by local cistern owners fearing for their own business. On the other hand, local merchants and ship-owners who needed this basic

---

17   Appadurai, Arjun, *Après le colonialisme. Les conséquences culturelles de la globalisation* (Lausanne: Payot, 2015), p. 29.

18   Gelvin, James L., *The Modern Middle East: A History* (New York and Oxford: Oxford University Press, 2005), pp. 231–7.

19   See, for example, Boyar, Ebru and Kate Fleet, *A Social History of Ottoman Istanbul* (Cambridge and New York: Cambridge University Press, 2010), pp. 272–3, 309–13.

resource for their daily lives as well as business repeatedly invested large sums into water-supply projects conducted jointly with the state.[20]

Similarly, in the field of education, it seems that local merchants had pressed the Ottoman government to open a middle school (*rüşdiye*) in the mid-1870s. As teaching was mostly in Ottoman Turkish, only a handful of local notables sent their children to the school which was otherwise frequented by the offspring of Ottoman officials.[21] Hence, notables aspiring to educate their sons in Arabic beyond the customary Qur'anic schools proceeded to found another, privately funded school in the early twentieth century.[22]

Transformation could, of course, also be framed in terms consciously rejecting notions of modernization or even Westernization. Thus, in Imamic Yemen, there was a concerted effort to distance Imamic government institutions from the earlier Ottoman modernization efforts and to Islamize institutions at least outwardly. This was done, for example, by returning to an Islamic terminology, i.e. by calling the Ministry of Finance *bayt al-mal* and by re-introducing Islamic taxes (or rather abolishing most non-Islamic taxes). This notwithstanding, there was marked continuity in state and urban administration, and even some, albeit very modest, efforts at building roads or schools which was elsewhere couched in terms of modernization.[23] However, these activities were

---

20 Low, Michael C., "Ottoman infrastructures of the Saudi hydro-State: the technopolitics of pilgrimage and potable water in the Hijaz", *Comparative Studies in Society and History*, 57/4 (2015), p. 961; c.f. Trabulsi, Muhammad Yusuf Muhammad Hasan, *Jidda: Hikayat madina* [Jeddah, Story of a City], 2nd ed. (Riyadh: al-Madina al-Munawwara li-l-tiba'a wa-l-nashr, 1429/2008), pp. 140–2.

21 Sabban, Suhayl, *Nusus 'uthmaniyya 'an al-awda' al-thaqafiyya fi 'l-Hijaz: al-Awqaf, al-madaris, al-maktabat* [Ottoman Texts Relating to the Cultural State of the Hijaz: Pious Foundations, Schools and Libraries] (Riyadh: Maktabat al-Malik 'Abd al-'Aziz al-'amma, 1422/2001), pp. 154–5; among these notables was apparently 'Umar Nasif; Sabban, Suhayl, "Jidda fi watha'iq al-arshif al-'uthmani" [Jeddah in the Ottoman Archive](unpublished manuscript, prepared as part of project of Encyclopedia of Jeddah, n.d. (2005?)), p. 42; at least, books and other materials were ordered, Başbakanlık Osmanlı Arşivi (hereafter BOA), MF.MKT 37/11, 2 Cemaziülahır 1293 (24 June 1896); Amin, Bakri Shaykh, *al-Haraka al-adabiyya fi 'l-mamlaka al-'arabiyya al-su'udiyya* [The Cultural Movement in the Kingdom of Saudi Arabia] (n.p., 1392/1972), p. 145. The short account in Trabulsi, *Jidda*, p. 436, is very inaccurate.

22 Freitag, Ulrike, "The Falah School in Jeddah: civic engagement for future generations?", *Jadaliyya* (http://www.jadaliyya.com/pages/index/21430/the-falah-school-in-jeddah_civic-engagement-for-fu).

23 On the continuities in the financial administration, see al-Khutabi, Arwa, "The Financial Policies of the Yemeni Imams (1918–1962)", Ph.D. Dissertation, Freie Universität Berlin, 2014.

linked to quite different political and moral concepts of statehood, one considered to be 'modern', the other decidedly building on Islamic norms.[24]

The Evolution of Urban Governance

In order to understand urban dynamics and state-society relations, but also how states intervened in the cities, it is important to consider how cities were governed. Two main, complementary levels can be discerned which provide different perspectives on urban dynamics. As the organisation mostly goes back to Ottoman times, the late Ottoman model needs to be briefly introduced.[25]

On the most basic level, Ottoman cities were divided into quarters (*mahalle* or *hara*), which were headed by quarter heads called *muhtar* in Turkish and *'umda* or *shaykh al-hara* in Arab provinces.[26] Other influential people in the quarter consisted of the *shaykh* of the local mosque, the leading local notables (often merchants and *'ulama'* or Sufi sheikhs) who formed part of a more or less informal council. The *'umda* often came from a well-reputed family of the quarter, but was usually not one of the leading notables of the wider city. The quarter as the basic administrative unit of the city served as an important locus of local solidarity. The *'umda* was responsible for local security, commanding night guards and holding the right to temporary arrests of suspects. He, as well as the sheikh or important notables also settled local disputes and organised neighbourhood help.[27]

Seen from the perspective of central administration, cities were usually part of larger administrative units, many of which were subject to fairly frequent reorganisation. Thus, to give the example of Jeddah in 1887, it was the capital of

---

24   C.f. Cooper, Frederick, *Colonialism in Question: Theory, Knowledge, History* (Berkeley: University of California Press, 2005), p. 149.

25   There were numerous modifications to how Ottoman cities were governed, for an outline of the classical age, but mostly of the different phases during the Tanzimat era, see Ortaylı, İlber, *Tanzimat Devrinde Osmanlı Mahallî İdareleri, 1840–1880* (Ankara: Türk Tarih Kurumu Basımevi, 2000). The following depiction is thus simplified.

26   Lewis, Bernard, "Baladiyya", in *The Encyclopaedia of Islam*, 2nd ed., ed. Peri J. Bearman et al. (Leiden: E.J. Brill, 1954–2009), vol. 1., pp. 972–5.

27   Lévy-Aksu, Noémy, *Ordre et désordres dans l'Istanbul ottomane (1879–1909)* (Paris: Éditions Karthala, 2013), pp. 215–75; al-Messiri-Nadim, Nawal, "The concept of the Hara: a historical and sociological study of al-Sukkariyya", *Annales Islamologiques*, 15 (1979), 323–48; Freitag, Ulrike, "When festivals turned violent in Jeddah, 1880s-1960s", in *Violence and the City in the Modern Middle East*, ed. Nelida Fuccaro (Stanford, CA: Stanford University Press, 2016), pp. 63–74, with further references in note 7, pp. 250–1.

the *sancak* of Jeddah, one of three *sancak*s of the province of the Hijaz with the capital Mecca.[28] There had, for quite some time, existed various councils on the level of the city of Jeddah about which we know rather little, even before the institutionalisation of partly elected, partly appointed provincial councils and municipalities in subsequent laws since 1854.[29] The responsibilities of the newly created municipalities concerned buildings, roads and public spaces, water provision, lighting, cleaning and sewage, transport, supervision and improvement of markets, slaughterhouses etc., the guarding of public morality and police service, supervision of brothels, care of orphans and unemployed, fire service etc.[30] However, a major problem was that the provincial administration (as well as other state institutions such as the military) intervened in municipal decisions and often took responsibility for larger-scale or prestigious projects. One example from Ottoman Jeddah is the repair of the city wall as an urban work of major importance in 1879–80. It involved members of local councils (although it is unclear which ones), the local as well as the imperial military authorities, a state engineer and, last but not least, the Ministry of Finance.[31] Based on his research on late Ottoman Damascus, Grallert concludes that the municipalities were situated at the "intersection of local, regional, and imperial civil and military bureaucracies as an administrative unit staffed with notables hardly able to satisfy the contradictory demands levelled upon them".[32] While Saßmannshausen in his discussion of late Ottoman Tripoli seems much more optimistic about the civic engagement and possibilities

---

28   *Hicaz Vilayeti Salnamesi: 1305 Sene-i Hicriye* (Mekke-i Mükerreme: Vilayet Matbaası, 1305/1888).
29   Osmanoğlu, Ahmed E., "Hicaz Eyaletinin Teşekkülü (1841–1864)", M.A. Dissertation, Marmara University, 2004, p. 43; Young, George, *Corps de droit ottoman: recueil des codes, lois, règlements, ordonnances et actes les plus importants du droit intérieur, et d'études sur le droit coutumier de l'empire ottoman,* 6 vols. (Oxford: Clarendon Press, 1905), vol. I, pp. 36–95, 99–105. For Istanbul see Gül, *Emergence*, pp. 40–71.
30   Young, *Corps*, I, pp. 70–1. Although the provincial law on which this is based was abrogated in 1877, the provisions for the municipality of Istanbul were based on it, c.f. Young, *Corps*, vol. VI, p. 152.
31   BOA, I. DH. 826/66580–01, 6 Cemaziülevvel 1298 (17 January 1881).
32   Grallert, Till, "To Whom Belong the Streets? Property, Propriety, and Appropriation: The Production of Public Space in Late Ottoman Damascus, 1875–1914", Ph.D. Dissertation, Freie Universität Berlin, 2014, p. 156. For a good description of the various intersecting levels of government intersecting see Büssow, Johann, *Hamidian Palestine: Politics and Society in the District of Jerusalem 1872-1908* (Leiden and Boston: Brill, 2011), pp. 41–100.

of the municipal council, it would seem for Jeddah that it had not very much say in important affairs, probably not least for lack of funds.[33]

This is important in so far as this finding is supported by what can be traced in the sources about Ottoman Jeddah and many other cities; it also, more pertinently, applied to the post-Ottoman situation as well. If anything, the role of centrally appointed officials and/or of state ministries in urban affairs increased practically everywhere in the former Ottoman realms, whether under national or under foreign rule. While it is not possible to rehearse regulations in a dozen or so successor states of the empire, it is worth noting that, in Turkey, appointment rather than election of municipal assemblies was decreed in 1924.[34] Eddé has shown for Beirut that, while the manpower of and expenditures for the municipality certainly increased during the French Mandate, so did control by the state over the *baladiyya*. Effectively, this meant not only increased French control and consequently loss of independence of the – in Beirut still elected – city council. It also meant that, for example, the local police force came under the orders of the provincial authorities, rather than, as formerly, the head of the municipal council. Overall, this resulted in increased power for the central government at the expense of the municipality, even if Eddé admits that the financial, technical and human resources of the *baladiyya* increased.[35] A somewhat similar system of colonial "guidance" of local officials can be observed in the British Mandates, for example in Haifa.[36]

After the fairly turbulent Sharifian interlude, which was marked mainly by the last years of World War I and the conflict with Ibn Saud, Jeddah capitulated to the latter in December 1925. It had, during the last year of Hashemite rule, served as de facto capital, although this does not seem to have much affected local management. However, the almost continuous war conditions – first as a result of World War I and then of the confrontation with Ibn Saud – caused severe economic hardship for most of the population. With the fall of Jeddah at the end of 1925, all of Hijaz became part of Saudi Arabia. In 1926, a constitution for the region was passed, containing provisions for various administrative bodies, a legislative council as well as municipal bodies. Thus, municipalities were "attached to the senior local administrative official" – presumably of the Department of Internal Affairs, that supervised the Municipality of Mecca,

---

33   Saßmannshausen, Christian, "Reform in Translation: Family, Distinction, and Social Mediation in Late Ottoman Tripoli", Ph.D. Dissertation, Freie Universität Berlin, 2012, pp. 216–53.
34   Gül, *Emergence*, p. 80.
35   Eddé, "Beyrouth", pp. 255–99.
36   Seikaly, *Haifa*, pp. 52–9.

the capital of the Kingdom of the Hijaz.[37] The Administrative Council of Jeddah, as well as that of Medina, consisted of the governor (*qa'immaqam*), his assistant, the chief officials and four notables chosen and nominated by the King (of Hijaz and Sultan of Najd).[38] These were indeed notables of longstanding importance, even if the inclusion of Shaykh 'Abdallah b. Muhammad al-Fadl, a merchant of Najdi origin, indicates a certain shift in power relations among the notables.[39] However, the explicit provision that all decisions had to be royally approved, and their implementation overseen by the Viceroy, shows an extraordinary desire for central control similar to what could be observed elsewhere.[40]

A new element was the introduction of "general municipal councils", consisting of landlords, craftsmen and notables, who were again appointed by the King and had the task of overseeing the work of the municipality.[41] Leading municipal officials were charged with regularly coordinating among themselves in a Municipal Administrative Committee.[42]

The internal system of *'umda*s was kept, but once again put under increased control, at least theoretically (there is no information on the implementation). They and their collaborators in the running of the quarter were, according to a decree of late 1927, to be selected on the basis of their good reputation, their ability to read and write, and knowledge of their quarter. Their first duty was the settlement of local conflicts and the upkeep of security.[43] However, both police force as well as the newly introduced religious police could report to higher authorities if they felt that matters under their supervision were not dealt with speedily by the *'umda*s. The *'umda*s were charged with assisting the police and judiciary when certain inhabitants were requested by these authorities. Furthermore, they had to convey government decrees to the population. Presumably, this concerned cases such as the following, reported by the British

---

37 The British Library (hereafter BL), India Office Records (hereafter IOR)/L/PS/12/2099, *Constitution of the Hejaz*, encl. in weekly letter 228 of 14.7.1932 from Secretary, Political and Secret Dept. India Office to Foreign Office, Art. 13. Which of these provisions were part of the original arrangements, and which were amended later, is not clear, see Hope Gill's accompanying letter, 18 May 1932.
38 BL, IOR/L/PS/12/2099, Art. 32.
39 *Umm al-Qura*, 145, 23 September 1927.
40 BL, IOR/L/PS/12/2099, *Constitution*, Art. 34–5.
41 BL, IOR/L/PS/12/2099, *Constitution*, Part VIII, Art. 62–76.
42 BL, IOR/L/PS/12/2099, *Constitution*, Part IX, Art. 77–79; c.f. *Umm al-Qura* 133, 1 July 1927, "Nizam da'irat al-baladiyya" (Mecca), p. 3; about the *Majlis al-shura* see *Umm al-Qura*, 135, 15 July 1927.
43 *Umm al-Qura*, 157, 16 December 1927.

consul: "a regulation has been cried in the bazaar in Jedda but not published in the press, which seems to mean that unmarried men are not to live in the same houses as married couples. Fortunately Jedda has no low comedians to improve the occasion".[44]

The centralisation – here under national, rather than colonial rule – also manifested itself in the appointment of a new *qa'immaqam* who came from the Najd region (from where the Saudi family hails, rather than from the Hijaz) after the death of the old *qa'immaqam* in 1932. Perhaps crucially, this occurred at a time when local discontent was on the rise and there were even suggestions that plots were hatched by Hashemite loyalists against the Saudi rulers.[45]

Centralisation was not just a matter of royal control of decisions and appointments on all levels of administration, including the municipalities, but also, perhaps more critically, of finance: from September 1928, the new Saudi Finance Minister, 'Abdallah Sulayman, had to authorise any expenditures by the city of Jeddah. The municipality had just been authorised to raise new taxes when urban lands were registered. It was, however, apparently not authorised to use this revenue independently.[46] This was most likely the result of the massive financial crisis of the new Saudi government and an attempt to lay hands on any resources available anywhere.[47] Thus, local merchants were also recruited to cover notorious budget deficits, as had already been practiced in Ottoman and Hashemite times.[48] In 1931 a report from the now Saudi-controlled city stated: "In Jeddah the populace was in a poor way, while the landlord and merchant classes were exasperated almost beyond measure by the extortions of Abdullah Suleiman".[49]

---

44 The National Archives, London (hereafter TNA), Foreign Office (hereafter FO) 371/21905, *Jeddah Report, May 1938*. For lists of what was allowed and forbidden, see, for example, TNA, FO 104/609/5, *Jeddah Report, August 1928*, p. 34.

45 BL, IOR/L/PS/12/2073, *Jedda Report, May-June 1932*; BL, IOR/L/PS/12/2073, *Jedda Report, July-August 1932*.

46 TNA, FO 104/609/5, *Jeddah Report, September 1928*, p. 35. This seems to be based on a regulation concerning the directorate-general of finance, 7 Rabi' al-thani 1347 (21 September 1928), see BL, IOR/L/PS/12/2099, *Constitution*, Art. 7, 12. About the increase of sources of income and land registration, *Umm al-Qura*, 197, 5 October 1928, p. 3.

47 See the speech about the economic crisis by the King on 28 Jumada al-thani 1350 (10 November 1931), Middle East Centre Archives, St. Antony's College, Oxford (hereafter MEC), Philby Collection GB165-0229, 1/4/4, c.f. MEC, Philby Collection GB165-0229, 5/2/11/7, Economics in Arabia, with a detailed report on the economic crisis 1931–33.

48 For an example from Sharifian times, see TNA, FO 371/10809, *Jeddah Report, July 21–August 1925*, p. 323.

49 BL, IOR/L/PS/12/2073, *Jeddah Report, September-October 1931*, p. 3.

Overall, one can conclude that local administration and finances came under closer state control in most of the former Ottoman realms, while outwardly many of the earlier structural elements persisted.

Unifying Ideologies: Nationalism and Islam

Both in Turkey and in Egypt, the post-war governments emerged as the result of national struggles against foreign occupation, albeit with different degrees of independence. It is hence not surprising that nationalism became the banner under which state policies were advertised. Similarly, the mandated territories developed a language of national liberation – of varying degrees of moderation and radicalism. Turkey was clearly the only state (at the time) which advocated an entirely secular nationalism – ironically after having driven out most of the non-Muslim population. In most other cases, nationalism incorporated some measure of the Islamic legislation, mostly in family law.

Saudi Arabia (as well as the Yemen) chose the opposite approach, namely a decidedly Islamic orientation. In Saudi Arabia, this was based on the extension of the puritan Wahhabi interpretation of Islam from the Najd to all parts of the country. This was enforced by a new institution, which was not just to discipline the local population but also the – even more radical – warriors of Ibn Saud, the so-called *Ikhwan* who abhorred the religious and moral state of the Hijaz. The so-called *Hay'at al-amr bi-l-ma'ruf wa-l-nahy 'an al-munkar*, better known as religious police, was imported from the Najd. In September 1926, this successor to the Islamic institution of market control (*hisba*) made its first appearance in Jeddah, with the local head in Mecca being the son of a Hijazi *'alim*. By 1927, the committees in the Hijaz were subordinated to the Najdi *'alim* 'Abd al-Malik b. Ibrahim al-Shaykh, presumably to pacify Najdis suspicious of more liberal Hijazi religious practices.[50] British reports give a sense that this religious police acted rather unevenly and tended to be most active when the King or Viceroy were in town.[51] Major campaigns were conducted against

---

50   Darat al-Malik 'Abd al-'Aziz (DARA), Watha'iq wataniyya 2295, *letter by the ra'is diwan al-niyaba al-amma*, 16 February 1346/15 August 1927, for the announcement of the undated founding through a decision by the *'ulama'* see document no. 192. Steinberg, Guido, *Religion und Staat in Saudi-Arabien: Die wahhabitischen Gelehrten 1902–1953* (Würzburg: Ergon, 2002), pp. 411–14; Kostiner, Joseph, *The Making of Saudi Arabia, 1916–1936: From Chieftaincy to Monarchical State* (New York: Oxford University Press, 1993), p. 110.

51   TNA, FO 104/609/5, *Jeddah Report, September 1928*, p. 36; TNA, FO 371/13728, *Jeddah Report, December 1928*; BL, IOR/L/PS/12/2073, *Jeddah Report, July 1934*, p. 2; BL, IOR/L/PS/12/2073,

the consumption of alcohol, smoking, listening to music, three dimensional depictions of persons, the shaving of beards and football. In a sense, we have here the local manifestation of a national, Islamically oriented re-education campaign (notably in the non-Najdi territories of Saudi Arabia).

Public morals were also a major theme at a national conference of urban representatives in June 1931, next to pilgrimage, economics and general affairs.[52] This was to impress on them the importance of urban authorities ensuring regular attendance of prayers, the closing of shops during prayer times, the prohibition on smoking and drinking, on shaving beards, speaking to unrelated women etc.[53]

Besides such direct instruction of office-holders, the media were used to imbue the national creed. Thus, *Sawt al-Hijaz* (The Voice of Hijaz) ran an article on dress on August 16, 1939 under the beautiful title "Unification of dress. A sign for the moral harmony in this Arab homeland".[54] In 1930, Ibn Saud had declared the Najdi headdress with *ghutra* (and without *'iqal*) instead of the customary Hijazi turban as mandatory for anyone working in government service.[55] Incidentally, the language of "Arab homeland" shows that even the Islamically-oriented Saudi state was not immune from allusions to national (i.e. Arab) notions of identity. Indeed, the question of national dress, known as an important tool in nation-building in the Middle East, not least in the Ottoman empire, but also in post-war Iran and Turkey (which advocated very different styles of dress from the one described here) was to exercise the minds of people in present-day Saudi Arabia for a while.

In particular, silk applications on dresses and facial hair incited the Najdi *'ulama'*,[56] while the question of the Islamic legality of wearing a turban became a matter of a heated debate in the pages of the weekly *Umm al-Qura* in

---

Jeddah Report, December 1934, p. 3; BL, IOR/L/PS/12/2073, *Jeddah Report, April 1936*; BL, IOR/L/PS/12/2073, *Jeddah Report, August 1936*.

52   BL, IOR/L/PS/12/2085, *Hejaz-Nejd Annual Report 1931*.
53   Londres, Albert, *Pêcheurs de perles* (Paris: Albin Michel, 1931), pp. 32–4.
54   "Tawhid al-zayy. Mazhar min mazahir al-insijam al-khalqi fi hadha al-watan al-'arabi", *Sawt al-Hijaz*, 399, 16 August 1939.
55   Yamani, Mai, "Evading the habits of a life time: the adaptation of Hejazi dress to the New Social Order", in *Languages of Dress in the Middle East*, ed. Nancy Lindisfarne-Tapper and Bruce Ingham (Richmond, Surrey: Curzon, 1997), pp. 55–66. This is quoted by al-Rasheed and Steinberg but gives no dates and is rather general; al-Rasheed, Madawi, *A History of Saudi Arabia* (New York: Cambridge University Press, 2002), p. 201; Steinberg, *Religion und Staat*, p. 550. TNA, FO 371/15289, *Jeddah Report, December 1930*. Unfortunately, it is not clear, when the *thawb* was made mandatory.
56   Steinberg, *Religion und Staat*, pp. 550–1.

the early 1930s.[57] This was embedded in the wider discourse on Islamic morality, propounded not only by *'ulama'* but by the King. Besides rejecting a wide range of 'traditional behaviours', this was also used as a pretext to reject demands for "reform".[58]

In Jeddah (as well as other Saudi Arabian cities), the introduction of the *Hay'at al-amr bi-l-ma'ruf* marked an unprecedented intrusion of a state institution into people's private lives. To some extent, this might be compared structurally to state imposition of secularization, which was part of Turkey's nationalist agenda, and which found echoes in many MENA countries, be it under the auspices of colonial rule (such as in Algeria) or national governments (Iran and even Afghanistan). The imposition of dress-codes and the enforced removal of veils is clearly an expression of a more intrusive type of state which developed in this period.

The Changing Realms of Labour and Political Organisation

The interwar period saw in many places the emergence of new forms of self-organisation of civil society. Obviously, this is something with older roots. Thus, some mutual aid societies began in the late nineteenth century, and some of these are regarded as the first labour organisations. First secret associations, such as the Young Ottomans, forecast the later development of parties. The real game-changer for political as well as labour organisation was the declaration of the constitution in 1908, although the experience was cut short by the growing authoritarianism of the Young Turks and the wars of the second decade of the twentieth century.[59] Port cities and metropoles, such as Istanbul, Alexandria, Cairo, Beirut and Aden, were the initial starting points of labour organisation as they required large numbers of labourers in the ports as well as in the emerging industries.

In the interwar period, the actual possibilities of self-organisation depended very much on the respective political circumstances. The immediate end of the Great War saw a flurry of activity by workers as well as former students in Turkey. While Atatürk initially attempted to integrate urban workers into the

---

57   *Umm al-Qura*, 401, 19 August 1932, with references to earlier contributions to the debate.
58   *Umm al-Qura*, 647, 30 April 1937; BL, IOR/L/PS/12/2073, *Jedda Report, May 1937*.
59   For a cursory survey with useful references see Man, Fuat, "The perception of the relationship between trade unions and politics in Turkey: a tracking on the related acts", *Mediterranean Journal of Social Sciences*, 4/9 (2013), pp. 214–16; c.f. Beinin, *Workers and Peasants*, pp. 77–80.

nationalist movement and invited them to participate in political meetings, independent activism was not tolerated for long. The Kurdish rebellion of 1925 also led to a clampdown on the wider labour movement, as well as independent parties and political organisations thereafter.

In other metropoles of the former Ottoman empire, labour unions began once again to emerge, albeit under difficult circumstances.[60] However, in remote provinces such as the Hijaz but possibly also provincial towns, the traditional guild system continued unabated. Thus, in a labour conflict in Jeddah harbour about who was responsible for the passage of goods through customs in 1928, it was the *qa'immaqam*, local merchants and the sheikh of the guild of porters who negotiated a settlement, much like they would have done in the nineteenth century.[61] Probably the main difference was that the guilds, which acted as a kind of mediator to local government, were more prone to accept compromise than unions that were decidedly representatives of workers' interests.

Besides unions, nationalism and political parties were the other main new features of civic organisation, although they had made a brief appearance after 1908. One needs to be cautious not to expect too rapid a transition from the politics of notables to party politics, and needs to consider the political constellations. Thus, Atatürk converted the Müdafaa-i Milliye Cemiyeti (Defence of Rights Group), basically a nationwide association of his supporters, into the Cumhuriyet Halk Fırkası (later Cumhuriyet Halk Partisi, the People's Republican Party) in September 1923. Apart from the Terakkiperver Cumhuriyet Fırkası (Progressive Republican Party), founded in 1924 and closed the following year, and a short-lived "experiment with a 'tame' opposition party in 1930", Turkey remained a one-party state until after World War II.[62] In this context, both the party as well as trade unions and other organisations that would usually be counted among the civil society, such as the Türk Kadınlar Birliği (Turkish Women's Union), became instruments of the state rather than means to express collective interests of societal groups vis-à-vis the state.

---

60   Beinin, Joel and Zachary Lockman, "1919: labour upsurge and national revolution", in *The Modern Middle East: A Reader*, ed. Albert Hourani, Philip S. Khoury and Mary C. Wilson (London and New York: I.B. Tauris, 1993), pp. 395–428; as well as Beinin, *Workers and Peasants*, pp. 84–92.

61   TNA, FO 371/13010, *Jeddah Report, October 1928*; for earlier disputes e.g. TNA, FO 195/1943, Alban to Currie, 18 February 1896, Alban to Currie, 23 March 1896; TNA, FO 195/2286, Monahan to Chargé d'Affaires, 2 July 1908; TNA, FO 195/2320, Monahan to Lowther, 23 February 1909.

62   Zürcher, Erik Jan, *Turkey: A Modern History*, 3rd ed. (London: I.B. Tauris, 2004), pp. 160, 176.

Even where the struggle for independence caused (relative) mass mobilisation such as in Egypt, or in Palestine where the struggle against the project of a Jewish homeland created through immigration mobilised masses, representatives of the leading notable families were usually among the leading figures when it came to the formation of parties and the formulation of political goals. Saying this does not dismiss the importance of lower class mobilisation and populist politics.[63] Indeed, Khoury has shown in much detail how different interest groups crystallized around, and were mobilised by, different notables, and how in a kind of generational change younger and at times lesser notables came to represent new groups of urban professionals. At the same time, youth organisations and gangs absorbed and channelled the demands of other sectors of the urban population.[64]

While, in the Levant and Egypt, the interwar period was a time during which political parties and other civil organisations emerged, organised political activity was fairly subdued in the Hijaz. There is one body which called itself al-Hizb al-Watani (The National Party), consisting of a group of leading notables. This was formed early in October 1924, after the fall of Ta'if to the forces of Ibn Saud. The city had been plundered and many inhabitants massacred following its surrender in September 1924.[65] The party was the result of a gathering of Hijazi nobility, including members of the Sharifian family, 'ulama' and chief merchants. Its aim was basically to replace Sharif Hussayn and avoid a similar massacre to that which had taken place in Ta'if. This was based on the assumption that such a change in ruler would placate Ibn Saud. The notables seized the opportunity to establish almost a constitutional monarchy, in response to the many political grievances which had emerged with regard to maladministration under King Hussayn, as already mentioned above. British reports support the claim that life became more difficult: The only extant bank ceased to function,[66] water supplies had become scarce on a number of occasions,

---

63 For an overview of the debate see the contributions by Gershoni, Gelvin, Lockman and Khoury in *Rethinking Nationalism in the Arab Middle East*, ed. James P. Jankowski and Israel Gershoni (New York: Columbia University Press, 1997).
64 Khoury, Philip S., *Syria and the French Mandate: The Politics of Arab Nationalism, 1920–1945*, 1st ed. (Princeton: Princeton University Press, 1987); c.f. Wien, Peter, *Iraqi Arab Nationalism: Authoritarian, Totalitarian and Pro-Fascist Inclinations, 1932–1941* (London and New York: Routledge, 2006).
65 Vassiliev, Alexei, *The History of Saudi-Arabia* (London: Saqi, 2000), pp. 261–2; for the party see Nasif, Husayn Muhammad, *Madi al-Hijaz wa-hadiruhu* [Hijaz, Past and Present] ([s.n.], 1349/ 1930), pp. 120–43. On the changeover of power see also TNA, FO 371/10014.
66 TNA, FO 371/5242, *Political Report by Col. Vickery, period June 22-July 2, 1920*.

taxes were raised on various goods and services,[67] censorship was rife and infrastructural improvements, such as the building of lighthouses to improve the harbour, were rejected.[68] Given the confrontation with Ibn Saud which overshadowed all other concerns, however, any concrete reform measures were put aside also by the National Party.

After the Saudi takeover in December 1925, there was little room for political manoeuver, with many leading notables initially leaving the city for Suakin or Aden. British reports mention occasional disturbances, for example in December 1928 in Ta'if when followers of Ibn Saud got upset by smokers and destroyed a number of shops. They were also said to have killed the local *qadi* who refused to sentence a smoker, causing considerable unrest.[69] By the late 1920s, and with the worsening international economic situation, a number of exiles started to organise and to coordinate with discontented exiles notably from the 'Asir region.[70]

It is not surprising that Saudi authorities were extremely suspicious of a conspiracy against them in the cities of the Hijaz, and arrested a number of relatives of the opposition ringleaders. Furthermore, they attempted to prevent any larger gathering that could be used for political purposes. One coincidental 'victim' of this was the game of football, which had arrived in the late 1920s with Javanese pilgrims and very quickly gained wide popularity among young men. It was quickly prohibited, partly for suspicions that it was un-Islamic, partly – according to a British report – for "the fact that it brings young men together in clubs".[71] Thus the type of youth organisation that has been described for Baghdad and Damascus which could evolve into a political and at times paramilitary force had no chance of developing in Jeddah. In the light of strict control on state institutions and tight press-censorship, independent political expression by social groups could hardly develop.[72]

---

67 TNA, FO 371/6524, *Jeddah Report, April 1–10, 1921*, pp. 528, 534; TNA, FO 371/7718, *Jeddah Report, January 1–20, 1922*, p. 4; TNA, FO 371/7718, *Jeddah Report, February 11–28, 1922*, pp. 18–20.; TNA, FO 371/7718, *Jeddah Report, April 21-May 10, 1922*, p. 44.

68 TNA, FO 371/8946, *Jeddah Report, November 1–29, 1923*, p. 179. On the problems in Hashemite times see also al-Harbi, Dalal bte Mukhlid, "al-Awda' al-dakhiliyya fi Jidda fi fatrat al-hisar 1343-144 h./1925 m. min khilal sahifat "Barid al-Hijaz"" [The Internal Affairs of Jeddah during the Siege 1343-1344 h./1925 through (a reading of) the newspaper "Mail of Hijaz"], *al-Dar'iyya*, 47–48 (2010), 123–84.

69 TNA, FO 371/13728, *Jeddah Report, December 1928*, p. 48.

70 Vassiliev, *History*, pp. 282–5.

71 BL, IOR/L/PS/12/2073, *Jeddah Report, May-June 1932*.

72 TNA, FO 104/609/5, *Jeddah Report, August 1928*; TNA, FO 371/13728, *Jeddah Report, April 1929*.

Developmentalism in Urban Planning

The overwhelmingly dominant notion of developmentalism was closely linked to a more interventionist state, but also to the nationalist and Islamic ideologies dominating the period. As mentioned before, there were widely differing degrees of state planning. The most radical approach was clearly the construction of the new capital, Ankara, in Turkey, based on "the most recent principles of the art of urbanism".[73] "By building an entirely new city (next to a smaller old one), the state ... [became] the agent of the nation", argues Çınar.[74] In this case, the projected image was one of modernism, secularism, and Turkish nationalism. The central "nation square" with the parliament, the official guesthouse, a restaurant, bank and the central station, not forgetting a monument of the new republic's founder at its centre, was emblematic of this approach. This was where official ceremonies, commemorative gatherings as well as public executions were held.[75] Indeed, squares – rather than mosques – became the new 'natural' centres of cities serving as "platforms" for those in power, while older cities, most notably Istanbul, were neglected.[76]

Houston rightly remarks that many of the impulses behind this representative and nationalist way of urban planning were quite typical of the time and were also shaping the re-arrangement of cities elsewhere in the Middle East, such as Baghdad and Tehran. There was one important difference, however: new Tehran was "built on and over the old city" through widening the streets, establishing large squares and roundabouts, often decorated with statues of the monarch.[77]

Not only the nation states were interested in a representative re-structuring of urban spaces, but also the Mandate powers, notably in the major cities. Thus, the French in Beirut were set on implementing a "plan of enlargement and beautification". It was put in place in 1920 and translated into practice since 1931. Its basic principles of urban recording and development were thought to

---

73 Atay, Falih Rıfkı, *Çankaya: Atatürk'ün Doğumundan Ölümüne Kadar*, pp. 488–9; cited after Kaçar, Duygu, "Ankara, a small town, transformed to a nation's capital", *Journal of Planning History*, 9/1 (2010), p. 47. Kaçar's article also shows the early architectural plans for Ankara.
74 Çınar, "The imagined community", p. 154.
75 Çınar, "The imagined community", pp. 155–62.
76 Gül, *Emergence*, p. 79. On public spaces c.f. Turhanoğlu, F. Ayşın Koçak, "Spatial production of Ankara as capital city of republican Turkey", *Journal of Interdisciplinary Social Sciences*, 5/5 (2010), pp. 312–15.
77 Houston, Christopher, "Ankara, Tehran, Baghdad: three varieties of Kemalist urbanism", *Thesis Eleven*, 121/1 (2014), p. 65.

be transferable between cities almost anywhere in the French empire.[78] With reference to French plans in Damascus, Neep argues that this model had been initially developed in the French metropole, "but only in the colonies did urbanists find a suitable climate in which to implement their grand designs for city planning and public health".[79]

Obviously, "grand designs" could be better realised in new towns, such as Qamishli in the Jazira region of Syria.[80] Here, certain Western notions of the 'Oriental' or 'Islamic' city, such as the separation of religious and socio-economic groups, were taken into account by planners such as Danger. Both in Damascus and Aleppo, the picturesque old cities were rarely touched, unless events such as fires invited such initiatives. New initiatives in these locations concentrated on the outskirts.[81] Here, urbanist models such as garden cities, parks and other spaces dedicated to a healthy and hygienic life were introduced by French and British urban planners. These concepts had often emerged in international urbanist debates in the late nineteenth century and already been tested in Cairo prior to World War I.[82] In Haifa, a Central Town Planning Commission was established in 1921, even though, as in the case of Beirut, it only started effective work after 1929 and, even then, seems to have been overshadowed by the central authorities in Jerusalem, which initiated a master plan for Haifa in 1930.[83] In Baghdad, the British were much slower – the first proper master plan was only passed in the 1950s, which is similar to developments in the Saudi cities of Riyadh and Jeddah (where the first overall master plan was only written in 1959). Overall, it seems that urbanist visions were diffused unevenly, so that one cannot assume an imperial master-vision that should be applied, although traces of this may, of course, be found in the French notions of separating ethno-religious groups in Syria and in certain North-African cities.[84]

78 Eddé, Carla, Franck Friès, Marlène Ghorayeb and Jade Tabet, "Damas, Beyrouth, regards croisés", in *Damas: miroir brisé d'un Orient arabe,* ed. Anne-Marie Bianquis (Paris: Autrement, 1993), pp. 136–45; c.f. Prestel, Joseph B., "Feeling Urban Change: Debates on Emotions in Berlin and Cairo, 1860–1910", Ph.D. Dissertation, Freie Universität Berlin, 2014.
79 Neep, Daniel, *Occupying Syria Under the French Mandate: Insurgency, Space and State Formation* (Cambridge: Cambridge University Press, 2012), p. 132. A very similar argument is put forward by Eddé, Friès, Ghorayeb and Tabet, "Damas, Beyrouth, regards croisés", pp. 136–45.
80 Neep, *Occupying Syria*, p. 146.
81 Neep, *Occupying Syria*, pp. 152–3.
82 Prestel, "Feeling Urban Change", Ch. 6.2.
83 Seikaly, *Haifa*, p. 62.
84 On the colonial city, see King, Anthony D., *Colonial Urban Development: Culture, Social Power, and Environment* (London and Boston: Routledge and Kegan Paul, 1976).

STATE-SOCIETY RELATIONS AND URBAN DEVELOPMENT 47

In addition, as King has pointed out, the urban landscape was and is even in a colonial setting "a terrain of discipline and resistance",[85] in which transnationally circulating models were adapted and negotiated.[86] Finally, it needs to be remembered, once again, that notions of master plans and massive urban remodelling were not exclusive to the imperial situation, but already implemented in Cairo under Khedive Ismail in the 1870s.[87]

If Jeddah or Saudi Arabia has not been mentioned in this section, it is simply because larger scale urban planning, which Jeddah had undergone to some extent in the last quarter of the nineteenth century, only returned after World War II. Before the influx of oil money, the country simply was too poor to invest in anything much beyond the basic infrastructure discussed in the next section. There were occasional bouts of larger ideas: thus, in 1936, a visit by the Egyptian economist Talaat Harb prompted renewed speculations about road building, air traffic and paved roads. "In Jedda", the British consul wrote,

> urban development is in the air. We are promised two new boulevards, and Fuad Bey Hamza, our premier advocate of modernity, is said to have even larger schemes. Meanwhile, January witnessed one achievement, the creation of miniature Champs Elysées, without the trees, outside the Medina gate. Two parallel roads, 200 or 300 yards long, marked out with oil drums and neatly bordered with drains, were made to carry traffic, one-way of course, to and from the desert. They were oddly set with reference to the gate and they have not so far been surfaced [...].[88]

There was some refurbishment in the harbour area that same year with a few new government buildings, but otherwise, no major urbanisation projects were undertaken, in spite of some speculation about the building of a new port and even an airport.[89] Rather, there was a kind of 'bricolage' when basic needs, most notably in the fields of water and health, became urgent. This is

---

85 King, Anthony D., "Writing transnational planning histories", in *Urbanism: Imported or Exported?*, ed. Joe Nasr and Mercedes Volait (Chichester, UK and Hoboken: Wiley-Academy, 2003), pp. 3–4. This is borne out by the different reactions in Damascus and Beirut to French urbanist suggestions in the 1960s, See Tabet et al., "Damas, Beyrouth, regards croisés", p. 137.

86 King, "Writing transnational planning histories", pp. 4–5.

87 Abu-Lughod, Janet L., *Cairo: 1001 Years of the City Victorious* (Princeton: Princeton University Press, 1971), p. 109.

88 BL, IOR/L/PS/12/2073, *Jedda Report, January 1936*, pp. 1–2.

89 BL, IOR/L/PS/12/2073, *Jeddah Report, May 1936*. For the expectations of business in aviation, electrification, telegraph etc. see the documents in Ministère des Affaires étrangères

not surprising in a state which remained, until the 1950s when oil revenues began to flow, basically stripped of cash.

The Question of Health and Hygiene

Health and hygiene had been central concerns related to the pilgrimage since the latter half of the nineteenth century. While, initially, European powers had been mostly concerned with the spread of cholera, and enforced the introduction of a quarantine regime for the Red Sea, this concern with health – not only of Europeans but also of pilgrims – caused a heightened interest also in wider sanitary conditions in the Hijaz, including healthcare and the provision of clean drinking water. This prompted relatively wide-spread public works in the port city, although they fade in comparison to investments in cities such as Istanbul, Beirut or Alexandria.[90] During the troubled Hashemite times, it seems that little was invested by the authorities into urban infrastructure. Obviously, the continued provision of the city with water, from a source on the foothills of Mecca by aqueduct, as well as the condenser which had been first inaugurated during Ottoman times, was of vital concern.[91] The water question became even more vital as refugees from Mecca and Ta'if fleeing the Saudi advance swelled the city's population.[92]

With the establishment of Saudi rule, there was a need felt to improve pilgrimage provisions, not just for reasons of Islamic legitimacy but also for the vital income generated through pilgrimage. Thus, while the repair of the old condenser was still contemplated in May 1926, by summer 1927 a new machine had been ordered.[93] Apparently, technical difficulties persisted with the condenser, so that by summer 1932, the government was considering closing the condensers and relying exclusively on the water from the Meccan foothills. The installations of the water source, seven miles out of town, had been renewed in the autumn of 1931.[94] Apparently, optimism was fuelled by the prospecting of

---

(hereafter MAE), Centre des Archives diplomatiques de Nantes (hereafter CADN), 2_MI_3299 and 2_MI_3300.

90 For an overview see Pétriat, Philippe, "For pilgrims and for trade: merchants and public works in Ottoman Jeddah", *Turkish Historical Review*, 5/2 (2014), 200–20.

91 TNA, FO 371/7718, *Jeddah Report, January 1922*.

92 al-Harbi, "al-Awda' al-dakhiliyya fi Jidda", pp. 140–1, 162; TNA, FO 371/10809, *Jeddah Report, July 21-August 10, 1925*, p. 325.

93 TNA, FO 371/11442, *Jeddah Report, April 1926*, p. 385; TNA, FO 371/12250, *Jeddah Report, July 1927*, p. 466; TNA, FO 371/13010, *Jeddah Report, December 1927*, p. 486.

94 BL, IOR/L/PS/12/2073, *Jeddah Report, May-June 1932*, p. 4; BL, IOR/L/PS/12/2073, *Jeddah Report, June 1933*, p. 2; *Umm al-Qura*, 352, 11 September 1931.

an American engineer for water and minerals.[95] By summer 1933, water from the source reached Jeddah again, and a British report indicates the widespread official as well as local interest in the matter: "The event was celebrated on the 26th by a ceremonial inauguration, at which local dignitaries, the Minister of Finance and a crowd of some thousands were present".[96]

In a quite revolutionary move, water could be taken free of charge from a tank on the edge of town, the only charges raised were for its transport to the individual houses. Even if matters remained somewhat complicated, given that, in 1937, it is reported that the drinking water was polluted with animal dung, the topic fades into the background in the newspapers and consular reports, indicating a temporary solution to a long-standing vital problem for the urban problem and visitors.[97]

While there were protracted negotiations between the Hashemite King and the British regarding the implementation of earlier quarantine regulations, the health situation in the city seems to have been dire. Jeddah only had one working hospital at the time, and Egyptian and Syrian doctors and health officials, sent for the pilgrimage in late 1924 with ample staff and equipment, were welcomed and – in the Syrian case – even incorporated into the local administration.[98] Health services remained minimalistic in early Saudi times.[99] From both newspapers and consular reports, it appears that the Saudi state insisted on licensing doctors, pharmacists and midwives, presumably with view to licensing fees. In any case, Jeddah did not attract many medical practitioners: the first dentist, a Turk, seems to have settled in Jeddah only in 1938.[100] Interestingly, only the visit of an Arab medical mission (possibly from Egypt) spurred the government to renew its interest in a reasonable state of the quarantine stations.[101] Hence a report by a visitor from 1932 who complained that money was available for motor transport and the upkeep of the royal family, but neither for schools nor hospitals and dispensaries, seems to support the impression, emerging from other sources, that there was very little investment.[102] This is in marked contrast to, for example, the attention given to national health and education by the Turkish government. The latter used classical tools of

---

95   *Umm al-Qura*, 337, 29 May 1931.
96   BL, IOR/L/PS/12/2073, *Jedda Report, August 1933*.
97   TNA, FO 371/20842, *Jedda Report, September 1937*.
98   TNA, FO 371/20842, *Jedda Report, September 1937*, pp. 141–3.
99   TNA, FO 371/11442, *Jeddah Report, August 1926*.
100 TNA, FO 104/609/5, *Jeddah Report, April 1928*, FO 371/21905, *Jeddah Report, May 1938*.
101 TNA, FO 371/23271, *Jeddah Report, May 1939*.
102 Dame, Louis P., "A trip to Taif", *Neglected Arabia. Arabia Calling*, 163 (Oct.-Dec. 1932), p. 11.

governmentality, such as surveys, and access to the population via the quickly proliferating state institutions to combat the spread of diseases.[103]

Transport

Transport within Jeddah was easily possible on foot, or by beast of burden. By the late 1920s, bicycles became a desirable means of transport as well as a source of tax income for the cash-stripped state.[104] Indeed, Saudi memoirs discussing the 1940s to the 1960s mention the bicycle as a very attractive alternative to long marches on foot in smaller or more remote Saudi towns and villages.[105]

More important were the connections by sea and inland to Mecca, which presented major challenges. The Ottomans had invested quite heavily in expanding the port area and harboured plans to extend the Hijaz railway to Jeddah to facilitate the travel of pilgrims. However, the latter project was stopped by the war. Discussions of this project were revived in 1932, but came to nothing, probably due to financial constraints.[106] Instead, motor transport of pilgrims became an obvious alternative. British reports as well as local newspapers abound with reports on motor transport between the two cities and the difficulties its organisation encountered. There were various attempts to organise it centrally through the government, or to organise a joint company by a number of investors which was to be a national endeavour.[107] Of course, this quickly caused frictions between the state and notables as well as between notables on finances, licenses for car imports etc.[108] In spite of these obstacles, the American consul reported in January 1928 that Jeddah had about 500 cars and that the old pilgrims' route to Mecca was to be turned into a proper road.

---

103   Evered, Emine Ö. and Kyle T. Evered, "Sex and the capital city: the political framing of syphilis and prostitution in early republican Ankara", *Journal of the History of Medicine and Allied Sciences*, 68/2 (2013), 266–99.

104   TNA, FO 371/13728, *Jeddah Report, February 1929*.

105   Atmaca, Nushin, "Saudische Lebensgeschichten: Die 'Generation des Aufbaus' im Spiegel zeitgenössischer Autobiographien", M.A. Dissertation, Freie Universität Berlin, 2012, pp. 54, 90–91.

106   MAE, CADN, 2_MI_3229, Krajewski to French Ministry of Foreign Affairs (22/29 December 1922), letter to Maigret, 3 November 1932.

107   al-Harbi, "al-Awdaʿ al-dakhiliyya fi Jidda"; TNA, FO 371/11442, *Jeddah Report, March 1926*; TNA, FO 371/11442, *Jeddah Report, September 1926*; *Umm al-Qura*, 151, 4 October 1927; *Umm al-Qura*, 152, 11 October 1927.

108   TNA, FO 371/13010, *Jeddah Report, February 1928*.

STATE-SOCIETY RELATIONS AND URBAN DEVELOPMENT   51

Already, transport time had apparently been reduced from 24 to two hours and prices had become fixed.[109] Besides cars, motor buses were imported on a relatively large scale and started to supplant the caravans, causing some unrest among the Bedouin in the surrounding areas.[110] By 1947, the demand for roads within the walled city was among the strong reasons for demolishing the city wall.

Education

As mentioned before, education was not high on the Saudi development agenda. In Ottoman times, a middle school (*rüşdiye*) and a private Arab school had been established in Jeddah, mainly as a result of local pressure and investment. These schools seem to have lived on, the former *rüşdiye* being characterised by a British report of 1926 as an elementary school.[111] The newspaper *Umm al-Qura* noted on 29 July 1927 the establishment of an "educational council" (Majlis al-Ma'arif) which, shortly thereafter, announced the unification of curricula.[112] Given that, seven years later, there were still as many as one primary and one secondary state school in Jeddah, this seems to have been an activity more geared towards pacifying the Wahhabi establishment than towards the systematic building of an educational system.[113] Besides a number of Qur'anic schools, the private *Madrasat al-Falah* remained the major school in Jeddah, catering to the needs of about 700 pupils.[114] The world economic crisis, as well as a downturn in the pearling industry which had formed the base of its

---

109   National Archives and Records Administration, USA (NARA), M722,17 (Saudi Arabia 890f, 1910–1929, American Consulate, Aden Arabia (Vice Consul in Charge Aldridge), 23 January 1928 to Secretary of State; TNA, FO 371/13728; *Jeddah Report April 1929*; BL, IOR/L/PS/12/2073, Sir A. Ryan to Sir John Simon, 9 May 1933; BL, IOR/L/PS/12/2073, *Jedda Report, April 1933*, Eastern (Arabia) Confidential 30 May 1933, Sir A. Ryan to Sir John Simon, 5 June 1933, *Jedda Report, May 1933*, Eastern (Arabia) Confidential June 28, 1933. About the building of roads see also MAE, CADN, 2_MI_3229, 11 April 1939, 4 December 1939.
110   van der Meulen, Daniël, *Don't You Hear The Thunder: A Dutchman's Life Story* (Leiden: Brill Academic Publishers, 1981), p. 86; TNA, FO 371/20842, *Jeddah Report, September 1937*; TNA, FO 371/20842, *Djeddah Report, November 1937*; about tarmacking of road see BL, IOR/L/PS/12/2085, *Hejaz-Nejd Annual Report 1930*.
111   TNA, FO 371/11442, *Jeddah Report, September 1926*, p. 411.
112   *Umm al-Qura*, 140, 19 August 1927.
113   TNA, FO 371/11442, *Jeddah Report, September 1926*, 411–12; BL, IOR/L/PS/12/2085, *Saudi Arabia Annual Report 1933*; BL, IOR/L/PS/12/2085, Sir A. Ryan to Sir John Simon, 28 April 1934.
114   BL, IOR/L/PS/12/2085, *Saudi Arabia Annual Report 1933*, p. 37.

founder's wealth led to an interesting initiative by local merchants: they suggested to Ibn Saud a special import tax "for the benefit of the schools and a girls' school". "The merchants were to be entrusted with the collection of this tax and the administration of the proceeds".[115] This suggestion, which was accepted, illustrates both the need for (and existence of) private initiative in the educational sector as well as Ibn Saud's willingness to cooperate. This happened, *nota bene*, at a time when the spread of state education with a clear focus on nation building was an important concern of governments from Turkey to Egypt, and when, as in Syria and Palestine, schools became important focal points of student political mobilization.

It seems that, apart from the above intervention, Ibn Saud shunned the confrontation with the Wahhabi *'ulama'* on an issue that was of little immediate concern to him. If money was to be invested in education, it was in areas deemed necessary for the state. This is evidenced by the founding, in 1930, of two schools, one for flying and the other for wireless communication.[116] Both wireless connections and air traffic were considered part of the strategic project of integrating and controlling the country through improved communications and a more intense postal service. This assumed even more importance against the backdrop of the *Ikhwan* revolt in northern Saudi Arabia.[117] The improvement of telephone lines a decade later probably served the same purpose.[118] Given the recent establishment of the kingdom and its very basic infrastructure, infrastructural improvements became crucial to the very survival of the new state. In contrast, the provision of services to the population was of secondary importance.

Conclusion: The Expansion of the State through Development

Returning to the overarching question of how state-society relations present themselves in the interwar Middle East, it may be concluded that the period was marked by a good degree of continuity from Ottoman times. This includes not just concrete institutional continuities, but also a desire by the state – now in the garb of a (nascent) nation-state rather than an empire – to expand its control and grip on society. This found its expression in new modes of urban

---

115   BL, IOR/L/PS/12/2085, *Saudi Arabia Annual Report 1935*; BL, IOR/L/PS/12/2085, Sir A. Ryan to Sir John Simon, 29 February 1936, p. 42.
116   *Umm al-Qura*, 307, 24 October 1930.
117   MAE, CADN, 2_MI_3229, Maigret to French Ministry of Foreign Affairs, 22 September 1931, 4 May 1932, 24 August 1932.
118   TNA, FO 371/21905, *Jedda Report, July 1938*; TNA, FO 371/24588, *Jedda Report, April 1940*.

planning as well as more specific types of urban development. On the flip side, Middle Eastern societies also continued to develop new forms of organisation, such as associations, parties and trade unions, but also, for example, sports clubs which, again, had begun to emerge in late Ottoman times, notably after 1908. Their room for manoeuvre was often curtailed in more than one way, even in ostensibly democratic regimes as the one in Egypt.

The expanding domains of the state were particularly observable in the fields of health, education and services. The case of Jeddah, which has taken centre-stage in this chapter, demonstrates the dramatic differences between the various parts of the former Ottoman empire – the notion of a "colonial welfare state" developed by Thompson for Syria was not applicable in Saudi Arabia (this changed with the onset of oil wealth after World War II).[119] It is exactly this lack of state funds which shows the (partial) convergence of the interests of the state with those of the elite, notably where vital infrastructures were concerned. Thus, even without the type of new, nationalist middle classes aspiring to the "national modernist developmentalist ethos"[120] which were found elsewhere, the answer to the question of convergence and difference of interests between state and society remains ambiguous.

Finally, it seems important to draw attention to the growing competition between the state and the city for the primary affiliation of the population, which Holston has highlighted.[121] This was a continuous process which did not begin in the interwar period and might, in a number of cases, still continue today, and be it only in form of multiple notions of belonging. It was certainly stronger in cases of rigorous urban reconfiguration and weakest where, for different reasons, the state had to enter partnerships with local urban elites in order to push its developmentalist agenda.

Overall, it would seem that state-society relations in cities developed in a complex interplay of state interventionism, local conditions and transnational professionalism. It is only if these different factors are integrated that we can grasp the common and the specific in urban development, and understand how at times contradictory terminologies of state-led developmentalism might still reveal some common ground.

---

119   Thompson, *Colonial Citizens*, pp. 155–6.
120   Ryzova, Lucie, "Egyptianizing modernity through the 'New Effendiya': social and cultural constructions of the middle class in Egypt under the monarchy", in *Re-Envisioning Egypt: 1919–1952*, ed. Arthur Goldschmidt, Amy J. Johnson and Barak A. Salmoni (Cairo and New York: The American University in Cairo Press, 2005), p. 146.
121   Holston, James, *Insurgent Citizenship: Disjunctions of Democracy and Modernity in Brazil* (Princeton: Princeton University Press, 2008), pp. 22–3.

CHAPTER 3

Beirut's Musical Scene: A Narrative of Modernization and Identity Struggles under the French Mandate

Diana Abbani

When American missionaries asked the Arab philologist and *Nahda* poet Sheikh Nasif al-Yaziji (1800–71) to write Arabic hymns for them to be sung to European melodies with a western orchestra and chorus, he replied "We have beautiful Arabic rhythms [in which] to compose your hymns if you wish. We have no interest in your melodies that resemble the barking of jackals during winter nights!"[1] A century later, Salam al-Racy (1911–2003), a Lebanese writer of folk literature, who reported this incident, tried unconsciously to excuse al-Yaziji's response by explaining that "Oriental [al-sharqiyyin] ears were still not accustomed to harmonized music [al-harmuni al-musiqiyya]",[2] thereby implying that it was only in his day "Oriental ears" learned to listen to and appreciate European classical music! This anecdote summarizes the discourse duality, the changes in taste and the struggles around musical modernization that took place in the musical field in Beirut and the region for more than a century.

From the nineteenth century, Beirut had undergone many changes, from the reforms of the Tanzimat (1839–76), to its becoming the capital of its province (*vilayet*) in 1888 and the main port city in the Levant, undergoing urban transformation, political and administrative change and, after the Great War (1914–18), becoming a French Mandate.[3] All these changes were reflected in the discourse of the emerging intellectuals who argued about the meaning of modernity, European values, and reform. Music, too, formed part of this modernity discourse and was seen as part of the process of progress and modernization.

---

1 al-Racy, Salam, *Li'alla tadi'* [For Fear That It May Be Lost] (Beirut: Dar Nawfal, 1995), p. 66.
2 al-Racy, *Li'alla tadi'*, p. 66.
3 For a more detailed account of the economic, social and urban development of Beirut, see Davie, May, *Beyrouth et ses faubourgs (1840–1940): une intégration inacheveé* (Beirut: CERMOC, 1996); Hanssen, Jens, *Fin de Siècle Beirut: The Making of an Ottoman Provincial Capital* (Oxford: Oxford University Press, 2005); Sehnaoui, Nada, *L'occidentalisation de la vie quotidienne a`Beyrouth, 1860–1914* (Beirut: Dar an-Nahar, 2002), and Eddé, Carla, *Beyrouth, Naissance d'une capitale (1918–1924)* (Paris: Actes Sud, 2009).

Following Pierre Bourdieu's approach, this chapter aims to map the musical production in Beirut during the Mandate period by studying the musical scene as a field of forces and a field of struggles where concepts of civilisation (*tammadun*), music and culture (*tathqif, tahdhib*) were interlinked and circulated among different scholars.[4] My aim is to examine the factors involved in this process in a larger socio-political context and, moving beyond the fixed Orient-Occident dichotomy, to investigate questions of identity which were central to conversations about music and art in general.[5]

While *Nahda* scholarship mainly focuses on literary modernity and questions of subjectivity, few works deal with aesthetics and artistic fields. Recently, several works have related modernization to tastes and class distinction, demonstrating how the formation of a new modernity and ideas of nationalism were linked to material culture and gradually brought about the creation of tensions inside society.[6] Applying this approach to the musical field, I seek here to trace the conflicts generated in the musical scene, while linking it to questions of enlightenment, progress, and modernization. It is also associated with the emergence of a new educated class willing to take part in the civilizational narrative and trying to create a new modern identity based on its cultural past.

The first part of this chapter focuses on the production of music itself, showing how the emergence of a new 'middle class' and the introduction of new technologies and new forms of entertainment were interlinked and changed musical practices during the Mandate period. The second part analyses, through the examination of musical criticism in the Beiruti press, the ways in which Beiruti intellectuals discussed questions of modernity in their musical discourse. My aim is to examine how music was integrated into modernization

---

4   Bourdieu, Pierre, *The Field of Cultural Production: Essays on Art and Literature*, ed. Randal Johnson (New York: Columbia University Press, 1993), p. 30.
5   Bourdieu, *The Field of Cultural Production*, p. 29.
6   This literature includes the work of Abou-Hodeib, Toufoul, "Taste and class in late Ottoman Beirut", *International Journal of Middle East Studies*, 43/3 (2011), 475–92; Khater, Ahram, *Inventing Home: Emigration, Gender, and the Middle Class in Lebanon, 1870–1920* (Berkeley and Los Angeles: University of California Press, 2001); Pollard, Lisa, "The family politics of colonizing and liberating Egypt, 1882–1919", *Social Politics*, 7/1 (2000), 47–79; Russell, Mona, *Creating the New Egyptian Woman: Consumerism, Education, and National Identity, 1863–1922* (New York: Palgrave Macmillan, 2004); Watenpaugh, Keith, *Being Modern in the Middle East: Revolution, Nationalism, Colonialism, and the Arab Middle Class* (Princeton and Oxford: Princeton University Press, 2006) and Ramadan, Dina, "The Aesthetics of the Modern: Art, Education, and Taste in Egypt 1903–1952", Ph.D. Dissertation, Columbia University, 2013.

debates and how this in turn gradually brought about a change in the status of music which became perceived as a route to progress and a marker of 'taste'.

Beirut Musical Production: Cosmopolitism, Education and Mutations

New Modern Class, New Way of Life

From the end of the nineteenth century, with its integration into the world economy and the proliferation of economic and political migration, Beirut became a cosmopolitan city and a new urban 'modern' middle class, composed mainly of intellectuals, merchants, and bureaucrats, took shape under the Mandate.[7] Made up of educated men and women, this new urban class shared the same cultural and economic capital, new interests and new aspirations, and the same way of life with greater access to commodities and places of entertainment. The intellectual and cultural elite of Beirut gathered together with other business and professional elites in salons, theatres, and cafés where they shared their ideas. They adopted a cosmopolitan lifestyle with a 'modern' culture mixing traditional practices with a 'modernist' attitude, and sought to adopt westernized behaviour in their intellectual and cultural activities, which revolved around literature, music, fashion, and art.[8]

With the emergence of this new class and the increase of European influence, Beirut witnessed the opening of new bars, restaurants, theatres, and *café-chantants* (singing-cafés) from which music, talks, and laughter were heard. Some theatres began to present plays and concerts for European and Beiruti customers, animated foreign films were screened, and cinemas became trendy places under the Mandate. The old town was filled with shows by jugglers, acrobats, magicians and mime artists, as well as musicians and singers from neighbouring cities, as well as from Egypt and Europe.[9] Young boys shouted out the news on the streets announcing the arrival of these artists. Beirut became more and more noisy, especially during the night when bars and theatres were filled with crowds animating the city.

The diffusion of new popular forms of entertainment imported from Europe, such as the music hall, theatre and cinema, influenced the musical scene during the Mandate period. They replaced the previous places of entertainment in private gardens or the streets, and became agents and sources of

---

7   Abou-Hodeib, "Taste and class in late Ottoman Beirut", p. 476.
8   Sehnaoui, *L'occidentalisation de la vie quotidienne à Beyrouth, 1860–1914*.
9   As proved by the numerous adverts in newspapers such *Lisan al-Hal* or *al-Ma'rad*.

influence on musical production and aesthetics. Beirut witnessed the gradual transformation of the old *café-chantants* into *café-concerts* following the Parisian model.[10] Whereas in the old *café-chantants*, the singer was paid directly by the café owner or the clients, the newly-established *café-concerts*, new locations of production, were concert halls and places of consumption to which access was obtained by purchasing a ticket. Listening to music was, therefore, no longer reserved for official, private or occasional ceremonies but was now linked to an economic activity.[11]

With the emergence of the European-style concert, and especially after World War I, artists became more independent, presenting their music to a wider public at prefixed prices. Thus, the status of musicians and singers gained in importance and changed from what Jean During calls "craftsman entertainment"[12] to a professional performer of music, an artist. Moreover, and with the gradual emergence of a new urban and elitist class, a new audience with new musical interests and values was being formed. Unlike the society of the nineteenth century, this new urban public was much more open to music and its practitioners, and was more interested in music that became art (*fann*).

The development of these new forms of entertainment led to the appearance of new mediators: the record companies or theatre managers, such as the Beiruti notable Salim Agha Kraydiya (1848–1935). A key figure of Beirut's cultural life, Kraydiya can be considered as the godfather of theatre and cinema in Beirut at the beginning of the twentieth century. Encouraged by the governor (*wali*) of Beirut, he built, together with his partner Salim Badr, one of the first theatres in the Levant, the famous Beiruti theatre Zahrat Suriya (around 1887), constructed following the design of Austrian theatres. He then financed the building of other theatres and supported them financially: the Crystal Theatre (1901), which followed the design of the Egyptian Opera House and attracted the finest European and Egyptian actors and singers; al-Dik Theatre and Cinema (1909), which specialized in the entertainment of European, Turkish and Russian troops; al-Masrah al-Jadid (1909) which became the Bellevue Cinema in 1924; and the Chef d'œuvre (1920) which became the Royal Cinema.[13] It was said that Kraydiya named most of these theatres after his horses: Crystal was

---

10   Lagrange, Frédéric, "Musiciens et poètes en Égypte au temps de la Nahda", Ph.D. Dissertation, Paris VIII University, 1994, p. 90.
11   Lagrange, "Musiciens et poètes en Égypte au temps de la Nahda", p. 90.
12   During, Jean, "Question de gout, l'enjeu de la modernité dans les arts et les musiques de l'Islam", *Cahiers d'ethnomusicologie*, 7 (1994), p. 38.
13   *Masarih Bayrut wa tawarikhiha* [Beirut's Theatres and its History] (Beirut: Dar al-tafahum lil tiba'a wal nashr wal-tawzi', 2006), p. 82.

the name of one of his best horses and al-Dik and Bellevue were the names of his own personal horses. As for the Chef d'œuvre, it was the name of the first steam car that entered Beirut.[14]

The opening of European-style entertainment places, in particular that of the Grand Theatre (Teatro al-Kabir) in 1927, was intended to turn Beirut into a modern city. The inauguration of the Grand Theatre was a major event in the history of Beirut's cultural life, as it formed part of the official reconstruction and renovation of downtown Beirut, a process which was part of the shaping of Beirut as a modern city. Poet and theatre lover, Jacques Tabet, built the theatre with the support of the French and local authorities, under the direction of Yusuf Aftimos, the leading Lebanese architect and urban planner during the first half of the twentieth century. It was part of a commercial centre that housed a hotel, rental apartments, offices and shops. With two balconies and machinery for stage sets, the theatre had the ability to accommodate 630 seats and an orchestra and hosted, in particular, European performances. It became one of the main symbols of Beirut's modern cultural life, located in this downtown area that turned at night into a leisure district where local traditions of entertainment coexisted alongside European music and performances. These new places where occidental music was played offered a new musical taste identified with the new modernized upper and intellectual class. At the same time, folk traditions[15] continued to exist alongside these new cultural expressions. In this atmosphere, several local members of the bourgeoisie attempted to create musical clubs and institutes to promote 'modern Oriental and/or Arabic music', and to protect the rights of musicians, with a focus on Western instruments and musical genres.

Beirut had direct contact with European music through the presence of many musicians and musical instructors – often Europeans, especially pianists, and Russian musicians who came to Beirut after the Bolshevik Revolution[16] – who gave private classical music courses. Learning music became a sign of modernity. Many wealthy families brought the piano into their homes as a sign of modernity and elitism, and learning this instrument was especially

---

14 *Masarih Bayrut wa tawarikhiha*, p. 101.
15 We follow the musicological difference between folk music (the traditional music that existed at the beginning of the twentieth century, based on oral transmission with unknown composers which had been performed over a long period of time), popular music (music distributed to a large audience mainly through the music industry), and art music (the 'classical' music in the region).
16 Kayali, Zeina Saleh, *La vie musicale au Liban de la fin du 19ème siècle à nos jours* (Paris: Geuthner, 2015), p. 63.

approved of for girls.[17] Moreover, we see the increasing use of European instruments (piano, accordion, harmonica), especially in the private sphere and among young people. Newspapers and magazines reflected this growing interest in music and were filled with concert announcements and artists' photos, as well as articles evaluating and criticizing the musical scene.

Many European and Egyptian artists, as well as local and Levantine ones, started to present European-style concerts in Beiruti theatres, such as the poet and monologist 'Umar al-Z'inni (1898–1961) or the cantor, musician and composer of several nationalistic anthems Mitri al-Murr (1880–1969). A few musicians also began to give lectures about music, in particular on the origin of oriental music or the difference between oriental and occidental music, as Chikri Afandi al-Suda or Wadi' Sabra (1876–1952) did. These musicians were part of the intellectual circle and used to play for the elite or during theatrical performances. We have little information about al-Suda, who died around 1920, but his name was often mentioned in the press as a great musician who lectured about music, its origin and the organisation of its musical theories and notation system.[18] Sabra, who studied music in Paris, too, appeared frequently in the press as a skilled musician who had graduated from the Paris Conservatoire and who had as his goal the reconciling of Western and Eastern music. The press greatly praised Sabra who was seen as the equal of any foreign musician[19] and who "combined a perfect knowledge of the 'noble' French music and the beautiful and wonderful oriental one. He is the symbol of the spiritual union between France and Lebanon".[20] In 1911, he achieved a first in the city: a piano competition for his female students with a jury of local and foreign experts and attended by notables and intellectuals from the city.[21] During the Mandate period, Sabra became one of the key figures in Beirut's musical life. He received the support of French and local authorities and participated in various cultural, intellectual and political events.

Dar al-Musiqa *and the Institutionalization of Music*

Fascination with European musical education combined with his goal of reconciling Western and Eastern music led Wadi' Sabra to open Dar al-Musiqa

---

17 Poché, Christian, "Vers une musique libanaise", *Les cahiers de l'Oronte*, 5 (1965), pp. 118–19.
18 *Lisan al-Hal*, 16 March 1903, no. 4248.
19 *Lisan al-Hal*, 26 June 1901, no. 3755.
20 *Al-Barq*, 8 July 1921, no. 1306.
21 *Lisan al-Hal*, 11 June 1911, no. 6673.

(the House of Music) in 1910, which became the National School of Music (Madrasat al-Musiqa al-Wataniyya) in 1925 and the official Conservatoire (Madrasat al-conservatoire) in 1929.[22] Here, European musical theories were taught and new methods of music education were developed.[23] The inauguration of this local and occidental-style musical institute marked a shift in Beirut's musical history with the initiation of formal westernization of musical traditions. It also introduced the institutionalization and professionalization of its modern musical scene and the beginning of different local attempts to define "a modern oriental art music" based mainly on western music.[24] Before the opening of this institute, musical education was based mainly on oral tradition and limited to the private sector; amateurs and professional musicians learned oriental and local music under the direction of established musicians. But with the opening of this institute, the profession of musician was established and the notion of an artist began gradually to be formed.

The institute's main goal was to develop local music, and it had a 'civilizing' mission to guide society towards progress. Its musical education was based on the promotion of European art music considered to be the main international music. Through this learning, the institute was to help Beirutis to form a modern society[25] and to contribute to the creation of a 'modernized' artistic taste that would lead ultimately to the acquiring of a 'national' taste – even though this national taste was not completely defined. The creation of this institute was motivated by a desire to define what constituted modern oriental music and to participate in the production of musical knowledge. The kind of music the Beiruti should be producing and enjoying was slowly being defined. It was a music based on Western techniques and practices 'translated' to produce a local modern and artistic music. This process of 'translation' was not new to the region but was part of the *Nahda* movement and the elite's struggle over education. It thus fitted seamlessly into the *Nahda* narrative by following other educational and artistic attempts to translate Western practices in order to create and produce a new local modern culture, particularly given that the primary concern of *Nahda* intellectuals was to revive the arts as part of the desire for progress and a progressive nation.[26]

---

22 *Lisan al-Hal*, 5 November 1929, no. 10666.
23 Poché, "Vers une musique libanaise", p. 118.
24 Sabra, Wadi', "al-musiqa al-sharqiyya" [The oriental music], *al-Mashreq*, October 1929, pp. 17–21; February 1929, pp. 96–100; and March 1929, pp. 196–9.
25 *Lisan al-Hal*, 16 June 1922, no. 8951; and 8 March 1929, no. 10499.
26 Sheehi, Stephen, *Foundations of Modern Arab Identity* (Gainesville: University Press of Florida, 2004), and Ramadan, "The Aesthetics of the Modern: Art, Education, and Taste in Egypt 1903–1952", p. 11.

This attempt to define and create a new local music was part of a larger discourse defining local identity. At the time of its opening, the institute presented itself as a Syrian Beiruti school within the Ottoman empire aiming to revive oriental music through Westernisation. Later on, during the Mandate, it became the representative of the newly-established Lebanese state and tried to shape a new musical language distinct from the prevailing Egyptian or folk music. It was for this reason that Sabra's project received the support of Beirut's intellectuals and the official authorities (first Ottoman and then French).

The location of the school is also very significant. It was located in the 'cultural and educational centre' of Beirut, the neighbourhood of Zuqaq al-Blat. This area had been the centre of the new educational movement since the expansion of Beirut in the mid-nineteenth century[27] and it was here that Beirutis and European missionaries opened many schools and educational institutes. The opening of the musical institute in this area reflected its educational vision and its mission to educate and to lead society to progress and enlightenment.

Since its inauguration the institute had promoted Western music at the expense of Oriental music. However, this ideological project aimed at modernizing society was not supported by all and when the Lebanese and the French authorities started officially to support and finance the institute in 1926, the city faced a major debate over the future of the institute, its functions and its importance for the society. Some intellectuals and members of the parliament called for its closure, accusing it of being merely an obscene coffee house, or of encouraging Western music while sacrificing Oriental music, providing 40 European music courses and only two Arabic music lessons. Other intellectuals defended the institute as a beacon of modernism and progress and called for the support and promotion of music and fine arts in general, which they perceived as necessary for the survival of civilized nations. This institute needed to be protected because "it is useful for the country and essential on the path of the new modernization".[28]

This major debate about the institute's future, involving issues of identity and the nature of society, found its way into the press of the time and was manifested by an open quarrel between the *oud* player and director of the Oriental Music Club (Nadi al-Musiqa al-Sharqi) in Beirut, Alexi al-Ladhqani (1907-?70), one of the fiercest opponents of the institute, and the newspaper *Lisan al-Hal* (The Tongue of the [current] State), a staunch defender of Sabra, his institute and his ideas. The newspaper published a long article entitled "al-Madrasa al-Musiqiyya: A-Bayrut tuharib al-Funun al-jamila?" (The school of Music: does Beirut fight against fine arts?). The article summarized the main points of disagreement

---

27 Hanssen, *Fin de Siècle Beirut,* p. 163.
28 *Lisan al-Hal,* 10 December 1926, no. 9925.

between the opposing sides and fiercely accused those who were in favour of its closure of hindering the country's progress and modernization.[29] The quarrel ended eventually with the triumph of the institute and the government's decision to keep it open. This incident marked a shift in the history of music in Beirut: the authorities officially supported Sabra's project and the Westernization of music became the main line followed by the local conservatory, from which graduated Beirut's next musical generation of the 1940s and the 1950s.

The Impact of the Record Industry and Musical Mutations

Before the era of the phonograph, concerts of professional singers were reserved for the elite and for special occasions. With the rise of the record industry and the diffusion of the phonograph, such music was gradually extended to the rest of society and was no longer reserved for the wealthy class, a similar process occurring in Egypt.[30] During the 1920s, 78-rpm records became less expensive and more accessible to a much wider audience. The diffusion of the phonograph to private homes also contributed to the transformation of gender boundaries: more women joined the musical scene and the latest female singers who used to perform in cafés now entered private houses via musical records.[31]

Gradually, the phonograph and the record industry contributed to a change in the status of musicians and in the musical taste of society. It also played a part in the identity affirmation of the new emerging intellectual class. Music professionals were no longer dependent on musical patronage but followed the record companies. The popularity of different artists grew, and their economic and social prestige increased.[32] Under the Mandate, the concept of an *adib* (a man of letters) musician developed. Beirut experienced the diffusion of literary gatherings combining music with literature and art. The stars of these literary meetings were singers and composers who were considered as educated artists (*udaba'*), such as ʿUmar al-Zʿinni, Mitri al-Murr, the Flayfel brothers (with their military brass band) and Wadiʿ Sabra. They all participated in the intellectual and cultural life of Beirut and started to publish their songs and notations in newspapers or separated publications.

Furthermore, the music itself was affected by the record industry, from the technical aspects of recording to the need to record a large number of songs

---

29   *Lisan al-Hal*, 10 January 1927, no. 9941.
30   al-Racy, Ali-Jihad, "Musical Change and Commercial Recording in Egypt, 1904–1932", Ph.D. Dissertation, University of Illinois at Urbana-Champaign, 1977, p. 65.
31   Lagrange, "Musiciens et poètes", p. 191.
32   al-Racy, "Musical Change and Commercial Recording in Egypt", p. 134.

that was commissioned by the record companies. The 1920s saw the diffusion of new musical forms in Beirut imported mainly from Egypt: the Egyptian *taqtuqa* (light songs), the operetta and satirical monologues and dialogues – the only genre, together with the nationalist anthems, that was mainly developed by local artists such al-Zʿinni, the Flayfel brothers and Mitri al-Murr. These three types formed the popular and commercialised music (music aimed at wide popular appeal and driven by the music industry). As noted by Frédéric Lagrange, this music was designed for entertainment and leisure, like the French *musique de variétés*.[33] It was based on simple melodic forms, with simple but varied texts, expressing social and political demands in a dialectal language. This *musique de variétés* was often characterized by its simple melodies inspired by Western music and the use of the piano or other Western instruments.

Indeed, the use of the piano was essential since it was a sign of modernism. That is why many supporters of the modernization musical discourse, like Wadiʿ Sabra or the Flayfel brothers, supported its use and its introduction into the Beiruti musical scene. Oddly, these supporters of the Westernization of music were not accused of erasing their traditions or compromising their music. Rather, they were seen as nationalists who wanted to rationalise their music and turn it into a science. They helped to modernize their society and therefore contributed to the progress of the nation. The music itself was not a criterion of authenticity, but the text was. Thus this contradiction can be explained by their choice of classical or colloquial language expressing topics affecting daily life.

ʿUmar al-Zʿinni represented perfectly this new modern educated popular poet and *chansonnier* mixing Western music with satirical colloquial texts. Known as the poet of the people and the Molière of the Orient, he reproduced and expressed the ideas and problems of the Beirutis regardless of class or education, creating a kind of mass culture. In his songs, ʿUmar al-Zʿinni criticized the French Mandate and the political elite, as well as the society, its obsession with modernization and its decadence at all levels. In *Shubban shik* (Chic Young Men) he mocked young men obsessed with imitating European attitudes and way of life and depicted in an ironic way these men, interested only in money and appearance. His first target was the westernised (*tafarnuj*) of the society. For him, *tafarnuj* was evident in the effeminacy of men and the numbers of women filling the streets and the ball rooms, as well as the abuse of alcohol and gambling and the use of foreign languages (French or English words). He alluded to this *tafarnuj* by using French terms such as "chic" and

---

33   Lagrange, "Musiciens et poètes", pp. 215–16.

"sympatique", in opposition to various popular expressions (such as "Mnakol qanes / we eat without paying"), to mark this contrast in society. He was also one of the first to criticize class and gender distinction. For example, in his song *Law kun hsan*, he used the horse as a way to criticize the excesses of the rich, as well as economic and social inequalities. He parodied the miserable reality of low-income people in Lebanon, while horses lived in comfort in the stables of bourgeois families. He wished to live like a horse, for it was well treated. He would even obtain better care and privileges inaccessible to an ordinary Beiruti man. He was also among the earliest singers and poets to support the cause of women. But his vision presented a contrast, reflecting the ambivalence of the position of many Beiruti intellectuals about the condition of women. On the one hand he called for the liberation of the "honourable woman" from her veil and submission in *Maskina l-bint al-mastura* (Poor Decent Girl), but on the other, this liberation had limits, for the Beiruti woman had to respect the traditions of her society. Thus he distinguished between two kinds of women: the immoral and careless woman who totally followed the European way of life, leaving her family and her husband in order to run behind the attractions of her time, epitomised in his song *Laylit 'ursi* (The Night of My Marriage); and the one who kept her honour and followed the traditions of her society while caring for her family and her husband.

Al-Z'inni gained huge success during the 1920s and the 1930s both among the intellectuals and the populace, and his songs were widely disseminated and listened to by all Beirutis. He became an example followed by several popular singers imitating his satirical monologues such as Laure Daccache, Elia Bayda and Sami al-Sidawi.

Emerging patriotic songs (like those of Mitri al-Murr or the Flayfel brothers) emphasized the history and glory of the Arab, glorifying the nation, mainly Syria, and Arab leaders such as Prince Faisal or the martyrs. In *Nashid al-shuhada* (the Anthem of Martyrs) Mitri al-Murr exalted the Arab martyrs who died during the Franco-Syrian War that took place in 1920 between the Hashemite rulers of the newly established Arab Kingdom of Syria and France and ended with the defeat of the Arabs during the Battle of Maysalun in July 1920. This anthem reflects the rise of nationalism in songs. Martyrs were represented as the protectors of Arab rights and dignity, and the Great Men of the nation. They are the liberators who stimulated the somnolent and motivated patriotic feelings. Al-Murr calls the Syrian to follow the example of these martyrs and fight against the injustice afflicted by the enemy. Thus the cult of the hero, the martyrs in this case, became a manifestation of patriotic worship. These songs called for an Arab awakening and solidarity, rejecting foreign domination and creating a collective imagined Arab or Syrian identity, history and solidarity.

They also boasted about the bravery and dignity of the Arabs and their refusal to accept humiliation, as well as their role as protectors of the nation. The hero of this nation for al-Murr was the King Faisal (1885–1933), who was idealized in *Nashid Faysal* (the *Anthem of Faisal*). Faisal was the king of Greater Syria in 1920 who led the fight against the French. He was represented as the saviour and the liberator of his nation, the one who brought victory despite all the difficulties. The future was full of hope with him. Indeed, Syria, led by King Faisal, became the nation sought by many singers and poets. Moreover, the Arabs were called in *Siru lil Amjadi* (March to the Glory) to restore their glorious past, when they used to dominate the world. Thus, they must unite and sacrifice to protect their history and restore their glory by taking up arms. This patriotic song aimed to raise self-esteem among Arabs. Thus it undertakes its 'work of national education' and becomes an integral part of the affirmative discourse trying to define a 'national identity'.

Famous poets wrote the texts of these nationalist and patriotic songs in classical Arabic, but the music of European and Ottoman anthems were the main sources of influence for these musical compositions. Yet these composers and singers were and are still considered patriotic and nationalistic personalities working for the 'national' cause of the country.

All these musical mutations posed a challenge to the social and aesthetic musical norms and slowly brought about changes in the musical field. The new kind of *musique de variétés* composed to fit the recording medium dominated the scene and eclipsed the former traditional concert (the *wasla*). Moreover, the 78-rpm records became a primary source for musical learning leading to the fixating of oral musical tradition in recorded discs and the gradual disappearance of improvisation.[34] The music was no longer limited to a particular place and a specified class category. And slowly by the beginning of the 1940s, Beirut experienced the gradual transformation of the musical language: the *wasla* and improvisation were gradually abandoned, and certain forms of songs disappeared (such as the *mawwal Baghdadi* or the former *qasida*),[35] while others gained popularity (like the monologue, anthems and light songs). The sung musical phrase became simpler with an increase of Western influence. The musical ensemble (*takht*) also gradually disappeared with the diffusion of local orchestras. The role of musicians became more established, and the importance of composers increased.

---

34 al-Racy, "Musical Change and Commercial Recording in Egypt", p. 84; and Lagrange, "Musiciens et poètes", pp. 191 and 217.

35 The *mawwal Baghdadi* was an improvisatory vocal genre extremely popular in early twentieth-century Beirut and the *qasida* was a vocal form based on classical Arabic poetry.

These social and cultural transformations of musical production paralleled a mutation of the discourse over music and its role in society. Always seen through the prism of its function and benefits, music was regarded as a tool of progress and education, and no longer simply an object of entertainment. Through an analysis of the press and musical criticism, I will now trace how the intellectual elite approached and perceived this musical production, focusing on the ways in which certain intellectuals talked about music to access modernity and on the way they used the notion of taste in music to construct class boundaries. Faced with a moment of crisis and trying to defend their positions, these different writers had varied opinions and different interests. But they all participated in the creation of a musical discourse and played a part in this identity struggle because music was considered an educational tool and a "barometer" of progress.[36]

Music in the Eyes of Beiruti Intellectuals

Music as a "Barometer" of Progress and Modernity

Since the beginning of the twentieth century, Beirut's intellectuals and its elite tended to consider music and fine arts as a symbol of modern advancement. Music was seen as a powerful medium capable of reaching society, with an ability to educate and refine it. In this context, and borrowing an expression developed by Dina Ramadan in her analyses of the Egyptian artistic field,[37] music was now a "barometer" of progress and modernity, which could also define and shape the desire to be a nation. Because of its educational aspect, music was also an indicator of success in this identity crisis. The emergent intellectual class in Beirut saw and defined itself as an educated generation of knowledge with the role of modernizing the rest of society.[38] For them, music had the role of and ability to refine local taste and create an appreciation of the "beauty and perfection", which is an important quality of the "civilized nations".[39]

In this civilization struggle, an original authentic and pure past needed to be created and found, in contrast to the current state of decadence and

---

36   Ramadan, "The Aesthetics of the Modern: Art, Education, and Taste in Egypt 1903–1952", p. 136.

37   Ramadan, "The Aesthetics of the Modern: Art, Education, and Taste in Egypt 1903–1952", p. 136.

38   Abou-Hodeib, "Taste and class in late Ottoman Beirut", p. 477.

39   Ramadan, "The Aesthetics of the Modern: Art, Education, and Taste in Egypt 1903–1952", p. 89.

backwardness. The question of "authenticity" (*asala*) was the central concern for musical producers in Beirut. The terms *asala*, *turath*, and *tammadun* were therefore used and combined in musical writings and discussions. In a time when the definition of a local identity (Oriental (Sharqiyya), Arabic, Syrian or Lebanese) was still not clear, the search for origin, sources of influence and inspiration, became central. In their quest for legitimacy and a glorious past, different authors tried to link their music to the Arabic music of the Abbasids or of Andalusia. Some also tried to link it to Greek or Byzantine roots. In a few articles dealing with the history of music and the 'golden age of Arabic music' this music was presented as having being, once, more advanced (*mutamaddina*) than European music. But it had deteriorated into a state of barbarism (in contrast to *tamaddun*), and had thereby lost its pre-eminence. In these articles, there is a call to revive Arabic music in order for it to regain its lost place and glory.

During the 1920s, the daily newspaper *Lisan al-Hal* re-published several articles extracted from Egyptian and American Arabic journals on music and Arabic singing emphasizing the importance of Arabic civilisation. An article from the Egyptian newspaper *al-Muqtataf* (the Selected) on the history of the Arabic music was republished on its front page.[40] In the introduction, Arab singing was presented as an aspect of Arab modernity and civility reflecting the beauty of its literature, desires and sentiments. In another article taken from the Arab-Argentinian newspaper *al-Salam* (The Peace), Arabic music was described as stagnant during the *Jahiliyya*, but with Muslim civilisation, it found growth and progress.[41] The newspaper considered these articles as significant publications retracing the musical history of the region while emphasising its golden age. Thus, its re-publication in Beirut could contribute to the education of Beirut literate class. At the same time, it could provide an authentic history of the musical traditions, which could be considered as a main source for musical revival and modernization.

On another hand, like furniture and domestic supplies advertisements,[42] concerts and musical announcements often stressed the innovative side of the artists and the fact that they met the needs of the age. Sometimes such advertisements underlined the 'oriental' authenticity of the artists, while many tried to relate singers, composers and music compositions to the occidental world. Thus we often find in the press the use of expressions such as "the noble artist", "the nationalist", "the modernist", "the innovative", "the one who studied in

---

40   *Lisan al-Hal*, 13 December 1928, no. 10428.
41   *Lisan al-Hal*, 29 January 1929, no. 10471.
42   Abou-Hodeib, "Taste and class in late Ottoman Beirut", p. 484.

Europe" or "the one who knew great success in Europe or the United-States".[43] The link with Europe or America was considered to be a sign of modernity, and sometimes even a guarantee of good quality. During the Mandate, different adverts also stressed the 'national' character of the product or singer in order to distinguish them from those imported from Europe. Their attitude is ambivalent. On the one hand, they highlighted the importance and the greater value of Western products, but on the other, they wanted to emphasise the local aspect and the authenticity of their music and musicians.[44]

From the beginning of World War I and during the Mandate period music, as a tool of progress, became more associated with nationalism. Intellectuals argued more explicitly that this medium had the benefit of being able to bring society together and create a taste for a national art. For example, during a ceremony for the Chams al-Barr society, a charitable society established in Beirut in 1870, the Jewish feminist and journalist, editor and founder of the magazine *al-'A'ila al-Mahjouba* (The Veiled Family), Esther Azhari Moyal (1873–1948), delivered a speech entitled "Nahdatouna" (Our renaissance) in which she linked the revival of music and arts to national revival.[45] She called for equal education for men and women based on the love of the country and the nation, for the promotion of socio-economic development of agriculture and local industry, and for the establishment of a local workforce, which would lead to the enrichment of society. Such developments would eventually allow for the revival of the arts as the country's artists would now be able to devote their time to the arts without being impeded by the need to make a living, for, she argued, the poet would no longer be obliged to write for anyone, nor would the musician need to flatter the rich: "This will enable the emergence of scientists, poets, musicians, singers, photographers, sculptors and writers who will complete the artistic *Nahda* that we have already begun with great difficulty".[46]

Esther Azhari Moyal praised the efforts of "modern" poets and singers who began the revival of the arts:

> Who can deny the existence of a real progress in our poetry and our song? Poetry, which was once composed of rhymes and metrics, has embraced,

---

43 *al-Ma'raḍ*, 18 March 1923, no. 191; 22 November 1923, no. 260; 6 January 1924, no. 271; 17 June 1926, no. 502.
44 Abou-Hodeib, "Taste and class in late Ottoman Beirut", p. 484.
45 Azhari, Esther, "Nahdatuna" [Our renaissance], *Al-Hasna'*, 1/9 (June 1912), 408–15. For a different and complete translation see Moshe, Behar and Benite Zvi Ben-Dor, *Modern Middle Eastern Jewish Thought: Writings on Identity, Politics, and Culture, 1893–1958* (Waltham Massachusetts: Brandeis University Press, 2013), pp. 38–47.
46 Azhari, "Nahdatuna", pp. 408–15.

with the modern poet, a field of complex and emotional senses. Our singer, formerly passive and narcissistic, used to wait to find his lover. But now he is proud of his love to which he is ready to devote himself.[47]

Thus, according to Esther Azhari Moyal, the "obsolete" themes of love and sadness that were very popular and prevalent at the time and strongly criticized by the intellectuals would be increasingly abandoned. She called for this musical revival to continue, while forsaking indecent love songs, and instead encouraging enthusiastic melodies that insisted on the love of the country and the nation:

> I'm eager for the day when young men and young women will be able to play and sing Arabic tunes while clearing the Arabic music from its contaminations. [...] This is how we found an Arab and Eastern modernity based on inherited virtues of our ancestors, as well as love and excellence of the work. This will allow us to reach an honourable place among modern societies.[48]

Thus, it was argued, music based on the local culture but incorporating new Western technologies and musical techniques, should not be perceived as a simple medium of entertainment, but as a tool for modernization and a reflection of modernity. It should not be taught in schools merely for leisure purposes but rather because it was part of fine arts, and because it could "refine the senses, educate the feelings, stir the emotions, teach munificence and generosity, and finally because it allows the enrichment of the soul".[49] Ironically, however – as shown later in the chapter – 15 years after Esther Azhari Moyal's speech, the journalist Karam al-Bustani was still criticizing the musical scene and formulating the same arguments and criticisms, proving once again that the taste of the masses did not always follow the aspirations of the intellectual elite that tried constantly to find ways to modernize its music in order to follow the spirit of the time.

How to Modernize Our Music?

While some Beiruti musicians and intellectuals were interested in modernizing music, the question for many of them was quite how to do this. There was constant criticism in the press of the current state of the music, described as being decadent and debauched, and of the lack of music theory and music

---

47 Azhari, "Nahdatuna", pp. 408–15.
48 Azhari, "Nahdatuna", pp. 408–15.
49 *Lisan al-Hal,* 23 November 1921, no. 8184.

education – the concept of 'lack', as demonstrated by Stephen Sheehi, being a fundamental component of the *Nahda* narrative and its subjectivity debates.[50] Moreover, popular music, especially the Egyptian *taqatiq*, became perceived by some intellectuals as being associated with depravity and of easily arousing the feelings of uninformed listeners. In contrast, 'art music', combining pleasure and reason, was seen as 'serious' and meaningful music intended to address scholars or knowledgeable listeners. But what this 'art music' was was not easy to define.

For some musicians and critics, like Wadi' Sabra, who were attracted by the technological dominance of the West, Western music was synonymous with an art that had to be associated with and adapted to Eastern music in order to create a new classical Arabic music.[51] For others, traditional Oriental music was the only source of good music; it merely needed to be revivified. Those who advocated the use of Western music regarded their own musical tradition as aging and they wanted to see it evolve towards the acquisition of a "universal standard".[52] Indeed, the European art music with its notation system and dominant notoriety was accepted as the International music (*al-musiqa al-ʿalamiyya*) and viewed as the ultimate advancement and sophistication. They therefore chose to follow the European tonal harmonic system and started to introduce systematic elements from European music schools. Those who opposed this acculturation, however, like Alexi al-Ladhqani, presented a sentimental and romantic vision of Oriental music that was to be based on local and regional musical tradition.[53] But both groups aimed to modernize Arabic music and to 'rationalize' musical practice and thus set it within the European notation system, to keep it as a unified heritage and preserve its musical legacy in written sources. For both groups, the modernization of music was only reachable by organizing more conferences on music, writing down musical theories and publishing more specialized books.

In 1932, the journalist and editor of *Lisan al-Hal*, Karam al-Bustani (1894–1966) clearly articulated the demands of the intellectual elite in an article published on the front page of the newspaper and entitled "The song we

---

50   Sheehi, *Foundations of Modern Arab Identity*, p. 75.
51   Sabra, "al-musiqa al-sharqiyya", pp. 196–9.
52   al-Racy, Ali-Jihad, "Music in contemporary Cairo: a comparative overview", *Asian Music*, 13/1 (1981), p. 11.
53   We do not have any writing for Alexi al-Ladhqani, but we know that he aggressively opposed Sabra's project and that he followed the ideas and ideology of the Beiruti music theorist Iskandar Shalfoun, who lived most of his life in Egypt and was a fierce defender of traditional Oriental music and its revival from within.

want today. We've had enough of elegies and lamentations. Bring us joy and excitement".⁵⁴ In this article, he discussed the appearance of a new movement in Lebanon and Syria which criticised and re-evaluated the current state of Arabic music, in particular that of Egypt that had dominated the Levantine musical scene. For al-Bustani, the style of singing and the melodies themselves failed to entertain the public since they were mostly slow and depressing melodies. The public therefore rejected this music as stagnant and turned instead to a new modern music. But the new popular music diffused by the record industry did not correspond either to al-Bustani's expectations. He was, therefore, surprised to see the composers "refusing to follow the course of modernism" and wondered if this was due to a lack of musical skills and thus fear of failure, or simply to conservatism.

For al-Bustani, the modern young man was bored by Arabic music and preferred that of the West:

> One cannot blame him with all this modernization surrounding him: he sees the change in his food, his clothes, his social, moral, intellectual and sentimental life. He asks the same of music and singing, but cannot find it. How can we ask him to enjoy music from a time when the lover was away and out of reach, and the singer used to console himself by singing about his desire and hope to see the lover whilst describing his passion and his lovesickness? How can we force him to enjoy all this while his lover is in front of him and in his arms: at the school on the same bench, in the car and on the train, in his office and his shop, in the restaurant and the cinema, in the street and the dancing cafes [al-maqahi al-raqisa]? Today's times are different from those of yesterday!⁵⁵

Al-Bustani therefore demanded songs expressing the desires of this new generation and matching their tastes, songs such as those of 'Umar al-Z'inni. The "Syrian-Lebanese", he claimed, rejected the Egyptian songs because of their stagnation, something that for him also explained the stagnation of the Egyptian record market that had dominated the Beiruti and Syrian markets. The backwardness of such music was linked, al-Bustani argued, to 'Eastern societies' (al-sharqiyyin) tendency to sentimentality and melancholy. 'Eastern

---

54   al-Bustani, Karam, "al-Ghina' al-ladhi nuriduhu al-yawm: shabi'na nadban wa-'awilan, fa-hatu mafrahan wa-muhamissan" [The song we want today. We've had enough of elegies and lamentations. Bring us the joy and the excitement], Lisan al-Hal, 27 June 1932, no. 11325.
55   al-Bustani, "al-Ghina' al-ladhi nuriduhu al-yawm".

people' were more imaginative than creative, the beauty of their environment provoking feelings of love, and their music was more sentimental than rational. Further, the political situation produced a constant feeling of helplessness and defeat among the population, who saw their country humiliated and occupied by foreigners. This in turn lead the Arab to indulge in melancholic and plaintive songs.[56]

Al-Bustani's response to this situation was to call for the modernization of music, for Western music was more cheerful and enthusiastic corresponding perfectly to the soul of the century. Indeed and despite the French domination, Beirut and the region had experienced various reforms and the introduction of technological advancement from the beginning of the century. Thus, the city followed different measures of modernization in order to access progress and development. Music had to follow these same rhythms because times had changed and "we have had enough of elegies and tears".[57] The presence of singers and composers like 'Umar al-Z'inni meant that a change was possible. 'Umar al-Z'inni galvanized the people with his moral, social and political criticism because he reflected their feelings: "He provokes us with his injuring sarcasm, but we applaud him as he touches our hearts with this sad situation. Besides, it is not too surprising, since he lives with us, shares the details of our popular life and knows what upsets and affects us".[58]

Good Taste/Bad Taste: The Creation of Class Boundaries

Engaged in a mission of educating society, the intellectual elite sought to refine the musical taste of the populace by imposing their own musical and cultural taste (*dhawq*). The notion of *dhawq*, used recurrently in the press, constituted an important element in the musical and artistic discourse of the period. As Toufoul Abou-Hodeib has shown, the term *dhawq* itself had different meanings, from the actual sense of taste to moral values, such as *adab*. Even the term *adab* contains a double meaning, referring both to manners and to the aesthetics of literature.[59] Abou-Hodeib argued that the question of taste was not a new concept discovered by nineteenth-century intellectuals, but what was new was its extension to the whole of society, and its integration into the social reform project of *Nahda* intellectuals. The concept of taste as social reform was thus opened up to a wider audience and used extensively as a marker

---

56   al-Bustani, "al-Ghina' al-ladhi nuriduhu al-yawm".
57   al-Bustani, "al-Ghina' al-ladhi nuriduhu al-yawm".
58   al-Bustani, "al-Ghina' al-ladhi nuriduhu al-yawm".
59   Abou-Hodeib, "Taste and class in late Ottoman Beirut", p. 480.

of class and as an indicator of an authentic modernity different from European modernity.[60]

From the beginning of twentieth century, the concept of good taste/bad taste was gradually being shaped in the press, and it became a more recurrent theme during the Mandate period.[61] Articles urged people to attend musical and theatrical performances while criticizing the audience and calling for more civilized behaviour and less rowdiness in the theatres. Emphasizing the role and importance of theatre and 'art music' in the construction of a modern civilized nation, they focused on the notion of taste by presenting cultural practices and behaviours in the musical and artistic scene aimed at cultivating society and refining its behaviour. Some Beiruti intellectuals also regarded 'art music' as not the domain of the populace (*al-ru'ā'*) whose poverty led them to this kind of profession, but argued that it should be in the hands of the intellectual elite, that is those who had good taste.

Different articles criticized the elite and the populace, the upper and the lower classes of the society structure. They criticised the upper elite for their blind imitation of the West with their Europeanised (*tafarnuj*) attitude, and the lower classes for their vulgar behaviour. In doing so, intellectuals defined good and bad taste distinguishing between different lifestyles and social classes. On one hand, we have 'popular' taste (of the upper and lowers classes), which preferred novelty and consumption, and on the other, the 'modern' taste of the intellectuals who privileged the local authentic tradition and moderation. An example of division of taste is provided by the attacks on the *café-chantants*, which became a prime target of elite criticism which associated them with moral corruption and perceived them as immoral and dangerous for the society. Full of debauchery, they were uncivilised and contributed to the regression of society, while, in contrast, the new noble intellectual theatre symbolized a new form of noble culture. The Beiruti newspaper, *Lisan al-Hal*, which presented itself as "the spokesman of the nation" whose duty it was to address the problems of society,[62] often criticized the existing musical scene and considered it to be depraved and "uncivilised", while it promoted the development of literary theatre and classical music. In an article published in 1927, the editor criticized the proliferation of *café-chantants* in the city. For him, these were places of obscenity and houses of secret prostitution corrupting the young, especially those under 18 years of age. He blamed the authorities and asked the

---

60   Abou-Hodeib, "Taste and class in late Ottoman Beirut", p. 480.
61   Abou-Hodeib, "Taste and class in late Ottoman Beirut", p. 477, and Ramadan, "The Aesthetics of the Modern: Art, Education, and Taste in Egypt 1903–1952", p. 13.
62   *Lisan al-Hal*, 8 February 1901, no. 3639.

government to follow the example of Turkey and Italy by prohibiting access to them. He also criticized parents who had a primary role as educator, especially "at a time when European modernity has ravaged us, preventing us from choosing and deciding independently".[63]

The aim of such press articles was to educate the common people to listen to and to appreciate 'good' music and to adopt appropriate behaviour in places where music was performed. In his analyses of the question of taste, Pierre Bourdieu relates cultural practices (like music) to ways of life and the judgment of beauty. Thus the class concept is connected to the cultural capital gained at home and at school, and not only to economic capital.[64] In this sense, a class became a community of tastes sharing the same aesthetic views and cultural background. Thus, beauty is not considered as a pure taste but an acquired one. It is also a marker of class, separating individuals into groups.[65] Following this definition, we can see here that the intellectual elite tried to impose its taste on the rest of society and thus tried to impose its authority through cultural capital. While criticizing the musical scene and popular behaviour, it engaged not only in an educational mission of civilisation and progress, but also in a class struggle. Having the ability to recognize taste and reproduce it, the elite possessed cultural capital, which was considered to be more important than economic capital in this quest to construct a modern and civilized society. Thus the intellectual elite sought to define a modern taste based on local and on European culture. Its role was to bring this modern taste to the masses and initiate them into civilized behaviour that would allow access to progress.[66]

The elite thought that the only way to access their vision of modernity was to keep some form of distinction from Europe while placing value on their own local culture and heritage. This led them to direct constant criticism at locals who mindlessly imitated the Europeans, and at the subsequent degeneration of taste in society. Fascinated by the novel and the trendy, the Beiruti had more and more access to imported commodities. The press often criticized attempts to look wealthier and to imitate Europeans:

> Beirut adores the West and loves flowing into its arms [...], she exaggerates in her borrowings from the West and neglects her Orientalism

---

63   *Lisan al-Hal*, 3 February 1927, no. 9960.
64   Bourdieu, Pierre, *Distinction: A Social Critique of the Judgment of Taste*, trans. Richard Nice (Cambridge, MA: Harvard University Press, 2002), pp. 2–3.
65   Bourdieu, *Distinction: A Social Critique of the Judgment of Taste*, pp. 2–3.
66   Ramadan, "The Aesthetics of the Modern: Art, Education, and Taste in Egypt 1903–1952", p. 121 and Abou-Hodeib, "Taste and class in late Ottoman Beirut", p. 477.

[sharqiyataha]. What a pity, she looks almost like a nouveau rich. She abandoned her precious heritage based on customs, manners and language, to buy obsolete rags full of vices from foreign countries. This pushes her to imitation and the loss of her Eastern virtues, without being able to capture the beautiful features of European cities.[67]

This kind of 'national' criticism is typical of *Nahda* thoughts. Many intellectuals believed that modern Western science combined with local traditions was the main route to form the bases of a national identity.[68] There was a need to save the local cultural heritage not only from the threat of Europe but also from the locals who threatened local culture and its uniqueness by their mindless imitation of the West or through their inertia.

The views of the intellectual elite, however, did not necessarily reflect those of the populace they criticised. Indeed, the barrage of criticism in the press had the unintended result of giving a voice to those normally unheard, the 'uncivilized' audience (in fact, the majority of the society) that laughed loudly during performances, interacted with the actors and insisted on eating seeds and peanuts and smoking *shisha* during the shows.[69] This audience preferred comic plays with musical performances between the acts, while the intellectual elite preferred learning and hearing Western classical music and intellectual plays. Recorded songs, too, proved that society preferred more popular and light songs that addressed their everyday life.

The diffusion of phonographs and the activity of the record industry, as well as the proliferation of theatres and concert halls, led to the spread of light music and short songs performed in an attractive style, perfectly adapted to the needs of the new music industry. Popular songs were in high demand. This led disc companies and theatre groups to choose popular and vernacular productions. The classical language (*fusha*), the favoured domain of the urban elite, was slowly discarded.[70] It was thus the new entertainment industry that dominated the musical scene and largely influenced the cultural tastes of the

---

67 al-Bustani, Karam, "Bayrut ta'du Nahwa al-gharb" [Beirut runs towards the West], *al-Ma'rad*, 26 January 1927, no. 554.
68 Makdisi, Ussama, "Rethinking Ottoman imperialism: modernity, violence and the cultural logic of Ottoman reform", in *The Empire in the City, Arab Provincial Capitals in the Late Ottoman Empire*, ed. Jens Hanssen, Thomas Philipp and Stefan Weber (Beirut: Orient-Institut, 2002), p. 43.
69 Wajdi, Qasim, "al-tamthil fi Suriyya, Lubnan, Falastin, sharq al-Urdun" [The theatre in Syria, Lebanon, Palestine and East Jordan], *al-Masrah*, 14 October 1926, pp. 14–25; 'Awwad, Toufic, "Fi Dur al-Tamthil" [In theatres], *al-Bayan*, 23 March 1930, no. 318.
70 Fahmy, Ziad, "Media-capitalism: colloquial mass culture and nationalism in Egypt, 1908–18", *International Journal of Middle East Studies*, 42/1 (2010), p. 83.

masses with its simple lyrics and popular language, much more than the intellectual elite who mainly addressed a minority. This led to the increase in cultural tensions between the masses, the mass-media industry and the intellectual elite, who opposed the use of the vernacular and popular music and criticised the mass media as vulgar, without taste and dangerous for the development of society.[71]

Conclusion

In this chapter, I have attempted to present the mutations in the musical scene and to analyse the role that music played in the construction of modern Beiruti society during the Mandate period. Based on an interdisciplinary approach relating music to socio-political and economical changes, the study of the musical field allows us to situate musical practices within the wider *Nahda* discourse. During a crucial moment of identity reconstruction and the development of modern society, music was seen as a tool of modernization and as a marker of progress and a measure of civilisation. Intellectuals formulated sophisticated analyses, taking music as an essential tool to access modernity, and thus arguing for its educative and aesthetic qualities. This kind of musical discourse has been reproduced, almost identically, from the beginning of the twentieth century, and, surprisingly, is still in circulation today.

Music thus became part of the modernity debates, and questions arouse about how to modernize it. The status of musical aesthetics changed in society, and music was no longer a despised profession, at least in 'modern' intellectual or elitist circles. Such intellectuals used the notion of good taste in music to evoke a new kind of culture based on local tradition and European development. Moreover, the cultural elite aggressively attacked popular songs that it considered dangerous to the nation. However, despite the criticism of the intellectual and the cultural elite these songs attained increasing success among the general population (regardless of class or education), creating, once again, a tension between the intellectual elite and the masses.

Finally, it is interesting to note that throughout this entire period, certain famous and much recorded Beiruti singers, such as the famous tambour player and singer Muhyeddine Ba'yun or the singers Farjallah Baida and Youssef Taj, never appeared in the press at all. As for women singers, their names were almost entirely absent from the pages of the press. Apart from European or Egyptian artists, the only local female singers who were mentioned were those

---

71 Fahmy, "Media-capitalism", p. 83.

who took part in European-style concerts. One cannot help but notice that the only singers and musicians mentioned in the press were those who belonged to the intellectual or elite circles and whose music was a modern Occidental music which was considered worth referring to in the press. This raises the question of why such famous singers, whose great fame and popularity in the period is well known, were never mentioned. Perhaps this was due to their not being 'modern' enough for the pages of the press, or because they did not fit the 'modern' criteria set by the intellectual elite.

CHAPTER 4

Tourism and Mobility in Italian Colonial Libya

Brian L. McLaren

From February 26 to March 14, 1925, Major Valentino Babini carried out a *raid automobilistico* from the coastal town of Tripoli to the oasis settlement of Ghadames on the edge of the Saharan desert.[1] Babini was accompanied by art critic and writer Raffaele Calzini, who published a book, *Da Leptis Magna a Gadames*, that chronicled this sometimes perilous journey in the form of a travel diary.[2] The two were joined in this excursion by a second military officer, nine soldiers, one military photographer, and one civilian filmmaker and photographer who had been commissioned to document the experience. The group traveled this route of some 600 kilometers in each direction with a convoy of five trucks equipped with 1,000 liters of water and over 500 liters of gasoline – a quantity that was said to be sufficient to last up to ten days of travel in this pre-desert region. The map drawn by Babini, which documented his successful negotiation of a challenging physical landscape, has the appearance of a carefully planned military operation. This fusion of a motorized tourist excursion with the military surveillance of the territory should be no surprise, as the south-western region of Tripolitania had only recently returned to Italian control. This was due to the efforts of General Rodolfo Graziani, who just over a year earlier led a successful mission to capture this oasis settlement as part of the so-called reconquest of Tripolitania initiated by Governor Giuseppe Volpi.[3] The drawing also reveals the treacherous terrain of a region that until that time had been deemed impassable, even by the most modern motorized vehicles available.

This excursion was conducted in preparation for a similar, though far more symbolic, trip that took place just three months later, in late-May of 1925.

---

1 Babini, Valentino, "Relazione del raid", Archivio Storico Ministero degli Affari Esteri (hereafter ASMAE), Ministero dell'Africa Italiana (hereafter MAI) 3–154, Fascicolo – Raid automobilistico, 16 March 1925. Note that "*raid*" is an English word that was used in Italian to reference an adventurous form of travel that was a hybrid of a military raid and a sporting or leisure-based car rally.
2 Calzini, Raffaele, *Da Leptis Magna a Gadames* (Milan: Fratelli Treves Editori, 1926).
3 Del Boca, Angelo, *Gli italiani in Libia. Dal fascismo al Gheddafi* (Bari-Rome: Giuseppe Laterza e Figli, 1991), pp. 36–7. The capture of Ghadames took place from 7–15 February, 1924.

This trip transported Volpi, who had just stepped down as governor, from Tripoli to Ghadames and back in a total of ten travel days. The former governor was joined by an entourage of distinguished guests that included his wife and daughter, General Graziani and his wife, the duke of Spoleto and his wife, and the contessa Lina Bianconcini Cavazza – who directed the Bolognese artisanal company, *Aemila Ars*. The rhetorical dimension of this trip is clearly evident in a telegram sent by Volpi to the Minister of the Colonies immediately following his return to Tripoli, which stated: "this *raid* has demonstrated that the Tripoli-Ghadames route can be completed in five days and that the extreme western territory [of the colony] is perfectly safe".[4] Despite the precarious hold that Italy held over the Fezzan region, which was not stabilized until at least 1932, this tourist excursion was intended to reflect a freedom of movement that, it was hoped, would spur economic expansion. At this early stage of the development of this colony, it was argued that the presence of Italian and foreign travelers was highly desirable. In the book, *La rinascità della Tripolitania*, which commemorated the four years of the governorship of Volpi (1921–25), the tourism industry was presented as having the potential to be the most important factor in the industrial expansion of the region. Tourism was also discussed in this volume in relation to the "politics of transportation", where it was seen as a "new source of prosperity and movement for the Colony".[5]

Of particular interest in this case is the fact that the establishment of colonial order by the Italians was tied to the creation of infrastructures of transportation that would eventually support the tourist experience of the region. However, the principle of movement in Libya was more than just a propelling mechanism for a modernization process that fostered increasing levels of mobility for Italians. It was closely tied to the indigenous politics that put an equivalent effort into the control of the local populations. In his book, *Mobilities*, British sociologist John Urry speaks of the explicitly class-based experience of mobility in our contemporary culture, with those of greatest wealth, what he calls the "mobile elite", being able to escape the confines of a single home and nationality. Notably, Urry also speaks about the opposite tendency, stating: "most attempts at restricting the 'right' to mobility have been associated with forms of state intervention that stigmatize certain groups on the basis of color, religion, ethnicity or cultural practice".[6] In reference to the arguments of Urry, this chapter will assert that while the relationship between

---

4 Telegram from Volpi to the Minister of the Colonies, ASMAE, MAI 3-154, 31 May 1925.
5 *La rinascità della Tripolitania. Memorie e studi sui quattro anni di governo del Conte Giuseppe Volpi di Misurata* (Milan: Casa Editrice A. Mondadori, 1926), pp. 511–12.
6 Urry, John, *Mobilities* (Cambridge, UK and Malden, MA: Polity Press, 2007), p. 205.

social class and mobility applied to Libya during the Fascist period, degrees of mobility – and especially the restriction of movement – were more clearly mapped in relation to racial and cultural difference. This is especially true of tourist mobilities. While for the Italian and foreign "guests", the experience of mobility transported them to another place and another culture, for the Libyan "hosts" the tourist system tied them to the land and to their history according to an unchanging vision of their cultural past.[7]

Tourism and Colonization, 1911–1933

The close connection between colonial order and mobility was evidenced in some of the earliest measures that were initiated by the Italian authorities to modernize and restructure the region. This process began in January of 1912, just under three months after the Italian invasion and initial conquest.[8] It was at that time that the Ministry of Public Works commissioned the engineer, Luigi Luiggi, to make recommendations to improve the administrative structure as well as the physical infrastructure of the city of Tripoli. The latter of these concerns involved the reorganization of the port, the introduction of water and sewer systems, the regularization of streets, and the construction of public and private buildings in the city and its surrounding oasis.[9] One of the key components of the proposal was a master plan, whose organization was based upon the most modern principles of urban planning. Just like French and British colonial cities, the expansion of Tripoli was to be ordered by creating a new garden city for the metropolitan populations separate from the indigenous one. The street network was based upon the existing routes, with an additional connecting road that was likened to the "Ring" in Vienna, the boulevards of Paris and the crescents in London. In addition to the new street system, a series of tramways were proposed that would make for easy movement between home and work in a manner that was "like all other modern cities".[10] Notably, in

---

[7] These terms are used in reference to the ground-breaking book, Smith, Valene (ed.), *Hosts and Guests: The Anthropology of Tourism* (Philadelphia: University of Pennsylvania Press, 1977).

[8] The Italian invasion of the Ottoman province of Tripolitania began on October 4, 1911 and concluded in early November of that year. See Ahmida, Ali Abdullatif, *The Making of Modern Libya. State Formation, Colonization and Resistance, 1830–1932* (Albany: State University of New York Press, 1994), p. 103.

[9] Luiggi, Luigi, "Le opere pubbliche a Tripoli", *Nuova Antologia*, 47/ 965 (1 March 1912), 115–30.

[10] Luiggi, "Le opere pubbliche a Tripoli", p. 123.

discussing the master plan in the journal *Nuova Antologia*, Luiggi does not fail to assert the value of Tripoli as a tourist destination. With its modern villas, hotels and *pensioni*, it was seen to be less costly than the cities of Cairo or Algiers, while offering all of the benefits of a "mild climate and brilliant sun".[11]

In the years immediately following its adoption in January of 1914, the master plan of Tripoli was largely unrealized due to ongoing political instability. This situation changed following Volpi's appointment as governor and the launching of a series of rather brutal military operations that began in January of 1922.[12] The "rebirth" of the region under his direction was thus closely tied to military conquest, which, like the development of a viable local economy, was an equally necessary precondition for the facilitation of tourism. In this effort, a great emphasis was placed on public works projects, such as the improvement of the infrastructure and the construction of a network of public institutions. These projects had both practical and propagandistic value, as they provided the amenities that were needed to create a more modern and efficient colony, while giving an important visual corollary to the Italian military and administrative presence in the region. With the improvements to roads and modes of transportation, the intention was to assure military and civilian movement within the colony while also improving its connection with Italy and Europe.[13] These projects included the restructuring of the port and the creation of wide tree-lined network of streets. Improvements to the infrastructure of Tripoli were, at least in part, conceived from the viewpoint of their political message – the intention being, among other things, to "communicate the sense of a stable reconquest".[14]

The modernization of the street and road systems continued under the governorship of Emilio De Bono, who took office in July of 1925. These advances are largely attributable to the greater level of security provided by the ongoing military campaigns of Graziani – which were eventually able to claim the area from the central coastal region south to the oasis of Jufra and the 29th parallel.[15] With regard to the public works program, over the course of his governorship

---

11   Luiggi, "Le opere pubbliche a Tripoli", p. 127.
12   The reconquest of coastal areas of Tripolitania was done through a series of military campaigns between January 1922 and November 1924. See Romano, Sergio, *Giuseppe Volpi. Industria e finanza tra Giolitti e Mussolini* (Milan: Bompiani, 1979), pp. 102–12. For a more detailed account see Del Boca, *Gli italiani in Libia. Dal fascismo a Gheddafi*, pp. 5–76.
13   Queirolo, Ernesto, "La politica delle comunicazioni", in *La rinascità della Tripolitania. Memorie e studi sui quattro anni di governo del Conte Giuseppe Volpi di Misurata* (Milan: Casa Editrice A. Mondadori, 1926), pp. 259–83.
14   Queirolo, "La politica delle comunicazioni", p. 259.
15   Del Boca, *Gli italiani in Libia. Dal fascismo al Gheddafi*, pp. 93–103.

almost 600 projects were completed, including the improvement of ports, the extension of water and sewer systems, and the creation of a network of schools, post offices, hospitals, and government and military offices.[16] The result of this building campaign was the enhancement of public services in the city of Tripoli and the extension of these amenities to smaller centers along the coast and into the interior.[17] Equally important to the modernization program was the improvement of transportation infrastructure, including the road that followed the Mediterranean coast. Also enhanced were the roads south and west of Tripoli, which linked towns like Jefren, Nalut and Ghadames that became important tourist destinations.[18] Notably, the level of advancement of this system was still quite provisional, as the 1929 Italian Touring Club guide to the colonies advised that while exploring these regions, travelers should seek the permission of the relevant government offices, bring along sufficient water, provisions and a kit of medical supplies, and be accompanied by a translator.[19]

FIGURE 4.1   *View of* raid automobilistico *of Rodolfo Graziani along the Mediterranean coast at Sirt, June 1931, Central State Archive, Rome – Photographic Archive of Rodolfo Graziani.*

16   Piccioli, Angelo, "L'opera di S.E. Emilio De Bono in Tripolitania", in *Vigor di vita in Tripolitania (anno 1928-VI)* (Tripoli: Ufficio Studi e Propaganda del Governo della Tripolitania, 1928), pp. 17–22.

17   Bertarelli, L.V., *Guida d'Italia del TCI, possedimenti e colonie* (Milan: Tipografia Capriolo e Massimino, 1929), pp. 330–1, 335–6, 340.

18   Piccioli, Angelo, "Le comunicazioni", in *Vigor di vita in Tripolitania (anno 1928-VI)* (Tripoli: Ufficio Studi e Propaganda del Governo della Tripolitania, 1928), pp. 75–85. See also Fantoli, A., "Le strade della Tripolitania", *Le vie d'Italia*, 40/4 (April 1934), 274–87.

19   Bertarelli, *Guida d'Italia del TCI, possedimenti e colonie*, pp. 174–5.

With the appointment of Marshall Pietro Badoglio as governor of the regions of Tripolitania and Cyrenaica in January of 1929, the colony of Libya and its related politics took a decisive step toward unification. It was under the guidance of Badoglio that the continuing military operations of Graziani were concluded in January of 1932 after the complete "pacification" of these two regions. Notably, in June of 1931 Badoglio took part in an even more elaborate *raid automobilistico* with General Graziani, then vice-governor of the region of Cyrenaica. In this case, the group traveled from Tripoli to Benghazi and back – a trip of 1,125 kilometers in each direction – in a total of six travel days. The excursion was made with a prestigious group of government officials and business leaders, including Undersecretary of the Colonies Alessandro Lessona, and officials from the Automobile Club of Benghazi.[20] This commemoration of the unification of Libya into a single colony free of rebellion was, in fact, a well-staged propaganda event. The complete suppression of rebel forces was not officially declared until some seven months after this voyage was completed.[21] A published account of the trip makes the intersection of commercial, tourist, and military discourses quite clear, stating: "the *raid* we are speaking of ... establishes new currents of traffic, serving internal commerce as much as tourist propaganda, while even enhancing the security of military surveillance".[22] The photographs taken of the event testify to the juxtaposition of tourism and colonial politics, with one particularly compelling image showing a small military plane encountering its long convoy of vehicles along the rugged coastal region of Sirt.

The rhetorical dimension of the voyage of Graziani is a demonstration of the deep ideological investment of the Italian colonial administration under Badoglio in the principle of mobility. This commitment was physically evidenced in the creation of an efficient system of movement of goods and people.[23] These projects included extending the existing road system in the more populated regions along the coast – including the upgrading of the coastal road between Zuwarah, Tripoli and Misratah. On the interior, continued improvements were made to existing roads connecting Tripoli with Ghadames and new roads were introduced in the newly claimed territories.[24] The new infrastructure served

---

20 "Da Bengasi a Tripoli in automobile. Come 38 macchine nel deserto annunciano che la Libia è unificata", *Giornale d'Oriente* (28 June 1931).
21 Del Boca, *Gli italiani in Libia. Dal fascismo a Gheddafi*, pp. 207, 213.
22 "Da Bengasi a Tripoli in automobile".
23 Piccioli, Angelo, *La nuova Italia d'oltremare l'opera del fascismo nelle colonie Italiane* (Milan: A. Mondadori Editore, 1933), p. 914. See also Pellegrineschi, A.V., "Le nuove strade della Libia", *Rivista delle Colonie Italiane*, 7/11 (November 1933), p. 888.
24 Fantoli, "Le strade di Tripolitania", p. 279.

to improve the means of travel and the level of public amenities available. Quite naturally this system was closely tied to its tourist development. Among the buildings executed by the municipality was a series of eight hotels that were constructed throughout the colony.[25] While most of these were of a modest size, this was the beginning of what would become a substantial network of accommodation that would make travel possible in the most remote locations. By the end of the Badoglio era, these facilities were linked through a growing number of organized tourist itineraries – the longest of these involving a journey of over 1,500 kilometers in 15 days. The mode of transportation for these excursions were Saharan motor coaches which could comfortably carry up to four people in the most demanding climate.[26] The result of this effort at improving the tourist system in Libya during the governorship of Badoglio was

FIGURE 4.2 *Resettlement camp, Marsa Brega, ca. 1930, ASMAE, MAI, Volume 5, Materiale recuperato al nord, Pacco 30.*

25   These hotels were constructed in Agedabia (1932), Cyrene (1932), Ghadames (1931), Homs (1931), Jefren (1930), Misratah (1930), Sirt (1933) and Zuwarah (1930). See "Tripolitania e Cirenaica – notiziario d'informazioni economico-agrario, politico, militare ecc., di dette Colonie", Archivio Centrale dello Stato-Presidenza del Consiglio dei Ministri (hereafter ACS-PCM) 1931–33 – 17.1.6267.

26   Piccioli, "La valorizzazione turistica", in *La nuova Italia d'oltremare l'opera del fascismo nelle colonie Italiane* (Milan: A. Mondadori Editore, 1933), p. 1564.

what Angelo Piccioli described as "a perfect system of accommodations in a climate that has no winter".[27]

At the same time that the Italian authorities under Badoglio were expanding and improving the systems of transportation for Italian and foreign visitors, these same government and military officials were pursuing and equal and opposite strategy for the Libyans – whose freedom of movement was severely restricted. As part of this effort the local populations were under constant surveillance, as is evident in the monthly dispatches sent to the Minister of the Colonies in Rome, which were especially concerned with cross-border movements.[28] Particular attention was paid to the members of the Senussi order in the region of Cyrenaica who, under the charismatic leadership of 'Umar al-Mukhtar, proved to be the greatest threat to the establishment of colonial order. In response to this threat, in May of 1930 – and with the approval of Mussolini – Governor Badoglio called for the forced evacuation of around 100,000 Libyans from the Jebel Akhdar region.[29] In addition to responding to the political problem of their unregulated movement, this large scale forced migration was conducted for the purpose of resettlement of the region by Italian agricultural colonists. As a result, these native families and all of their belongings were marched some 1,100 kilometers from the fertile northeast to the coastal region of Sirt, where they were put into resettlement camps like Marsa Brega – which housed over 20,000 individuals in carefully ordered ranks of tent structures. Due to the severe strain of the journey and the poor sanitary conditions of the various camps, it is estimated that over the course of several years, more than 30,000 individuals died.[30]

The absolute restriction of movement in the social and political arena was supported by a parallel set of initiatives in the economic and cultural realm, where Libyans were engaged in menial and labor intensive occupations, such as the "native" artisanal industries. Indeed, the Volpi administration undertook a significant preservation program that was aimed at improving the local economy. In this effort the Italian authorities founded the Government Office

---

27   Piccioli, "La valorizzazione turistica", p. 1564.
28   "Tripolitania e Cirenaica – notiziario d'informazioni economico-agrario, politico, militare ecc., di dette Colonie", ACS-PCM, 1931–33 – 17.1.6267.
29   Del Boca, Angelo, "L'infamia delle deportazioni", in *Gli italiani in Libia. Dal fascismo a Gheddafi*, pp. 174–232.
30   Del Boca, "L'infamia delle deportazioni", p. 183. Del Boca estimates that around 40,000 died in Cyrenaica from the military efforts and internment camps. Ahmida's estimate is closer to 50,000 individuals, as he asserts that only 35,000 survived the migration of 85,000–100,000. See Ahmida, *The Making of Modern Libya*, p. 139.

of Indigenous Applied Arts in January of 1925, with the mission to study these industries, make proposals for their expansion, and promote their sales through exhibitions and displays.[31] In attempting to improve the artistic production of local craftsmen – who were seen to be practicing an "unclear and impure" interpretation of Arab art – this office provided information, such as representative patterns taken from the indigenous craft industries of Algeria, Tunisia and Morocco, and brought in master craftsmen from these French colonies. This public agency was also active in improving the organizational structure and economic system of these industries. The improvements involved, among other things, financial support for acquiring raw materials and the systematic upgrading of the quality and cost of these commodities. The colonial intervention in this area led to the creation of a School of Indigenous Arts and Crafts in 1931, which was directly involved in a program of instruction.[32] In this effort, there is a striking contrast between the economic measures that were taken to insert the Libyan artisanal industries into modern mechanisms of commerce and exchange and the cultural effort to create a static set of artistic practices that conformed to what the Italian authorities argued were the purest form of the indigenous arts.

A Modern Tourist System, 1934–1940

With the appointment of Italo Balbo as governor in January of 1934, this contrasting approach, which saw Italian and foreign travelers as part of a modern system of transportation at the same time that the mobility of the Libyans was under the strictest level of control, was brought to new levels. The first step in this process was a series of administrative reforms that called for the unification of the regional governments of Tripolitania and Cyrenaica into a single authority.[33] These changes represent a consolidation of Balbo's powers in governing the colony and the creation of a system of government analogous to that found in Italy. The logical conclusion of the modernization of Libya

---

31 Rossi, Francesco M., "Le piccole industrie indigene", in *La rinascità della Tripolitania. Memorie e studi sui quattro anni di governo del Conte Giuseppe Volpi di Misurata* (Milan: Casa Editrice A. Mondadori, 1926), p. 517.

32 See "Progetto per la trasformazione dell'Ufficio di Arte Applicata in Azienda Autonoma", ASMAE, Archivio Segreto, Cartella 209, Tripolitania IV, Ufficio di Arte Applicate.

33 Bruni, Giuseppe, "Il nuovo assetto politico-amministrativo della Libia", in *Viaggio del Duce in Libia per l'inaugurazione della litoranea. Anno XV. Orientamenti e note ad uso dei giornalisti* (Rome: Stabilimento Tipografico Il Lavoro Fascista, 1937), pp. 1–14.

FIGURE 4.3 *Mussolini motorcade at Tobruk during inauguration of* strada litoranea, *1937, Author's collection.*

during the Balbo era was reached in December of 1939, with the approval of legislation that officially incorporated the four coastal provinces of Tripoli, Misratah, Benghazi and Derna into the territory of the Kingdom of Italy.[34] In conjunction with the administrative and legislative changes that were aimed at bringing metropolitan standards to Libya, Balbo made a substantial effort to apply this same measure to the public works infrastructure. The architectural and planning implications of this initiative were evidenced in the creation of a Building Commission, which was formed in February of 1934, just over one month after his arrival in Libya.[35]

In addition to these general improvements which modernized the public infrastructure of Libya, the Balbo administration undertook one notable endeavor that was conceived and executed at a monumental scale – the construction of the *strada litoranea*. This project involved the completion of the remaining portion of just over 800 kilometers of the coastal highway that stretched from Tunisia to Egypt. Construction began in October of 1935 and was completed

---

34 This legislation was Regio Decreto Legge of January 9, 1939 n. 70, which incorporated the four provinces of Libya into metropolitan Italy. For a detailed discussion of the debate concerning this law, see ASMAE, MAI – Direzione Generale Affari Politici, Cartella 54–6.

35 Bucciante, G., "Lo sviluppo edilizio della Libia", in *Viaggio del Duce in Libia*, pp. 4–5.

by February of 1937, just a few weeks before Mussolini's visit to Libya.[36] The *strada litoranea* was the logical outcome of the political reforms that had unified Libya into a single administrative, military and civic entity, providing an artery that gave physical and metaphoric form to this new reality. It was also intended to facilitate commercial development of this colony and respond to military demands. In so doing, this road was not only built according to the most modern standards, it also contained amenities like the roadside facilities that provided gas and lodging for travelers.[37] As a major transportation artery that validated Fascist proclamations of the Roman origins of the region, the *strada litoranea* was a central element in Mussolini's March 12–21, 1937 visit to Libya. Indeed, his travel itinerary followed the length of the just completed artery, beginning near Tobruk at the eastern border with Egypt and traveling through Benghazi and Tripoli to Zuwarah and the western border with Tunisia. The images that captured the events associated with this visit communicate the importance of this artery as a powerful expression of the colonial order that was imposed on this North African context.

At the same time that the Balbo administration vigorously pursued a policy of modernization of systems of transportation and movement that would provide various forms of mobility for a Western audience, they were also deeply committed to a seemingly opposite program gauged at preserving the indigenous culture of the Libyans. The most comprehensive articulation of the indigenous politics by Balbo can be found in the presentation "La politica sociale verso gli arabi della Libia", that he made at the Alessandro Volta Foundation in Tripoli in 1938.[38] Although recognizing the need for a "vigilant defense of the manners" of the Libyans, he did not hesitate to speak of the eradication of "those old retrograde customs that oppose themselves to the social evolution of these same populations".[39] The qualified support of native customs was particularly true for religious practices, which were tolerated "as much as they are vital and derive from the laws of the Prophet", and prohibited if they were understood as "deviations of religious fanaticism".[40] This meant that while the Libyans were allowed, within certain limits and within the confines of religion and the family, to practice according to their traditions, all larger forms of

---

36 While the entire length of this highway was listed at 1,822 kilometers, by their own admission this project involved only 813 kilometers of new construction. See *La strada litoranea della Libia* (Verona: Officine Grafiche A. Mondadori, 1937), p. 33.

37 *La strada litoranea della Libia*, pp. 127–34.

38 Balbo, Italo, "La politica sociale fascista verso gli arabi della Libia", *Convegno di scienze morali e storiche. 4–11 ottobre 1938-XVI. Tema: L'Africa. Vol. 1* (Rome: Reale Accademia d'Italia, 1939), pp. 733–49.

39 Balbo, "La politica sociale fascista verso gli arabi della Libia", p. 746.

40 Balbo, "La politica sociale fascista verso gli arabi della Libia", pp. 738–9.

FIGURE 4.4 *Muslim colonization village of Alba (al-Fager), Libya, 1939, The Mitchell Wolfson Jr. Collection – Fondazione Regionale Cristoforo Colombo, Genoa.*

social and political organization were regulated by the dictates of the colonial administration.

Although the indigenous politics of Balbo was largely consistent with the previous policies, it amplified these measures by introducing a corporativist structure to the colonial context. This resulted in the creation of a set of parallel organizations and practices for the local populations, thus giving form to the racial discourse practiced in Italy's African colonies that called for separation of metropolitan and colonial. These initiatives were also aimed at exercising control over the local populations through concretizing stereotypes about the religious devotion of Muslims, their patient dedication to menial forms of labor, and the domestic role of their women. One example is the Women's School for Instruction and Work. This program was comprised of a series of separate institutions located in major towns, such as Tripoli, Homs, Misratah, Benghazi and Derna – the intention being to prepare Muslim women for their role in family life. The courses of study included general instruction in subjects such as language, religion, domestic economy and hygiene, and specific training in domestic skills such as cooking, sewing and weaving.[41] A second is

---

41 For a more detailed outline of the curriculum of this school and the general perception of Muslim women by the Italians, see "L'evoluzione delle condizioni della donna musulmana in Libia", pp. 1–8, ASMAE, MAI 5, Pacco 14, Fascicolo 182.

the Hassun Pasha Karamanli Orphanage and Shelter, which provided the local populations with training in agricultural development.[42] While these initiatives were initially in the form of subsidies for Libyan entrepreneurs, by 1939 they were expanded to include the creation of a series of agricultural towns – such as, Alba (al-Fager) in eastern Libya which consisted of a modest series of buildings that included public services and a mosque.[43] However, these Muslim agricultural villages conformed to neither the patterns of settlement nor the farming practices of the indigenous peoples and, as such, failed to achieve any significant results.[44]

The tourist exploitation of Libya during the governorship of Balbo was an extension of the modern social and political agenda of the colonial regime. Indeed, the development of a well-organized and efficient tourist system was premised on the modernization program that saw the construction of an infrastructure of roads and public services. However, the considerable financial investment that the Balbo administration made in the improvement of the road network was not an isolated gesture. The creation of a paved system of highways designed according to the most modern standards was undertaken in conjunction with a substantial program for the construction of new tourist facilities that was initiated in the first days of Balbo's governorship. In 1934 four new hotels began construction and four others were substantially renovated, all under the direction of the colonial administration.[45] It was during this same period that the project for the *strada litoranea* was being planned and a series of improvements in the road network in the Libyan interior were undertaken. These two initiatives resulted in the creation of a coordinated system of modern roads and hotels that described two basic itineraries that soon became the most desirable tourist experiences in this colony. The first of these reinforced Libya's Mediterranean status, following the *strada litoranea* from Zuwarah on the west to Tobruk on the east, linking Libya's largest cities of Tripoli and Benghazi and the major archeological sites of Sabrata, Leptis Magna, Cyrene and Apollonia. The second route explored Libya's African and Saharan setting,

---

42   Balbo, "La politica sociale fascista verso gli arabi della Libia", pp. 741–2.
43   Cresti, Federico, "Edilizia ed urbanistica nella colonizzazione agraria della Libia (1922–1940)", *Storia Urbana*, 11/40 (1987), 220–5.
44   Segrè, Claudio, *Fourth Shore. The Italian Colonization of Libya* (Chicago: The University of Chicago Press, 1974), pp. 144–57.
45   Bucciante, "Lo sviluppo edilizio della Libia", p. 5. The new hotels constructed during the Balbo era were eight in total; the Berenice in Benghazi (1935); the Cussabat (1936); the Derna (1937); the Rumia in Jefren (1934); the Nalut (1934–5); the Tobruk (1937); and the Uaddan (1934–5) and the Mehari (1934–5) in Tripoli. The renovation projects were the Ain-el Fras in Ghadames (1934–5); the Sirt (1934–7); and the Gazzelle in Zliten (1935).

traveling south from Tripoli deep into the interior, passing through Jefren and Nalut and ending in the oasis settlement of Ghadames.

In addition to creating these and other tourist facilities, the Balbo administration was responsible for the foundation of a centralized authority for the control of all tourist related activities. This effort culminated with the creation of the Libyan Tourism and Hotel Association (ETAL) in May of 1935. As a state sponsored corporation, this group provided the services of a travel agency, organizing tourist itineraries involving all forms of travel. It acted as tour operator, providing car and motor coach transportation throughout the region.[46] The ETAL was also responsible for the management of the 18 hotels that belonged to the Libyan government and the municipality – including the most prominent hotels in Tripoli, Benghazi and the Libyan interior – and supervising a network of entertainment facilities that included a theater and casino. Finally, this group handled its own publicity campaigns, producing publications like brochures, guide books, and postcards and organizing displays at exhibitions and fairs in Italy and abroad. By the end of the 1930s, the tourist system of the Libyan Tourism and Hotel Association comprised a network of 18 hotels located throughout this colony, numerous affiliated entertainment and tourist facilities in Tripoli and Benghazi and several offices dedicated to promoting the travel services of this organization. In so doing, the tourist system was closely tied to the colonial administration's efforts to bring this region up-to-date with the standards of the metropole in order to incorporate it into the larger Italy. Through the supervision of this network by a centralized authority whose point of reference was clearly metropolitan, a certain standard of services and amenities were almost universally available throughout the colony.[47]

The experience of modernity, an experience that supported various forms of mobility, was quite literally suffused throughout the tourist system of the Libyan Tourism and Hotel Association, which attempted to provide a network of modern travel services that met the expectations of the Italian and foreign traveler. While one of those expectations was providing a well-organized system, of equal importance was creating a comfortable setting that was familiar to the tourist. This group thus provided a series of amenities and tourist related activities that effectively transported the metropolitan context to Libya.

---

46   ETAL, "Realizzazioni fasciste. Gli sviluppi del turismo Libico", ASMAE, MAI 5, 5, Fascicolo 18.
47   All of the hotels in Libya were published in *Annuario a Alberghi d'Italia* (originally called *Gli alberghi in Italia*), a guide book to hotels in Italy put out by ENIT on a yearly basis. Ente Nazionale Industrie Turistiche, *Annuario alberghi d'Italia, 1939* (Milano: Turati Lombardi E.C., 1939).

One such example is the Uaddan Hotel and Casino in Tripoli, which was referred to in the tourist literature as a "jewel of modern African architecture".[48] As the only luxury class hotel in this colony, the Uaddan provided extensive support facilities that included a 500 seat theater and a gaming casino while only accommodating 50 guest rooms.[49] One of the major initiatives that provided an experience of modernity in this hotel were the activities of the Theater and Performance Service of the ETAL. This group brought in actors and musicians from Italy to provide forms of entertainment that principally appealed to a highly cultured Western audience.[50] The idea of mobility in this case not only applied to its cultural program – which was entirely Western – it was also reflected in its architecture. The highly polished wood surfaces of the Teatro Uaddan provided an opulent but appropriate context for these performances, which would seem more typical in the metropole than in the colony.

The tourist system in Libya during the Balbo era was also a product of the indigenous politics that both conceptually and physically restricted the indigenous populations. Indeed, the modern network of tourist activities and facilities that reached the most remote locations in this colony was not necessarily an end in itself so much as it provided a mechanism for the experience of the Libyan environment and culture – an experience that was, after all, the motivation for travel in this region. An interest in authenticity in the experience of indigenous culture extended to the meeting places and recreation facilities which, according to a press release from 1938, were: "one of the most appreciated attractions for the foreigner".[51] The most well-noted of these tourist settings was the so-called Arab Café, located in the Artisanal Quarter of the nineteenth-century Suq al-Mushir just inside the walls of the medina of Tripoli adjacent to the castle and the Karamanli Mosque.[52] Operated by the ETAL, this facility presented "characteristic" Arab musical and dance performances in a setting that one commentator argued "fully reproduces the suggestive local environment".[53] Not unlike the broader restoration project of Balbo in Libya, this "authentic" experience was assembled according to the same logic that pervaded the Italian intervention in the Libyan artisanal industries. Indeed, in

---

48   Brunelli, Claudio, "L'organizzazione turistica della Libia", *Rassegna Economica delle Colonie*, 25/3 (March 1937), p. 328.
49   Vicari, Eros, "L'Ente turistico ed alberghiero della Libia (E.T.A.L.)", *Gli Annali dell'Africa Italiana*, 5/4 (December 1942), pp. 963, 965, 971.
50   Vicari, "L'Ente turistico ed alberghiero della Libia", p. 971.
51   Untitled report of the Ente turistico ed alberghiero della Libia, (1938) 4, ASMAE, MAI 4, 29, Fascicolo 210.
52   Bucciante, "Lo sviluppo edilizio della Libia", p. 4.
53   Vicari, "L'Ente turistico ed alberghiero della Libia", p. 971.

FIGURE 4.5 *View of Yifran Hotel and surroundings, from* Itinerario Tripoli-Gadames, *1938, Author's collection.*

response to a lack of qualified local musicians and dancers the ETAL created an Arab music school to train the Libyans.[54] The Arab Café of the Suq al-Mushir is thus the embodiment of a political policy that sought to restrict the physical and cultural movement of the Libyans by fixing them to a timeless interpretation of their culture for the benefit of a Western audience.

An equally compelling example of tourist mobility during the governorship of Italo Balbo was provided by an itinerary that, just like the excursion of Volpi, brought foreign travelers from Tripoli to the edge of the Saharan desert. With the creation of the Libyan Tourism and Hotel Association, the pre-Saharan hotels in Yifran, Nalut and Ghadames were an integral part of a continuous tourist experience. In the 1938 guide book *Itinerario Tripoli-Gadames* this experience was characterized as providing an efficient and comfortable means of travel supported by hotels which, in addition to being carefully contextualized to their site and the local architecture, provided "the most comfortable hospitality".[55] This guide book also offers a systematic description of the itinerary that provided a five day return trip to Ghadames with an overnight stay

---

54 "Relazione tecnica del Direttore Generale al bilancio dell'esercizio, 1936–37", 23, ASMAE, MAI 4, 29, Fascicolo 210.

55 ETAL, *Itinerario Tripoli-Gadames* (Milan: Tipo-Litografia Turati Lombardi, 1938), p. 29.

FIGURE 4.6 *Tourists in the courtyard of 'Ain el-Fras Hotel, Ghadames, 1935, The Mitchell Wolfson Jr. Collection – Fondazione Regionale Cristoforo Colombo, Genoa.*

in Nalut. In contrast with the adventurous and sometimes dangerous experiences of the 1920s, in this publication the difficult realities of travel in this colony had been rendered invisible. Indeed, the series of watercolor images that accompany the text provide a narrative thread that creates the impression that travel in this region is almost effortless. One such example is the image of Yifran that counterposes a modern automobile in the foreground with the brilliantly white Rumia Hotel on the distant hillside.

The final hotel along this organized travel itinerary was the Hotel 'Ain el-Fras in Ghadames. The building responds to the formal language of the city, which is a complex labyrinth of narrow passages, covered courtyards and terraces shaped by dense walled structures, by creating a massive exterior wall that sheltered a series of courtyard spaces. Indeed, when looking closely at the arcaded wings that flank the central body of this building, there is an unmistakable connection between this element and the main courtyards of the town. This relationship can also seen in the interior spaces of the hotel, whose timber ceilings, rich wall coverings and minimal use of furnishing was intended to suggest the distinctive spaces of the indigenous houses – which were themselves highly desirable tourist sites. Through the direct incorporation of native forms, the building and its pre-Saharan context formed a continuous experience for the foreign tourist. The attempt to simulate the indigenous culture through architecture was enhanced by the fact that the entire hotel staff was dressed in local costume.[56] Such tourist spaces were the apotheosis of the racial prejudices that defined the Libyans and their culture as primitive and backward. As evidence of this tendency, the image the Berbers was constructed in the tourist literature – through an unchanging stereotype of their cultural past – as "more severe, more rigid, more bound to the observance of law" than the Arab populations.[57] The 'Ain el-Fras Hotel, just like the larger tourist system of the ETAL, was thus a combination of the most modern of tourist mobilities with carefully curated indigenous spaces – where the Libyans and their culture were put on display.

Conclusion

In a final reflection on tourist mobility in the Italian colony of Libya, it is interesting to consider the changing circumstances within the tourist system brought on by the conditions of war. On the 10th of June 1940, Italy entered World War II and almost immediately the English army initiated a series of raids against Italian positions in eastern Libya. On the 28th of June, Governor and Air Marshall Italo Balbo was shot down by friendly fire over the skies of Tobruk and soon after he was replaced as governor general and commander of the Italian troops in North Africa by General Graziani.[58] The war effort did not go well for the Italians, as by January of 1941 the towns of Tobruk and Bardia were taken by the English troops. With no small amount of irony, immediately following the Allied victory, Italian prisoners of war were marched across a bridge that was constructed as an instrument and symbol of Italy's colonial domination. Soon after, the fate of this colony, and of all of its tourist facilities, was placed in the hands of the German command of General Rommel, who continued the North African campaign that ended in May of 1943 with the German and Italian surrender.[59] During this time of military struggle a number of the tourist facilities of the Libyan Tourism and Hotel Association were damaged by the Allied raids, while others were requisitioned as residences for the German command. Perhaps the most poignant of these was the Arab Café of

---

56   Vicari, "L'Ente turistico ed alberghiero della Libia", p. 966.
57   ETAL, *Itinerario Tripoli-Gadames*, p. 13.
58   Del Boca, *Gli italiani in Libia: Dal fascismo a Gheddafi*, pp. 295–304.
59   Clark, Martin, *Modern Italy, 1871–1982* (London and New York: Longman Group Limited, 1984), p. 286.

the Suq al-Mushir which was used by the German consul for meetings of the National Socialist Party.[60]

While the impact of the North African military campaign on the Italian tourist system might be seen as the product of an exceptional condition, in reality the wartime situation merely exposed its uncompromising and inexorable logic. As subjects of the colonial tourist system the Libyans provided its essential content. At the same time, in reflecting a timeless vision of their culture they validated the discriminatory practices of Italy's colonial mission – and thus rendered unarguable their own "immobility". Moreover, under the auspices of the safety and political stability of the colonial state it was only Italian and foreign visitors who were accorded the liberating potential of what Urry calls the "right to mobility".[61] This freedom of movement was thus inevitably tied to and dependent upon the restriction of movement of the Libyans – enforced by the regime of violence that allowed Italy to maintain its fragile hold on this North African colony. It thus should be no surprise that during the last moments of Italian control – under the threat of the Western Desert campaign – there was revealed a certain form of symmetry with the *raid automobilistico* of Major Valentino Babini, as tourist mobilities returned to their origins in the military control of the territory.

---

60   Vicari, "L'Ente turistico ed alberghiero della Libia", p. 973.
61   Urry, *Mobilities*, p. 205.

CHAPTER 5

The Call of Communication: Mass Media and Reform in Interwar Morocco

Emilio Spadola

For two decades Middle East and North Africa media scholars have emphasized the transformative power of technical communications. To be sure, the Arab revolutions and social media have garnered the greater public attention, yet the best media scholarship has emphasized deeper regional histories of technological media and social change. Eschewing claims of new media's total novelty, scholars are now better able to address historical continuities of media and politics linking the present to earlier twentieth century political and social movements. This chapter continues that effort by examining transformations in communications media and the intertwined emergence of nationalism and modern Islamic reformism in interwar urban Morocco.

Extending and applying Benedict Anderson's seminal reading to particular sites and media forms, MENA scholars have generally argued for linking mass communications and nationalism.[1] Similar analyses of Islamic reformism, as well as more recent Islamic revivalist movements, point to the crucial role of mass communications, both visual (print included) and aural, in refiguring notions of public authority and piety.[2] Overall, the historical contemporaneity

---

1 Anderson, Benedict, *Imagined Communities,* rev. edition (London and New York: Verso, 2006 [1983]).
2 Scholarship emerging in the 1990s focused primarily on print. Work in the 2000s has focused on a broader array of media. See Atiyeh, George N., *The Book in the Islamic World: The Written Word and Communication in the Middle East* (Albany and Washington, D.C.: State University of New York Press, 1995); Eickelman, Dale, "Mass higher education and the religious imagination in contemporary Arab societies", *American Ethnologist,* 19/4 (1992), 643–55. See also, Eickelman, Dale, *Knowledge and Power in Morocco: The Education of a Twentieth-Century Notable* (Princeton: Princeton University Press, 1985); Eickelman, Dale F., and Jon W. Anderson (eds.), *New Media in the Muslim World: The Emerging Public Sphere,* 2nd ed. (Bloomington: Indiana University Press, 2003); Hirschkind, Charles, "Experiments in devotion online: the YouTube Khutba", *International Journal of Middle East Studies,* 44/1 (2012), 5–21; Hirschkind, Charles, *The Ethical Soundscape: Cassette Sermons and Islamic Counterpublics* (New York: Columbia University Press, 2006); Messick, Brinkley, "On the question of lithography", *Culture and History* (Copenhagen, Denmark: Museum Tusculanum Press), 16 (1997), 158–76;

of nationalist and Islamic reformist thought and practice suggests a shared historical matrix of mass consciousness and communications, defined in the broadest sense of material and symbolic circulation and exchange among large-scale anonymous populations.[3]

The case of interwar Morocco is illustrative, as young reform-minded Muslim leaders worked in the name of both the modern nation and Islam, sharing a conjoined project of specifically *social* reform under the misguidance of the new sovereign colonial state. Indeed, the reformist arguments detailed in this chapter pointed to a key demand for, and creation of, mass actions by which a colonial state and eventual independent Morocco would cultivate proper communications, and thus summon up Moroccan subjects' identification with Moroccan society as such. James L. Gelvin evokes this disciplinary and *communicative* project in noting that the modern consolidation of the nation-state system coincided with mass consciousness of "society" as a putatively uniform and unified (because wholly interconnected) collectivity:

> The world system of nation-states had a created a world in which individual societies were conceived of as essential and autonomous entities with their own collective interest. It was a world in which the state had the responsibility to promote that interest by organizing, regularizing, and advancing its citizenry for that end. Conversely it was a world in which

---

Messick, Brinkley, *The Calligraphic State: Textual Domination and History in a Muslim Society* (Berkeley: University of California Press, 1993); Robinson, Francis, "Technology and religious change: Islam and the impact of print", *Modern Asian Studies*, 27/1 (1993), 229–51; Schulz, Dorothea Elisabeth, *Muslims and New Media in West Africa: Pathways to God* (Bloomington: Indiana University Press, 2012); Spadola, Emilio, *The Calls of Islam: Sufis, Islamists, and Mass Mediation in Urban Morocco* (Bloomington: Indiana University Press, 2014).

3 The vast majority of twentieth-century Western scholarship assimilated nationalism to an ostensible secular trend from which Islam would all but disappear. More nuanced readings point to interdependencies of Islam and nation as objects of new consciousness and administration. For the Muslim world in general, and Indonesia in particular, the classic text remains Siegel, James T., *The Rope of God*, rev. edition (Ann Arbor: University of Michigan Press, 2000 [1969]). Studies of the MENA emphasize the interwar reform or 'reinvention' of Islam and its classical institutions (law, the Caliphate, etc.) attending the modern nation-state system's consolidation. See Gershoni, Israel and James P. Jankowski, *Redefining the Egyptian Nation, 1930–1945* (Cambridge: Cambridge University Press, 1995); Messick, *The Calligraphic State*; Gelvin, James L., "Secularism and religion in the Arab Middle East: reinventing Islam in a world of nation-states", in *The Invention of Religion: Rethinking Belief in Politics and History*, ed. Derek R. Peterson and Darren R. Walhof (New Brunswick: Rutgers University Press, 2002), pp. 115–30. On the intertwining of religion and nation in Morocco, see Spadola, *The Calls of Islam*.

the citizenry had to internalize the notion of collective interest so that its activities would be directed toward the realization of that interest.[4]

As Gelvin suggests, nationalist and Islamic reformist organizing rested heavily on the efficacy of communications, as reformers aimed to persuade, summon and call populations to "internalize" – to *respond to* and *accept responsibility for* – unprecedented reforms and norms. Indeed, reform largely meant teaching individual subjects to identify themselves as one among many interconnected, serial national "Moroccans" regardless of other traditional social distinctions.[5]

My argument in this chapter, then, highlights these links: that nationalist thinkers in interwar Morocco developed an awareness (1) of communication *itself* as a structural and mobile force for making and unmaking the Moroccan society and its national fortunes, and (2) of *communicability,* or consciousness of this new force, as a moral quality of modern national subjects. For nationalists in Morocco and elsewhere in the MENA, the interwar expansion of global communications meant that communication and its effects required conscientious social adaptation and political domestication; in short, reformists saw both personal and social awareness of communication as the condition for weaving individual bodies into the social body. No better sign of this nationalist concern is the very ubiquity of the consciousness-raising "call" as grounding logic and strategy of large-scale modernist efforts. The continuity of "the call" in MENA mass politics from the interwar period to the present, whether in print, radio, or social media movements, suggests a continuing awareness of communication and communicability and its effects across disparate social, religious, and political domains.[6]

---

4   Gelvin, "Secularism and religion in the Arab Middle East", p. 119.
5   For discussions of this developing logic of universal consciousness in the interwar Muslim world, see Siegel, *The Rope of God,* pp. 68–133; Anderson, Benedict, "Nationalism, identity, and the logic of seriality", in Benedict Anderson, *The Spectre of Comparisons: Nationalism, Southeast Asia and the World* (London and New York: Verso, 1998), pp. 29–45.
6   This argument extends my analysis of Muslim politics of the call in Spadola, *The Calls of Islam.* This argument coincides with but also departs from literature on MENA social movements and mobilization. See Beinin, Joel and Frédéric Vairel (eds.), *Social Movements, Mobilization, and Contestation in the Middle East and North Africa,* 2nd ed. (Stanford: Stanford University Press, 2013); White, Jenny B., *Islamist Mobilization in Turkey: A Study in Vernacular Politics* (Seattle: University of Washington Press, 2002); Wickham, Carrie Rosefsky, *Mobilizing Islam: Religion, Activism, and Political Change in Egypt* (New York: Columbia University Press, 2002). Whereas Social Movement Theory in the MENA is breaking key ground in emphasizing these movements' heterogeneity and the pre-existing 'networks' they draw from,

The Emergence of Nationalist Reformism

Morocco is often treated as marginal to Middle Eastern political history; arguably, it presents certain historical exceptions. From the fifteenth century till twentieth-century colonial rule, the lands and peoples of what is now the modern Moroccan nation-state resisted Ottoman control, forming rather an independent Muslim sultanate legitimated by Sharifian descent. Claims that the premodern Sa'adi and 'Alawi dynasties' political theological power signaled a distinctly national identity, however, are questionable at best.[7]

Like late Ottoman provinces, the 'Alawi sultanate was in no sense organized or conceived as a unitary nation bound to a modern centralized territorial state.[8] As with Middle Eastern states, widespread modern nationalist claims

---

its continued emphasis on activists' strategies takes for granted such movements' distinctly modern technical social and political conditions of possibility. While acknowledging that interwar Moroccan nationalism was hardly *sui generis*, this chapter highlights the truly novel material conditions and *consciousness* of mass communication itself that marked reformists' concerns. These conditions are, of course, historically specific to modernity, having defined the nation form, and indeed 'the social' itself, as a unitary body in Europe only since the nineteenth century. See below, and the work of Foucault's student Donzelot, Jacques, *L'Invention du social: essai sur le déclin des passions politiques* (Paris: Éditions du Seuil, 1994).

7 On the historical formation of the pre-modern Sharifian sultanate, the formative work remains Geertz, Clifford, *Islam Observed* (Chicago: University of Chicago Press, 1968). Recent historical studies, however, provide detailed correctives. See Cornell, Vincent J., *Realm of the Saint: Power and Authority in Moroccan Sufism* (Austin: University of Texas Press, 1998); Kugle, Scott, *Rebel between Spirit and Law: Ahmad Zarruq, Sainthood, and Authority in Islam* (Bloomington: Indiana University Press, 2006).

8 Thus while James A.O.C. Brown writes of a precolonial "Morocco", he warns that "the use of the terms 'Morocco' or 'Moroccan' to indicate or describe a political entity or geographical area before the modern period is problematic", Brown, James A.O.C. "Morocco and Atlantic history", in *The Atlantic World*, ed. D'Maris Coffman, Adrian Leonard and William O'Reilly (London: Routledge, 2015), pp. 187–206. To put it in stronger terms, it is wholly anachronistic: premodern sultans' religious influence in the region, itself vastly broader than their political rule, did not translate to the kind of novel identitarian claims made in the name of a nation after World War I. Unfortunately, Brown considers it acceptable to speak of "Morocco" starting with the sixteenth century Sa'adian dynasty. A more thorough reading should make clear that the political unity of the state under the sultan as guarantor of law and religion imagined such subjecthood as comprising personal webs of connection rather than abstract unity. For recent historians' arguments for the colonial era construction and imagining of a unified Moroccan people and identity, whether under the sign of culture or Islam, see Burke, Edmund III, *The Ethnographic State: France and the Invention of Moroccan Islam* (Berkeley: University of California Press, 2014) and Wyrtzen, Jonathan, *Making Morocco: Colonial Intervention and the Politics of Identity* (Ithaca: Cornell University Press, 2015).

would circulate in urban Morocco only in the early interwar period, under French and Spanish colonial rule. This is not to repeat dubious claims of the precolonial sultanate's isolation or its anachronistic survival.[9] In point of fact, religious and state reform efforts demonstrated increasing integration of local political and religious thought with Mashriqi and European streams. Efforts by sultan, scholar, and Sufi Mawlay Sulayman (d. 1822) to reform popular Sufi practices of singing and dancing at saints' tombs were conversant with, if not inspired by, Ibn 'Abd al-Wahhab's teachings.[10] From the late nineteenth century on, the movement of merchants, pilgrims, and official state delegations from the 'Alawi sultanate east, as well as the increasing volume of Mashriqi journals moving west brought the pan-Islamic thought of al-Afghani and 'Abduh.[11] Among an increasing number of reform-minded scholars,

9 Nineteenth- and twentieth-century colonial scholars in particular overstated the region's geographic and cultural isolation from political and religious discourse in the Mashriq, basing the public case for colonial rule in part on its putatively medieval character and thus its need for assistance in modernizing. Writing in the early independence period, the scholar of nationalism John Halstead would characterize the precolonial state structure as "medieval ... anachronistically surviving into the twentieth [century]", Halstead, John, *Rebirth of a Nation: The Origins and Rise of Moroccan Nationalism, 1912–1944* (Cambridge, MA: Harvard University Press, 1967), p. 184.
10 While Mawlay Sulayman famously sent a delegation of scholars to Arabia to learn more of Ibn 'Abd al-Wahhab's thought, he was hardly an advocate. He himself was a member of the Tariqa Tijaniyya; in his view, singing, dancing, and "crowding" merely exceeded the proper forms of shrine visitation and emulation owed to great Muslim "Friends of God and the Saints [*al-awliya' wa-l-salihin*]". Further reform efforts were discontinued after his death. See El-Mansour, Mohamed, *Morocco in the Reign of Mawlay Sulayman* (Wisbech, UK: Middle East and North African Studies Press, 1990). Mawlay Sulayman's *khutba* calling for reforms is reproduced by 'Alawite historian Abu al-Qassim al-Zayani (d. 1833) in his *Al-Turjamana al-kubra fi akhbar al-ma'mur barran wa bahran* [Grand Collection of Reports of the World by Land and Sea], ed. Abdelkarim al-Filali (Rabat: Dar Nashr al-Ma'rifa, 1991), pp. 466–70. I thank Fatima Ghoulaichi for calling my attention to this resource. For a partial translation see Ghoulaichi, Fatima, "Of Saints and Sharifian Kings in Morocco: Three Examples of the Politics of Reimagining History through Reinventing King/Saint Relationship", M.A. Dissertation, College Park, MD, University of Maryland, 2005, pp. 52–6.
11 Nineteenth-century European economic and military incursions also prompted 'Alawite sultans to seek bureaucratic and military reforms modeled on French and British as well as the Ottoman empire's reformed (*nizami*) armies. These efforts, however, as Amira K. Bennison describes, were "small in scale and of relatively short duration and impact". See Bennison, Amira K., "The 'New Order' and Islamic order: The introduction of the Nizami army in the western Maghrib and its legitimation, 1830–73", *International Journal of Middle East Studies*, 36/4 (2004), 591–612, quote p. 608. For the most complete

Abdallah al-Sanussi returned to Morocco from his studies at Al-Azhar; a decade later, Abu Sha'ib al-Duqqali, a student of Muhammad 'Abduh, and himself dubbed "Abduh of the Maghrib", brought contemporary Salafi teachings to Morocco's Qarawiyyin.[12] These scholars' differing fortunes reflect the shifting local conditions and growing receptivity to socio-religious reform. Al-Sanussi, arguing against the Sufi saint veneration upholding local religious hierarchies, fell under attack from Fassi 'ulama' and returned to a more sympathetic audience in the Levant.[13] Al-Duqqali, receiving the patronage of new sultan and scholar 'Abd al-Hafidh, would win favor among younger scholars by denouncing local sumptuary and sacrificial practices and uprooting a myrtle tree serving as a sacrificial shrine.[14] Nevertheless, these more radical reformist thinkers had little impact on an urban social order defined by distinct Sufi orders and hierarchies and Sharifian nobility. Despite later historical and biographical claims, local audiences were not prepared to identify as, or celebrate, "Morocco" and "Moroccans" as a source of belonging or object of governance.[15]

Nationalist reforms and calls to (and celebrations of) common belonging to "the Moroccan People" would emerge following World War I, notably among a young generation of thinkers consciously adopting titles to distinguish

---

catalog of reforms, see Al-Manuni, Mohammed, *Madhahir yaqdhat al-maghrib al-hadith* [Aspects of Modern Morocco's Awakening], 2 vols. (Dar al-Bayda': Sharikat al-Nashr wa-l-Tawzi' al-Madaris, 1985).

12   Berque, Jacques, "Cà et là dans les débuts du réformisme religieux au Maghreb", *Extrait des études d'orientalisme dédiées à la mémoire de Lévi-Provençal* (Paris: Maisonneuve et Larose, 1962), pp. 471–94.

13   Laroui, Abdallah, *Les origins sociales et culturelle du nationalism marocain, 1830–1912* (Paris: Maspero, 1977), p. 206. On reforms articulated in the dominant local idiom of sharifian Sufism, see Bazzaz, Sahar, *Forgotten Saints: History, Power, and Politics in the Making of Modern Morocco* (Cambridge, MA: Harvard University Press, 2010).

14   Berque, "Cà et là dans les débuts du réformisme", p. 480.

15   Sahar Bazzaz identifies an independence-era biographer's spurious attribution of nationalism to Sufi reformist Muhammad al-Kattani in denouncing the consumption of tea and sugar. The motivation was neither a boycott (as later nationalists would enact against tobacco) nor national reform, but rather a pious concern for the addictive effects. See Bazzaz, *Forgotten Saints*, pp. 99 and 109, n. 73. A more general indication of resistance to any notion of 'general public' or common identity is the outrage in Fez prompted by Sultan 'Abd al-'Aziz's attempt in 1901, all but forced by British creditors, to impose a flat tax (*tartib*) on all subjects. This venture in centralizing and monopolizing authority sought to overturn the longstanding class privileges, tax exemptions and even legal sovereignty, of the quasi-nobility, the *shurafa'* (Bazzaz, *Forgotten Saints*, p. 95).

themselves from older religious institutions and social categories.[16] In Fez, Rabat, Salé, and other urban centers young elites schooled in new francophone *collèges musulmans*, formed alumni groups of "Jeunes marocains", on the nationalist inspiration of the Young Turks.[17] At al-Qarawiyyin in the heart of the medina, 'Allal al-Fassi and others preached not just Salafi doctrine, but "neo-Salafiyya" (*al-salafiyya al-jadida*), explicitly bound to nationalist reform.[18] Among the key efforts were the founding of new "free schools" (*madaris hurra*), secondary schools outside French administrative control, in Fez, Salé, Rabat, and Marrakech.[19] Neo-Salafis and *Jeunes marocains,* familiar with Salafi journals *al-Shihab* and *al-Najah* in Algeria, and *al-Mu'ayyid* and *al-Manar* in Egypt, likewise submitted articles under pseudonyms.[20] Indeed, through the 1920s nationalist expression within Morocco remained surreptitious, kept to personal correspondence or, as with Al-Fassi's broadsheet, *Umm al-Banin*, to clandestine press with limited circulation.[21] Beginning in 1930, however, reformist thinkers would turn outward to summon a mass public through novel forms of protest, the formation of mass political parties, a larger-scale nationalist press, and new public forms of royal ceremony.

---

16 Terem, Etty, *Old Texts, New Practices: Islamic Reform in Modern Morocco* (Stanford: Stanford University Press, 2014). Etty Terem's recent study rightly argues against "subsum[ing] late nineteenth century thinkers and twentieth century nationalists under one ideological rubric, the Moroccan salafiyya movement" (p. 9). Nevertheless, Terem also writes that late nineteenth-century thinkers "were deeply convinced that the sanctity of the shari'a was being violated and that the renewal of religion (*tajdid*) was necessary for the revival of Moroccan society" (p. 53). While agreeing with Terem in general, my point here is that the terms *Moroccan* and *society* were not internal to reformists' discourse, as neither term would find common usage for several decades. See note 44 below.
17 Halstead, *Rebirth of a Nation*, pp. 206–8.
18 Al-Fassi, 'Allal, *Al-Harakat al-istiqlaliyyah fi-l-maghrib al-'arabi* [Independence Movements of the Arab Maghreb] (Tangier: 'Abd al-Salam Jasus, 1948), p. 135; Abun-Nasr, Jamil, "The Salafiyya movement in Morocco: the religious bases of Moroccan nationalist movement", *St. Anthony's Papers*, 16 (1963), p. 99.
19 French Protectorate officials contemptuously named these *"msids renovées"* (after Qur'anic elementary schools, *msids*) but the free schools in fact departed sharply from the mnemonic methods of Qur'anic schooling, combining French and Arabic instruction, and Qur'an and Hadith studies, with contemporary European political theory. See Girardière, E., "L'école coranique et la politique nationaliste au Maroc", *France méditerranéenne et africaine*, 1 (1938), 99–109.
20 Halstead, *Rebirth of a Nation*, p. 125.
21 Souriau-Hoebrechts, Christine, *La Presse Maghrebine: Libye – Tunisie – Maroc – Algérie: évolution historique, situation en 1965, organisation et problèmes actuels* (Paris: Editions du CNRS, 1975), p. 86.

This shift toward nationalist thought is familiar to historians of Morocco; Jonathan Wyrtzen in particular has traced it convincingly not only through the colonial state's bureaucratic management, classification, and representation of populations as "Moroccan", but also through Moroccan reformists' adoption and communication of these logics to urban social groups.[22] His work thus helps us grasp more precisely how, in Gelvin's words, reform-minded Moroccans aimed strategically to induce distinct social groups, conventionally organized by kinship and tribe, geographic proximity, and religious loyalties, "to internalize the notion of collective interest" based on the ideally uniform and unified nation. If, as Wyrtzen shows, such efforts were contemporaneous with expanding infrastructure, speed, and scale of communication, I want to press the argument further to argue that scholarly interpretations of reform as a task *of communication* was shared by nationalist and Islamic reformists themselves; to reform required "calling" different local groups to *society*, first and foremost, Moroccans. Thus in examining how young urban elites imagined themselves as "neo-Salafis" and "young Moroccans", we must grasp not merely the modernist political messages *in* these media, but the acceleration and expansion of mass mediated communication *as message*. In doing so we may discern how reformists sought to control communication itself as the source of social – which is to say, both material and spiritual – unity.

Communication and the Promise of Unity

Scholars of Moroccan modernity rightfully point to the expanding access to print publications in the latter part of the nineteenth century. In addition to the increasing volume of imported material, from the 1860s onward the print technologies of lithography (1865) and moveable type (1906) were installed in Morocco. The technology, initially monopolized by the sultan Sidi Muhammad (r. 1859–73), would find increasing use only after the 1880s, as private printing houses and individual operations expanded to produce tens of thousands of volumes.[23] Yet the effects of print on the social and political consciousness of the growing readership should not be overstated: publication of religious texts remained solely the purview of wealthy *shurafa'* and notables, and Sufis and scholars expanded their readership and prestige by following traditional

---

22 Wyrtzen, *Making Morocco*.
23 Sufi literature (biographies, apologetics, *hizb* literature) and jurisprudence comprised half of all printed books in the sultanate between 1865 and 1920, with Sufi biography as the most "visible literature" available, with 38,000 copies. See Abdulrazak, Fawzi, "The Kingdom of the Book: The History of Printing as an Agency of Change in Morocco between 1865 and 1912", Ph.D. Dissertation, Boston University, 1990, pp. 231, 224.

genres.[24] Political literature too pursued recognizable themes of anti-European jihad, with "much if not all ... reform literature appear[ing] during the French Protectorate".[25] Ultimately, Fawzi Abdulrazak considers the precolonial era of printing "as a transition leading to the eventual democratization of books, and to modernity".[26]

Acceleration and expansion of communications, including transport, are among "the most radical transformations" marking early colonial rule.[27] Within two decades, state and private railways, an advanced highway system, seaports and airports, print and photography, telephony and telegraphy, and radio broadcast linked the interior cities with the Atlantic coast, and growing numbers of Moroccans with Europe, the Middle East and the world.[28] The decade of nationalism's public emergence, 1925–1935, witnessed an especially rapid increase and consolidation of communications technologies as well as an increase in their use by Moroccans of multiple classes.[29]

These technologies exceed the category of "print-capitalism" that Anderson linked to national consciousness, yet the forms share basic qualities of

---

24 Abdulrazak, "The Kingdom of the Book", p. 214.
25 Abdulrazak, "The Kingdom of the Book", p. 235. Abdulrazak notes publishers' general disinterest in mass markets for the first two or so decades, with a handful of "small capitalist" family or one-person operations eventually accounting for all marketed volumes (Abdulrazak, "The Kingdom of the Book", p. 181). Although printing permitted individual scholars to serve as editors, the continued involvement of scribes in publication suggests that the shift from scribal to early print witnessed relatively little change in the mode of production or the speed and scale of distribution, which remained bound to conventional overland transport.
26 Abdulrazak, "The Kingdom of the Book", p. 191.
27 Wyrtzen, *Making Morocco*, p. 87.
28 Regarding the development of transport in Morocco, Frédéric Abécassis writes, "One of the most striking aspects of Morocco for nineteenth century European travelers was without a doubt its archaic transport system". He continues to argue that "the system of transport in precolonial Morocco cannot be separated from [its] social organization". See Abécassis, Frédéric, "La mise en place du réseau routier au Maroc", *Aperçu historique* (2009) (https://halshs.archives-ouvertes.fr/halshs-00435869). Estimates of typical speeds in the precolonial sultanate range from four km/hour (approx. 2.5 mph) or 30 km/day (approx. 18.6 miles) for commerce to six mph for wheeled military vehicles in the service of the sultan. See Bousser, M., "Les transport au Maroc et leurs tarifs de l'origine à nos jours", *Bulletin économique du Maroc*, 3 (January, 1934), p. 201; Aflalo, Moussa, *The Truth About Morocco: An Indictment of the Policy of the British Foreign Office with Regard to the Anglo-French Agreement* (London: John Lane, 1904), p. 126.
29 By 1933, the French Protectorate had constructed 5,996 km of highways and 1,088 km of standard gauge railway, *Bulletin économique du Maroc* (January, 1934), p. 203.

mass communication, of multiplicity and simultaneity, which his reading emphasized. Specifically, Anderson focused on the way mass production and dissemination of multiple copies in simultaneous, distant circulation, made possible a consciousness of oneself sharing the "empty, homogeneous" time and space of other distant readers or recipients of the text.[30] To imagine oneself as equivalent addressee among potentially tens of millions whom one could never possibly know was, for Anderson, the very ground of national longing and national belonging. Or, as media historian Michael Warner observes of modern mass publics more generally, by virtue of grasping communications "as addressed to us and as addressed to strangers", we learn to place ourselves among "indefinite others". "The benefit of this practice", Warner writes, "is that it gives a general social relevance to private thought and life. Our subjectivity is understood as having resonance with others, and immediately so".[31] By Anderson's reading, this sense of immediacy (or, better, simultaneity) is of course *technologically* mediated: the nation, insofar as it can be imagined *as* a community, is an effect of mass communication.[32]

Such logics can very well describe the dynamics of national publics already formed; but what of nascent mass societies? It is this key conjunction between nation-building and mass communication that media historian Armand Mattelart identifies with French social thinkers' "invention of communication" in the long nineteenth century from the Revolution to World War I.[33] Mattelart's capacious definition of *communication* of course matches its early modern use meaning not only circulation of "information", but also the great mobility of commodities and bodies that came to power industrial capitalism both in France and its colonies, including the emerging nation-state of Morocco. For

---

30 The first edition of *Imagined Communities* focused on time. In rewriting subsequent editions Anderson focused on the spatial homogeneity necessary for thinking simultaneity and thus the nation. See Anderson, *Imagined Communites*, rev. edition, Ch. 10.

31 Warner, Michael, *Publics and Counterpublics* (New York: Zone Books, 2005), p. 77.

32 James L. Gelvin writes of nationalist thinkers in interwar Syria who "redirected their focus away from local concerns to the national arena". See Gelvin, James L., *Divided Loyalties. Nationalism and Mass Politics in Syria at the Close of Empire* (Berkeley: University of California Press, 1998), p. 21. This distinction between the "local" and "national" was not fixed, however: the national became the site of locality *par excellence* as new technological connections and bureaucratic structures bound distant people, objects and events together by a sense of simultaneous presence. Through the fact and feeling of simultaneity, what took place afar could feel entirely local. The nation-state as a whole came to constitute one's locale.

33 Mattelart, Armand, *The Invention of Communication*, trans. Susan Emanuel (Minneapolis, Minn.: University of Minnesota Press, 1996).

Mattelart, the networking of France was not random, but rather a conscious exercise in the production of social control. Communication denotes "the mastery of movement by Reason", that is, both a "system of thought and power" as well as a "mode of government" at once centralizing and decentralizing.[34] The linking of communication and governance points up the concept's extension beyond technical structure and practice to encompass modern governmentality, that is, both managing individual subject production and vast social engineering.[35] By the end of the nineteenth century, Mattelart writes, "communication was to be the sacred standard by which the power of a people is measured, along with its social well-being, its prosperity, its civilization, and the degree of civil and political liberty that it has attained".[36]

While Mattelart studied France, the universal claims and global circulation of this "sacred standard", like Anderson's "nationness", were certainly not lost on political and social reformers of the historical Middle East and North Africa. Hence, reformers emphasized the management of communication as not merely one reform among others but rather as the condition for all possible reforms.[37] Which is to say, modern reformists did not merely learn about

34 Mattelart, *The Invention of Communication,* pp. xiv, xi. Mattelart and others note that *cybernetics*, a term virtually synonymous with Euro-American communication studies, has a lengthy etymology linked to governance, from Plato's discussion of skill in steering (*kubernētikē*) or "the art of governing", to the nineteenth-century French physicist André-Marie Ampère's use of "la cybernétique" as "the science of government". See Mattelart, *The Invention of Communication,* p. 223; Johnson, Christopher, "'French' cybernetics", *French Studies,* 69/1 (2015), p. 64; Wiener, Norbert, *Cybernetics; Or, Control and Communication in the Animal and the Machine,* 2nd ed. (New York: MIT Press, 1965 [1961]).

35 Foucault, Michel, *Security, Territory, Population: Lectures at the Collège de France 1977–1978,* ed. Michel Senellart, trans. Graham Burchell (New York: Picador, 2007).

36 Mattelart, *The Invention of Communication,* p. 57.

37 As the chapters of this volume attest, this regulation of communication marked such diverse and seemingly contrary practices as anti-colonial activism, the regulation and standardization of Islamic practice, tourism, public health and sanitation, vitality of the tourism industry, the emphasis on team sport, and the Miss World competition. In his study of late nineteenth- and early twentieth-century colloquial Egyptian media and nationalism, Fahmy characterizes advocacy of Fusha over colloquial Arabic by staunch modernists from Muhammad 'Abduh to Naguib Mahfuz as somehow closer to a "traditionalist" (if not "classical traditionalist") view. See Fahmy, Ziad, *Ordinary Egyptians: Creating the Modern Nation through Popular Culture* (Stanford: Stanford University Press, 2011), pp. 7, 185, n. 31. This is a puzzling misreading: advocating the standardization of language, indeed, the regulation of communication more generally, marks modernists' desire to construct modern subjects and societies. Indeed, Fahmy quotes a statement by Mahfuz that specifically compares language to a social disease (both of course are

or express aims through new communicative channels; they sought large-scale interventions and institutions on the political, social, and religious scale these technologies produced and now demanded as conditions of global recognition and political survival.

The reference to "religious" scale may seem awkward (we are not accustomed to speaking of "mass religion" as we do mass society or mass politics). Yet, coming to grips with new speed and scale of communications affected all areas of collective social life.[38] Indeed, for modernists, communicative networking of a national territory would guarantee not only its political-economic unity, but more importantly, the very possibility of the social, that is, the *moral-spiritual* coherence of its citizens as a collective.[39] This communicative fact of modern reform undergirds the ubiquity of "calls" to novel mass publics voiced through mass communicative channels across interwar Middle East and North Africa; in interwar Morocco it informed such disparate reformist concerns as the regulation of public Sufi rituals, and the production of a new national holiday celebrating the 'Alawite sultan, whom nationalists now named as their "king" (Arabic *malik*, French *roi*).

To reiterate, national coherence in the age of mass communication would involve reforming not only social and political and religious institutions, but also familiarizing people with a collective made possible by virtue of mass communication itself. Such efforts would demand addressing not only particular established and defined groups, but reaching *people* despite *social*

communicable): "The colloquial is one of the diseases from which the people are suffering, and of which they are bound to rid themselves as they progress. I consider colloquial one of the failings of our society, exactly like ignorance, poverty, and disease", Fahmy, *Ordinary Egyptians*, p. 181.

38 On the changing "pace, pattern, and scale" of modern communications, see McLuhan, Marshall, *Understanding Media: The Extensions of Man*, critical edition W. Terrence Gordon (New York: Gingko Press, 2003 [1964]); McLuhan, Marshall, *The Gutenberg Galaxy: The Making of Typographic Man*, new edition (Toronto: University of Toronto Press, 2011 [1962]). McLuhan's theories, dismissed as pop eccentricity through the 1970s and 1980s, regained favor with the rise of digital communications. MENA historians Gelvin and Green likewise emphasize scale, intensity, and acceleration of connections as the defining features of modern communicative technologies. See Gelvin, James L. and Nile Green (eds.), *Global Muslims in the Age of Steam and Print* (Berkeley: University of California Press, 2013), pp. 1–22. Other key texts on speed and scale in modernity include Schivelbusch, Wolfgang, *The Railway Journey: The Industrialization of Time and Space,* rev. edition (Berkeley: University of California Press, 2014 [1986]); Virilio, Paul, *Speed and Politics*, new edition, trans. Mark Polizzotti (Cambridge, MA: MIT Press, 2006 [1977]); Derrida, Jacques, "No apocalypse, not now (full speed ahead, seven missives, seven missiles)", *Diacritics*, 14/2, *Nuclear Criticism* (1984), 20–31.

39 Mattelart, *The Invention of Communication*, p. 26.

definitions. To reform (or form) individuals to be capable of inserting themselves into or "internalizing" this new society, such individuals would need to identify themselves precisely *as one of a mass*, as one of potentially millions of identical or serial subjects receiving the same message at the same time. Such an effort to reach out and awaken would thus not just convey the message of reform, but of a novel mass collective – the message of mass communication itself.[40]

Nationalism, Islam, and Reforms of Communication

Sacralizing Communication

In recalling the interwar Moroccan reformist movement, the Fassi nationalist leader Mohammed Hassan al-Wazzani would describe Salafiyya and nationalism as "twin da'wa movements"; the *"da'wa wataniyya"* and *"da'wa salafiyya"* were inseparable as they shared the fundamental aim of "reforming the individual and the society".[41] Al-Wazzani was familiar with the classical Islamic traditions of reform and renewal. But as a Sorbonne-educated political scientist and personal secretary of Shakib Arslan in Geneva, he, more than any other nationalist thinker, brought European political thought, and more specifically strongly republican or statist liberalism to bear on Moroccan reformism.[42] Certainly, as editor of two of Morocco's first nationalist newspapers, he advocated for establishing and controlling mass communication in constructing and conveying Islamic and nationalist calls to the reform of "Moroccan society".

We may begin identifying these efforts by examining al-Wazzani's celebration of communication itself as enacted by its master, "the caller". A collection

---

40   For an argument regarding the formation of a collective despite social differences, Siegel, James T., *The Rope of God*. For Siegel's description of the cultural emergence of mass audienceship, which he calls "overhearing", linked to Indonesian nationalism, see Siegel, James, *Fetish, Recognition, Revolution* (Princeton: Princeton University Press, 1997).
41   Al-Wazzani, Mohammed Hassan, "Harakat al-nahda al-sharqiyya" [The East's renaissance movement], in *Mudhakarat hayat wa jihad: Al-tarikh al-siyasi li-l-haraka al-wataniyya al-tahririyya al-maghribiyya, al-juz' al-awal* [Memoirs of a Life and Struggle: The Political History of the Moroccan Nationalist Liberation Movement, vol. 1] (Beirut and Fez: Dar al-Nahda al-'Arabiyya and Mu'asasat Mohamed Hassan al-Wazzani, 1982), pp. 330, 323.
42   I gather this orientation from his published writings, which includes a translation of the French Republican thinker Charles Dupont-White's *L'individu et l'état*. Al-Wazzani, Mohammed Hassan, *Dirasat wa ta'mulat, 2: Hurriyat al-fard wa sultat al-dawla* [Studies and Reflections, vol. 2: The Freedom of the Individual and the Powers of the State] (Beirut and Fez: Dar al-Nahda al-'Arabiyya and Mu'asasat Mohamed Hassan al-Wazzani, 1987).

of al-Wazzani's political writings, composed during and after a period of imprisonment and exile (November 1937–May 1946), includes a brief (one page) commentary, "Who is 'the Caller'?"[43] The caller (*al-daʿiya*), he writes, is first of all to be distinguished from a more familiar figure, the preacher (*al-khatib*):

> Whereas the preacher is limited to preaching, the caller believes in his thinking and calls others to it through writing, preaching, everyday conversation, and rigorous efforts in his private and public life – indeed by all communicative means possible. He is a writer, a preacher, an interlocutor and an example [*qudwa*], influencing others through his action and his very person [*bi shakhsihi*].[44]

Al-Wazzani begins to define the "caller" by contrasting him with an established religious authority; the preacher is similar to be sure, but different enough to warrant a separate defined category. In particular, the caller is more *communicative* than the preacher. Whereas the preacher "merely preaches", that is, merely communicates in *one* setting and one medium, the caller communicates *all* the time and "by all ... means possible". This function transcends any distinctions between public and private; he communicates everywhere, continuously, by virtue of his specific efforts, but also by simply being an "example", in his very "person". The caller's position and personhood as *exemplar* is important; it reinforces not merely a notion of continual communication, but the defining feature of the person being his communicative capacity. This capacity derives from his being more (and less) than a specific person: the caller as example is unique, outstanding, but also a model – no one in particular. The caller as example is both within the community and abstracted from it, reduced or elevated to a signifier.

This fact of being both someone to emulate and no one in particular, being part of the social fabric and distinct from it, is held to be salutary; it makes *reform of* "society" possible.

> The caller is also a social doctor, treating illnesses of selves [*al-nufus*] and reforming the corrupt conditions of society. A discerning critic who dedicates his life to the reforms that God wills, he is companion, friend, and

---

43 Al-Wazzani, Mohammed Hassan, "Man huwa al-daʿiya?" [Who is 'the Caller'?], *Dirasat wa taʾmulat, 5: Al-Islam wa-l-mujtamʿ wa-l-madaniya* [Studies and Reflections, vol. 5: Islam, Society, and Civilization] (Beirut and Fez: Dar al-Nahda al-ʿArabiyya and Muʾasasat Mohamed Hassan al-Wazzani, 1987), p. 36.

44 Al-Wazzani, "Man huwa al-daʿiya?", p. 36.

brother to rich and poor alike, and to young and old ... with love in his heart and blessings flowing from his gaze and consolation given by his tongue and hands. These are absolutely necessary qualities for the caller, being among the gifts of heaven and spirit.[45]

Note that al-Wazzani does not describe the particular set of reforms that God wills: there is no *content* yet to the call, only the caller's communicative capacity. This capacity allows him to relate to everyone, to transcend differences of age or class. Rather than treat particular people within particular kinship webs or institutions, the caller simply treats "selves" who, connected by proper and not "corrupt" exchanges, constitute "society". The caller, communicating by example, transcending differences, embodies communication itself. More specifically, the caller embodies the kind of communication that links everyone and anyone without regard to differences. He embodies *mass* communication – the type appropriate to a modernist imaginary of "society" comprising not corporate social groups, but a mass of single individuals.[46]

Embodying mass communication distinguishes a caller from preacher. Nevertheless, the caller bears religious or sacred (heavenly) power. Al-Wazzani's description of the caller's blessings "flowing from his gaze" evokes a Sufi saint dispensing *baraka* by his touch. Perhaps Sufi saints, as more liminal figures, offer a more appropriate metaphor for mass communication. In any case the distinction from the preacher is important: whereas readers would likely link a preacher's communicative authority to an institution (the mosque) and its collectivity, the caller operates beyond institutions, communicating everywhere, all the time – in "empty, homogeneous" space.

While the caller bears heavenly or saintly gifts, Al-Wazzani explicitly describes the caller as a political figure:

> Far more than someone merely gifted in rhetoric and speaking, the caller is a commander in his milieu, political chief in his region, and a true leader and visionary for those who follow him. [...] For without a doubt

---

45 Al-Wazzani, "Man huwa al-daʿiya?", p. 36.
46 According to linguist Jaroslav Stetkevych, the term "society" (*mujtamiʿ*), used in the contemporary sense of large-scale and abstract body rather than a particular gathering, only gained currency (that is, *circulated* widely) in the MENA in the early interwar period. Stetkevych, Jaroslav, *The Modern Arabic Literary Language: Lexical and Stylistic Developments* (Publications of the Center for Middle Eastern Studies. Vol. 6) (Chicago: University of Chicago Press, 1970), p. 25. On French thinkers' post-Revolutionary discourse on 'society', see Donzelot, *L'invention du social.*

he will have a psychological influence and spiritual preeminence with a true connection to God as well as recourse to rational analysis of historical experiences and current conditions of the community.[47]

Notably, al-Wazzani seems unsatisfied by the possibility of reducing the caller to one recognizable authority figure; "commander", "chief", "leader", and "visionary" do not suffice. Rather, the caller's mass communicative power, linking spiritual power with rational knowledge, religion with modern science, encompasses them all. Thus, if the call and the caller as such are well established in Islamic traditions, al-Wazzani thinks these must be highlighted and emphasized. The caller must be redefined for the new age of communication – in which communication, a novel force of political and social life, takes on the sacral duty of making the national society itself possible.[48]

"The Life of the Press is the Best Indicator of the Life of the Nation"[49]

For Moroccan reformists power and necessity of mass communication would emerge in the early 1930s, more starkly perhaps after reformists' initial failed attempts to summon a specifically *national* public to a sustained cause. Moroccan nationalists first emerged publicly in mid-May, 1930, with public protests organized against the "Berber *dahir*" or French indigenous law, which removed certain so-called Berber tribes from the legal reach of shariʿa courts, and placed them under "customary law" courts overseen by the Protectorate judiciary.[50]

---

47 Al-Wazzani, "Man huwa al-daʿiya?", p. 36.

48 We might be tempted to read Clifford Geertz's "warrior saint", which he identified with Moroccan Islam, as a premodern precedent for the political-theological power of "the caller". This equivalence could be read differently, however. Specifically, Geertz took the postcolonial king Mohammed V as such a model, yet Mohammed V, as this chapter begins to show, emerged within an age newly marked by mass communicative power. While I agree that the connection is compelling, it is forged only by Geertz's reading the modern king's (and state's) contemporary powers of mass communication back onto an incompatible history. See Geertz, *Islam Observed*, pp. 8–9. See Spadola, *The Calls of Islam,* Ch. 3, for the 1970s apotheosis of the Moroccan monarch Hassan II as "caller".

49 *Majallat al-Maghrib*, July 1932, p. 9.

50 Adria Lawrence argues that while the movement described here was reformist, it was not nationalist. Rather, she argues, Moroccans like al-Wazzani viewed their movement within the scope of French universalism, which would be abandoned for Moroccan nationalism only with the founding in 1944 of the still extant Istiqlal [Independence] Party. See Lawrence, Adria, "Rethinking Moroccan nationalism, 1930–44", *Journal of North African Studies*, 17/3 (2012), 475–90. While I agree that reformists shifted strategies from working with to rejecting French colonialism, it should be clear that I disagree with Lawrence's overall assessment. Indeed I find no conflict between French-inspired liberal universalism and

The *dahir* of May 16 in fact only modified a Protectorate *politique bérbère* enforced since 1914, but it drew the attention of Abdellatif Sbihi, a Protectorate translator, and he alerted students at his former school, the *Collège musulman* in Rabat.[51] More specifically, Sbihi and his cohort recognized it as a breach of the 1912 Treaty of Fez, and an attempt to divide and rule Morocco. The group of nationalists in Rabat and Salé, along with *Jeunes marocains* in Fez, took their protest public.

Curiously, however, urban Moroccans failed initially to respond to the young Moroccans' anti-*dahir* call. According to Kenneth Brown, while Sbihi and his peers in Rabat spoke in the language of nationalism, their audiences did not:

> [Sbihi] told [the *Collège* students] about the Dahir by which, he argued, the French were trying to divide Morocco. He did talk about Islamic law, but spoke of *territorial division*. Then he went to Fez and talked to people. Soon he saw that his way of presenting the threat in terms of a single territory that should not be torn apart was not understood by the people. For them he had to say: 'Islam is being violated in its very being'.... That excited the people.[52]

Articulated as an attack on religion the protests drew considerable attention from audiences listening, we may assume, as *Muslims* rather than *Moroccans*. Not surprisingly, then, the protests that followed took a familiar form within a familiar place, that is, in mosques as group recitations of *Ya al-Latif*, a call to God in times of calamity. Formed in familiar terms the anti-*dahir* protests spread quickly from city to city; yet they also subsided quickly. A single issue and this form of protest could not sustain a nationalist movement.[53]

The Berber *dahir* protests forced nationalists to consider new strategies, among them a new push for nationalist publishing. That the protests sparked a global Muslim response was itself due to the young nationalists' international publishing efforts. Nationalist Mekki Naciri published articles in Cairo, where an Egyptian-Moroccan Muslim coalition formed; in Europe, articles signed

---

theories of nationhood, the very sovereignty of each nation depending after all on its distinction from other comparable polities. See Anderson, *The Spectre of Comparisons*.

51   Lafuente, Gilles, *La Politique berbère de la France et le nationalisme marocain* (Paris: L'Harmattan, 1999), p. 187.

52   Brown, Kenneth, "The impact of the Dahir Berbere in Salé", in *Arabs and Berbers*, ed. Ernest Gellner and Charles Micaud (London: Duckworth, 1973), p. 209, original emphasis.

53   For an extensive reading of the *dahir* protests as a key turning point in nationalist thought and strategy, see Wyrtzen, *Making Morocco,* pp. 1–5 and Ch. 5.

by the new *Comité d'Action Marocaine* and criticizing the *dahir* appeared in Shakib Arslan's *La Nation arabe*.[54] A number of longer essays were published as well, including an essay written by al-Wazzani writing as "Mouslim Barbari".[55] Within Morocco, however, the protests led only to the French Protectorate's intensified censorship efforts.[56]

Colonial prohibitions notwithstanding, a subsequent brief and busy period between 1932 to 1934 would find young urban Moroccans communicating their call to nationalist reform with increasing intensity and effect. Working with international sponsors and collaborators, youth established a nationalist press in both Arabic and French; organized a political party explicitly formulating demands in the name of the Moroccan nation; organized boycotts of popular public Sufi festivals and ecstatic rituals; and finally, created, planned, and carried out a new holiday in honor of the youthful Sharifian Sultan Sidi Mohammed comprising simultaneous celebrations across all major cities of the French Protectorate.

In developing an independent French and Arabic press, nationalists navigated prohibitions on Moroccan-owned press. With the aid of Shakib Arslan, nationalists in Fez enlisted Jean-Robert Longuet, grandson of Karl Marx, to edit the francophone journal *Maghreb* in Paris in 1932. In the same month in Rabat, Mohammed al-Salih Missa, an Algerian national employed by the Protectorate as a court translator, established an Arabic literary journal, *Majallat al-Maghrib* (*The Maghrib Journal*). Although officially unaffiliated with nationalists (and thus free of the restrictions they suffered), the journal soon found a compatible nationalist readership across North Africa and in multiple cities inside Morocco.[57] During the following summer in Fez, Mohammed Hassan al-Wazzani began editing *L'Action du Peuple* (Arabic *'Amal al-Sha'b*, The People's Action). Like the Parisian *Maghreb,* this paper appeared in collaboration with French socialists, evading Protectorate suppression by enlisting George Hertz to sign as the paper's publisher. In both cases, however, the French leadership

---

54 Abun-Nasr, "The Salafiyya movement in Morocco", p. 95.
55 Barbari, Mouslim [al-Wazzani, Mohammed Hassan], *Tempête sur le Maroc, où, les erreurs d'une "politique berbère"* (Paris: Éditions Rieder, 1931).
56 French concern with nationalists' communications is indicated by the sharp increase in the volume of books, pamphlets, and periodicals banned in the French Protectorate zone. See Ladreit de Lacharrière, J., "A l'assaut du Maroc français", *L'Afrique Française: Bulletin du Comité de l'Afrique Française*, 42/9 (September 1932), p. 516.
57 Baida, Jamaa, "Mohamed Salih Missa", in *Ma'lamat al-maghrib*, vol. 21 (Salé: Matba' Sala, 2005), pp. 7343–4.

was nominal. Moroccans researched, penned, and edited the journals, with some adopting pseudonyms.[58]

Though Moroccan literacy remained low, the journals' authors, as Mattelart's history suggests, assumed the mass medium itself to be the key sign of national progress. "The life of the press", the first issue of *Majallat Al-Maghrib* intoned, "is the best indicator of the life of the nation".[59] The journal framed its intervention as "a call to reform" (*daʿwa li-l-islah*). To be sure, both journals addressed educated strata, but the educated comprised a part of the new audience of "Moroccans", no longer distinguished by class or family or origin; the object of reform, and thus the audience to summon, was Moroccan "society" (*mujtamʿ*) bounded by "the nation" or "homeland" (*al-watan*), and comprising "the general public" (*al-ʿumum*), and "the people".

Far from guaranteeing national consciousness, young nationalists viewed older forms of status, including those based on education or wealth, as potential obstacles to identifying oneself with, and thus fulfilling one's duty to, the Moroccan nation. An early issue of *Majallat* was themed the "duty of the wealthy to the nation [*al- watan*]". Aiming to "publically address the wealthy" and their disregard for the needy, the author asks, "Why has the community shrunk from obeying our call?" ("ihjam al-umma ʿan talbiyat daʿwatina").[60] The author offers an explanation by emphasizing older cultural habits and loyalties. The wealthy of Morocco today still follow local religious practices of shrine visitation, "spending generously for the tombs of the dead and sparing little for the shacks of the living".[61] The author singles out the wealthy of Fez, a city founded by a *sharif* (Moulay Idriss II) and centered on his tomb. The author exhorts wealthy Fassis to think of divine reward for generosity, in which God "'raises high your esteem'" ("rafʿa laka dhikrak") as God raised high the Prophet Muhammad's name (6; Qur'an 94:1). Yet, being the standard bearers of older social and religious ethics, those addressed are *unconscious*: their failure to respond comes "not from miserliness, nor incapacity", but from a lack of understanding of the value of dedication to the "general public" ("al-ʿumum"). (The term is distinct from an older term for 'commoners', *al-ʿamma*). Wealthy Moroccans' "sacred responsibility" to this body is, in the author's view, the basis for collective awakening and progress:

---

58   Halstead, John, "The changing character of Moroccan reformism 1921–1934", *Journal of African History*, 5/3 (1964), 435–47.
59   *Majallat al-Maghrib*, July 1932, p. 9.
60   *Majallat al-Maghrib*, September 1932, p. 4.
61   *Majallat al-Maghrib*, September 1932, p. 4.

> Truly exertion for the good of public works [*fi sabili al-mashariʿ al-ʿumumiyya*] is the first condition for awakening and the strongest foundation for progress. Indeed exertion is the first duty we teach the self to accept.... We Muslims will not cast off our gloom but by our charitable giving [*al-infaq*] and sacrifice of money. Now to lead the nation to this sacred responsibility we should seize all opportunities and all available means to demonstrate sincere dedication to society [*ikhlas li-l-mujtamʿ*].[62]

The author is urging readers to respond to the newspaper's call, and in doing so to take greater responsibility. For what? The audience is addressed as "we Muslims", but the collective is not the *umma*. The journal calls, via mass communication, to a new community referred to as "society", an Arabic term of universal and bounded belonging only thinkable by virtue of mass communication. The nationalist author is teaching readers to recognize the origin of a call in society, coterminous with the "general public".[63] That is to say, readers must learn to respond to a call the origin of which, occupying "empty homogeneous" space, is no place in particular, and thus requires a new kind of awareness. To recognize that you cannot see the origins of what calls you is to develop consciousness of this new, distinctly mass-mediated, national community. The newspaper claims to voice that call, or what amounts to the same, to alert readers to the fact that society itself is calling. That is to say, the call will originate, quite literally, from within a sphere of mass-mediated communication. It is not merely the mass medium of the call that matters here, but mass communication that calls – the call of communication itself.

Communicability and Sufi Reform

If nationalists sought to use mass communication to raise Moroccans' consciousness of belonging to a mass political (that is to say, national) collectivity, commentary on reforms of Sufi practices pursued a similar aim. Whereas precolonial reformist literature focused on what constituted true, legitimate (*shariʿi*) Sufi doctrine and ritual, nationalist critiques of Sufism often focused on the material consequences of Sufism for a nation in need of unity and eventual independence. We are certainly familiar with MENA nationalists'

---

[62] *Majallat al-Maghrib*, September 1932, p. 5.
[63] On the emergence of the modern public as an abstract body distinct from crowds, see Tarde, Gabriel, "The public and the crowd", in *On Communication and Social Influence: Selected Papers*, ed. Terry N. Clark (Chicago: University of Chicago Press, 2010 [1969]), pp. 277–94.

criticisms of collaborationist Sufi leaders and of the divisions sown by institutions demanding particularistic, rather than mass, loyalty. But still another set of nationalist concerns with Sufism, harder to place in conventional narratives of reform, emphasized the dire political effects of Sufi rituals newly situated within national and global spheres of mass communication.[64]

That nationalists viewed Sufi rituals less as religious practices and more as large-scale social and political forces is illustrated by an assessment of the problem by the nationalist Mohammed al-Sqalli writing in *Majallat al-Maghrib*. Examining the annual pilgrimage (*mawsim*) of urban and rural Moroccans to Meknes to celebrate the local saint Mohammed bin 'Isa in conjunction with the Mawlid al-Nabi, al-Sqalli focused on the sheer quantity of pilgrims:

> This year I estimated the number of participants gathered at the rendezvous at no less than 200,000. If we further estimate the expenditure per person, including the round-trip transportation, at 100 Francs, we reach a total of 20 million Francs (20,000,000). This is a significant fortune, which, if spent on science and charity, would surely bring great benefits.[65]

The quantification of Sufi ritual says nothing of the doctrinal qualities of Sufism; if he emphasizes the benefits of science and charity, we are nevertheless a long way from the Islamic reformism of Morocco's early Salafis. Al-Sqalli's quantification of the participating masses reveals rather a keen interest in the force, and potential monetization, of communication through which such masses form, i.e., a keen interest in mass communication. Significantly, this critique depends on a capacity to imagine the pilgrimage as a total system. As such it follows the channels of the new highways and railways linking disparate small towns and cities into a national system. Within this system, participants no longer mark particular social groups, but rather are reduced to serial repetitions of a generic national subject – to consumers of mass transport. To see Sufism as system and its participants as generic subjects is to think in terms of a network of connections and of the people transmitted as all equally "communicable".[66] Such an imaginary is no doubt encouraged by means of mass communication

---

64   As a writer lamented in the June 3, 1905, issue of pan-Islamist journal *Al-Mu'ayyad*, "The public festivals [of Egypt's Sufis] are no longer but profane celebrations and objects of curiosity for infidels".

65   "Mawsim al-'Isawa", *Majallat al-Maghrib*, July 1933, p. 9.

66   The realization in nineteenth-century Europe that railways formed a vast *network* rather than separate, unrelated parts, sparked the standardization of time and time zones. See Schivelbusch, *The Railway Journey*.

increasingly available to Moroccans of all classes.[67] Adopting that large-scale "sociological imagination" or panoptic gaze, the nationalist author sees not Sufism as such but rather the circulation of communicable subjects, "the masses". From this perspective reforming the nation means coming to awareness of that communicability in order better to channel (in this case, monetize) its force. This is Sufi reform for an age of mass communication.

The relationship of Sufism to forces of mass communication was made yet more explicit in a set of articles published in the first issues of the Fez-based journal, *L'Action du Peuple*, edited by Mohammed Hassan al-Wazzani. In the late 1920s, nationalist leaders Fez, Rabat, and Salé had organized boycotts of public rituals among underclass adepts of the 'Isawa and Hamadsha Sufi orders. These rites, during which adepts fell into trance and slashed their skulls with hatchets, or sacrificed and then consumed a raw sheep, had met with some Protectorate bans based on public hygiene.[68] In this at least, nationalists and the colonial state were aligned. Yet the Protectorate, acting in the name of "custom", also saw significant political and economic value in these rituals; they named annual festivals like the Mawsim al-'Isawa, which included such rites, as official state holidays to be honored and attended by high-level Protectorate officials. And in the popular tradition of Orientalist art and literature, French filmmakers and photographers recorded the public rites for metropolitan film reels and popular magazines; touring companies featured them as key local attractions for the thriving tourism industry.[69]

---

67 Between 1924 and 1932, the number of riders in fourth class (which included the great majority of Moroccans) rose from approximately 177,590 to over 1,010,137, *Bulletin économique du Maroc*, July 1933, p. 38.

68 Brûnel, René, *Essai sur la confrérie religieuse des 'Aîssâoûa au Maroc* (Paris: Librarie Orientaliste Paul Geuthner, 1926), p. 110. In the "frissa" (meaning "prey" in dialectal Arabic) adepts took on the character of animals, ripping apart sacrificial sheep or goats given by devotees as alms to the saint. It was extremely popular in Fez, being held as many as 30 times a year by an individual team.

69 Note that the French tourism industry took particular interest in Morocco's urban and natural offerings, but also its cultural performances, with "traditional Muslim holidays" included among the "principle attractions of Moroccan tourism" (*Bulletin Economique du Maroc*, April, 1938, p. 124). In the early 1930s, in the midst of a global economic crisis, the number of international visitors served by French tour companies more than quadrupled from 9,503 in 1929 to 45,808 in 1932 (*Bulletin Economique du Maroc*, July 1933, p. 16). The growing tourism industry also added to the railway traffic, with special train cars for tours increasing volume from 2,847 tourists in 1931 to 8,247 in 1934, despite a drastic loss of market share to automobile-based tours, which far exceeded railway in their geographic range (*Bulletin Economique du Maroc*, April 1935, p. 136).

Should it be any surprise that such Sufi rituals, and the technical communications that expanded their reach, prompted the ire of Moroccan nationalists? For nationalists affiliated with *L'Action du Peuple*, this was not merely insulting. Arguing that such rites had been of relatively muted scope and appeal before colonization, one unsigned article noted that "with the establishment of the Protectorate the means of transport multiplied and the bloodthirsty throng [...] could stream into the unfortunate city of Meknes, pillage the cemeteries and perform before a shocked humanity the most repugnant and most shameful demonstration that history has ever recorded".[70] Thanks to mass communication, previously local ritual practices now gathered national significance; indeed, the nation's reputation is at stake on a *global* stage:

> Beyond the Aïssaoua who head toward Meknes the number of sadistic spectators has risen steadily. The zeal of tourists and filmmakers has transported the image of these ignominies beyond the hills and seas to all four corners of the world, as if it were the present style in our country and defined the evolutionary social stage of our people.[71]

Here the global view is explicit; in the view of the newspaper, the Sufi rites are dangerous because they are bad publicity. And bad publicity could have real consequences for claims of independence.

It is worth emphasizing here that nationalists' reformist efforts concerned not only Sufi rites themselves but, more broadly, the communicative media that now amplified their scale within Morocco and extended them beyond its borders to a global audience. We may grasp the more general significance of this fact by recalling the anthropologist Talal Asad's persuasive description of Islam as a "discursive tradition", or debate, regarding, among other issues, "apt performance" of ritual.[72] According to Asad, an imagined unity and uniformity of Islam's discursive tradition emerged for Muslim reformist thinkers only in modernity, with the "development and control of communication techniques that are part of modern industrial societies".[73] From this chapter's argument we can better understand how reformists in the age of mass communication considered ritual performance differently than had reformists. That is to say, insofar as mass communications refigured the conditions of the tradition, it

---

70 *L'Action du Peuple*, August 18, 1933, p. 2.
71 *L'Action du Peuple*, August 18, 1933, p. 2.
72 Asad, Talal, "The Idea of an Anthropology of Islam" (Washington, DC: Georgetown University Center for Contemporary Arab Studies, Occasional Papers Series, 1986), p. 15.
73 Asad, "The Idea of an Anthropology of Islam", p. 16.

established novel conditions by which to judge what *constituted* apt performance. The forming and *performing* of unified national societies were inseparable in nationalist and reformist Muslim politics. Nationalists' concern with mass communicative spread of underclass Sufi performance concerned, literally, the public *image* of Morocco. That is, a segment of underclass Sufis gathered a new power to speak for the nation of Morocco as a whole.[74] Morocco being vulnerable to international recognition based on mass communications, reform would entail grasping this very force of the masses' communicability.

The Throne Holiday

Moroccan nationalists' production of a novel ceremony honoring the 'Alawite sultan, Sidi Mohammed (later King Mohammed V) would aim to do just that, by focalizing and centralizing the communicative powers of masses on a novel, national scale. This approach came to fruition around a tactical call articulated in 1933, to which, reformists hoped, Moroccans across classes and social differences would respond: a new "Royal Holiday" (*'id maliki*) in 1933.

In the July 1933 issue of *Majallat al-Maghrib* Mohammad Hassar, a young Salé nationalist writing under the pseudonym "A Moroccan" (and here we see pride in the anonymity of a mass identity) recommended a new celebration to recognize "the day of His Majesty's ascension to the throne" as a specifically "national holiday" (*'id watani*).[75] The idea provoked much interest, and the September 1933 issue of *Majallat al-Maghrib* ran with an explicit call for the "Royal Holiday" (*'id malaki*), outlining not only the specific steps to be taken in preparation for the event but also its significance for Morocco's developing unification. *L'Action du Peuple,* quickly joined the call, and articles detailing and heralding the holiday (*La Fête du Trône*) appeared in the two journals for the next six weeks.

The call, according to nationalists and Protectorate officials, marked a qualitative transformation. Despite the short time available for organization, nationalists from Marrakech to Fez to Rabat and Salé indeed managed to

---

74 The danger of Sufi crowds' capacity to speak for the nation rests on the same conditions by which, as Gelvin describes, nationalists in Damascus formed "demonstrating communities" before the amir Faisal. Gelvin notes a crucial shift in the attention of the ceremonies from the amir himself (as in older ceremonial forms of petition) to the attending crowds who were now meant to stand for (demonstrate the presence of) the larger public imagined community. See Gelvin, *Divided Loyalties*, Ch. 6. It is significant therefore that the term *mudhahara,* meaning "street demonstration", came into common usage only after World War I. Berque, Jacques, *French North Africa: The Maghrib between Two World Wars,* trans. Jean Stewart (New York: Praeger Publishers, 1967), p. 82.

75 "Hukumatuna", *Majallat al-Maghrib*, July 1933, p. 12.

summon the masses to express their loyalty and love for Sidi Mohammed on a new scale. This fact was not lost on Protectorate officials, who would indeed emphasize the new capacity to command at a distance: "Rare were the ancestors of Sidi Mohammed – in fact he may be the only one – whose Vizirs were able to order the commemoration of such an event *on the same day, in every city of the Empire*".[76]

Voiced by nationalists, the call did garner support, leading to an unprecedented popular response to the sultan as celebrity. Not surprisingly, French officials by summer 1934, noting nationalists' success and momentum, sought to stop the movement by exiling and jailing leaders and banning any independent Moroccan press.

Later in 1934, nationalists' capacity to summon crowds provoked the French colonial state's swift and decisive punishments (jail and exile for the main nationalists) and utter suppression of a nationalist press for the next three years. Yet the Protectorate soon adopted and legally instituted the Throne Holiday, praising it as the continuation of a "tradition established by the ancient Sultans", with "the double merit of satisfying the natives and of celebrating the benefits of the French Protectorate";[77] the main benefits of 1934 were, specifically, the French military's "pacification" of the colony's "lands of dissidence" (*bled al-siba*) and establishment of complete territorial rule. Yet nationalists, rather than decrying the change, vigorously supported it. Identifying the Protectorate's power with that of the throne which symbolized it, they lauded the "extension" of Sidi Mohammed's "effective authority [*nufudh*] over the farthest reaches of the kingdom".[78] This convergence of nationalist with colonial aims bespeaks a yet more fundamental link in the political logic of communication as an object of governance. That is to say, the nationalists' construction of the Throne Holiday celebrated the sultan's simultaneous long-distance command and control, a simultaneous long-distance call made possible by the means of mass communication.

Conclusions

MENA media scholars have documented very well how transformations of communication have shifted political and social conditions in the twenty-first

---

76 *L'Afrique française*, 1935, p. 92 (emphasis in original).
77 *Bulletin Official*, no. 1149, November 2, 1934, p. 1124.
78 "Nazra 'ama 'ala al-'am al-madi" [Overview of the past year], *Majallat al-Maghrib*, April–May 1934, p. 5.

century; indeed, the very characterization of the 2011 Arab uprisings as "Twitter revolutions" or "Facebook revolutions" suggests an awareness of the force of communication itself. If MENA historians have linked older media transformations to the emergence of national identities, an equivalent consciousness of communication itself has not been identified. My aim in this chapter has been to do just that: to identify in nationalist thought an implicit and explicit concern with communication itself as an object to be managed and controlled. Mass communications would not be merely incidental to the formation and reform of the defining mass political bodies of the age, i.e., nation-states. Rather, insofar as national consciousness required a sense of simultaneous co-presence at a distance, a sense of being connected from afar, mass communications constituted the defining conditions of any legitimate, globally recognized political body.

This binding of mass communication and modern political belonging helps explain the ubiquity of "the call" as the quintessential act of modern reformism. Nationalist and reformist calls entwine technical communications with critical questions of personal responsibility and belonging at times when old social fabrics are stretched and torn to accommodate new forms of identity and community. Insofar as interwar reformists sought to call people via mass-mediated communications to a mass-mediated political community, they predicated belonging on an awareness of mass communication itself as a moral force. As evidenced by the issues raised in this chapter and other chapters in this volume, communication and communicability – the shared capacity among a range of people and objects and ideas for rapid ("viral") proliferation – concerned far more than mere technology, or indeed "the media" as a narrow field of journalism or mass entertainment. Rather, by reforming communication itself nationalist thinkers meant to build societies and subjects now defined by its material and moral powers.

CHAPTER 6

Doctors Crossing Borders: The Formation of a Regional Profession in the Interwar Middle East

Liat Kozma

"These conferences may be political, they may be social, they may be scientific, they may be artistic, they may be industrial, economic or sportive", wrote Egyptian pan-Arab intellectual Muhammad ʿAli ʿAluba in an April 1939 special issue of *al-Hilal* on Arabism and Islam in reference to regional and all-Arab professional and organizational conferences. "When the different Arab nations agree on the production of such conferences, their provisioning and their continuous existence, these conferences bring together these nations that speak the same language, turn them into a united block worthy of high status among the nations, and groom them to become a powerful actor on the world stage". It is the bureaucracy at work bringing men and women together, the face-to-face exchanges fostered in these conferences, he argued, that creates the kind of Arab solidarity that would later be translated into political action. When Arab solidarity becomes concrete, in these multiple arenas and various contexts, Arab politics is born.[1]

I start with ʿAluba's observation as it allows us to think of Arab politics in the interwar years as being formed and developed in the context of regional professional networking gatherings, one of which was the medical conferences. The mundane routine of middle-class professional networks enabled these men to imagine an Arab nation in ways that had not existed before. These conferences, I argue here, were indeed arenas for political socialization, but they were building on and supplementing a much deeper infrastructure of shared educational venues, literary exchanges, and only after these were shared networks formed: the professional conferences.

This chapter examines networks and interconnections between medical doctors, and looks at the formation of a transnational professional identity.

---

* Research for this paper was funded by the Israel Science Foundation [grant number 440/15]
1 ʿAluba, Muhammad ʿAli, "Ahmiyyat al-muʾtamarat al-ʿarabiyya fi nuhud al-muslimin wa-l-ʿarab" [The importance of the Arab conferences in the awakening of the Muslims and the Arabs], *al-Hilal: ʿAdad mumtaz al-ʿArab wa-l-Islam fi-l-ʿasr al-hadith* [al-Hilal: Special issue – The Arabs and Islam in the Modern Age] (Cairo: Dar al-Hilal, 1939), pp. 51–3, quoted from p. 51.

These connections were formed, first, through educational paths, that crossed in medical schools in the region (particularly Istanbul, Cairo and Beirut), and in student missions to specific European medical schools. These connections were later reinforced in the scientific and medical press, and from the 1930s, through regional medical conferences. These conferences, and the transnational connections they forged, were built on an existing infrastructure of professional and interpersonal relations.

Further, the chapter seeks to contribute to the study of Arab nationalism, the formation of the middle class in the Middle East, and to the history of the medical profession, all of which are normally studied in parallel trajectories for Egypt, Syria, Palestine, Lebanon and Iraq. Pan-Arabism is mostly a post-World War II political movement, but pan-Islamic, pan-Arab and pan-Eastern networks and political agendas had already been formed in the 1930s. These networks filled up the political vacuum created by the collapse of the Ottoman empire, and were developed in an attempt to create anti-colonial solidarity and support networks. Thus, while historians concentrate on case studies throughout the region, the interconnections in which they were embedded have been largely overlooked. This chapter takes medical doctors as an example of these transnational processes.

Theoretical Framework: A Transnational History of the Professions

Sociologists and political scientists, among others, have been trying, in the last decade or so, to integrate present-day globalization processes into their understanding of the professions and of the formation of professional communities. Their insights can help us conceptualize interwar regional, pan-Arab and transnational processes as well. The incorporation of such a transnational analytic framework complicates more traditional understandings of professional communities, which are normally bound by epistemic nationalism or presume universality with minor national variations – and thus leave transnational networks and processes outside of the picture.

Sociologies of the professions center on the relationship between practitioners, users, universities and the state: practitioners seek to identify, carve out and protect an area of exclusive competence in order to maximize financial and status rewards. Users' demands and expectations shape professional practices. States grant licenses and thus influence the legal status of professionals, while universities produce the knowledge-base for the professions and provide the necessary credentials. The interplay between these different actors creates variations in the knowledge base of the professions, variations in professional standards and different constructions of professional responsibility and practice.[2]

Transnational communities are networks established around similar practices of education, occupation, leisure and friendship.[3] Transnational professional associations and university degrees provide credentials that enable supra-national professional mobility. In consequence, supra-national networks, licensing and regulatory systems are becoming a topic of sociological research, but not so much of historical investigation.[4] These transnational university programs, licensing procedures and associations, moreover, are not as new as sociological analysis would have us believe.

A transnational history of professions therefore entails the examination of international professional institutions, the transnational mobility of scholars and the politics of transnational exchange in other realms. A shared educational foundation in specific international schools, and internationally-recognized degrees, form the basis for such transnational professional communities. Sociologies of the professions can help us examine the professions as status groups – networks of people who perform interaction rituals among themselves and arrive at a common conception of their identity, purpose and status. Education serves the purpose of closure of the occupation and monopolization. It also forms group identities and gives members symbolic tokens to use in guiding and idealizing their activities, and creates bonds among those who participate in this schooling ritual.[5]

International professional meetings create nodes and modes of collaboration and occasions for communication and diffusion across national borders. These are opportunities for exchange of ideas, methods and political strategies between center and periphery and between different centers of knowledge production. The location of these encounters and their attendees also help mapping relevant centers as well as distinctions between center and periphery.

---

2 Burrage, Michael, Konrad Jarausch and Hannes Siegrist, "An actor-based framework for the study of the professions", in *Professions in Theory and History: Rethinking the Study of the Professions*, ed. Michael Burrage and Rolf Torstendahl (London: Sage Publications, 1990), pp. 203–25.
3 Altan, Özlem, "The American Third World: Transnational Elite Networks in the Middle East", Ph.D. Dissertation, New York University, 2006, p. 27.
4 Faulconbridge, James R. and Daneil Muzio, "Professions in a globalizing world: towards a transnational sociology of the professions", *International Sociology*, 27 (2011), pp. 139–45.
5 Collins, R., "Changing conceptions of the sociology of the professions", in *The Formation of Professions: Knowledge, State and Strategy*, ed. Rolf Torstendahl and Michael Burrage (London: Sage, 1990), pp. 24, 36–8.

In our case, regional medical conferences were part of a wider process of cross-border socialization and exchange of people and ideas.[6]

Following this conceptual model, in what follows, I examine medical education, professional medical journals and medical conferences to show how a professional community was formed regionally and transnationally. Specific schools created networks and social and professional common ground, which combined national identity and middle class professional identity. Journals, published in Cairo, Beirut, Damascus and Jerusalem, enabled year-round exchange of knowledge. The annual conferences, then, were literally conceptualized as pilgrimages, and served to consolidate shared identities among Arab medical doctors. The tools that help us trace the rise of national professions can help us here explain how such communities were formed regionally as well.

Fragments of Pan-Arabism

Pan-Arabism is paradoxically studied within the confines of individual Arab states and transnational or even comparative studies of Arab nationalism are rare. As Israel Gershoni argues, new professional classes had an active role and were central to the popularization of Arab nationalism. Throughout the Middle East, schools produced generations of new professionals who served in the state bureaucracy, the education system and literary and journalistic enterprises. This generation forged ties across the Arab world. Inter-Arab cultural associations and the institutionalization of inter-Arab professional meetings, workshops and congresses were also carried out by teachers, lecturers, students, engineers, lawyers, journalists, writers and activists. The Arab press addressed Arabic readership across the region.[7] A modern transnational middle class was therefore formed in the Middle East, educated in Europe or in the region, which formed regional networks.[8]

---

[6] Heilbron, Johan, Nicolas Guilhot and Laurent Jeanpierre, "Toward transnational history of the social sciences", *Journal of the History of the Behavioral Sciences*, 44/2 (2008), pp. 147–50.

[7] Gershoni, Israel, "Rethinking the formation of Arab nationalism in the Middle East, 1920–1945: old and new narratives", in *Rethinking Nationalism in the Arab Middle East*, ed. Israel Gershoni and James Jankowski (New York: Columbia University Press, 1997), pp. 18–22.

[8] Eppel, Michael, "The elite, the effendiyya, and the growth of nationalism and pan-Arabism in Hashemite Iraq 1921–1958", *International Journal of Middle East Studies*, 30/2 (1998), pp. 229–32.

The option of Pan-Arab nationalism competed with two other political-cultural alternatives: the post-Ottoman nation-state and pan-Islamism. Increasingly in the 1930s, the Arabic language and the common colonial experience led Arab intellectuals throughout the region to embrace pan-Arab ideology – which, unlike the pan-Islamic alternative, was also attractive to Christian, and to a lesser extent, Jewish minorities. They often did not see this Arab identity as replacing the Egyptian, Syrian or Iraqi one, but rather as supplementing it. They conceptualized neighboring Arab nations as siblings, and often saw Egypt as the older brother and a leader – of both the Arabic cultural revival and pan-Arabism as a political movement.[9]

Pan-Arabism in Iraq, Palestine or Syria, for example, owed its existence to the mobility of intellectuals across newly-created borders. In the 1920s the Iraqi state lacked skilled professionals and encouraged the arrival of Arabic-speaking civil servants, teachers and university professors from Egypt and the Levant. Since Iraq's publishing industry was modest in the early 1920s, Iraqis read mostly Arabic publications produced outside Iraq. Lebanese and Egyptian writers dominated the Iraqi print market, and Iraqis published articles in the Egyptian and Lebanese press. Iraqi pan-Arabism reflected a cultural market and constant movement of teachers, writers, journalists, and printed products from and to Iraq.[10]

Similarly, Syrian government schools encouraged students to memorize nationalist Arab poetry and study Arab history and civilization. Since Syria had very few published authors, students learned texts by Egyptian poets and thinkers, as well as literary production from elsewhere in the Arab world. Such a curriculum, already in the 1920s and 1930s, reinforced a national identity stretching beyond Syria's frontiers.[11] Palestinian intellectuals were similarly dependent on the Lebanese and Syrian markets for teachers and for literary production.[12] In all of these places, then, tensions between the local and the regional shaped political agendas as well as group identities.

Medical doctors were part of this growing professional middle class, and were uniquely positioned to forge regional connections. Unlike lawyers, for

---

[9] Gershoni, Israel and James Jankowski, *Redefining the Egyptian Nation, 1930–1945* (Cambridge: Cambridge University Press, 1995), pp. 117–43.
[10] Bashkin, Orit, *The Other Iraq: Pluralism and Culture in Hashemite Iraq* (Stanford: Stanford University Press, 2009), pp. 149–56.
[11] Khoury, Philip S., "The paradoxical in Arab nationalism: interwar Syria revisited", in *Rethinking Nationalism in the Arab Middle East*, ed. Israel Gershoni and James Jankowski (New York: Columbia University Press, 1997), p. 277.
[12] Ayalon, Ami, *Reading Palestine: Printing and Literacy, 1900–1948* (Austin: University of Texas Press, 2004).

example, their professional expertise was universal and was not bound to specific locale or legal circumstances. Medical journals were established in Arabic in the early twentieth century, in Cairo, Beirut and Damascus, and circulated throughout the region. Medical schools in Cairo, Beirut, Damascus and Istanbul trained most of the doctors in the region. The pan-Arab outlook they might have shared with their middle-class peers was further reinforced through shared socialization, the circulation of texts, and the annual conferences.

Regional Medical Education

Schooling is relevant to our story as a site in which certain forms of capital are internationalized and reproduced, and in which students shared a common language and common tastes.[13] The story of medical education in the Middle East is usually narrated as separate, rather than connected, developments: the foundation of state-sponsored schools – Abu Zaʻbal in Cairo and the Ottoman military medical school, both founded in 1827, and the Ottoman civilian medical school founded in 1838; the foundation of Beirut's medical schools at the Syrian Protestant College (1867) and St. Joseph (1883); the Ottoman medical school of Damascus (1903), which followed the Istanbul curriculum, and its reincarnation as the Arab Medical School in 1919 by Faisal's Arab government, as part of the Syrian University; and the foundation of the Iraqi medical school in 1927.[14] These schools contributed to the formation of new elites, whose cultural capital relied mostly on modern scientific training. From Ottoman modernizing projects, designed to create a medical cadre for the Egyptian

---

13 Altan, "The American Third World", pp. 25, 135.
14 On these individual schools see, for example, Herzstein, Rafael, *Université Saint Joseph de Beyrouth: fondation et fonctionnement de 1875 à 1914* (Brussels: Le Cri Edition, 2008); İhsanoğlu, Ekmeleddin, *Al-Muʾassasat al-sihhiyya al-ʻuthmaniyya al-haditha fi Suriya: al-mustashfayat wa-kulliyyat Tibb al-Sham* [Modern Ottoman Medical Institutions in Syria: Hospitals and the Syrian Medical College] (Amman: Lajnat taʾrikh bilad al-Sham, al-Jamiʻa al-urduniyya, 2002); Demirhan Erdemir, Ayşegül, "The importance of Ḥaydarpāshā Medical Faculty (the first Turkish medical faculty) (1903–1933) from the point of view of Turkish medical history and some original results", *Hamdard Islamicus*, 20 (1997), 61–75; al-Hashimi, Hashim Makki, *Taʾrikh wa-muhattat: Sira dhatiyya tuʾarrakh li-kulliyyat al-tibb al-ʻiraqiyya* [History and Stepping Stones: An Autobiography Telling the Story of the Iraqi Medical College] (Beirut: al-Muʾassashah al-ʻArabiyah li-l-Dirasat wa-l-Nashr, 2009); Panzac, Daniel, "Médicine révolutionnaire et révolution de la médicine dans l'Égypte de Muhammad Ali: le Dr. Clot-Bey", *Revue des mondes musulmans et de la Méditerranée: les Arabes, les Turcs et la révolution française*, 52/53 (1989), 95–110.

and Ottoman armies, to missionary schools spear-headed by colonial regimes and finally schools founded by mandatory states within newly formed bodies, these stories are normally disconnected.

Already in the early nineteenth century, however, the story of the formation of the medical profession is a transnational and a regional one. The teachers at these schools were brought from Britain, Germany, the United States and France. Beginning from the 1810s, student missions from Cairo and Istanbul received several years of medical instruction in European medical schools, where they met fellow students from the Ottoman empire.[15] In the late nineteenth and early twentieth centuries, students from the Ottoman and later mandatory Middle East continued to travel to European medical schools, in Lyon, Montpellier, Paris, Geneva and Lausanne, for their schooling or medical training. They thus forged transnational and regional connections – that future research will have to address in more detail. Between 1833 and 1889, for example, 329 doctors from the Middle East, North Africa and the Ottoman Balkans had graduated from Paris University's medical school alone.[16]

This connection lasted to the twentieth century. In the acknowledgments to her 1928 dissertation on bilharzia in Iraq, Iraqi-born Endjun Nevuea-Lemaire (née Yamlki) presented her work as third in a series of dissertations submitted to the Paris faculty of medicine: "I would be very happy", she wrote, "if this modest contribution to the study of bilharzia in Iraq would be able to contribute, even slightly, to the wellbeing of my native land".[17] Fathallah 'Akrawi, in his own acknowledgments, similarly paid tribute to his Iraqi peers: "Although few in number in the Paris faculty of medicine, the Iraqi students who currently pursue their medical studies have decided to write their dissertations as a series of works on hygiene in Iraq and on the various diseases endemic to this country ... The honor has fallen to us to write the second".[18]

The student bodies of Haydarpaşa and Qasr al-'Aini have not been researched yet, but it is safe to assume that they drew students from across the region as well. Founded in 1827, Egypt's medical school was the first to teach scientific biomedicine in Arabic. It was established, first and foremost, to serve

---

15 Sonbol, Amira el-Azhary, *The Creation of a Medical Profession in Egypt, 1800–1922* (Syracuse: Syracuse University Press, 1991), pp. 74–6.
16 Panzac, Daniel, "Les docteurs orientaux de la faculté de médecine de Paris au XIXe siècle", *Revue du monde musulman et de la Méditerranée*, 75/76 (1995), 295–303.
17 Nevuea-Lemaire, Endjun, "La bilharziose vésicale en Iraq", Dissertation, Faculté de Médicine, Paris, 1928, avant-propos.
18 'Akrawi, Fathallah, "Etudes sur la peste en mesopotamie", Dissertation, Faculté de Médicine, Paris, 1928, avant-propos.

Mehmed Ali Paşa's military. Its founder, French surgeon Antoine Bartholomey Clot, also known as Clot Bey, insisted, from very early on, on Arabic as the language of instruction, in order to create a self-sufficient medical education that would not be dependent on the importation of French instructors and textbooks. From the 1830s, it attracted students from neighboring provinces, including Mt. Lebanon, which had its own medical schools, founded by French and American missionaries only in the late 1860s. Dr. Ilias Khuri, in his speech in the 1937 medical convention, traced these connections back to 1828, when the patriarch Yusif Astfan sent his nephew to study medicine in Egypt; and then groups of students who were sent there in the late 1830s and early 1860s.[19] Lebanese ophthalmologist Shakir al-Khuri narrates in his memoirs his experiences as a student in Qasr al-'Aini around 1870 as a series of intercultural gaps and misunderstandings.[20]

For the missionary schools of Beirut we have a clearer picture. Although most students came from Mt. Lebanon, many travelled to Beirut from Egypt, Anatolia, Iran, Iraq and the Balkans, and then returned home, or sometimes travelled further and ended up settling elsewhere.[21] Palestine's Arab medical profession before 1948 relied almost exclusively on graduates of the Syrian Protestant College (and later the American University of Beirut, AUB) and to lesser extent, St. Joseph, and the Ottoman schools of Damascus and Istanbul.[22] Iraqi students similarly travelled to the Levant and to Europe before the 1927 foundation of Baghdad's medical school.[23]

---

19 "Al-Kalima alati alqaha bi-ism al-jama'iya al-tibbiyya al-lubnaniyya amin sirr al-duktur Ilias Khuri", [A speech delivered by Dr. Ilias Khuri, the secretary general of the Lebanese Medical Association], *Al-Majalla al-Tibbiyya al-Misriyya*, 20 (January 1937), p. 53. See also Bourmaud, Philippe, "Ya doktor: Devenir médecin et exercer son art en 'Terre sainte', une expérience du pluralisme médical dans l'Empire ottoman finissant (1871–1918)", Ph.D. Dissertation, Université Aix-Marseille I, 2007, p. 137.

20 al-Khuri, Shakir, *Majma' al-Masarrat* [The Compound of Delights] (Beirut: Matba'at al-Ijtihad, 1908), pp. 213–307.

21 Verdeil, Chantal, "Naissance d'une nouvelle élite ottomane. Formation et trajectoires de médecins diplômés de Beyrouth à la fin du XIXe siècle", *Revue du mondes musulman et de la Méditerranée*, 121–122 (2008), 217–37; Verdeil, Chantal, "L'empire, les communautés, la France: les réseaux des médecins ottomans à la fin du XIXe siècle", in *Hommes de l'entre-deux: parcours individuels et portraits de groupes sur la frontière de la Méditerranée XVIe–XXe siècle*, ed. Bernard Heyberger and Chantal Verdeil (Paris: Les Indes Savantes, 2009), pp. 133–50.

22 Reiss, Nira, *The Health Care of Arabs in Israel* (Boulder: Westview Press, 1991), p. 36.

23 al-Fattal, Sa'ad, "Sir Harry Sinderson Pasha and Iraq's first medical school", *Journal of Medical Biography*, 21/3 (2013), p. 165.

These regional and transnational networks, which had their roots in the late Ottoman period, became a possible threat in the colonial era. In a different context, the establishment of the medical school in Baghdad in 1927 had the declared aim of realigning networks of medical authority to the British political orbit and distancing local practitioners from pan-Arab regional networks.[24] For similar reasons, the British considered the establishment of a British university in Palestine, which, unlike the Hebrew University, would target Arab students. Its "social and national ideal" would not be pan-Arabism, but rather "Palestinianism". Zionist objections and lack of funds nipped all of these initiatives in the bud.[25]

At the Syrian Protestant College, renamed the American University of Beirut in 1921, medical students formed networks, which transcended newly-formed borders. They attended classes together, and participated in extracurricular activities, such as sports, plays and literary clubs; and returned home speaking differently, adopting more formal Arabic and different styles, as well as new perceptions of themselves in a rapidly changing world. Students from the Sudan, Iraq, Palestine and Transjordan met for the first time at the AUB, and thus practiced and lived inter-Arab unity, which created an infrastructure for transnational identity. The AUB provided officials for the former Arab provinces of the Ottoman empire which had no equivalent educational institution. Students from the region enrolled at the AUB, and upon their return, were integrated into the upper echelons of the public and private sectors. Dozens of students were annually funded by their governments to attend the AUB.[26] The AUB's sports team was an opportunity for comradery which crossed national borders and represented the AUB in sports events in Egypt, Palestine, Transjordan, Cyprus and Greece. The students' journal *al-ʿUrwa al-Wuthqa* (literally: The Firmest Bond) openly advocated Arab nationalism, at least from 1936.[27] The caricatures

---

24   Dewachi, Omar, *Ungovernable Life: Mandatory Medicine and Statecraft in Iraq* (Stanford: Stanford University Press, 2017), pp. 17–19, 65–70; Bashkin, *The Other Iraq: Pluralism and Culture in Hashemite Iraq*, p. 239.

25   Ofer, Pinhas, "A scheme for the establishment of a British university in Jerusalem in the late 1920s", *Middle Eastern Studies*, 22/2 (1986), 274–85. The quote of an unofficial memorandum is from p. 277.

26   Kalisman, Hilary Falb, "Bursary scholars at the American University of Beirut: living and practising Arab unity", *British Journal of Middle Eastern Studies*, 42/4 (2015), pp. 600–2; Altan, "The American Third World", p. 46.

27   Penrose, Stephen B.L., *That They May Have Life: The Story of the American University of Beirut, 1866–1941* (Beirut: American University of Beirut Press, 1970), pp. 283–8; Anderson, Betty S., *The American University of Beirut: Arab Nationalism and Liberal Education* (Austin: University of Texas Press, 2011), pp. 128–33.

FIGURE 6.1 Medical students rushing to attend their seven o'clock morning class only to find no teacher present, from The Medical Society Gazette of the American University of Beirut, 2/3 (February 1929).

(figs. 6.1 and 6.2), taken from the journal of the AUB's medical school, offer a glimpse of students' shared experiences, and the shared venue they nurtured to joke and complain about the difficulties of medical studies.

For these schools to attract students regionally as well, their training had to be recognized by other governments. In the late Ottoman period, the Syrian Protestant College had to struggle to have its degrees recognized by the Ottoman authorities. In 1926, after a decade in which the students were examined only by their teachers after the withdrawal and eventual collapse of the Ottoman empire, an international board was invited to examine the medical students, in order to make the examinations more acceptable to various government authorities. It was composed of the director of the military hospital in Beirut and another French officer, the director of health for Palestine, the director of hospitals for the Baghdad governorate and the acting director and another professor from Qasr al-'Aini.[28]

---

28   Penrose, *That They May Have Life*, pp. 226–7; İhsanoğlu, *Al-Mu'assasat al-sihhiyya*, pp. 58–9.

FIGURE 6.2 *A fifth-year student faithfully doing his daily work. The nurse: You still can do some more! Why not sweep and scrub the floor. Fifth-year student: All right! I cannot answer you before June, from* The Medical Society Gazette of the American University of Beirut, *2/4-5 (June 1930).*

The Damascus medical school, founded in 1903 as an Ottoman institution, reopened as an Arab school in 1919, recruiting its professors from among the former Ottoman military doctors and the Arab assistant instructors of the pre-War medical school. Due to their Ottoman training and service in the Ottoman administration and military, many of them had little command of literary Arabic, and were criticized for this by the Syrian press. Their professional and scientific collaboration with the school's foreign personnel further cast a shadow over their loyalty. At the same time, the Damascus medical school was the only one that taught classes in Arabic, alongside some classes in French and presented itself as a beacon of Arab pride.[29]

The medical journals published in these capitals, to which I turn now, built on pre-existing ties and networks. They were the products of medical schools

---

29   Blecher, Robert Ian, "The Medicalization of Sovereignty: Medicine, Public Health, and Political Authority in Syria, 1861–1936", Ph.D. Dissertation, Stanford University, 2002, pp. 170–2, 184–6.

and of national medical associations. The infrastructure created by shared education provided them with regional authorship and readership.

Medical Journals

Arabic-language medical journals were venues for regional conversations and mutual learning. Given the Anglo-Saxon bias of medical instruction in the region, the publication of medical research in Arabic was politically significant. The first medical journal in Arabic, *Yaʿsub al-Tibb* (The Chief of Medicine) (1860–62), published by the Egyptian medical school, was short-lived, and so were most of its predecessors in the late Ottoman years. Most of them were private, and addressed the educated public, and not merely doctors. Such were, for example, Shibly Shumayl's *al-Shifaʾ* (The Cure) (1886–88) and Ibrahim al-Yaziji's *al-Tabib* (The Doctor) (1884–85).

Medical textbooks translated and authored in Cairo in the 1830s and 1840s for Mehmed Ali Paşa's medical schools, the first Arabic translations of modern biomedicine, had limited circulation in the Levant as well, and the self-trained Lebanese doctor Michel Mishaqa testifies to having read them.[30] More generally, the proliferation of the Arabic press during the second half of the nineteenth century included serious engagement with science and medicine. As Ami Ayalon has shown, many of these early Arabic printed journals were consumed throughout the region. Readers in Palestine, for example, were exposed to printed texts published in Beirut, Istanbul and Cairo; and major Arab newspapers employed agents in Palestine's major cities. Subscribers' lists, agents' lists, and letters to the editors attest to the geographical scope of journals' readership – in the Middle East and the diaspora.[31]

The interwar period witnessed a proliferation of a specific kind of medical journal – ones published by medical associations or medical schools in Cairo, Beirut, Damascus, Baghdad and Jerusalem. These targeted the Arabic-reading medical community, while highlighting regional conversations and collaborations. These were, for example, *al-Majalla al-Tibbiyya al-Misriyya* (The Egyptian Medical Journal) (1918), published by Qasr al-ʿAini medical school, *al-Majalla al-Tibbiyya al-ʿIlmiyya* (The Medical and Scientific Journal) (1923),

---

30 See, for example, Mishaqah, Mikhaʾil, and W M. Thackston, *Murder, Mayhem, Pillage and Plunder: The History of Lebanon in the 18th and 19th Centuries* (Albany: State University of New York Press, 1988), p. 158.

31 Ayalon, Ami, "Modern texts and their readers in late Ottoman Palestine", *Middle Eastern Studies*, 38/4 (2002), pp. 22–7.

published in Beirut and *Majallat al-Ma'had al-Tibbi al-'Arabi* (The Journal of the Arab Institute of Medicine) (1924), published by the Damascus faculty of medicine. Unlike earlier journals, these were markedly scientific. They enjoyed decades-long existence, targeting specifically Arabic-reading medical doctors, and highlighting Arabic as a language of scientific innovation. Alongside purely scientific articles, all of these journals published articles on Arabic terminology and debated the pros and cons of neologisms vs. transliterated loanwords. They also read and debated the linguistic choices of medical journals in neighboring Arab lands. The Syrian journal, *Majallat al-Ma'had al-Tibbi*, for example, criticized its Iraqi and Lebanese counterparts for their reliance on foreign terminology and their errors in Arabic. It was indeed the journal most reliant on Arabic neologisms and terms.[32]

Majallat al-Ma'had al-Tibbi al-'Arabi likewise declared the publication of medical research in Arabic as one of its main aims, and urged "every Arab doctor" to publish his work in the journal instead of, or in addition to, its publication in European languages. The journal's editors repeatedly lamented the scarcity of Arab doctors' contributions. Its wish to become a communication hub for doctors of Arab countries was not met with articles from Arab colleagues outside of Syria, and it continued to rely, at least in part, on translations from French.[33] The Egyptian medical journal similarly reminded its readers of the importance of publication in Arabic, in addition to publication in French, English or German.[34]

The publication of articles in Arabic was not merely a goal in its own right – its aim was to place medical research produced in the Middle East at the forefront of modern medicine. Arab doctors, the editor of *Majallat al-Ma'had al-Tibbi al-'Arabi* proclaimed in January 1930, should stop waiting for Western doctors to research the endemic diseases of the East, but should rather publish their own research in Arabic and thus encourage Western doctors to study

---

32 See, for example, Khatir, Murshid, "Al-Majalla al-tibbiyya al-Baghdadiyya" [The Baghdadi Medical Journal], *Majallat al-Ma'had al-Tibbi al-'Arabi*, 5 (March 1928), pp. 190–3; Khatir, Murshid, "Majallat al-Jama'iya al-tibbiyya al-lubnaniyya" [The Journal of the Lebanese Medical Association], *Majallat al-Ma'had al-Tibbi al-'Arabi*, 11 (March 1937), pp. 570–6.

33 See for example, "Fatihat al-sana al-rabi'a" [An introduction to the fourth year], *Majallat al-Ma'had al-Tibbi al-'Arabi*, 4 (January 1927), p. 4; "Fatihat al-sana al-khamaisa" [An introduction to the fifth year], *Majallat al-Ma'had al-Tibbi al-'Arabi*, 5 (January 1928), p. 4; "Fatihat al-sana al-sadisa" [An introduction to the sixth year], *Majallat al-Ma'had al-Tibbi al-'Arabi*, 6 (January 1929), p. 4.

34 "Al-Lugha al-'arabiyya wa-nasibuha min nashr al-thaqafa al-tibbiyya" [The Arabic language and its share in the dissemination of medical culture], *al-Majallah al-Tibbiyya al-Misriyya*, 15 (1932), pp. 191–3.

Arabic and benefit from Arab science, as they had during the golden age of Arab medicine.[35] The journal of the Egyptian Medical Association similarly called for a locally produced tropical medicine. Most foreign research of "our" diseases, claimed the editor, was defunct, as it did not take into account local economic, social and cultural factors which affected disease etiology, which only a local researcher would know.[36]

Founded in November 1945, the journal of the Palestinian Medical Association defined itself, in its opening editorial, as a communication link between Arab doctors in Palestine and the neighboring countries. Invited to congratulate it, representatives of the Egyptian, Iraqi and Jordanian medical associations expressed similar sentiments and hoped that the new journal would become an ambassador, a link or a nexus – connecting Palestine to other Arab countries.[37] In a later editorial, Dr. Ahmad Sururi defined the journal's goal as introducing Palestine's doctors to challenges facing their colleagues in neighboring Arab lands and exposing medical developments in Palestine to Arabic-reading medical communities in neighboring countries.[38]

Beginning from the 1920s, face-to-face interactions supplemented this written exchange of ideas. When Palestine's doctors travelled to Damascus or Beirut, they met their former classmates. Iraqi doctors had already studied with some of their peers, in Paris or Istanbul. These shared rituals and employment opportunities thus created a shared professional community.

The Medical Conferences

It is no coincidence that it was Egypt that initiated regional medical conferences. The Egyptian Medical Association took the lead in the interwar period because of the transformation the Egyptian medical profession was undergoing at the time, which was not paralleled in neighboring countries. Qasr al-'Aini lost its centrality in initiating Egyptians to the medical profession shortly after the 1882 British occupation. As Amira Sonbol and Hibba Abugideiri have

---

35 "Fatihat al-sana al-sadisa" [An introduction to the sixth year], *Majallat al-Ma'had al-Tibbi al-'Arabi*, 6 (January 1930), p. 4.

36 "Ahmiyyat al-bahth al-'ilmi fi amradina al-mutawattina" [The importance of research on our endemic diseases], *al-Majalla al-Tibbiyya al-Misriyya*, 18 (April 1935), pp. 142–3.

37 "Kalimat al-'adad" [This issue's introductory words], *Majallat al-Jama'iya al-Tibbiyya al-'Arabiyya al-Falastiniyya*, 1 (1945), pp. 1–4.

38 al-Sururi, Ahmad, "Kalimat al-'Adad", *Majallat al-Jama'iya al-Tibbiyya al-'Arabiyya al-Falastiniyya*, 1 (1946), pp. 85–6.

shown, the British saw the school as defunct, and Anglicized its teaching staff and its language of instruction. The Egyptian Medical Association, founded following the 1919 Revolution, saw it as its role to re-Egyptianize the medical profession, through legislation, through a bilingual (Arabic and English) journal and through Arabization of medical instruction. None of Egypt's neighbors had such a long history of instruction and professionalization. Under French or British mandates, moreover, none had the institutional backing of a semi-independent government that the Egyptian medical profession had enjoyed.[39]

One of the means that Egyptian doctors employed in order to establish their professional status was to prove their competence in medical research. The fields of parasitology and tropical medicine were promising niches to prove their professional specialization and their worthiness alongside their European colleagues and particularly in medical disciplines that were created and monopolized by European doctors stationed in Europe's colonies.[40] As noted above, in a 1935 editorial of the Egyptian Medical Journal (*al-Majalla al-Tibbiyya al-Misriyya*), for example, the editor explained that scientific research on tropical disease conducted by Western scientists was often oblivious of factors relevant to the spread of disease, such as local customs, education, nutrition, agricultural factors and weather conditions. A tropical disease research center, argued the editor, would provide the Egyptian doctors with an opportunity to study their own diseases and ways of combating them, and then implement this knowledge in their own country.[41]

As part of this growing emphasis on tropical medicine, Egypt hosted, in 1928, the first international congress of tropical medicine held after World War I.[42] The Egyptian Medical Association took the initiative, and asked the Egyptian government to back it, both politically and financially. King Fuad agreed to sponsor the conference. The date chosen was the centennial of the foundation of the Egyptian medical school. The Dutch Medical Association, which had already started preparing a similar initiative, graciously withdrew and

---

39   Sonbol, *The Creation of a Medical Profession*; Abugideiri, Hibba, *Gender and the Making of Modern Medicine in Colonial Egypt* (London: Ashgate, 2010).
40   Chiffoleau, Sylvia, *Médecines et médecins en Egypte: construction d'une identité professionnelle et projet médical* (Paris: L'Harmattan, 1997).
41   "Ahmiyyat al-bahth al-'ilmi fi amradina al-mutawattina", *al-Majalla al-Tibbiyya al-Misriyya*, 18 (1935), pp. 142–3.
42   On the pre-war tropical medicine conferences, see Neill, Deborah J., *Networks in Tropical Medicine: Internationalism, Colonialism, and the Rise of a Medical Specialty, 1890–1930* (Stanford: Stanford University Press, 2012).

allowed their Egyptian colleagues to take the lead.[43] The declared purpose of the conference was to promote the progress of hygiene and medicine, gaining knowledge, establishing relations with foreign medical doctors and familiarizing them with Egyptian medical research. The aim of the conference was thus to place Egypt firmly on the international map of medical research and to declare that, in this quintessential colonial realm of knowledge, Egyptians could write back at the colonial gaze and participate in scientific debates as equals.

Participants from the region included both colonial medical officials and local medical doctors; in the case of Palestine, these were both Arabs and Jews. It hosted a total of 2,400 participants and 400 lectures, 258 of which concentrated on Egypt. The railway company offered tours to Luxor, Aswan and Palestine. In framing it within a narrative of the international history of medicine, the conference looked back to ancient Egypt, to Mehmed Ali Paşa as the founder of the Egyptian medical profession, and to the future, embodied in the inauguration of a new building for the faculty of medicine. Professor Kawamura, a Japanese representative, expressed his admiration for the "harmonic utilization of modern science" in Egypt's ancient civilization.[44]

Beginning from 1931, the annual conference of the Egyptian Medical Association was held, usually alternately, in Egypt and in a neighboring Arab city – 1931 in Beirut, 1933 in Jerusalem, 1935 in Damascus and 1938 in Baghdad. The last one was finally termed the first Arab medical conference. The 1946 conference in Aleppo was called the eighteenth Arab medical conference, thus Arabizing all previous conferences in retrospect. The selection of the hosting cities thus followed, with the exception of Jerusalem, the chronology of the foundation of medical schools in the Arab-speaking world, starting with Cairo and Beirut and continuing with the late-comers, Damascus and Baghdad – both now mandatory semi-independent schools. The inclusion of Jerusalem is not coincidental and can be ascribed to two factors – first, the large numbers of Palestinian doctors, third only to Egypt and Lebanon; and second, a show of solidarity with the Palestinian brethren in their struggle for their homeland.

One hundred and fifty doctors participated in the 1931 conference in Beirut, 300 in later conferences and 800 participated in Cairo's 1945 conference. Participants came mainly from Egypt, Syria, Lebanon and Palestine, and a handful joined them from Jordan, Iraq, Yemen, Sudan and Saudi Arabia. The doctors and their families enjoyed reduced rates in hotels, at tourist attractions and on

---

43 "Introduction", *Congrès international de médicine tropicale et d'hygiène: comptes rendus* (Cairo: Imprimerie Nationale, 1929), p. 7.

44 *Congrès international de médicine tropicale et d'hygiène*; Sonbol, *The Creation of a Medical Profession in Egypt*, p. 172; Chiffoleau, *Médecines et médecins en Egypte*, p. 92.

train and steamship fares.⁴⁵ During the conference they enjoyed not only scientific lectures but also musical performances, dinners and tea parties, hosted or attended by mandatory or independent state officials, such as Egyptian government ministers, French and British High Commissioners and public health officials. In addition, they enjoyed excursions – to the pyramids, the Dead Sea, the Umayyad Mosque of Damascus or the Abraham River – depending on their host country, of course.⁴⁶

Through these encounters, in lecture halls, by the pyramids or on steamship or train rides, connections between doctors working throughout the region were created or reinforced. Thematic discussion of shared concerns, be it malaria or rural hygiene, further strengthened the exchange of ideas and a sense of shared destiny and shared mission.

In 1933, the Egyptian Medical Journal (*al-Majalla al-Tibbiyya al-Misriyya*) explained the choice of hosting the medical conference in Jerusalem stating: "We share customs, cultures, history and religions, serving scientific knowledge on the one hand, and the Arabic language on the other".⁴⁷ In 1934, Dr. Ali Basha Ibrahim explained that these conferences allowed Egyptians to get to know their neighbors.⁴⁸ Before the conference in Damascus, the Egyptian Medical Journal (*al-Majalla al-Tibbiyya al-Misriyya*) portrayed it as a hajj to the capital of the Umayyads.⁴⁹ In 1938, Dr. Yusif 'Arqatnaji, the director of public health in Damascus, spoke of the conference as a microcosm of the ties that connect the sons of the Arab nations, and Ilias Khuri, the doctor in chief of the French hospital in Beirut and the secretary general of the Lebanese Medical Association, spoke of a shared Arab medical renaissance which connected the peoples of the Nile, the Euphrates, the Barada and the Jordan rivers. Speakers invoked

---

45   "al-Mu'tamar al-tibbi al-tasi' bi-l-Qahira" [The ninth medical conference in Cairo], *Al-Majalla al-Tibbiyya al-Misriyya*, 19 (1938), p. 694.

46   "al-Mu'atamar al-sanawi al-khamis" [The fifth annual conference], *Al-Majalla al-Tibiyya al-Misriyya*, 21 (1932), p. 519.

47   Hasan, 'Abd al-Ra'uf, "Iftitahiyya: al-mu'tamarat al-tibbiyya al-misriyya wa-in'iqaduha fi al-buldan al-'arabiyya al-mujawara" [Editorial: The Egyptian medical conferences and holding them in the neighboring Arab countries], *al-Majalla al-Tibbiyya al-Misriyya*, 16 (April 1933), pp. 211–12.

48   "al-Mu'tamar al-sanawi al-sabi' bi-l-uksur" [The seventh annual conference in Luxor], *al-Majalla al-Tibbiyya al-Misriyya*, 21 (1934), p. 301.

49   Hasan, 'Abd al- Ra'uf, "Iftitahiyya: al-mu'tamar al-sanawi al-thamin li-l-jama'iya al-tibbiyya al-Misriyya" [Editorial: The eighth annual conference of the Egpytian Medical Association], *al-Majalla al-Tibiyya al-Misriyya*, 18 (1935), pp. 167–8.

their shared past under the Umayyads of Damascus, Harun al-Rashid's Baghdad and Hamdanid Aleppo.[50]

The third conference in 1930 launched a series of meetings for the unification of medical terminology, on the basis of Dr. Sharaf's 1,000 page English-Arabic dictionary, in collaboration with colleagues from neighboring countries. These discussion followed debates already held in the medical press, and their proceedings were published in these journals, and further debated until the following year.[51] The first meeting of the *Lajnat Tawhid al-Mustalahat* (Terminology Unification Committee) started with a conflict between the Egyptian doctors, who wanted to take Sharaf's dictionary as a starting point, and non-Egyptians, who claimed to have found multiple errors, and that it relied on foreign words even when Arabic equivalents do exist. The linguistic tensions between representatives of different countries reflected also a linguistic-institutional tension between two active language academies – *al-Majmaʿ al-ʿIlmi al-ʿArabi* (The Arabic Scientific Academy) in Damascus, founded in 1919, and *Majmaʿ al-Lugha al al-ʿArabiyya* (The Arabic Language Academy), founded in 1934, in Cairo. The names of these first two language academies indicate an intention to represent the entire Arabic-speaking world.[52] Lebanese doctors who visited the Egyptian medical conferences, moreover, noted that despite the rhetoric of Arab revival, most of the talks were held in English, and speakers blamed the paucity of Arabic scientific terminology for their failure to conduct the discussion in Arabic – a statement which was on par with one of the conferences' main objectives. The terminology panels, then, were among the only ones to be held in Arabic.[53]

---

50   "Khitab al-Duktur Yusif ʿArqatanji" [Dr. Yusif Arqatanji's talk], "Khitab al-Duktur Ilias Khuri" [Dr. Ilias Khuri's talk], *al-Majalla al-Tibbiyya al-Misriyya*, 21 (1938), pp. 244–6.

51   Chiffoleau, *Médecines et médecins en Egypte*, p. 94; "Tawhid al-mustalahat al-tibbiyya fi al-lugha al-ʿarabiyya bi-muʾtamar al-jamaʿiya al-tibbiyya al-misriyya" [The unification of medical terms in Arabic, at the Egyptian Medical Association meeting], *al-Majalla al-Tibbiyya al-Misriyya*, 17 (1934), pp. 470–1; "Jalsat tawhid al-mustalahat al-tibbiyya al-ʿarabiyya fi al-muʾtamar al-sanawi al-sadis li-l-jamaʿiya al-tibbiyya al-Misriyya" [The session dedicated to the unification of Arabic medical terminology at the sixth annual conference of the Egyptian Medical Association], *al-Majalla al-Tibbiyya al-Misriyya*, 16 (1933), pp. 467–8.

52   Chaoqun, Lian, "Language Planning and Language Policy of Arabic Language Academies in the Twentieth Century: A Study of Discourse", Ph.D. Dissertation, University of Cambridge, 2015, pp. 21–3.

53   "The third conference of the Egyptian Medical Society", *The Medical Society Gazette*, 11 (1930), p. 21; al-Khuri, Ilias, "Ma raʾaytu wa-samiʿatu fi al-muʾtamar al-Misri al-sabiʿ" [What I saw and heard at the seventh Egyptian conference], *al-Majalla al-Tibbiyya al-ʿIlmiyya*, 11 (1934), pp. 594–5.

The linguistic deliberations, over the years, were often technical in nature, and concentrated on whether to Arabize or translate, and which term would be most appropriate for different symptoms, diseases and medications. In addition, more substantial issues were raised. First was the Arabization of medical instruction in Egypt, which, as I noted earlier, had been held in English since 1882. Classroom instruction and textbooks were in English and Arabic terms were therefore not in circulation and available textbooks in Arabic were grossly outdated. As Egypt sought to present itself as the leader of the regional profession this was a situation that had to be remedied.[54] In Beirut as well, the language of instruction at the faculties of medicine was English and French – and students' requests to have at least some of the AUB's classes taught in Arabic was denied.[55] The association's journal, and then the exchange and circulation of medical journals between different medical associations, was to provide a partial solution and supply a growing body of medical texts in Arabic.[56]

A second challenge was how to unify medical terms among a group of doctors who met only once a year. A committee was formed of doctors from Baghdad, Damascus, Beirut and Cairo, who met annually to discuss the formation of a unified lexicon.[57] More importantly, perhaps, was the question of to what extent the Arabic language constituted a basis for professional identity, and, as I showed before, a conference which started as an *Egyptian* one (generously hosting their Arab neighbors), turned into an *Arab* conference, symbolically erasing its Egyptian origin in 1946.

Another challenge was Palestine, which also hosted the 1933 conference. The conference was held in the new and impressive YMCA building that had just been inaugurated. It hosted doctors from Egypt, Palestine, Syria and Lebanon, consuls and religious leaders – with the exception of Hajj Amin al-Husayni, the grand mufti of Jerusalem, whose absence was well noted. The guests visited

---

54 "Jalsat tawhid al-mustalahat al-tibbiyya al-'arabiyya", pp. 469–79; al-Wakil Bek, 'Abd al-Wahid, "Mahdar jalsat tawhid al-mustalahat al-'arabiyya, Baghdad" [Proceedings of the Arabic terminology unification session, Baghdad], *al-Majalla al-Tibbiyya al-'Arabiyya*, 21 (1938), pp. 777–8.

55 Anderson, *The American University of Beirut: Arab Nationalism and Liberal Education*, pp. 126–7.

56 "Qararat al-mu'tamar al-tibbi al-sanawi al-sabi' 'ashar" [Decisions adopted by the seventeenth annual medical conference], *al-Majalla al-Tibbiyya al-Misriyya*, 28 (1945), pp. 270–1.

57 Al-Ma'uf, Amin Basha, "Tawhid al-mustalahat al-tibbiyya fi al-lugha al-'arabiyya" [The unification of medical terminology in Arabic], *al-Majalla al-Tibbiyya al-Misriyya*, 20 (1937), pp. 1005–6.

the Jordan River and the Dead Sea, had tea by the beach, and were invited to a tea party by Jerusalem's mayor. The mufti invited them to watch the Nabi Musa celebrations, and the Egyptian consul invited them to dinner. They also visited Jerusalem's hospitals, the leper colony and Jerusalem's antiquities. Iraqi physician Fa'iq Shakir described the Hadassah infant care centers and school health services and noted especially anti-trachoma and anti-syphilitic measures. This excellent care for infants and children, he concluded grimly, would eventually lead to Zionist victory over Palestine.[58]

A report in the Lebanese Medical Journal concluded that the conference had an important social objective – bringing Arab doctors together in one place, allowing them to get to know each other, mingle, reach mutual understanding and form and reinforce friendships. Unfortunately, however, doctors of different countries socialized among themselves and there was no targeted effort to break these circles and force doctors to socialize with others; this objective was therefore not achieved. The author of the report further called for a Near Eastern conference that would not be initiated by the Egyptian doctors, but rather by a joint committee, or even by a Lebanese one – whose medical association was established 15 years before its Egyptian counterpart.[59]

As in the 1928 tropical medicine conference in Cairo, here as well both Jewish and Arab doctors participated, and the conference was covered both in the Hebrew and the Arabic press. The Palestinian Arab press noted particularly Dr. Rokach's opening speech, in the name of the Zionists doctors' association, which he delivered in Hebrew and for which he did not bother to provide a translation, except in English for the High Commissioner. Most of the audience could not follow the speech, but did notice the recurring term "the Land of Israel" (Eretz Israel, or Ard Isra'il), which they found to be extremely rude, and which spoiled the atmosphere of human solidarity. Interestingly, though, the high participation of Jewish doctors among the conference speakers was not deemed worthy of comment. It was Dr. Rokach's apparently political statement, which alienated most of those present, that seemed to have upset *Falastin*'s correspondent, and not the presence of Jewish doctors *per se*.[60]

---

58   *Palestine Post*, 9, 12 April 1933. For Shakir's account of his visit to Jewish health facilities on this occasion, see Shakir, Fa'iq, *Kitab al-Amrad al-Zahariyya* [The Book of Venereal Diseases] (Baghdad: Matba'at al-'Ahd, 1934).

59   "al-Mu'tamar al-tibbi al-sadis" [The sixth medical conference], *al-Majalla al-Tibbiyya al-'Ilmiyya*, 10 (1933), pp. 518–19.

60   "Iftitah al-mu'tamar al-tibbi fi al-quds" [The opening of the medical conference in Jerusalem], *Falastin*, 5 April 1933; "Fi al-mu'tamar al-tibbi: shu'ur insani 'ala hisab al-ghayr" [At the medical conference: humanitarian sentiment at the expense of the others], *Falastin*, 7 April 1933.

The question of Palestine came up again in later conferences. In a speech in Baghdad in 1938, Palestinian Arab doctor Rushdi al-Tamimi equated the Arab homeland to a human body, whose right hand lay in Egypt and its left hand in Syria, while its neck lay in Palestine, which was presently in peril and thus endangered the life of the entire body.[61] The 1945 Cairo conference took a strong stand on the question of Palestine. One of its resolutions included a boycott of Zionist pharmaceutical companies, and doctors pledged to refrain from prescribing their medications. In Aleppo in 1946, country representatives pledged a donation of a total sum of 50,000 pounds for the establishment of medical institutions in Palestine; these were never delivered.[62]

Conclusion

Histories of medicine in the Middle East are bound by epistemic nationalism and thus miss the transnational connections within which the medical profession was embedded. The formation of medical schools which attracted students regionally and appealed to Arabic- and Turkish-speaking students throughout the Middle East; scientific and medical journals that were published in Cairo, Beirut and Damascus, but circulated between these urban centers and beyond, and then the regional conferences, created a regional, or even pan-Arab, professional identity. These processes were facilitated by the accelerated mobility of people and ideas across the region, partly due to the railway, the steamship and motor transportation, which connected urban centers much more quickly and directly than ever before. This was an inter-Arab initiative that other professions would follow. It affirmed both Arab unity and Egypt's leadership role.[63]

Focusing on one group of middle-class professionals, this chapter offered a model for transnational histories of Arab nationalism and the Arab middle class. To write such histories, we need to look for other sites of interaction and for different modes of circulation, which created and fortified regional connections. Gender, class, ethnicity and politics might then serve as additional axes of analysis.

---

61 "Kalimat al-Duktur Rushdi al-Tamimi Bek" [Dr. Rusdi al-Tamimi Bek's talk], *al-Majalla al-Tibbiyya al-Misriyya*, 21 (1938), p. 257.
62 "al-Mua'amar al-tibbi al-'arabi al-sanawi al-thamin 'ashar al-mun'aqad bi-madinat halab" [The eighteenth annual Arab medical conference, convened in Aleppo], *Al-Majalla al-Tibiyya al-Misriyya*, 29 (1946), p. 150.
63 Chiffoleau, *Médecines et médecins en Egypte*, p. 95.

CHAPTER 7

There She is, Miss Universe: Keriman Halis Goes to Egypt, 1933

Amit Bein

The selection of Miss Turkey Keriman Halis as Miss Universe in 1932 was received with a wave of enthusiasm in her homeland. Her achievement was celebrated as a national victory for the young Kemalist Republic. In the previous three years since the inauguration of the Miss Turkey competition by the daily *Cumhuriyet* in 1929, the pageant was a matter of public controversy. But after Keriman Halis was crowned Miss Universe in a beauty contest held in Belgium in August 1932 the Turkish government hastened to embrace her as a national hero. Mustafa Kemal himself participated in a dance ball in her honor. The president of the republic proposed that she should add the surname Ece, or queen in old Turkish, which she indeed adopted formally after the adoption of the surname law in 1934. The Kemalist establishment meanwhile incorporated Keriman Halis into its propaganda and image management operations at home and abroad. Her person and the title she had won were presented as the result of the Kemalist modernist and secularist reforms in general and of the steps towards the emancipation of women in particular, as well as their validation. The European press too promoted a similar narrative. For instance, the Parisian daily *Le Matin* reported that the 18 year old Turkish beauty queen was a high school graduate who enjoyed playing the piano and whose favorite sport was tennis, all traits associated with western middle class tastes, as was her hair-style and dress which adorned the French journal's front page.[1] The *London Times* explained that Miss Universe was indeed "a symbol of the new freedom which Turkish women have won, and a proof to the world that Turkey has finally shaken off the shackles which kept her for so long from taking her place among civilized nations".[2] This was a music to the ears of the Kemalist leadership. The crowning of a Turkish woman as Miss Universe did not go unnoticed in the Arabic press as well. The Egyptian daily *al-Ahram*, for example, featured on its front page a story about her election and background

---

1 "La plus belle: Miss Turquie est élue Miss Univers au tournoi de Spa" and "L'élection de Miss Univers", *Le Matin* (Paris), 1 August 1932, pp. 1, 3.
2 "Feminism in Turkey", *The Times* (London), 12 November 1932, p. 11.

accompanied by a photo of her in evening dress, and in November 1932 reports in the press suggested that the Turkish beauty queen might be soon embarking on a tour of Syria and Egypt to meet and greet fans and help bolster the image of the Kemalist republic.[3]

Scholarly work on Keriman Halis and the uses and abuses of her fame by the Turkish government have generally ignored the fact that she eventually did indeed visit Egypt in 1933. What was initially planned as a short visit of less than two weeks eventually extended to more than three months of high profile and well publicized engagement with the Egyptian public at a time of strained relations between Ankara and Cairo. An examination of this hitherto overlooked episode in Keriman Halis's career and its intersection with Turkish-Egyptian relations in the early post-Ottoman period is instructive of various aspects of Kemalist Turkey's engagement with the most important former Ottoman territory in the Middle East. For one thing, examination of the visit offers an interesting vantage point on Turkey's efforts to cultivate a positive image of the Kemalist reforms in Muslim-majority societies in the region. For another, the Egyptian reactions to the visitor illustrate perceptions of Kemalist Turkey and reactions to its reforms in the largest and most important Arab country of the interwar period. And finally, the visit offers a counterpoint to the prevailing narrative in the historiography of the period according to which the Turkish and Arab elites of the period were all but consensually committed to efforts to distance their respective societies and states from one another. According to this prevailing narrative, lingering animosities from the late Ottoman period, Kemalist policies to dissociate Turkey from the Middle East, and hostile reactions in the region to secularizing and nationalist reforms in Turkey led by the early 1930s to the opening of a serious chasm between the Kemalist elites and their counterparts in the Middle East. There is no doubt that policies that were implemented by the Kemalist government since the mid-1920s were indeed very polarizing in Egypt and neighboring Arab countries. They came under scrutiny and were debated publically much more widely than could have been done under the single-party political order in Turkey itself. The alphabet and language reforms, as well as various policies of secularization and nationalization of Islamic worship, became topics of particular criticism by Arab nationalists, conservatives, and Islamists of various types and stripes. However, such critical perspectives and viewpoints on Kemalist Turkey

---

3 "Malikat al-jamal fi Turkiya untuhibat malika li'l-jamal fi al-'alam" [Turkish beauty queen elected Miss Universe], *al-Ahram*, 6 August 1932, p. 1; "Malikat al-jamal fi Turkiya", *al-Ahram*, 17 November 1932, p. 4; "Keriman Hanımın İzmir Seyahati İntibaları ..." [Impressions from Miss Keriman's visit to İzmir], *Cumhuriyet*, 26 November 1932, p. 1.

were neither consensual nor yet dominant in Egypt of the early 1930s, as they would become in the decades that followed. Examination of the events surrounding Keriman Halis's visit to Egypt only a few months before the ten year anniversary of the Republic of Turkey, and at a time by which the most radical Kemalist reforms were already being implemented, suggests that at that point in time there were many more nuances to Turkish-Egyptian relations than has often been reflected in the historiography of the period.[4]

The Royal Treatment

On February 20, 1933, the King and Queen of Italy were received with great fanfare in Cairo at the beginning of a short visit that was considered to be of great political importance. But whereas official Egypt was preoccupied with the arrival of the head of state of an important imperial power with shared borders and known regional ambitions,[5] many ordinary Egyptians were as much absorbed with the visit of a different type of royalty: Miss Universe. Keriman Halis arrived in Egypt ten days earlier than the Italian monarchs and by the time of their arrival her visit was supposed to wind down. Her initial plan was to spend only a couple of weeks in the Land of the Nile before departing for Europe en route to America to help promote the Turkish pavilion in the Chicago World Fair of 1933 and serve as an example of the rapid progress of women rights in Turkey.[6] But because the reception in Egypt was much more enthusiastic than expected, the beauty queen and her father, who served as her chaperon, made changes to their initial plans and eventually remained in the Land of the Nile three eventful months before heading back to their home in Istanbul in May.

The intense public interest in the visit of the Turkish beauty queen was put on full display from the moment she arrived in Egypt in early February 1933.

---

[4] For a broader discussion of the relations between Turkey and the Middle East in the early post-Ottoman period, see Bein, Amit, *Kemalist Turkey and the Middle East: International Relations in the Interwar Period* (Cambridge: Cambridge University Press, 2017).

[5] "Egyptians welcome Italian royal party: great political importance is attached to visit of King Victor Emmanuel", *The New York Times*, 21 February 1933, p. 22.

[6] "Dünya Güzeli Dün Gitti. Keriman H. Mısır ve Amerika Seyahatinde Milli Mahsullere Propaganda Yapacak" [Miss Universe left yesterday. Miss Keriman will promote Turkish-made products in her visits to Egypt and America], *Cumhuriyet*, 8 February 1933, p. 1; "'Hail! Women Progress East & West' by the Progressive Turkish Women of Chicago", in Ganz, Cheryl R., *The 1933 Chicago World's Fair: A Century of Progress* (Chicago: Illinois University Press, 2010), pp. 80–1.

At the docks in Alexandria, she was met by an enthusiastic crowd of hundreds of people who wished to catch a glimpse of the newly minted international celebrity as she disembarked from the steamship that brought her and her father from Istanbul. A welcoming committee on behalf of the organized Turkish community of Alexandria was in charge of publicizing her arrival and inviting the public to welcome her to Egypt. A reception in her honor later that day was attended by the Turkish consul general, Egyptian government and municipal officials, and important local notables and dignitaries. The Egyptian press willingly cooperated in trumpeting the arrival of Turkish Miss Universe with reports and photos splashed on the front pages of all the important periodicals, including highbrow dailies such as *al-Ahram*.[7] However, neither the local press nor Keriman Halis and her handlers expected the level of interest and enthusiasm that awaited her as she took the train to Cairo after a couple of days in Alexandria. As she arrived in the Egyptian capital's railway station she was astonished to see throngs of men, along with some women, clogging the station in anticipation to catch a glimpse of her. Only after a 30 minutes delay, in which the police worked to open for her a path out of the station, could the Turkish beauty queen be whisked away to her hotel in an automobile. The popular weekly *al-Kashkul* suggested that the crowd's curiosity was informed first and foremost by the fact that she was a Muslim and Easterner just like the majority of the people of Egypt and therefore they were very proud of her achievement. The journal commented, tongue-in-cheek, that since the interest in her was so intense her arrival might have well been declared the beginning of a National Women's Week.[8] There was little chance of that happening, but Egyptian feminists did hope to harness the public interest in the visiting Turkish beauty queen to their cause. The Egyptian Feminist Union, led by Huda al-Sha'rawi, thus dispatched a delegation to Keriman Halis's hotel to greet her and invite her to serve as the guest of honor of a fundraiser ball in their leader's private mansion. The Turkish beauty queen received them in between meetings with journalists, businesspeople, notables, and politicians, and before proceeding to visit the royal palace, where she was reportedly "the first Eastern woman"[9] to be invited to sign its official guestbook.

---

7   "Malikat al-jamal al-Turkiya fi Misr", *al-Ahram*, 12 February 1933, p. 1.
8   "Malikat al-jamal al-Turkiya!", *al-Kashkul*, 17 February 1933, p. 4; "Bi-munasabat ziyarat malikat al-jamal" [On the occasion of the beauty queen's visit], *al-Kashkul*, 17 February 1933, p. 14; "Usbu' al-mar'a" [Women's week], *al-Kashkul*, 17 February 1933, p. 22.
9   "Malikat al-Jamal al-Turkiya fi Misr" [The Turkish beauty queen in Egypt], *al-Ahram*, 13 February 1933, p. 1.

Keriman Halis's hectic first day in the Egyptian capital culminated with a reception and fancy dance party in her honor which was sponsored by a charitable organization of the Turkish community in Cairo, entitled the *al-Jam'iya al-Khayriya al-Turkiya* (Turkish Benevolent Society). This was a recently established charitable organization which was aimed at galvanizing common social bonds and identity among members of the Turkish colony in Egypt. The ball was held at the mansion of Hüseyin Remzi, the proprietor and editor-in-chief of the Turkish-Arabic bilingual weekly *Muhadenet/Mukhadana*, and a major proponent of Kemalism and Turkish nationalism in Egypt. His house and its surroundings were decorated with dozens of Turkish and Egyptian flags, giving the event an appearance of a semi-official celebration of the bilateral relations between the two states and societies. Crowds of curious onlookers lined the streets leading to the house in the hope of catching a glimpse of Keriman Halis and other celebrities among the A-list invitees, who included many of Cairo's famous men and women. The evening opened with toasts in honor of Keriman Halis by the host and a number of other dignitaries. Among them stood out the warm greetings of Saiza Nabarawi, a close friend and associate of Huda al-Sha'rawi in the Egyptian Feminist Union, and the editor-in-chief of the organization's mouthpiece *l'Egyptienne*. Nabarawi hailed Keriman Halis for being the first Muslim woman to be elected Miss Universe and thus becoming a great model for all "Eastern women". The allusion to the Turkish visitor as a source of pride to all the women of "the East", as well as the celebration of her status, was reported widely in the Egyptian press. The most popular periodical in the land, *al-Ahram*, reported on the party, its participants, and the speeches given in it, along with photos from the event.[10]

The astounding level of public interest soon convinced Keriman Halis and her handlers to extend her stay in Egypt and abandon her previous plans to visit America. Indeed, her schedule was full of daily events in her first few weeks in Egypt which included receptions, tea parties, and balls in which she served as the main attraction and the guest of honor. She was the toast of the town, with particularly high exposure to the Egyptian elites, and with reports and photos of her activities published widely in the press. On one occasion she was taken to parliament for a meet and greet with lawmakers and senior politicians. Before entering the building she was received by a large crowd of hundreds of men and women who were eager to catch a glimpse of Miss Universe. On another occasion, Prince Muhammad 'Ali, King Fuad's nephew, arranged for himself a private audience with the Turkish beauty queen and her

---

10   "Malikat al-jamal al-Turkiya fi Misr", *al-Ahram*, 13 February 1933, p. 1.

father. He subsequently shared his positive impressions of her with the press.[11] Her mystique and fame got to the point where the Minister of Education, Muhammad Hilmi 'Isa Paşa, remarked publically that the Egyptian people could learn a lot from adopting Keriman Halis as a role model and from listening to her message about feminine beauty and progress. His statement became fodder for satirical publications associated with the Egyptian opposition. The popular *Ruz al-Yusuf*, for instance, depicted the Minister of Education in one particularly stinging caricature as staring at a beautiful and young Keriman Halis, cross-eyed and in awe, and in another, as standing on the podium with a foolish look on his face while inviting Miss Universe to deliver a lecture on "the science of ... Beauty".[12]

But the interest in meeting the instantaneously famous visitor and newly minted celebrity was not limited to politicians or to the middle and upper classes. The respectable intellectual and journalist Muhammad Husayn Haykal, for instance, arranged for the daily *al-Siyasa*, in which he was the editor-in-chief, to host a reception in her honor. This was a highbrow publication that also doubled as the organ of the Liberal Constitutionalist Party (Hizb al-Ahrar al-Dusturiyyin). Keriman Halis was welcomed by him and some of his colleagues and associates as "a messenger of beauty from Ankara" and her visit was hailed as an expression of the strong bond and friendly relations between Turkey and Egypt. The Turkish visitor was received as warmly in less formal and more popular events as well. For instance, she was a guest of honor in concerts of the young singing sensation Umm Kulthum and of the famous singer Ibrahim Hamouda, and was the main attraction in the weekly women-only show in the successful night club of the famous 1930s belly dancer and movie star Badi'a Masabni.[13] All in all, Keriman Halis was time and again welcomed and hailed as both an "Eastern" and Muslim woman who was a source of pride for the women of Egypt and as an informal ambassador of goodwill on Turkey's behalf.

Egyptian feminists also saw Keriman Halis's visit as an opportunity to buttress their advocacy for women rights thanks to her celebrity and the example

---

11   "Fi majlis al-nuwwab: malikat al-jamal fi al-majlis" [In the House of Representatives: the beauty queen in the House], *al-Ahram*, 16 February 1933, p. 2; "Dünya Güzeli Mısır'da!" [Miss Universe in Egypt], *Cumhuriyet*, 23 February 1933, pp. 1–2.

12   "Wazir al-maarif ... wa-al-jamal!" [The Minister of Education and ... Beauty], *Ruz al-Yusuf*, no. 262, 20 February 1933, p. 3; *Ruz al-Yusuf*, no. 264, 6 March 1933, p. 2.

13   "Malikat al-jamal tasma'u Umm Kulthum" [The beauty queen in an Umm Kulthum concert], *al-Ahram*, 1 March 1933, p. 7; "Takrim malikat al-jamal fi Dar al-Siyasa" [Honoring the beauty queen by al-Siyasa], *al-Ahram*, 3 March 1933, p. 7; *al-Ahram*, 11 March 1933, p. 12.

set by her and her country. In the early 1930s it was not unusual for Middle Eastern feminists to view beauty contests as representations of women empowerment that could assist their struggle for emancipation. In this matter as in other women-related issues, Turkey was seen by many a Middle Eastern feminist as a progressive force for change that was trailblazing a path of potential modernization for all "Eastern women". In the Eastern Women's Conference held in Tehran in 1932, for instance, the Syrian feminist activist Nur Hamada expressed hope that the achievements secured by the women of Turkey would set a precedent for all the women of the Middle East and the non-Western world.[14] Prominent Egyptian feminists expressed similar views. Taking a cue from the Kemalist propaganda, they embraced Keriman Halis very publically as a symbolic representation of the advancement of women rights in Turkey and as a source of inspiration for women rights activists in Egypt. Among them was Safiyya Zaghloul, the widow of one of the most popular nationalist leaders in post-World War I Egypt and a political activist in her own right.[15] The so-called Mother of the Egyptians (*Umm al-Misriyyin*) invited Keriman Halis to a well-publicized meeting at her mansion, popularly known as the House of the Nation (*Bayt al-Umma*), to congratulate her personally and endorse her image of modernity for Muslim and "Eastern" women. Her friend and fellow nationalist feminist, Huda al-Sha'rawi, went a step further in her public endorsement of the Turkish visitor. She held in her private mansion a ball that also doubled as a fundraiser for the Egyptian Feminist Union, in which Keriman Halis was the main draw.[16]

Yet, even as she was welcomed in Egypt enthusiastically and mostly adoringly, a minor public debate developed regarding what made her famous in the first place: her looks. It involved the general question of how beauty should be evaluated and a more particular debate on whether Keriman Halis was that exceptional based on those standards of beauty. Some commentators objected to the use of looks as an acceptable yardstick to measure female attractiveness. They suggested that a woman's beauty should be evaluated by the positivity of

---

14   Weber, Charlotte, "Between nationalism and feminism: the Eastern Women's Congresses of 1930 and 1932", *Journal of Middle East Women's Studies*, 4 (2008), p. 94; Salami, Gholamreza and Afsaneh Najmabadi, *Nahzat-e Nisvan-e Sharq* [The Eastern Women Movement] (Tehran: Shirazeh, 2005), pp. 53, 59, 70, 82, 255.

15   For an extensive discussion of Safiyya Zaghloul's life and career, see Baron, Beth, *Egypt as a Woman: Nationalism, Gender, and Politics* (Berkeley: University of California Press, 2005), pp. 135–61.

16   "Malikat al-jamal fi Dar al-Ittihad al-Nisa'i" [The beauty queen in the Feminist Union's house], *al-Ahram*, 14 February 1933, p. 7; "Dünya Güzelinin Mısır Seyahatı" [Miss Universe's Egypt journey], *Cumhuriyet*, 20 March 1933, p. 5.

her character, as supposedly had been the common and well-tested practice until objectifying Western standards began influencing perceptions in Egypt and other Muslim-majority societies. In that sense, the celebrity Keriman Halis and her title were presented as a reflection of continued exposure to negative European social and cultural influences. Other critics demurred regarding the use of looks to determine beauty, but agreed that Keriman Halis was judged as beautiful based on European standards of female attractiveness whereas in Egypt and the East there were different standards for feminine beauty according to which she was merely elegant and fashionable rather than beautiful. The prominent intellectual Fikri Abaza took both the former and the latter critics to task. He suggested that beauty may be evaluated universally according to scientific methods based on shape and proportion of various facial parts and their relations to each other. He insisted that an application of this modern scientific method to Keriman Halis reveals that she is indeed universally beautiful, and added that the women of Egypt have much to learn from the way she carries herself so gracefully and honorably.[17] A number of celebrated male Egyptian poets concurred and wrote poems in which they hailed Keriman Halis's beauty and public conduct and insisted that she had proven worthy of her title and of her fame.[18]

But even among commentators who conceded that the Turkish beauty queen was deserving of her title, the nationalist sensibilities of some of them informed their judgement of her image. The journal *al-Kashkul*, for instance, agreed that the Turkish beauty queen "is very graceful and likeable", but suggested that "her beauty is not extraordinary, and those who visited San Stefano beach or Stanley Bay beach [in Alexandria], have seen plenty of young [Egyptian] girls who are more beautiful than her". Another popular periodical, *Ruz al-Yusuf*, attributed a similar view to none other than Huda al-Sha'rawi. Shortly after the feminist and nationalist leader hosted Keriman Halis in her mansion she purportedly remarked to friends and acquaintances that there were a great many Egyptian girls who were more beautiful than the reigning Miss Universe. According to the report in the press she went on to suggest that should the Egyptian Feminist Union organize a beauty pageant in Egypt, as it should, her assertion of the superior Egyptian beauty would be proven beyond

[17] Abaza, Fikri, "Jamal malikat al-jamal?!" [The beauty of the beauty queen?!], *al-Musawwar*, 24 February 1933, p. 2.
[18] "Tahiyat Misr ila' malikat al-jamal" [Egypt's salutation to the beauty queen], *al-Ahram*, 16 February 1933, p. 7; "Malikat al-jamal", *al-Ahram*, 18 February 1933, p. 7; "Ila' malikat al-jamal" [For the beauty queen], *al-Ahram*, 6 March 1933, p. 7; "Ila' malikat al-jamal", *al-Ahram*, 14 March 1933, p. 1.

doubt. The weekly *al-Kashkul* concurred, arguing that the women of Egypt, and particularly those of the upper classes, were indeed equipped by nature and through nurture with all the qualities that would ensure their success in international beauty contests.[19] The message to the Egyptian public was, then, that they could and should have their own beauty queen to cheer on and proudly display to the world the attractiveness of Egyptian women. Although welcomed heartily as a fellow Muslim and "Easterner", in this instance Keriman Halis was used as a foil for some nationalists and feminists in Egypt to both express their pride in their own countrywomen and indirectly to point to potential gains of international prestige through the participation in beauty pageants.

Two years later, in 1935, an important precedent was indeed set when Egypt too held its own beauty pageant. The elected Miss Egypt, Charlotte Wassef, indeed went on to win the Miss Universe title, three years after Keriman Halis achieved that feat and became an instant celebrity and a national hero in Turkey. In Egypt, however, it was the candidate who came second in the Miss Egypt contest that made a much greater splash and left a more important mark in Egyptian history. Doria Shafik, a young graduate of the Sorbonne and at the time a protégé of Huda al-Sha'rawi, shot to immediate celebrity among some and infamy among others because she was the first Muslim Egyptian contestant in a beauty pageant. Her fairytale story proceeded with her engagement to Ahmad al-Sawi Muhammad, a rising star journalist in *al-Ahram*. Their relations were destined to end abruptly shortly thereafter, but as long as they lasted the report on their marriage along with their photos were featured on the front page of *al-Ahram*, Egypt's newspaper of record. Interestingly, during Keriman Halis's visit two years earlier al-Sawi Muhammad published a column in which he admitted that before her arrival in Egypt he was opposed to the idea of beauty pageants but after meeting the Turkish beauty queen and observing her dignified conduct and personality he was won over by her and changed his mind about beauty pageants and queens. He was not an exception. In fact, the leaders of the Egyptian Feminist Union indeed invited Keriman Halis to their dance ball and fundraiser in the hope that she would have a similar effect on other men and women who would thus be more amenable to support their

---

19 "Malikat al-jamal al-turkiya!" [The Turkish beauty queen], *al-Kashkul*, 17 February 1933, p. 4; "Akhbar raqiya wa-ghayra raqiya" [Sophisticated and non-Sophisticated News], *Ruz al-Yusuf*, no. 262, 20 February 1933, p. 13; "Hal tuqam mubarat li'l-jamal fi Misr..!" [Will there be beauty pageants in Egypt?], *al-Kashkul*, 3 March 1933, p. 14.

vision of emancipation of women along similar lines to the Kemalist policies in Turkey.[20]

There was one main challenge to the image and credibility of the visiting beauty queen which she worked hard to refute, with some success. Questions raised about the "true purpose" of the visit and accusations in the press that it was part of a secret commercial undertaking to promote cosmetic products threatened to paint the Turkish visitor as a self-serving hypocrite on a disguised commercial tour. These negative rumors and commentaries were fed by early reports in the Turkish press according to which her visit to Egypt and the USA would help promote Turkish exports to these markets. The weeklies *Ruz al-Yusuf* and *al-Kashkul*, for instance, warned their readers not to be swayed by Arabian Nights type of stories about her, with which they were fed, because she was simply serving as a salesperson for unnamed foreign cosmetic companies.[21] After her arrival in Egypt Keriman Halis released statements aimed to refute the claims that she was aiming to help sell cosmetic products. She explained to the Egyptian press that all she wanted was to inspire Egyptian women to adopt hygienic practices and a healthy lifestyle with the ultimate goal of marrying and raising a family. She explained that many of the Egyptian women appeared to her to be overweight and therefore would benefit from taking better care of their bodies through a healthier diet and some physical activity.[22] Upon her return to Turkey in May, Keriman Halis was asked about these charges, as well as about reports of the sale of her signed photos to the public. She rejected out of hand the assertions that she traveled to Egypt to make money, insisting that she took only payments as reimbursement for her travel and living expenses. She was particularly adamant that she did not sell her photos. She explained that it was in fact the Egyptian Feminist Union that sold her photos, without permission, as part of its fundraising efforts.[23] The available sources make it hard to determine whether the beauty queen gained

---

20 al-Sawi, "Qala wa-dala" [Brief and useful], *al-Ahram*, 17 March 1933, p. 1; al-Sawi, "Ma qalla wa-dalla", *al-Ahram*, 20 February 1933, p. 7; "al-ustadh al-Sawi wa-'arusuhu" [Mister al-Sawi and his bride], *al-Ahram*, 6 September 1935, 1; "Untuhiba Miss Misr malika li'l-jamal fi al-'alam", *al-Ahram*, 1 October 1935, p. 1; Nelson, Cynthia, *Doria Shafik, Egyptian Feminist: A Woman Apart* (Gainseville: University of Florida Press, 1996), pp. 60–4.
21 *al-Kashkul*, 17 February 1933, p. 13; "Bayna al-suhuf wa-al-majalat" [In the newspapers and magazines], *Ruz al-Yusuf*, no. 263, 27 February 1933, p. 39.
22 "Dünya Güzelinin Mısır Seyahatı" [Miss Universe's Egyptian voyage], *Cumhuriyet*, 20 March 1933, p. 5.
23 Mekki Sait, "Dedikodulu Mısır Seferi: Keriman Ece Gördüklerini Anlatıyor ..." [The gossipy Egyptian voyage: Keriman Ece describes her observations], *Yedigün*, no. 12, 31 May 1933, p. 14.

any significant financial benefit from her Egyptian tour, or only covered her expenses, but it is beyond doubt that she and her representatives did strike some business deals. The luxurious Heliopolis Hotel, for instance, was able to lure her away from the Continental with the promise of free accommodation and meals. In return, the hotel received free publicity in the press as well as a steady stream of customers who frequented its cafeteria and tea lounge in the hope of catching a glimpse of Miss Universe. In another case, the Mahmud Fahmi cigarette company organized for Keriman Halis a well-publicized tour of its factory, where Egyptian cigarettes were manufactured with tobacco imported from Turkey. And in another instance, promoters of the increasingly popular sport of soccer invited Keriman Halis to hand out the trophy to the winning side in featured matches.[24] To what degree the celebrity of Keriman Halis translated into monetary gains for her or business partners is hard to tell, but it is clear that the accusations thrown at her neither dented her aura in Egypt nor discouraged various commercial interests from seeking to have some of that aura rub off on them.

The community most thrilled with Keriman Halis's visit, however, was undoubtedly the Turkish colony in Egypt, which was made up primarily of people of Anatolian background who chose to identify as ethnic Turks. The fact that the Turkish beauty queen was in fact of Circassian background was no secret, as was the Circassian backgrounds of some members of the Turkish colony in Egypt. She presented herself as a proud Turk who represented the Turkish nation and was generally accepted as such. At one point during her visit, however, statements attributed to her father regarding their ethnic identity threatened to create some difficulties for her. It happened after reports appeared in the Turkish press according to which she had participated in a meeting with Circassian dignitaries in Egypt during which her father purportedly expressed his great pride in his Circassian ancestry and identity. This was a potentially dangerous proposition in 1930s Turkey. It appeared to fly in the face of the campaign of cultural assimilation led by the Kemalist government, aimed at transforming the various ethnic minorities in Anatolia into proud sons and daughters of the Turkish nation. Furthermore, coming at a time in which the Turkish government and press were regularly accusing Circassian activists in the Middle East of plots against Turkey and its leader it could have

---

24 "al-al'ab al-riyadiya" [Sports], *al-Ahram*, 13 February 1933, p. 10; "Malikat al-jamal" [The beauty queen], *al-Ahram*, 20 February 1933, p. 7; Shechter, Relli, *Smoking, Culture and Economy in the Middle East: the Egyptian Tobacco Market, 1850–2000* (London: I.B. Tauris, 2006), p. 113; "Malikat al-jamal", *Filastin*, 17 February 1933, p. 2; "al-al'ab al-riyadiya", *Ruz al-Yusuf*, no 263, 27 February 1933, p. 41.

been interpreted as an outright subversive statement. Keriman Halis and her father therefore hastened to deny these reports out of hand. The beauty queen emphasized that her visit in fact was a long celebration of the Turkish republic and its people, exemplified by chants of adoration to Turkey and Mustafa Kemal wherever she visited. Keriman Halis was indeed largely perceived and received not only as the epitome of a modern Turkish woman but also as an informal ambassador of goodwill on Turkey's behalf. For example, when she visited the town of Mansoura in the Delta region, under the auspices of the local Turkish colony, she was received with chants of "Long Live the Gazi [Mustafa Kemal]! Long live Turkey! Long Live Miss Keriman!"[25] The beauty queen and her father indeed emphasized very emphatically to the Turkish press that they were proud and loyal children of the Turkish nation and that Keriman Halis's prolonged stay in Egypt was a great service to the Republic of Turkey, as well as to the Turkish colony in Egypt.[26]

Public Diplomacy

A careful examination of the initiators and organizers of Keriman Halis's visit to Egypt in early 1933 suggests that her perception as an informal representative of Kemalist Turkey was not unsubstantiated. Her visit to the Land of the Nile was in fact ancillary to broader Turkish efforts to repair Turkey's relations with Egypt and improve its image among the Egyptian public. It came about shortly after the outbreak of an embarrassing diplomatic crisis between Cairo and Ankara, which strained bilateral relations already marred by various disagreements and mutual suspicions. The visit was organized primarily by the proprietor of the Turkish-Arabic weekly *Muhadenet/Mukhadana*, in cooperation with the Turkish embassy and Turkish notables in Egypt. They hoped that the visit of Miss Universe would help divert attention away from troubles in the two countries' relations and put a proverbial beautiful face on Kemalist Turkey's image in Egypt, and thus produce a better atmosphere for a negotiated settlement of their disagreements.

The most immediate difficulty in Turkish-Egyptian relations at the time emerged from the so-called Fez Incident between Mustafa Kemal and the Egyptian ambassador to Turkey. The crisis began when at the end of a celebratory

---

25 "Mansure Bayram Yaptı" [Mansura celebrated], *Cumhuriyet*, 30 March 1933, pp. 1–2.
26 "Keriman Hanım Mısırdan Avdet Etti" [Ms. Keriman returned from Egypt], *Cumhuriyet*, 20 May 1933, p. 3; Mekki Sait, "Dedikodulu Mısır Seferi: Keriman Ece Gördüklerini Anlatıyor ...", *Yedigün*, no. 12, 31 May 1933, p. 14.

reception for the diplomatic corps, held by the Turkish government in Ankara on the occasion of Turkey's Republic Day in late October 1932, the president of the republic instructed that the headgear of the Egyptian ambassador should be removed and be taken away. Whether this was a friendly and good-humored request or a rude and undiplomatic order became a matter of dispute between the two governments. Initially the two sides sought to hide the incident from the public, but once reports about it were published in the London press in mid-November, with follow-ups in the Egyptian press, it soon escalated into a diplomatic spat between Cairo and Ankara. On the Egyptian side, accusations were made that Mustafa Kemal had no right to enforce the Turkish prohibition against wearing the fez on the Egyptian ambassador. The red headgear with the tassel had been banned in Turkey since 1925, but its equivalent, the *tarbush*, was proudly worn by the majority of the Egyptian elite and was considered by many of them as a national headgear.[27] The encounter between Mustafa Kemal and the Egyptian ambassador was therefore presented in the Egyptian press as an arrogant attack on Egypt's national honor. The Egyptian government thus demanded an official apology and assurances that similar incidents will not occur in the future. Turkey refused to issue an apology. And once Ankara decided in early December that the Egyptian press was crossing the line with personal attacks on Mustafa Kemal, the Turkish press began launching acerbic attacks on the Egyptian government regarding its temerity in allowing wild criticism of Turkey's leader and national hero. Relations appeared to be deteriorating fast. The Egyptian ambassador was called back to Cairo for consultations, and for weeks there was chatter that the two countries might even break off their diplomatic relations over the incident. Neither of the governments was interested in that eventually, nor was the British government, which was still the informal colonial overlord of Egypt. Finally, after long weeks of tensions a solution was worked out. Turkey did not issue any formal apology, but it reassured Egypt that in future it would respect the diplomatic prerogatives of its representatives in Turkey. By mid-January 1933 the affair was declared closed and the popular press reported that the brotherly relations between the two nations have been restored. And yet, tensions continued to simmer between the two governments in the aftermath of the crisis and in the weeks before Keriman Halis arrived in Egypt in early February.[28]

---

27 For a discussion of the controversy in Egypt regarding whether the *tarbush* should be considered the national headgear, see Jacob, Wilson Chaco, *Working Out Egypt* (Durham, NC: Duke University Press, 2011), pp. 186–92.

28 Şimşir, Bilal N., *Doğu'nun Kahramanı Atatürk* [Hero of the East: Atatürk] (Ankara: Bilgi Yayınevi, 1999), pp. 257–327; "al-Ghazi Mustafa Kemal Basha wa-al-tarbush" [The Gazi Mustafa Kemal Pasha and the fez], *al-Ahram*, 12 November 1932, p. 4; Abdullah Husayn,

The crisis over the fez in fact masked more serious reasons for tensions between the two governments, which went far beyond a diplomatic *faux pas*. To a degree they were partially the result of personal antipathy of King Fuad of Egypt toward Mustafa Kemal. But much more profoundly, they were the result of Turkey's attempts to assert its position as a major power in the Eastern Mediterranean, and the reluctance of the quasi-independent Egyptian government to support these ambitions and its unwillingness to afford the Kemalist republic a number of extraterritorial legal prerogatives that had been enjoyed by various European nations since Ottoman times.

Indeed, one of the bitterest disagreements between the two governments stemmed from Turkey's demand to be afforded capitulatory rights in Egypt. These agreements allowed citizens of signatory nations, the vast majority of them European, various special rights including exemption from the regular Egyptian judicial system and laws. Kemalist Turkey highlighted the abolition of similar Ottoman agreements as one of the greatest achievements of the republic. At the same time, Turkey insisted that although it was in favor of the abolition of all the capitulatory agreements in Egypt too, the extraterritorial prerogatives they entailed should in the meanwhile be extended to Turkish citizens in Egypt as well. Ankara protested that as things stood in the early 1930s, citizens of countries such as Italy, Greece, Denmark and Spain enjoyed unfair legal advantages and many more rights than those of Turkey. Cairo declined Ankara's demands. The Egyptian government refused to expand the application of the capitulatory agreements at a time in which their abolition was a central demand of all its political parties.[29] Furthermore, the Turkish case was particularly sensitive because of the long and broad social, economic, and cultural bonds between Anatolia and the Land of the Nile. Had Egypt budged, there were tens of thousands people in Egypt who could have potentially claimed Turkish citizenship and the jurisdiction of the Turkish secular legal codes rather than the Egyptian Islamic-based laws and regulations. Indeed, Turkey made a very explicit demand that its citizens in Egypt would not be subject to the sharia-based family law.[30]

"al-'alaqat bayna Misr wa Turkiya" [The Turkish-Egyptian relations], *al-Ahram*, 18 December 1932, p. 1; "Kardeş Mısır ve Türk Milletleri" [The fraternal Egyptian and Turkish Nations], *Cumhuriyet*, 9 January 1933, p. 1; "Taswiyat hadithat al-tarbush bayna Misr wa-Turkiya" [The settlement of the fez incident between Egypt and Turkey], *al-Ahram*, 16 January 1933, p. 7.

29 Brown, Nathan J., *The Rule of Law in the Arab World* (New York: Cambridge University Press, 1997), pp. 40–3.

30 The National Archives, London (hereafter TNA), FO 371/17029/904, Campbell to Simon, 1 April 1933.

The Egyptian government did not want to see the emergence of a new colony of foreign citizens whereas Turkey appeared to be encouraging such an eventuality. From an Egyptian perspective there were more than enough communities with foreign nationalities in Egypt as it was, such as the substantial Greek and Italian colonies. The possibility of Egyptians with Turkish ties opting for Turkish citizenship was even more worrying because of the economic and social importance of the so-called Turco-Circassian elite in Egypt, which the ruling family itself was part of. The establishment of Turkish benevolent societies in Egypt's major cities by residents with claims to Turkish citizenship appeared as part of a groundwork toward the establishment of a formal Turkish colony in Egypt. These benevolent societies played a central role in organizing and funding Keriman Halis's visit to Egypt.

Tensions resulting from Turkey's demand of capitulatory rights and their rejection were compounded by Egyptian steps to prevent the flow of significant *waqf* funds to Turkey. In Ottoman times, the revenue of significant Islamic endowments in Egypt were endowed by wealthy benefactors to support of various educational and charitable institutions in Anatolia. But in the interwar period the Egyptian government was taking steps to nationalize the *waqf* properties in order to channel any funds and revenues from them toward national goals set by the government. This was in fact in line with similar policies adopted by the Kemalist government from the early days of the republic. However, Ankara was very displeased when the Egyptian government began diverting toward local causes revenues of *waqf* properties in Egypt that were formerly supporting Istanbul University and a number of other institutions in the old Ottoman capital. Indeed, the issue came to a head in early 1933, with the Turkish government appealing to Britain to help in dissuading the Egyptian government from perusing a policy that disadvantaged Turkish institutions, but to no avail.[31]

The confluence of legal, financial, and political disagreements between the two governments was perhaps best epitomized in the controversy surrounding the Egyptian Prince Ahmed Sayf al-Din. He was a member of the Mehmed Ali (Muhammad 'Ali) dynasty and the former brother-in-law of King Fuad through his first wife. In 1898, as the marriage of then-prince Fuad and his wife was coming undone, Sayf al-Din accused the future king of abusing his sister and tried to assassinate him. Fuad survived the gun shots with only a large scar, which did not prevent him from becoming the sultan of Egypt in 1917 and its

---

31 TNA, FO 371/15376/913, Turkey: Annual report for 1930, 18 February 1931; TNA, FO 371/17029/904, Campbell to Simon, 1 April 1933; TNA, FO 141/764/1, Clerk to Simon, 13 May 1933.

king in 1922. His assailant was arrested and soon declared mentally infirm. In 1900 he was sent to England for indefinite institutionalization in a mental asylum. Prince Sayf al-Din remained confined to the psychiatric institution for more than a quarter of a century. All the while, his very substantial inheritance was entrusted to the administration of the Egyptian government. In 1925, however, the prince's Istanbul-based mother and her Turkish husband organized the escape of the long-term mental patient out of the institute and his travel across the English Channel and European borders all the way to Turkey. The Turkish government issued the travel documents for the now middle aged Egyptian prince. He was subsequently given legal status and residency rights in Turkey. Shortly thereafter his mother launched in Egypt a legal claim for sole guardianship over her son's substantial inheritance, yet again with backing and assistance from the Turkish government. Even as the legal proceedings were yet to take their course, Turkey awarded the prince full citizenship in 1927 despite the opposition of the Egyptian government and royal family. Cairo interpreted these moves as an attempt to stake a claim to significant properties in Egypt and as a dangerous precedent that might be repeated with other wealthy members of the royal family. The affair became more complicated still when Sayf al-Din was hurriedly married to a much younger Turkish woman, and claiming that he had regained his healthy mental state, lawyers on the couple's behalf launched a new legal case to restore all his properties to his control. The case became a major bone of contention between Egypt and Turkey, both because of the substantial inheritance at stake and because of the more general debate on whether members of the Egyptian royal family could assume Turkish citizenship and lay claim to properties in Egypt.[32]

The Egyptian government's suspicions about Turkey's intentions were further intensified because of Ankara's seemingly cozy relations with the most serious challenger to the Egyptian throne. Abbas Hilmi II, the former Khedive of Egypt who was deposed by the British government in 1914 because of suspicions about his loyalties during the Great War, maintained through the 1920s his claim to the rule of Egypt. The ex-Khedive divided his time between Turkey, Italy, Switzerland, and France. The Turkish government issued him residency and travel papers, which his uncle, King Fuad of Egypt, did not appreciate at all. The tensions were eased only in 1931, when the King and his nephew finally reached a compromise agreement. Abbas Hilmi formally dropped his claim

---

[32] "Egypt", *The Times* (London), 9 May 1898, p. 8; "Telegrams in Brief", *The Times*, 24 September 1925, p. 11; "The affairs of Prince Seif-Ed-Din", *The Times*, 3 November 1928, p. 11; Al-Sayyid Marsot, Afaf Lutfi, *Egypt's Liberal Experiment, 1922–1936* (Berkeley: University of California Press, 1977), pp. 110, 124; TNA, FO 141/760/8, Loraine to Simon, 13 December 1933.

to the Egyptian throne in May, and in return was granted Egyptian citizenship and a generous stipend from the Egyptian treasury.[33] King Fuad and his government believed that the agreement amounted to full retirement of the ex-Khedive from political life. They were therefore shocked and angered when only a few months later he mounted a public campaign for the throne of Syria with Turkey's encouragement and backing.[34]

In 1932 Turkey was concerned that the newly independent King of Iraq might be able to convince France to implement a political arrangement that would unite Syria and Iraq under his rule. This turned out to be a pipe dream. The French government had at the time no intention to transform Syria into a monarchy, and certainly not to reinstate King Faisal whom France had expelled from Damascus in 1920 and viewed as a British puppet. Nevertheless, as long as these possibilities appeared to be on the diplomatic table in early 1932, Turkey decided to promote the candidacy of a person it viewed as more amenable to its interests. Ankara did not want a British ally in a position of power in Syria, nor the political unification of Syria and Iraq and the establishment of a potentially powerful pan-Arab polity south of its borders. Abbas Hilmi was a well-known antagonist of the British, neither a member of Faisal's Hashemite family nor on friendly terms with his uncle the King of Egypt, and with a proven track record of cordial relations with Ankara. The Kemalist government thus saw him as a good candidate to serve as a spoiler for any design the British or pan-Arabists might have on uniting Syria with neighboring countries. Abbas Hilmi was duly invited to Ankara to meet with Mustafa Kemal and Prime Minister İsmet İnönü. Thereafter, he embarked on a tour of Palestine, Transjordan, Iraq, and Syria in an effort to garner support for his candidacy. The maneuvering enraged the Egyptian government in general and King Fuad in particular. They viewed the ex-Khedive's actions as a breach of the agreement of 1931 and blamed Turkey for it. Egyptian diplomats were instructed to communicate that displeasure to Ankara and ask that it cease its support for the Abbas Hilmi's candidacy. In response, the Turkish Foreign Ministry feigned surprise at the Egyptian displeasure, pretending to have expected King Fuad to be happy that one of his relatives might become the monarch of a neighboring country. The whole affair eventually became a moot point once the French

---

[33] "Yeni Bir Mücadele" [A new clash], *Cumhuriyet*, 19 January 1930, p. 1; "Eski Hidiv Mısır Kralı Mı Olmak İstiyor?" [Does the ex-Khedive want to be the King of Egypt?], *Cumhuriyet*, 2 August 1930, p. 3; "The throne of Egypt", *The Times* (London), 13 May 1931, p. 15; "Sabık Hidiv" [The ex-Khedive], *Cumhuriyet*, 22 July 1931, p. 3.

[34] 'Azmi, Mahmud, *Khabaya Siyasiya* [Political Mysteries] (Cairo: Jaridat al-Masri, 1939), pp. 96–8.

government clarified it had no intention to make any radical changes in Syria's political order. But the months-long affair added a lingering bitter taste to the already strained relations between Cairo and Ankara, only a few months before the Fez Incident and Keriman Halis's visit to Egypt.[35]

The tensions and mutual suspicions between the two states were palpable but by the early 1930s Turkey had a growing interest in improving the relations. The most immediate incentive was Ankara's desire to increase its mainly agricultural exports to Egypt at a time when the Turkish economy faced increasing challenges in the wake of the global economic crisis. Turkey exported to Egypt substantial volumes of tobacco, fruits, timber, and animal products. In the late 1920s, however, the volume and value of trade between the two sides decreased steadily, as both Egypt and Turkey were expanding their trade ties with other markets. The Turkish exports to Egypt thus declined from an estimated value of 6.5 million TL in 1925 to only 3 million TL in 1932. Turkish imports from Egypt declined even more dramatically during the same period, from an estimated value of 6 million TL in 1925 to less than 1.5 million in 1932. In view of the general deterioration in Turkey's exports to more important markets in Europe in the wake of the global economic crisis, Ankara was seeking to reverse the trend in its trade relations with Egypt.[36] In 1930, Turkey inaugurated a new steamship line between Istanbul and Alexandria, by way of İzmir and Piraeus. To increase the number of passengers and volumes of trade on its ships, the Turkish government by had 1933 opened in Alexandria an office of its Department of Exports, a branch of its state-owned bank, and a bureau of its semi-official travel and tourism agency. Because the Fez Incident threatened to derail these efforts, only days after it was resolved the Turkish government dispatched to Egypt a senior official in charge of economic affairs. Ankara was exploring the signing of a trade agreement that would decrease tariffs and custom dues, particularly on tobacco and opium, two of its most lucrative export commodities. The trade in opium was suffering additional difficulties because of Egyptian and British suspicions and informal accusations that the Turkish government was involved in the smuggling of other derivative drugs from the opium poppy,

---

35 "Gazi Hz. Abbas Hilmi Pş.yı Kabul Ettiler" [His Excellency the Gazi receives Abbas Hilmi Paşa], *Cumhuriyet*, 10 December 1931, p. 3; "Abbas Hilmi Pş.", *Cumhuriyet*, 6 January 1932, p. 1; "Abbas Hilmi Pş. Beyrut'tan Kudüs'e Hareket Etti" [Abbas Hilmi Paşa left Beirut en route to Jerusalem], *Cumhuriyet*, 28 December 1931, p. 3; "Abbas Hilmi Pş.", *Cumhuriyet*, 8 January 1932, p. 1; "Suriye Krallığı" [The Syrian monarchy], *Cumhuriyet*, 13 January 1932, p. 2; TNA, FO 371/16086/226, Loraine to Simon, 5 March 1932; TNA, FO 1011/61, Loraine to Simon, 16 March 1934.

36 Conker, Orhan, *Les chemins de fer en Turquie et la politique ferroviaire turque* (Paris: Librairie du Recueil Sirey, 1935), pp. 148–50.

or at least was turning a blind eye to the smugglers. Negotiations opened in 1931 failed to lead to an agreement largely because of the negative effects of the tensions between the two governments, but Turkey hoped that it might be reached in the wake of the Fez Incident as part of a broader effort to patch over the disagreements between the two sides.[37]

It was within this context of Turkish efforts to shore up relations with Egypt that Keriman Halis's visit to Egypt was initiated. Official Turkey and its surrogates in the organized Turkish community in Egypt viewed it as an opportunity to clear the heavy atmosphere in the relations between the two countries and thus facilitate the negotiations over important political, legal, and economic agreements with Egypt. The visit was seen at the same time as an opportunity to put a proverbial beautiful face on Kemalist Turkey and in the process energize pro-Kemalist elements in the Egyptian elites who were impressed and inspired by its reforms and accomplishments in general and its steps toward the emancipation of women in particular, as well as help galvanize the Turkish community and its social institutions in Egypt. The way the Turkish beauty queen was received in the Land of the Nile suggests that in Egypt too there was significant support for the efforts to improve the relations between the two states and societies.

Once Keriman Halis arrived in Egypt the reports on alleged Turkish slights to the Egyptian headgear indeed gave way to discussions of Turkish female fashion and beauty. The saturation of the Egyptian press with celebrity-type news reporting set a much less tense atmosphere than in the previous weeks when reports on crisis in the relations with Turkey dominated the news in Egypt. The social events organized in the beauty queen's honor by charitable organizations of the Turkish colony were well attended and were occasions for the celebration of their ethnic identity at a time in which Turkey hoped to gain for them a legal status of recognized foreign community with full capitulatory privileges. The Egyptian press did its part in publicizing these events as being hosted by the "Turkish colony" (*al-Jaliyya al-Turkiyya*) in Egypt's major cities. In the short term the visit was thus a great success that surprised even its organizers, as evidenced by its extension from a few days to three months.

At the same time, the causes for tension and disagreement between Turkey and Egypt were serious enough that the improved atmosphere failed to pave the way for any major bilateral agreement. It would take the emergence of Fascist Italy as a common threat following the invasion of Ethiopia in 1935, the

---

37 TNA, FO 141/751/16, Clerk to Henderson, 22 July 1931; "İbrahim Tali Bey Kahire'ye Gitti" [İbrahim Tali Bey travelled to Cairo], *Cumhuriyet*, 9 January 1933, p. 1; "Bayna Turkiya wa-Misr" [Between Turkey and Egypt], *al-Ahram*, 19 February 1933, p. 6.

death of King Fuad in 1936, and most importantly the granting of formal independence to Egypt in the wake of the Anglo-Egyptian treaty of 1936, to lead to a Turkish-Egyptian rapprochement. The two sides signed a treaty of friendship in 1937 and a number of agreements that settled their disagreements on various legal and trade issues. In 1938 the Turkish Foreign Minister visited Egypt and in 1939 the two countries took initial steps towards cooperation between their armies. Although several causes of tension persisted, such as the Egyptian king's toying with the idea of reviving the Caliphate and Egyptian suspicions towards Turkey's intentions in the Middle East, the bilateral relations between the two countries appeared on a path of improvement in the late 1930s, before World War II and its aftermath helped push them in very different geopolitical directions. The subsequent decades, in which Turkey distanced itself from the Middle East during the Cold War, were crucial in reshaping perceptions regarding the engagement of the republic with the region during the interwar period. Keriman Halis's visit to Egypt was only a small part in a larger puzzle of Turkish engagement in the Middle East in the interwar period based on pragmatic evaluation of the region's importance to Turkey's interests, even as the Kemalist government was implementing an ideological agenda that sought Turkey's social and cultural dissociation from the region. At the same time, even as Arab nationalist and Islamist ideological currents that were skeptical of Kemalism or outright hostile to it were on the rise in Egypt, it did not lack supporters either in 1930s Egypt. Keriman Halis's visit and the events surrounding it suggest that some assumptions regarding the rapid and willful dissociation between Turkey and the Middle East in the interwar period may need to be reassessed and recalibrated.

CHAPTER 8

Taking Health to the Village: Early Turkish Republican Health Propaganda in the Countryside

Ebru Boyar

In the second volume of his *Anadolu Notları* (Notes on Anatolia), which was first published in 1966, the famous novelist of the late Ottoman and early Republican period, Reşat Nuri Güntekin, describes the fight against flies and the popular attitude towards these creatures in an Anatolian town in 1935. Flies were regarded as one of the main transmitters of a range of diseases, in particular the devastating eye trachoma, known also as the Egyptian eye disease ("Mısır göz ağrısı"[1] or "Mısır göz hastalığı"[2]), which led to blindness. The disease was rampant, especially in southern and south-eastern Anatolia.[3] The fight against flies was thus vital but also very difficult, as Reşat Nuri Güntekin's account of his observations clearly demonstrates. In the small Anatolian town he describes, the municipality forced every shop to have a fly trap into which flies were enticed by a small piece of meat placed inside it. The municipality checked these traps "once or twice a day" to make sure that the shopkeepers were abiding by the municipal order. However

> As darkness fell and the time to close the shops arrived, the tradesmen took the traps outside into the street and released into the night air a cloud of the tens of thousands of flies which had been collected. Thus we performed our civic duty by carrying out the order of the municipality.

---

1 Duru, Dr. Muhittin Celal, *Sağlık Bakımından Köy ve Köycülük* [The Village from the Viewpoint of Health] (Cümhuriyet Halk Partisi Yayını, Klavuz Kitapları: VII) (Ankara: Sümer Matbaası, 1941), p. 194.
2 *Trahom Hakkında Halka Nesayih* [Advice to People about Trachoma] (Sıhhiye ve Muaveneti İçtimaiye Vekaleti Neşriyatından) (Dersaadet: Hilal Matbaası, 1340 [1924]), p. 3; Dr. Nuri Fehmi, *İnsanı Kör Eden Hastalıklardan Trahom Halk Kitabı* [A Popular Book about Trachoma, One of the Diseases that Blinds People] (Istanbul: Kader Matbaası, 1930), p. 5.
3 Ayberk, Nuri, *Türkiyede Trahom Mücadelesi* [The Fight against Trachoma in Turkey] (Istanbul: Kader Matbaası, 1936), p. 5.

After that the matter was one for our own conscience. Render unto Caesar what is Caesar's, and unto God what is God's.[4]

Güntekin rather cynically suggested that in order to prevent the shopkeepers from releasing the flies, that the government should pay them a small reward for every kilo of flies, as some municipalities paid for dead mice and dog tails. In this case, in Güntekin's opinion, the shopkeepers would abandon this 'charitable act' of freeing flies for the sake of profit and "the compassionate tradesmen would hand over to the municipality not only the flies but also, without noticing that they had by accident fallen into the traps, their own fathers".[5]

Although it remains unknown whether such a material incentive would have worked or not, this anecdote demonstrates that the successful implementation of such health policies depended not only on a sufficient body of capable health care personnel, medical infrastructure including hospitals and equipment, a developed sanitary system, a legal framework and the coercive force of the state, but also on the wholehearted cooperation of the population, which was key in any aspect of Republican governance. While the early Republican period is often presented in terms of clear-cut dichotomies, with the state and society clearly delineated one from the other, and a dominating role given to the state, conceived often as having the power to impose its will on a hostile population, this was in fact very much not the case. In contrast, this was a period of constant negotiation between state and society whereby the state sought to gain the support of its population and by so doing to ensure legitimacy for its government and the nation state building process. State health policies and public health practices are a particularly stark example of the state's inability to enforce policy and its reliance on winning support, particulary crucial in an area which involved intervention into the private lives of its citizens. The success of any improvement of health care thus depended largely on the state's success in being able to persuade the populace to buy into the new concepts of public health, to adopt them and to become willing propagators of such policies to the wider community.

The majority of this target population lived in small towns and villages. In the words of Dr. Zeki Nasır, who was a regular contributor to *Ülkü*, the journal of *Halkevleri* (People's Houses), "three quarters of the human capital of Turkey

---

4   Güntekin, Reşat Nuri, "Sinekler" [Flies], in *Anadolu Notları* [Notes on Anatolia], II (Istanbul: İnkılâp ve Aka Kitabevleri, 1966), pp. 28–30. The first volume of his observations of Anatolia was published in 1936 and the second volume was published for the first time in 1966.
5   Güntekin, "Sinekler", p. 31.

lives, produces, works and struggles in villages".[6] According to the 1935 census results, 12,355,376 Turkish citizens out of 16,157,450 lived in rural areas.[7] This figure represented 76.5 per cent of the entire population. According to the Ministry of Health and Social Assistance figures, by 1941, excluding Hatay, the number of villages was 37,941.[8] The most urbanized province (*vilayet*) of interwar Turkey was Istanbul, 85.5 per cent of whose population lived in the city centre and the towns attached to it. Istanbul was followed by İzmir of which 48 per cent of the population lived in urban areas. In the rest of the Turkish provinces, including Ankara (with only 23.9 per cent of its population in urban areas), less than 30 percent of the population lived in urban areas.[9] In reality, ever the majority of settlements described as 'urban' were not much more than villages.[10]

The most pressing problems for this mostly rural population were the rampant nature of diseases and poor living conditions which had dramatically lowered living standards and life expectancy. In response, the Ankara government had established the Ministry of Health and Social Assistance as early as 1920 during the Turkish National Liberation War (1919–1922) and before the establishment of the new republic. It had set out to develop public health policies and had prepared an extensive survey on health conditions in the areas under its control.

The new republic, however, suffered heavily from insufficient funds and health personnel. This led the government to develop a two-tier strategy which had a comprehensive legal and medical approach. On the one hand, policy makers saw their fight against disease as a total war covering the whole country, but, on the other, due to the limited resources, the campaign was focused on specific diseases and specific regions. Thus, certain areas became malaria, syphilis or trachoma zones and the majority of the funds and personnel were used there and their inhabitants provided with free medical care and drugs. Even though such diseases existed in other parts of the country, the state, both the central government and the municipalities, were not in a position to reach everywhere and/or to afford health services throughout. In consequence, in

---

6   Dr. Zeki Nasır, "Köylerimizin Sağlık İşleri" [The Health Issues of Our Villages], *Ülkü Halkevleri Mecmuası*, 2/7 (August 1933), p. 42.
7   Duru, *Köy ve Köycülük*, pp. 9–10.
8   Duru, *Köy ve Köycülük*, p. 16.
9   "Umum Nüfus Sayımının Son Neticeleri" [The last results of the general population census], *Belediyeler Dergisi*, 1/7 (December 1935), pp. 71–2.
10 See *Belediyeler* [Municipalities] (T.C. Dahiliye Vekâleti Mahallî İdareler Umum Müdürlüğü) (Istanbul: Holivut Matbaası, 1933).

some parts of the country doctors were a rare sight. An old peasant in the village of Saraycık in Kırşehir in central Anatolia remarked to the governor of Kırşehir, M. Saylam, who was touring the villages of the region in the spring of 1937: "I have got to this age and I have only seen the face of a doctor once. And he was only in our village because of the investigation of a murder".[11] Although in the interwar years there was a steady increase in the number of health personnel, these were far from sufficient and this was particularly so in the case of doctors.[12] Furthermore, for many doctors, even 'god forsaken' Anatolian towns, quite apart from villages, were not attractive destinations. During discussions in 1923 on the law for compulsory service for doctors (*Etibbanın Hizmet-i Mecburesi Kanunu*, no. 369) just after their graduation from the medical school, the Minister of Health and Social Assistance, Refik Bey (Saydam), explained that the impelling reason behind acceptance of this law was the fact that of the 380 or 390 *kaza*s (administrative districts) in the country, 150 or 160 were constantly without doctors, such jobs remaining vacant because however much extra salary and funds were given to these areas, doctors would not go because of the poor conditions of life there.[13] For Talat Bey, MP for Ardahan, this represented a major impediment to gaining the trust of the population. Claiming that doctors appointed to Ardahan either escaped from the town on the day they arrived or turned back half way to the province, he voiced his constituents' complaints: "Since we were joined to Turkey [Ardahan was returned to Turkey in 1921], will we not see a doctor?",[14] a complaint which could even have undermined Republican rule in Ardahan. The law was passed and as a result doctors were required to do two years of compulsory service in the country after graduation from medical school.[15] However, even after the enactment of

---

11 Saylam, M., *Köylüler Arasında 1* [Among Villagers 1] (Kırşehir: Kırşehir Basımevi, 1937), pp. 20–1.
12 For the numbers of health personnel employed in the Turkish public sector in the interwar years, for example see *İstatistik Yıllığı Üçüncü Cilt 1930* [Statistical Yearbook Third Volume 1930] (Istanbul: Ahmet İhsan Matbaası Limited, 1930), p. 121; *Dördüncü Cilt 1930/1931* [Fourth Volume 1930/1031] (Ankara: Hüsnütabiat Matbaası, 1931), p. 137; *Cilt/Volume 5 1931/32* [Volume 5 1931/32] (Ankara: Devlet Matbaası, n.d.), p. 131 and *Cilt 8 1935/36* [Volume 8 1935/36] (Ankara: Devlet Basımevi, n.d.), p. 144.
13 T.B.M.M. *Zabıt Ceridesi*, Devre: II, İçtima Senesi: 1, 29 Teşrin-i evvel 1339 (1923), Monday, p. 87.
14 T.B.M.M. *Zabıt Ceridesi*, Devre: II, İçtima Senesi: 1, 29 Teşrin-i evvel 1339 (1923), Monday, pp. 86–7.
15 In 1933, this law was amended and only those who were funded by the state and stayed in Leyli Tıp Talebe Yurdu had to perform compulsory service. The duration of this service was two-thirds of the period of their medical education. *Vekâletin 10 Yıllık Mesaisi* [Ten

the law, keeping doctors in the locations to which they had been appointed was not always possible.[16]

Apart from the problems of personnel, the fight against disease was an expensive venture,[17] particularly since the majority of medical equipment and drugs were imported. Although in time the state succeeded in producing the vaccines and serums essential for use against various widespread diseases, essential drugs such as quinine, atebrine and neosalvarsan had still to be procured from the international market. Quinine was imported and sold at a reduced price through Ziraat Bankası (the state agricultural bank) and in tobacco shops,[18] except in malaria zones where it was distributed free or on some occasions when malaria incidents had increased in rural areas.[19] Given that malaria was rampant all over the country, the fact that quinine had to be bought, even at a reduced price, could still make it unaffordable and thus unavailable for much of the population who needed it. This at least was the observation of a young idealistic member of the Milli Türk Talebe Birliği (National Turkish Students Association) who described how in a malaria-ridden village near İzmir which was not a part of a designated malaria zone, a woman begged him and his friends for quinine, saying "Sirs, you are from the city, you must have quinine in your pockets. For the love of God give me one or two tablets".[20] During World War II, even money did not remedy the scarcity of quinine and atabrine.[21]

Under these dire conditions, the need for the support of the population was essential to ensure that villagers followed their treatment regularly, thus preventing wastage of state resources and ensuring that diseases were either

---

Years Work of the Ministry], *Sıhhiye Mecmuası* (Türkiye Cümhuriyeti Sıhhat ve İçtimaî Muavenet Vekâleti), Special Issue (29 October 1933), pp. 26–7.

16   Emin Türk, "Köyümde Ne Gördüm" [What did I see in my village?], *Resimli Ay*, No. 10 (December 1929), pp. 8–9.

17   No Author, "Cumhuriyetin Sağlık, Bakım ve Yardım İşleri" [Health, care and assistance work of the republic], *Ülkü Halkevleri Mecmuası*, 2/9 (October 1933), p. 256.

18   Gönen, Dr. Remzi, *Sıtma Nedir? Nasıl Korunulur?* [What is Malaria, How to be Protected from It?] (Mersin Halkevi Sağlık Öğütler Serisi Sayı: 1) (Mersin: Yeni Mersin Matbaası, 1934), p. 9.

19   "İzmirde Sıtma ve Otomatik Telefon" [Malaria and the automatic telephone in İzmir], *Akşam*, 9 August 1929.

20   *Gezi Notları. Çanakkale-Bolayır, İzmir Köyleri, Orta Anadolu* [Travel Notes. Çanakkale-Bolayır, Villages of İzmir, Central Anatolia] (Milli Türk Talebe Birliği Yayımlarından Bitik No. 2) (Istanbul: Asri Basımevi, 1935), pp. 54–5.

21   *Sıtmadan Nasıl Korunacağız?* [How will We be Protected from Malaria?] (Sıhhiye ve İçtimai Muavenet Vekaletinden No. 86) (Ankara: n.p., 1943), p. 2.

prevented or contained. Such cooperation between the state and the society was highlighted by Dr. Zeki Nasır who wrote in 1933 that "in the civilised world today, state and society work in cooperation in all health and social matters. It is due to this cooperation that a nation's health, wealth and welfare increase".[22] In the same year, in the special issue of *Sıhhiye Mecmuası* celebrating the tenth anniversary of the declaration of the republic, the importance of the population's taking an active part in health matters was once more highlighted: "When this hygiene culture of the population increases, which it can be seen with pleasure has already begun, everyone will work harder to protect their own health and that of those around them and this will make the work of the state in health matters easier".[23]

This understanding already formed the backbone of the new republic's health strategy. In an interview given by the Minister of Health and Social Assistance, Refik Bey on 22 March 1921, the minister underlined the importance of social awareness and of society's support for the fight against syphilis, another rampant disease which decimated the Anatolian population:

> For the struggle with this [disease] the outcome absolutely cannot be assured by relying on medicine and doctors alone and by expecting hope only from them. It is necessary to add advice related to the family and the environment to the medical advice about the containment of contagion and damage resulting from the disease. It is important to understand that it is social organisation that most eases the work of the doctors. The organisation and order which are appearing for the good in our social strata will ease our work and will give the greatest assistance in the struggle with the diseases which threaten us today and in defeating them.[24]

Fighting against the Popular Mind-Set

Before all else, the state had to ensure that the population took their health conditions seriously, believed in the necessity of preventive public health measures and the benefits of modern medicine, and also abandoned popular

---

22 Zeki Nasır, "Halk Sıhhati" [Public health], *Ülkü Halkevleri Mecmuası*, 1/1 (February 1933), p. 74.
23 *Vekâletin 10 Yıllık Mesaisi*, p. 4.
24 "Refik Bey'le Mülakat" [Interview with Refik Bey], *Hakimiyet-i Milliye*, 22 March 1921, in *Türk Devrimi Mülakatları* [Interviews of the Turkish Revolution], ed. Sabahattin Özel and Işıl Çakan Hacıibrahimoğlu (Istanbul: Türkiye İş Bankası Yayınları, 2011), pp. 217–18.

superstitions and folk medicine. This was not an easy task. While both the republican and late Ottoman governments regarded syphilis, for instance, as one of the most devastating contagious diseases which, together with malaria, trachoma and tuberculosis, ravaged Anatolia, for most of the Anatolian populace this disease was not of such great concern. According to a booklet prepared by the Bursa Halkevi, the symptoms of syphilis, wounds or boils on mouth, lips, tongue and throat, were not taken seriously at all by the population, who simply regarded them as "some type of mouth sore" and carried on regardless.[25] Twenty odd years before this publication, the journalist Ahmed Şerif had visited various parts of the province of Kastamonu for his newspaper *Tanin* and had noted that the local population had "no feeling of disgust and hatred" for syphilis, which they referred to as "the disease 'that wanders from house to house'".[26] For them, syphilis was an ordinary occurrence of life and they were surprised about the state's interest in their painless, inconsequential boils. A similar attitude was evident over the first symptoms of trachoma, according to the 1933 educational booklet on the disease, which states that "the majority of ignorant people do not take seriously this disease which begins painlessly. They thus pay no attention to small burning and throbbing sensations. The disease begins to develop at full speed".[27] Similarly, the first symptoms of "şark çıbanı", oriental sore, also known as Aleppo boil (cutaneous leishmaniasis) which was rampant in Diyarbakır, Mardin, Urfa, Siirt, Maraş, Gaziantep, Elazığ and Malatya and transmitted by insects especially sand flies, flies and mosquitos, were ignored as the first appearance of oriental sore on the skin showed itself as a small red or pink mark which was taken as an unimportant flee or mosquito bite.[28]

Even when people took their diseases seriously, there was a dramatic lack of correct information about the nature of the diseases and how they were transmitted. This led the population to create their own medical information. Dr. Muhittin Celal Duru, who served as a Director of Health Propaganda and

---

25 *Zührevi Hastalıklar Nelerdir?* [What are Venereal Diseases?] (Bursa Halkevi Neşriyatı 9) (Bursa: Yeni Basımevi, 1937), p. 5.
26 Quoted in Boyar, Ebru, "'An inconsequential boil' or a 'terrible disease?' Social perceptions of and state responses to syphilis in the late Ottoman empire", *Turkish Historical Review*, 2/2 (2011), p. 112.
27 *Gözleri Kör Eden Trahom Hastalığı Hakkında Halka Nasihatler* [Advice to the Public about the Disease of Trachoma which Blinds Eyes] (Sıhhat ve İctimaî Muavenet Vekâleti Neşriyatından, No. 33) (Istanbul: Kâatçılık ve Matbaacılık A.Ş., 1933), p. 2.
28 *Şark Çıbanı (Yıl Çıbanı)* [Oriental Sore] (Sıhhat ve İctimaî Muavenet Vekâleti Neşriyatından, No. 77) (Ankara: Uğur Basımevi, 1941), p. 2.

Medical Statistics,[29] argued that "the villagers are so stricken by malaria ... that in order not to get malaria they are suspicious of everything and they apply every remedy in order to be saved from it".[30] Malaria was believed to be caused by a multitude of everyday things: yoghurt, eggs, cucumbers which had gone off, dirty water, dry cold, a very hot wind, the *hamam*, unripe plums, junk food, and the foul smells which emanated from swamps.[31] Similarly, there was a widespread belief that gonorrhoea, 'belsoğukluğu' in Turkish, literally meaning 'back cold', was transmitted via the *hamam* or was a result of getting cold on one's back or simply of sleeping at night without a cover.[32]

Apart from ensuring that the populace believed in the importance of the symptoms of diseases, that they learned about the main causes of such diseases and avoided unsanitary conditions which led to such diseases, there was a pressing need to persuade people to stop following old remedies and superstitions in treating and preventing disease. Writing about village life in the late 1940s, Mahmut Makal, an idealistic village teacher and proud graduate of a village institute, vividly described how villagers took care of their illnesses:

> According to them, they have a great many medicines, and use them all. A person, for example, who is bleeding in some part of his body immediately sprinkles earth on the wound to stem the flow of blood. Anyone who is wounded somewhere or other makes a poultice of an animal's droppings, and binds the wound up. Anyone who falls a victim to tuberculosis eats the flesh of a dog. Any who catches cold, and those who think they have fallen victims of erysipelas, bury themselves in the

---

29 Başbakanlık Cumhuriyet Arşivi, Ankara (hereafter BCA), 30 11 1 0 174 6 11, 8 March 1945, and BCA, 30 11 1 0 181 8 14, 12 March 1946.
30 Duru, *Köy ve Köycülük*, p. 93.
31 Duru, *Köy ve Köycülük*, p. 93; *Sıtma* [Malaria] (Kayseri Mıntıkası Sıtma Mücadele Heyeti 2) (Kayseri: Sümer Matbaası, 1938), p. 3; Arıkan, Dr. İzzet, *Köylüler için Sıtma Hakkında Kısa Bilgiler* [Concise Information for Peasants about Malaria] (T.C. Trakya Umumî Müfettişliği Köy Bürosu Yayını Sayısı 37) (Istanbul: Halk Basımevi, 1936), pp. 6–7; *Sıtma. Sıtmayı İnsanlara Geçiren Sivrisineklerdir* [Malaria. Mosquitos Transmit Malaria to Human Beings] (T.C. Sıhhat ve İçtimaî Muavenet Vekaleti Neşriyatından No. 65) (Ankara: n.p., 1939), p. 1.
32 *Zührevi Hastalıklar Nelerdir?*, p. 10; *Zührevî Hastalıklar Müptelalarına Öğütler ve Tavsiyeler* [Advice and Recommendations to Those Suffering from Venereal Diseases] (T.C. Sıhhat ve İctimaî Muavenet Vekâleti Neşriyatından, No. 69) (Ankara: n.p., n.d.), p. 4; Dr. Reşit Galip, *Dört Azgın Canavar* [Four Ferocious Monsters] (Istanbul: Devlet Matbaası, 1929), p. 8.

still warm and smoking droppings of a horse or an ass, and lie down in them.[33]

Although, according to Reşit Galip, pioneering doctor, defender of ideas about the development of villages and revolutionary Minister of Education between 1932 and 1934,[34] such beliefs and remedies did not always directly harm patients, they did lead to delays in receiving proper treatment or to totally ignoring the ailment. Thus while carrying amulets marked with pigeon or blackbird blood or tying a cotton thread with three knots around the ankles and wrists in order to prevent or treat malaria might not have any impact, either good or bad, on the disease itself, it did give people false hope and encouraged them to ignore the correct treatment given by health personnel. Covering open wounds with dried ox dung or smearing blood drained from a donkey's ear on areas affected by the skin disease erysipelas, on the other hand, could lead to very serious poisonous infections.[35] Such practices were so widespread in Anatolia that many years after Reşit Galip's publication, they had still not died out. In Kurtpala village in Sivas, those who were afflicted with erysipelas were made to swallow the sloughed skin of a snake wrapped in a cigarette paper. The powder of the snake skin or ointments made from it were used for erysipelas and many other diseases and snakes, both their skins and flesh, were used to cure malaria.[36] In search for a cure, the population went in vain to extremes in consuming things because of their supposed curative effects. In Safranbolu, a town in the north-west of Anatolia, for instance, recipes for the treatment of tuberculosis included eating boiled cormorant prepared with dog suet and coffee, eating snails and frogs, drinking milk of a mare or a donkey and drinking turtle blood.[37]

---

33 Makal, Mahmut, *A Village in Anatolia*, trans. Sir Wyndam Deedes (London: Valentine, Mitchell & Co. Ltd., 1965), p. 177; for its original Turkish, see Makal, Mahmut, *Köyümden* [From My Village] (Istanbul: Varlık Yayınları, 1952), pp. 106–7.

34 Hüseyin Namık, "Kaybettiklerimiz: Reşit Galip" [Our losses: Reşit Galip], *Ülkü Halkevleri Mecmuası*, 3/14 (April 1934), pp. 88–91; Oruç, Yener, *Atatürk'ün "Fikir Fedaisi" Dr. Reşit Galip. Günümüz Gözüyle* [Atatürk's Faithful Intellectual Follower Doctor Reşit Galip. From Today's Perspective] (Istanbul: Gürer Yayınları, 2007).

35 Dr. Reşit Galip, *Sıhat Koruma Bilgisi* [Information About Protecting Health] (Maarif Vekâleti Halk Kitapları Serisi No 4) (Istanbul: Devlet Matbaası, 1929), pp. 14–15.

36 Başar, Zeki, *Halk Hekimliğinde ve Tıp Tarihinde Yılan* [The Snake in Folk Medicine and the History of Medicine] (Ankara: Atatürk Üniversitesi Diş Hekimliği Fakültesi Yayınları, 1978), pp. 18–20.

37 Barlas, Uğurol, *Safranbolu Halk Hekimliği* [Folk Medicine in Safranbolu] (Karabük: Özer Matbaası, n.d.), pp. 95–6.

There were also less gruesome remedies. Natural springs, present almost everywhere in Anatolia, were believed to be curative for malaria.[38] In some places, erysipelas was treated by putting an "erysipelas stone" (yılancık taşı), on the wound.[39] This stone was not only used as a cure but also, in some places, for diagnosis. In Sinop, for instance, this stone, treated with a religious reverence, was placed on the wound. If the stone stuck to the wound, the wound was diagnosed as erysipelas, if it did not stick, it was not erysipelas.[40]

Apart from such dubious remedies, folk medicine did use ingredients which formed part of medical treatments for diseases, but did so either preparing them incorrectly or in insufficient amounts. Widespread use was made of incense (*tütsü*) containing mercury[41] in the treatment of syphilis in Anatolia, but such remedies caused "much death and disability".[42] Such incense and ointments mixed with mercury were dangerous, useless or insufficient,[43] and in interwar Turkey there was an increasing use of bismuth compounds, arsenobenzol, neosalvarsan and solusalvarsan for the treatment of syphilis while the use of medically prepared mercury ointments and injections had considerably decreased.[44]

Creating a Healthy Environment

One major problem the state faced was how to wean the population off inappropriate or positively dangerous folk remedies and onto modern medicine. Although the republican government passed laws allowing health personnel to use force to compel people to have health checks and to undergo enforced

---

38   Arda, Ramiz, *O Günler. Anılar (1928–1945)* [Those Days. Memoirs (1928–1945)], ed. Mustafa Özcan (Konya: Palet Yayınları, 2014), pp. 45–7.
39   Örnek, Sedat Veyis, *Sıvas ve Çevresinde Hayatın Çeşitli Safhaları ile İlgili Bâtıl İnançların ve Büyüsel İşlemlerin Etnolojik Tetkiki* [Ethnological Study of Superstitions and Sorcery Concerning Various Phases of Life in Sivas and its Surroundings] (Ankara: Ankara Üniversitesi Basımevi, 1966), p. 112.
40   Tanyu, Hikmet, *Türklerde Taşla İlgili İnançlar* [Beliefs of Turks Related to Stones] (Ankara Üniversitesi İlâhiyat Fakültesi Yayınları: LXXXI) (Ankara: Ankara Üniversitesi Basımevi, 1968), p. 153.
41   For a recipe including mercury, see Barlas, *Safranbolu Halk Hekimliği*, p. 44.
42   Talimcıoğlu, Şükrü Kamil, *Belsoğukluğu, Zührevi Hastalıklar, Frengi* [Gonorrhoea, Venereal Diseases and Syphilis] (Istanbul: Tefeyyüz Kitabevi, n.d.), p. 171.
43   Barlas, *Safranbolu Halk Hekimliği*, p. 44.
44   Talimcıoğlu, *Belsoğukluğu, Zührevi Hastalıklar, Frengi*, p. 175.

treatment, even jailing them if they rejected or ignored this,[45] this was not a complete solution. Not only did the government not have sufficient armed forces at its disposal to enforce such measures, but also such a persistent heavy handed approach would have alienated the peasants who were already suspicious of any state authority due to their experience under the late Ottoman empire. This concern about alienating the population was very evident in the regulation concerning the syphilis organization issued in 1934, the 9th clause of which warned officials that "in health checks, actions and behaviour which would offend people and incite a negative response to the organization fighting [against disease] must be avoided and especially in examinations of women, such matters should be paid attention to".[46]

Despite any such sensitivity in the application of the law, many public health related issues were in fact not covered by laws and regulations at all and in consequence change had to be brought about with the consent of the population. Obtaining this consent was a mammoth task. If the people did not believe in the merits of state health measures, they would simply behave as the tradesmen described earlier did with their fly traps. Persuasion, thus, was the most important element in the fight against disease.

The problems of reaching and persuading the people were nicely demonstrated by Dr. Fehmi, a malaria doctor and head of the malaria unit in Adana. Dr. Fehmi described his experience to Lilo Linke, who visited Turkey in 1935 and wrote an account of this journey in her book, *Allah Dethroned. A Journey through Modern Turkey*. Although in 1935, Dr. Fehmi was received by villagers with great respect, even, in his own words, being perceived as "a demi-god", ten years earlier his reception had been totally different. Then the peasants had wanted to stone him, for until that point the only people sent by the government were tax collectors or recruiting officers. When they learned that he was actually a doctor, "they were annoyed just the same. Was I not interfering with Almighty Allah who can strike a man with any disease he chooses?" But in the end he persuaded them by "talking with them in their own language":

> I asked them what they did when a dog attacked them, and when they answered: 'We throw stones at it and run for a stick', I said: 'Well, and what is

---

[45] For instance see "Umumî Hıfzıssıhha Kanunu. Kanun Numarası: 1593, Kabul Tarihi: 24/4/1930" [Public Health Law. Code No: 1593, The Date of Ratification: 24/4/1930], *T.C. Resmi Gazete*, No. 1489 (6 May 1930), pp. 8896–910.

[46] *Frengi Mücadele Teşkilâtının Vazifelerini Gösterir Talimatname. Tasdik Tarihi: 22.XII.1934* [The Regulation Containing the Duties of the Organization for the Fight against Syphilis. The Date of Approval: 22.12.1934] (T.C. Sıhhat ve İçtimaî Muavenet Vekâleti) (Ankara: n.p., 1935), p. 3 and reprinted in 1939, p. 5.

malaria but a million mad dogs raging in your blood, and what is quinine but a stick to beat them?' – And when they hesitated, I said: 'Can't Allah make animals of any size he pleases? Or are you so blasphemous as to doubt because your stupid eyes can't see them?' And that was the argument that finally convinced them.[47]

Dr. Fehmi's performance represented what lay at the heart of all the health propaganda of the period – to reason with peasants in a way they could understand and gain their trust, and thus persuade them to change their attitudes to disease, hygiene and medicine. The problem was in part, as the MP for Ardahan Talat Bey put it, "how can we prove to our people that we are a government of the people?"[48] Being a "government which is based on the people and exists for the people"[49] was an important distinction from the Ottoman regime for the republican elite and the state's concern for public health was an issue that was presented as a main signifier of this distinction.[50]

A 1936 booklet on malaria noted that it was now in the republic that "villagers ... began to see doctors bringing free malaria medicine to young people who passed out in the fields",[51] while another claimed that "when the new republic was being established, the health of the villager was considered before everything ... in no part of the world had any country given such help to the villager".[52] Aka Gündüz's play *Köy Muallimi* (Village Teacher) about how an idealist village teacher transformed a poor village of sick and ignorant peasants, so run down that "even the storks refrained from perching on the ruined

---

47 Linke, Lilo, *Allah Dethroned. A Journey through Modern Turkey* (London: Constable & Co. Ltd., 1937), pp. 249–50.
48 T.B.M.M. *Zabıt Ceridesi*, Devre: II, İçtima Senesi: 1, 29 Teşrin-i evvel 1339 (1923), Monday, p. 87.
49 Emin Türk, "Köyümde Neler Gördüm?", p. 9.
50 T.B.M.M. *Zabıt Ceridesi*, Devre: II, İçtima Senesi: 1, 29 Teşrin-i evvel 1339 (1923), Monday, p. 87. The distinction was underlined in a brochure on smallpox published in 1938 which explained that the reason for epidemics before the creation of the republic was the inability of the health administration to reach all parts of the empire, *Çiçek Hastalığı ve Çiçek Aşısı* [Smallpox and Smallpox Vaccine] (T.C. Sıhhat ve İçtimai Muavenet Vekaleti Neşriyatından No 59) (Ankara: n.p., 1938), p. 1.
51 Yılal, Dr. Mustafa Musa, *Sıtma Hakkında Köylüye Öğütler* [Advice to Peasants about Malaria] (T.C. Muğla Vilâyeti Köy Bürosu Yayın Serisi: 10) (Muğla: Halk Basımevi, 1936), p. 4.
52 Arıkan, *Sıtma Hakkında Kısa Bilgiler*, p. 5; a similar point was repeated in Atay, C., *Köy Muhtarlarının Ödevleri* [Duties of Village Heads] (T.C. Trakya Umumî Müfettişliği Köy Bürosu Yayım Sayısı 65) (Istanbul: Halk Basımevi, 1937), p. 7.

minarets and, without stopping, moved on to other places",[53] into a civilized urban centre. In the play, old folk songs recalled how the villagers, crushed by harsh living conditions and suffering from malaria and smallpox, had waited in vain for help from Istanbul from "the tyrant" (the sultan), but, on hearing that Mustafa Kemal Paşa had come to power, their hope rose, but they were still impatient for him to solve their problems quickly: "but let this matter not take long/ neither energy nor trust remains/ Help, the great Gazi Paşa/ rescue us, come quickly".[54]

One area of basic health care was hygiene. Cleanliness was "the first condition of health",[55] a view which was given religious weight in the Turkish *hutbe* (Friday sermon) book, prepared on the order of Mustafa Kemal Atatürk and sent to *imam*s, which stated that "the basis of religion is founded on cleanliness. Cleanliness comes from belief".[56] Arguing that in the poverty and run-down conditions of village houses, cleanliness and health were ignored and filth was "a natural condition", Duru wrote that even washing one's body with water, "a painstaking custom both in our national traditions and our religion" was neglected and "dangerous and harmful creatures such as lice, fleas and bedbugs have become unavoidable and inseparable from the villages and villagers".[57]

A lack of hygiene was not restricted to rural areas and cleanliness, bodily hygiene and clean food and water were major concerns throughout the country. Cleanliness and hygiene, together with fresh air and sun, were among the most important topics in education given to pregnant women and mothers about prenatal care and child rearing.[58] One publication explained that "babies want

---

53   Aka Gündüz, *Köy Muallimi* [Village Teacher] (Ankara: Hakimiyet-i Milliye Matbaası, 1932), p. 17. A copy of this play was presented by the author to Reşit Galip on 22 June 1932, with a handwritten and signed dedication, "to my highly esteemed brother Dr. Reşit Galip Beyefendi" (Turkish Historical Association Library, Ankara, A/I 4626).

54   Aka Gündüz, *Köy Muallimi*, pp. 16–17.

55   Ali Kami, *Musahabat-ı Ahlakiye ve Malumat-ı Vataniye* [Moral Conversations and Patriotic Information] (Istanbul: Kitabhane-i Hilmi, 1927), p. 53.

56   "Hutbe 5. Sağlığın Başı Temizliktir" [Friday sermon 5. The basis of health is cleanliness], in *Türkçe Hutbe. Diyanet İşleri Reisliği Tarafından Tertib Edilmiştir* [Turkish Friday Sermons. Compiled by the Presidency of Religious Affairs], second edition (Türkiye Cumhuriyeti Diyanet İşleri Reisliği Neşriyatından Aded 3) (Istanbul: Evkaf Matbaası, 1928–1346), p. 31.

57   Duru, *Köy ve Köycülük*, p. 101.

58   *Validelere Nasihat* [Advice to Mothers] (Türkiye Cumhuriyeti Sıhhıye ve Muavenet-i İctimaiye Vekaleti Şişli Etfal Hastahanesi 27) ([Istanbul]: Kader Matbaası, 1341 [1925]); *Annelere Nasihat* [Advice to Mothers] (Türkiye Cumhuriyeti Sıhhiye ve Muavenet-i İçtimaiye Vekaleti Neşriyat Şubesi Numara 21) (Ankara: Sıhhiye ve Muavenet-i İctimaiye Vekaleti

TAKING HEALTH TO THE VILLAGE 177

three things from their mothers ... mother's milk, attention and cleanliness". Of these "nothing could take the place of cleanliness and attention", while a mother's milk could be substituted by cow's milk.[59]

Cleanliness required changing unhygienic habits. The most important slogan for anti-tuberculosis propaganda was "Do not spit on the ground", a message sometimes accompanied by visual material.[60] İstanbul Verem Mücadelesi Cemiyeti (The Istanbul Society for the Fight against Tuberculosis) explained that when an ill person spat on the ground or coughed and sneezed without holding their hand or a handkerchief over their mouth, millions of microbes were scattered around and survived for long periods, particularly in dark and damp places.[61] For Dr. Osman Şevki (Uludağ), to spit on the ground was not only shameful and disgusting but was equivalent to "arson",[62] while for Kutkam, it was not simply a "very bad custom" but "a crime".[63]

Spitting thus produced germs which could be transported inside the house via footwear, hence the discouraging of wearing outdoor shoes inside. A series of paintings from the Ankara Hıfzısıhha Müzesi (Ankara Museum of Hygiene), reproduced in colour in *Sıhhi Müze Atlası* (the Atlas of the Museum of Hygiene), showed a father who, having stepped in spit, had entered his house carrying tuberculosis germs on the bottom of his shoes and had thus caused his baby son who was playing on the floor to become infected.[64] Some of these pictures were used in black and white in Kutkam's 1937 booklet on tuberculosis.[65]

Matbaası, 1926); *Annelere Nasihat* [Advice to Mothers] (Türkiye Cümhuriyeti Sıhhat ve İçtimaî Muavenet Vekâleti Neşriyatından No. 21) (Istanbul: Hilal Matbaası, 1929); *Annelere Öğütler* [Advice to Mothers] (T.C. Sıhhat ve İçtimaî Muavenet Vekâleti Neşriyatından No. 51) (Ankara: Selen Matbaası, 1938).

59   *Annelere Öğütler*, p. 51.
60   *İstanbul Verem Mücadelesi Cemiyeti Merkez Heyeti Raporu 1932* [The Report of the Central Committee of the Istanbul Society for the Fight against Tuberculosis 1932] (Istanbul: Kader Matbaası, n.d.), p. 20.
61   *İstanbul Verem Mücadelesi Cemiyeti Merkez Heyeti Raporu 1930–1931* [The Report of the Central Committee of the Istanbul Society for the Fight against Tuberculosis 1930–1931] (Istanbul: Kader Matbaası, n.d.), p. 15.
62   Dr. Osman Şevki, *Bursada Verem Dispanseri* [The Tuberculosis Clinic in Bursa] (Bursa: A. Refik Matbaası, 1932), p. 14.
63   Kutkam, İsmail Hakkı, *Köylülere Öğütlerim. Verem* [My Advice to Villagers. Tuberculosis] (T.C. Trakya Umumî Müfettişliği Köy Bürosu Yayım Sayısı 30) (Istanbul: Halk Basımevi, 1937), p. 6.
64   *Sıhhi Müze Atlası* [the Atlas of the Museum of Hygiene] (Sıhhiye ve Muavenet-i İçtimaiye Vekaleti) (n.p.: n.p., 1926), pp. 36–41.
65   Kutkam, *Verem*, on the unnumbered pages at the end of the book.

The campaign about cleanliness also included fighting against insects, presented in *Musahabat-ı Ahlakiye ve Malumat-ı Vataniye* (Moral Conversations and Patriotic Information), a 1927 school text book for fourth year of primary school children, as a citizen's primary duty.[66] "Karınca", the author of the column "Kadın ve Ev Hayatı" (Woman and Home Life) published in *Haftalık Mecmua*, whose readership was urban, regarded fighting insects and vermin as a major duty of a housewife, and stressed the importance of combatting cockroaches, believed to carry cancer microbes, bedbugs, transmitters of typhus, and fleas, transmitters of plague, not merely for the sake of the health of the family but also as part of the civilising mission: "A housewife, who is the guardian of the health of the family of which she is the head, must absolutely show no mercy to fleas, bedbugs, cockroaches and flies, mosquitos, mice. A housewife who does not declare fundamental and continuous war on pests neglects one of her most important duties".[67]

Of all the pests against which the population were to be mobilized, the most important were lice, flies and mosquitos. Lice were not, however, popularly perceived as dangerous and having lice was not seen as either shameful or harmful. Quite the contrary, seeing lice in a dream was interpreted as a sign of richness.[68] According to a popular saying "lice were found on brave young men, while fleas were found on dogs". Their presence in fact indicated an unclean body and lack of hair care. Quite apart from this, they transmitted, among other diseases, typhus from one human to another,[69] something only discovered in 1909.[70] Typhus fever became one of the major killers of Ottoman soldiers in the First World War and had a devastating impact during the National Liberation War.[71] The threat of lice was only truly understood in the First World War[72] and

---

66 Ali Kami, *Musahabat-ı Ahlakiye ve Malumat-ı Vataniye*, pp. 37–68.
67 "Ev Kadınının En Mühim Bir Vazifesi de Haşaratla Mücadeledir" [One of the most important duties of a housewife is the fight against vermin], *Haftalık Mecmua*, no: 10 (21 Eylül 1341 [1925]).
68 Güngör, Salâhaddin, "Yeni Bir Mücadele. Tifüsü Yeneceğiz" [A new fight. We will beat typhus], *Cumhuriyet*, 31 January 1940.
69 Dr. Reşit Galip, *Sıhat Koruma Bilgisi*, p. 17.
70 Özden, Akil Muhtar, "Tifüsün Bitle Geçtiğini Keşfeden Charles Nicolle" [Charles Nicolle who discovered the transmission of typhus by lice], published in *Akşam*, 20 February 1945, reproduced in Tevfikoğlu, Muhtar, *Âkil Muhtar Özden* (Ankara: Türk Kültürünü Araştırma Enstitüsü, 1996), pp. 167–9.
71 See Başustaoğlu, Ahmet, *Bir Nefes Sıhhat. Tevfik Sağlam'ın Yaşamı* [A Breath of Health. The Life of Tevfik Sağlam] (Istanbul: Türkiye İş Bankası Kültür Yayınları, 2012).
72 Güngör, "Yeni Bir Mücadele. Tifüsü Yeneceğiz".

it was then that publications, such as Neşet Ömer's book *Bitler. Bitlerin Ahval-i Hayatı ve Vesait-i İtlafiyesi. Lekeli Tifo ve Humma-i Racianın Bitler ile Sirayeti* (Lice. The Life of Lice and Ways to Destroy Them. Typhus Fever and Relapsing Fever Contagion via Lice), published in 1916, set out to explain the dire necessity of dealing with lice and the methods for doing so.[73] This struggle was of such great significance that it even took on an ideological tone, for at the All-Russian Congress of Soviets in 1919 Lenin declared "Either the lice will defeat socialism, or socialism will defeat the lice".[74]

One aspect of the anti-lice campaign was to strip lice of the popular image of being "found on brave young men". A 1938 pamphlet produced by the Ministry of Health and Social Assistance titled *Bit* (The Louse) declared that "A louse is not found on brave young men, it is found only on people who are dirty and do not look after their health",[75] a message echoed two years later by Selahaddin Güngör when he wrote that this image must finally be put to rest and, in very similar language, continued "a louse is not found on a brave young man, it is found on a dirty, foolhardy individual!"[76] The new image of the louse was summed up nicely by Reşit Galip in his book *Sıhat Koruma Bilgisi* (Information About Protecting Health), published for a popular readership by the Ministry of Education in 1929: "The louse is small, but its shame is very big".[77] This new negative image was repeated in a village wall newspaper published in 1934 by the Village Committee, organized under the Istanbul People's House. The title of the item on lice read "The worst thing: lice" and the piece continued:

> Be fearful of lice! Because they are one of the worst, dirtiest animals. Avoid lice, because once you catch them, it takes a great deal of your time to save yourself from them. Do not approach people with lice as they are disease-laden, filthy people, and they will then infect you with lice.[78]

---

73 Neşat Ömer, *Bitler. Bitlerin Ahval-i Hayatı ve Vesait-i İtlafiyesi. Lekeli Tifo ve Humma-i Racianın Bitler ile Sirayeti* [Lice. The Life of Lice and Ways to Destroy Them. Typhus Fever and Relapsing Fever Contagion via Lice] (Jerusalem: Matbaa-i Darüleytam-ı Suriye, 1332 [1916]).

74 Quoted in Starks, Tricia, *The Body Soviet: Propaganda, Hygiene and the Revolutionary State* (Madison: University of Wisconsin Press, 2008), p. 3.

75 *Bit. İnsanlara Lekelihumma gibi Tehlikeli Hastalıkları Geçirir* [The Louse Transmits to Human Beings Dangerous Diseases such as Typhus Fever] (T.C. Sıhhat ve İctimaî Muavenet Vekâleti Neşriyatından, No. 53) (Ankara: n.p., 1938), p. 5.

76 Güngör, "Yeni Bir Mücadele. Tifüsü Yeneceğiz".

77 Dr. Reşit Galip, *Sıhat Koruma Bilgisi*, p. 3.

78 Reproduced in Linke, *Allah Dethroned*, between pp. 172–3.

At the end of the 1938 pamphlet *Bit*, printed in a larger font and in bold, the final message was an order: "Protect yourself from and stay clean of the louse which brings the diseases typhus fever and relapsing fever to humans and is the enemy of health".[79] Five years later, during the Second World War when the Turkish army, although not actively fighting, had a large body of soldiers under arms, citizens were warned about dangers of lice by reminding them of the past:

> Fellow countrymen: in the days of this war our country finds itself in danger and under threat of typhus fever. We must all work together in the towns and the villages hand in hand to prevent a great epidemic of this disease. Always remember the thousands of victims of typhus fever among our people and in our army in the last World War and the Balkan War and be very frightened of the **Louse** which brings this disease. The enemy of the louse is **Cleanliness**. Cleanliness is the foundation stone of **health**.[80]

Another common insect with which the state had to struggle was the fly, popularly perceived as unpleasant but harmless, "not dirty but revolting" as one popular saying put it, or "small but disgusting".[81] For the driver of the horse cart into which Reşat Nuri Güntekin climbed in the Anatolian town described earlier, flies were totally harmless: "No harm", he said, "comes to humans from these poor little things. That is why almighty God has favoured these poor little creatures".[82] Writing in 1933, the journalist Nahid Sırrı (Örik) wrote in utter despair about a little girl whom he passed by on one of the dirtiest streets of Bağlım, a district of Ankara. The girl did not even bother to attempt to drive away the crowds of flies which landed on her face, attracted by a small wound below her lip. Nahid Sırrı speculated that this might be because she had not been taught the need to do this.[83]

---

79   *Bit. İnsanlara Lekelihumma gibi Tehlikeli Hastalıkları Geçirir*, p. 5.
80   *Lekeli Humma. Bitten Korkunuz! Bitten Sakınınız! Bu Tehlikeli Hastalığı İnsana Yalnız Bit Bulaştırır* [Typhus Fever. Only the Louse Transmits This Dangerous Disease to Human Beings. Be Afraid of the Louse; Keep Away from the Louse] (T.C. Sıhhat ve İctimaî Muavenet Vekâleti Neşriyatından, No. 93) (Ankara: n.p., 1943), p. 4. Repeated in Duru, *Köy ve Köycülük*, p. 201.
81   Tülbentçi, Feridun Fazıl (ed.), *Türk Atasözleri ve Deyimleri* [Turkish Proverbs and Idioms] (Istanbul: İnkılâp ve Aka Kitabevleri, 1963), p. 333.
82   Güntekin, "Sinekler", p. 28.
83   Nahid Sırrı, *Anadoluda. Yol Notları* [Travel Notes in Anatolia] (Istanbul: Kanaat Kitabevi, 1939), pp. 19–20.

FIGURES 8.1 A & B *On the left, the cover of a 1938 pamphlet on lice which reads "The louse-transmits to human beings dangerous diseases such as typhus fever". On the right, the cover of a 1943 pamphlet on lice which reads: "Typhus Fever- Only the LOUSE transmits this dangerous disease to human beings. Be afraid of the louse; keep away from the louse".*

For the state, however, the fly, far from being a harmless little creature, was a pestilential enemy whose presence, as Reşid Galip noted, denoted filth.[84] By the beginning of the 1930s, there was a consensus among Turkish medical professionals about the role of flies in transmitting trachoma microbes. In a 1930 publication, ophthalmologist Dr. Nuri Fehmi argued that flies could keep trachoma microbes alive in their bodies for up to 24 hours and transmitted them to healthy eyes.[85] This grave danger posed by flies was explained in a 1933 publication of the Ministry of Health and Social Assistance:

> Filthy flies are one of the greatest helpers in transmitting the disease [trachoma] from one person to another. These unclean creatures, who are the reason for the spread of many diseases, land on the eye of someone with trachoma, and then, with their feet infected by the pus in the eye of

84 Dr. Reşit Galip, *Sıhat Koruma Bilgisi*, p. 10.
85 Dr. Nuri Fehmi, *Trahom Halk Kitabı*, p. 12.

that person, land on the healthy eye of another man and easily transmit the disease there.[86]

Well before the role of flies in transmitting trachoma was proven, flies were already seen as the culprit of many diseases. Flies were "more dangerous than war planes" for "instead of bombs, they scatter, sow and leave everywhere all sorts of germs, microbes and bacillus of diseases and epidemics. Search no further for the reason for typhus, child diarrhoea, dysentery, cholera, tuberculosis".[87] In a talk on Ankara Radio in 1937 parasitologist Dr. Nevzad demonstrated the dangers of flies. Referring to a saying translated from French, "three flies eat an ox faster than a lion",[88] he advised his audience that "when a fly lands on you, receive it not like an ordinary insect but like a scorpion. Would you like a scorpion to wander around on your hand, on your face? But, in fact, a scorpion is a harmless animal in comparison to a fly".[89]

Like flies, the mosquito in popular perception was irritating but not dangerous. "The mosquito" in a popular saying "is weak but its noise tiresome".[90] In reality, mosquitos were the main transmitters of malaria which was rampant in Anatolia. The majority of Turkish soldiers during the National Liberation War had malaria.[91] The state set out to involve the population in the struggle against malaria and under the 1926 law on the disease, local people between the ages of 15 and 65 were made responsible for the removal of accumulated water, either by physical labour or financial payment.[92] A 1938 pamphlet on

---

86 *Gözleri Kör Eden Trahom Hastalığı Hakkında Halka Nasihatler* (1933), pp. 4–5.
87 Dr. Besim Ömer (trans.), *Yüzyıl Yaşamak İçün «22» Emr-i Sıhhiyede Bütün Hıfz-ı Sıhhat* [22 Commands about Hygiene in Order to Live a Hundred Years Long] (Istanbul: Ahmed İhsan Matbaası, 1927), p. 37. This book was translated from French.
88 Dr. Rüşdi Edhem (trans.), *Sineklerle Mücadele* [The Fight against Flies] (Istanbul: Hilal Matbaası, 1926), the front page has the line "Üç sinek bir öküzü, bir aslandan daha çabuk yer" [Three flies eat an ox faster than a lion].
89 Mekki Said, "'Üç Sinek Bir Öküzü Bir Aslandan Çabuk Yer!' Ankara Radyosunda Parazitolog Dr. Nevzadın Yaptığı Konuşmadan Parçalar" ['Three flies eat an ox faster than a lion!' Excerpts from parasitologist Dr. Nevzad's talk on Ankara Radio], *Cumhuriyet*, 15 Mart 1937.
90 Tülbentçi, *Türk Atasözleri ve Deyimleri*, p. 334.
91 *İstiklal Harbi Sıhhi Raporu. 336-337-338 Mudanya Mütarekesine Kadar* [The Medical Report of the Independence War. From 336-337-338 to the Armistice of Mudanya] (Türkiye Cumhuriyeti Müdafaa-i Milliye Vekaleti Sıhhiye Dairesi) (Istanbul: Matbaa-i Askeriye, 1341 [1925]), p. 20.
92 The 6th clause of "Sıtma Mücadelesi Kanunu. Numara: 839 (13 Mayıs 1926)" [The Law on the Fight against Malaria. No. 839 (13 May 1926)], *Resmi Gazete*, Year 4, No 384 (29 May 1926), p. 1472.

malaria explained that "to destroy a malaria nest wherever it is found is to close a grave which is open to strangle a citizen and to swallow a family", a graphic message repeated in 1941.[93] The danger of mosquitos was hammered home by the official in charge of operations against malaria in Thrace, Dr. Arıkan: "The mosquito is your biggest enemy because it infects you with malaria ... do whatever you can to kill mosquitos. Kill it before it kills you".[94]

For some, an effective campaign for cleanliness and against pests and vermin would automatically produce a healthier population, and one less inclined to superstitions. Atay, the Director of Culture in Kırklareli, argued that those villagers who attended to both public and personal hygiene would "neither be struck by jins, nor caught by fairies, nor encounter ghosts, nor see saints or those who have arrived at the divine truth. Nothing will happen to them. They will go through life upright, hale and hearthy, in the bloom of health".[95] In order to achieve the desired goal, however, a campaign against pests and vermin alone was not sufficient, for what was required was that people also made major changes in their way of life, from dietary and fashion preferences to drinking alcohol and womanizing. Propaganda was thus also aimed at lifestyle. Health museums featured warnings against the damaging effects of high heeled shoes on women's feet, legs, ankles and posture which read "Ladies do not be deceived by fashion. Do not sacrifice your health for elegance provided by non-healthy and non-medical shoes",[96] and the fashion for being slim was regarded as creating conditions for tuberculosis.[97] Here, the main target for such propaganda was the 'modern', and hence urban woman, but most of the state's concerns were directed at male lifestyle, regardless of urban-rural distinction.

Alcohol consumption and prostitution were considered major threats to public health. The most important reference point in campaigns against these was the religious command and precept of popular morality, "control your sensual desires [*nefis*]". Although the use of drugs, such as cocaine, morphine and heroin, was an increasing concern[98] and tobacco consumption was listed

---

93   *Sıtma. Sıtmayı İnsanlara Geçiren Sivrisineklerdir*, p. 7; Duru, *Köy ve Köycülük*, p. 96. It is possible that Dr. Duru was involved in the production of this pamphlet.
94   Arıkan, *Köylüler için Sıtma Hakkında Kısa Bilgiler*, pp. 17–19.
95   Atay, *Köy Muhtarlarının Ödevleri*, p. 28.
96   *Sıhhi Müze Atlası*, p. 25.
97   Dr. Osman Şevki, *Bursada Verem Dispanseri*, pp. 13–14.
98   Dr. Hikmet Hamdi Bey, *Sıhhî Müze Rehberi* [Health Museum Guide] (T.C. Sıhhat ve İçtimai Muavenet Vekâleti) (n.p.: n.p., 1931), pp. 49–53, originally published in Arabic script, Dr. Hikmet Hamdi Bey, *Sıhhi Müze Rehberi* (Sıhhiye ve Muavenet-i İçtimaiye Vekaleti) (Ankara: Vilayet Matbaası, 1340/1924); "Yeşilay Kongresi. Dr. Mazhar Osman Velileri, Muallimleri

among harmful habits,[99] alcohol, "a catastrophe for mankind"[100] and, according to Yeşil Hilal later Yeşilay (the Green Crescent), the national society which campaigned against the use of alcohol and other addictive substances, "the enemy of health and existence",[101] dominated the general discourse. Alcoholic beverages were described as damaging to physical and mental health, family life, public order and the economy.[102] According to Atay who wrote that in an environment in which it was believed that singing, playing musical instruments and dancing were forbidden by religion and laughing was religiously disapproved of, that which was actually religiously forbidden and prohibited in God's kingdom was alcohol, yet, in towns and villages, "when one refers to entertainment, the first thing that comes to mind is alcohol". And as a result, "we drink to exploding point, even until we make our heads and eyes explode. Then we turn on each other, a bloodbath ensues, houses are destroyed and families ruined".[103] There was concern about the trend of increasing alcohol consumption in villages. A 1941 publication on the harm of alcoholic beverages noted that before alcohol had been consumed more in towns but recently it had "regretfully" entered the villages and was drunk "on various pretexts".[104] Villagers of Muğla, thus, were urged to spend their money on quinine rather than on alcohol or cigarettes.[105]

Alcohol was also perceived as a factor in young men's frequenting of prostitutes, and thus contracting venereal diseases[106] which produced disastrous results for their wives and children. Young men were urged to control their desires, for, as a slogan in the *Sıhhi Müze Rehberi* (Health Museum Guide) put it, "a complete man is one who controls his sensual desires".[107] A man who

   ve Bütün Gençliği Beyaz Zehirle Mücadeleye Davet Ediyor" [The Congress of Yeşilay. Dr. Mazhar Osman invites parents, teachers and all the youth to the fight against the white poison], *Cumhuriyet*, 26 December 1937.
99 *Kalbimizi Koruyalım* [Let Us Protect Our Heart] (T.C. Sıhhat ve İçtimai Muavenet Vekâleti Neşriyatından No. 92) (n.p.: n.p., n.d.), pp. 6 and 8.
100 Dr. Hikmet Hamdi Bey, *Sıhhî Müze Rehberi* (1931), p. 44.
101 "Yeşil Hilâl. Cuma Günü İçkisiz Eğlence Tertib Ediyor" [Yeşil Hilal organizes a party without alcohol on Friday], *Cumhuriyet*, 19 May 1930.
102 *İspirtolu İçkilerin Sağlığa Zararları* [The Damage of Alcoholic Beverages to Health] (T.C. Sıhhat ve İçtimaî Muavenet Vekâleti Neşriyatından No: 76) (Ankara: Alâeddin Kıral Basımevi, 1941), *passim*.
103 Atay, *Köy Muhtarlarının Ödevleri*, pp. 31–2.
104 *İspirtolu İçkilerin Sağlığa Zararları*, p. 1.
105 Yılal, *Sıtma Hakkında Köylüye Öğütler*, p. 8.
106 *Zührevi Hastalıklar Nelerdir?*, p. 14.
107 Dr. Hikmet Hamdi Bey, *Sıhhî Müze Rehberi* (1931), p. 29.

TAKING HEALTH TO THE VILLAGE

could not do so was "for the most part subject to the tendency to sexual relations, becomes involved in sexual relations with immoral girls and, in this way, contracts venereal diseases".[108] The answer to this problem, or one of them, was sport.[109] It was necessary, a publication of the Bursa Halkevi on venereal diseases explained, to occupy young men, who were at threat of these diseases, were activities such as sports which were enjoyable and tired their bodies, and to marry them off as soon as the law allowed.[110]

"Awakening the Nation with Modern Techniques in the Matters of Health Protection"[111]

In order to combat the diseasescape it found itself faced with, the government of the new republic instituted a major propaganda campaign, run largely by the Ministry of Health and Social Assistance. This ministry, according to the 280th clause of the 1930 *Umumi Hıfzısıhha Kanunu* (Public Health Law), published books, posters and pamphlets to educate the population on health matters, including protection from contagious diseases and epidemics, child rearing and healthy living, set up health propaganda organisations and organised the showing of educational films. Such services were free. It also, if necessary, organised travelling health propaganda teams.[112]

Such propaganda efforts were not new. In the late Ottoman period, there was awareness of the necessity of the cooperation of the population in fighting against disease and education was considered an essential part of this.[113] But this awareness turned into a necessity and a well-organized policy with the republic not only because of the new state's understanding of governance but also due to its close following of developments in public health propaganda campaigns elsewhere in the world.[114] It is important to note that there was a very strong understanding that health propaganda should be conducted

---

108   *Zindelik Atlası. Çocuklar ve Delikanlılar için Zindelik Numuneleri* [The Atlas of Healthy Life. Health Lessons for Children and Young Men] (Istanbul: Muhit Neşriyat Limited Şirketi, 1930), p. 27 and for similar remarks see p. 17. Also see Zeki Nasır, "Halk Sıhhati", p. 75.
109   *Zindelik Atlası*, p. 6.
110   *Zührevi Hastalıklar Nelerdir?*, pp. 13–14.
111   No Author, "Cumhuriyetin Sağlık, Bakım ve Yardım İşleri", p. 253.
112   "Umumî Hıfzısıhha Kanunu", p. 8909.
113   Boyar, "'An inconsequential boil' or a 'terrible disease?'", pp. 118–19.
114   See for example, BCA, 30 18 1 1 22 75 9, 8 December 1926.

through many different channels simultaneously[115] and that it was necessary "not to tire of repeating it".[116]

Apart from the Ministry of Health and Social Assistance, other groups were also utilised in the propaganda campaign. While the Ministry of National Education, Village Bureaus, which were part of provincial administrations linked to the Ministry of Internal Affairs, the Republican People's Party branches, village committees organized under the People's Houses after the establishment of Republican People's Houses in 1932,[117] various civil society organizations such as societies for the fight against tuberculosis, Yeşil Hilal/ Yeşilay, Hilal-i Ahmer/ Kızılay (the Red Crescent), Himaye-i Etfal Cemiyeti (the Society for the Protection of Youth) and Milli Türk Talebe Birliği all contributed to propaganda campaigns, *muhtar*s in the villages, *imam*s, teachers, especially village teachers,[118] peripatetic health personnel, such as Dr. Fehmi himself, were accepted as the 'natural' soldiers in the national health propaganda army. Public meetings, which were easier to organize in villages, were held at which peasants were advised about health matters by experts and by teachers such as Recep Dalgır, a "head teacher" and member of a village committee of the Denizli People's House, who was photographed in 1937 giving a talk to peasants. The caption under the photo reads "while giving advice".[119]

Hygiene museums, similar to their various western counterparts, were opened. According to Refik Bey, the Minister of Health and Social Assistance in 1926, these museums gave information, in the form of easily understandable pictures and displays, on how to protect oneself from contagious and "social" diseases and about personal hygiene.[120] In 1933 it was reported that in nine years 685,927 people had visited the İstanbul Hıfzısıhha Müzesi (Istanbul Hygiene Museum).[121] Travelling health exhibitions in cities and

---

115 See for example, for syphilis see Duru, *Köy ve Köycülük*, p. 214; for trachoma, Ayberk, *Türkiyede Trahom Mücadelesi*, pp. 27–8.
116 "Sağlık İşleri. Bakırköy Kazası C.H. Partisince Sıtma ve Sağlık Koruma Savaşı Hakkında İkinci Kurultayca Kabul Edilen Çalışma Programı 10 Teşrisani 1933" [Health works. The work programme accepted by the Republican People's Party Bakırköy branch in the second congress about the fight against malaria and for the protection of health], *Belediyeler Dergisi*, 1/ 4–5 (September-October 1935), p. 74.
117 *C.H.P. Denizli Köycüler Komitası Köylerde. Birinci Teşrin 1937* [The CHP Denizli Village Committee in Villages. October 1937] (Denizli: Yeni Basımevi, 1937).
118 Aka Gündüz, *Köy Muallimi*, passim.
119 *C.H.P. Denizli Köycüler Komitası Köylerde*, p. 40.
120 *Sıhhi Müze Atlası*, preface.
121 No Author, "Cumhuriyetin Sağlık, Bakım ve Yardım İşleri", p. 259.

towns were organized and exhibition guides were printed and distributed freely.[122]

Where possible, educational films were shown. For instance, in 1931, in some parts of the province of Sivas, educational films, most probably foreign in origin, were shown free to the public, school children and soldiers. These films, which were regarded as having a positive impact on the public, had titles such as *Malaria, Child Care, The Danger of Flies, The Punishment of Negligence, The Means of a Long and Healthy Life, The Importance of the Head Cold, Hygienic Water* (possibly the 1920s *Drinking Health* produced by the US National Health Council), *The Early Diagnosis and Early Treatment of TB, Once Upon a Time They Were Three Friends, Syphilis*,[123] *New Methods of Fighting Against Malaria, The Value of Mother's Milk, Your Mouth,* and *Tommy's Tooth* (possibly the 1922 Disney short film called *Tommy Tucker's Tooth*).[124] According to a news item in *Cumhuriyet* from 1934, such films were shown free to people, army personnel, teachers and students in 49 provinces, nine "malaria combat zones" and through a travelling "pedagogy exhibition".[125] Radio was increasingly used as a medium to inform the population about health matters and talks, such as those by Selim Sırrı (Tarcan) on the importance of sports, Cemil Paşa (Topuzlu) on cancer and Hulusi Behçet on syphilis, were broadcast.[126] However, despite individual efforts, such as those of Kazım Paşa (Dirik), who was the governor of İzmir between 1926 and 1935 and who presented radios to some İzmir villages,[127] the accessibility of radios in rural areas was very limited in interwar Turkey.

The most easily accessed and circulated mediums of health propaganda were printed material, such as posters, books, booklets and brochures. Special informative brochures in simple Turkish were prepared and distributed; simple but effective posters were hung in *köy odaları* (village rooms), schools and other public spaces. Posters and informative booklets, aimed both at informing

---

122 No Author, "Cumhuriyetin Sağlık, Bakım ve Yardım İşleri", pp. 258–9.
123 This film, originally called *Il était une fois trois amis*, was produced in France in 1929. I would like to thank Liat Kozma for this information.
124 Dr. Hasan Tahsin, *Sıvas Vilâyeti Sıhhî ve İçtimaî Coğrafyası 1931* [Medical and Social Geography of the Province of Sivas 1931] (Istanbul: Hilâl Matbaası, 1932), p. 308.
125 "Sıhhi Propaganda. Yüzlerce Yerde Terbiyevi Filmler Gösterildi" [Health propaganda. Educational films were shown in hundreds of places], *Cumhuriyet*, 21 April 1934.
126 Yunus Nadi, "Spordan Neler Bekliyoruz?" [What do we expect from sports?], *Cumhuriyet*, 13 August 1931; "Radyo" [Radio], *Cumhuriyet*, 9 January 1933; "Radyo. Bu Akşamki Program" [Radio. This Evening's Programme], *Cumhuriyet*, 15 February 1935.
127 *Gezi Notları*, p. 24. Kazım Dirik was the General Inspector of Thrace between 1935 and 1941.

those who were to give talks to the population and also the people themselves, were published by both the Ministry of Health and Social Assistance[128] and various other local bodies, such as the general regional inspectorates and the Republican People's Houses.

Popular Language and Gruesome Pictures: Booklets and Brochures for Health Propaganda

Among such printed propaganda materials, booklets and brochures were especially important tools in reaching every part of Anatolia. Such material was cheap to print and easy to circulate. As an article in *Ülkü* explained, "thousands, hundreds of thousands of leaflets, pamphlets and works which were written in a popular language and published in order to enlighten and make the people aware about health, were distributed even to the most remote towns and villages".[129] Even though there was a low literacy rate in the Turkish countryside, such publications were still accessible as they were read aloud in village rooms, coffee houses, schools, mosques and village squares. Mahmut Makal, for example, described how, during an epidemic in the village, he read out two pamphlets published by the Ministry of Health and Social Assistance on "pure water supply" and "measles" at the school while his friend, the health officer, read them to villagers in the village room.[130] These brochures also gave the necessary information to those people who would then act as health propagandists.

Pamphlets published by the Ministry of Health and Social Assistance were distributed widely and free of charge, and although, being low budget publications, they were mostly of low quality, there were also some glossy ones. 50,000 copies of one such expensive publication, a brochure on trachoma which was embellished with many original coloured pictures, were printed in 1933 and distributed free, but the publication carried a stern warning: "After reading this book and understanding its meaning well, it is shameful and a sin to throw it away. Therefore, after reading it, it is important not to fail to give it to friends and acquaintances so that they can read it. This is the duty of every member of the nation".[131] This pamphlet went into a second edition in 1941, but this time it was smaller and the quality of the print was not as good, although it was still

---

128 Dr. Zeki Nasır, "Köylerimizin Sağlık İşleri", p. 45.
129 No Author, "Cumhuriyetin Sağlık, Bakım ve Yardım İşleri", p. 259.
130 Makal, *A Village in Anatolia*, p. 11.
131 *Gözleri Kör Eden Trahom Hastalığı Hakkında Halka Nasihatler* (1933), p. 8.

in colour, and there were fewer illustrations. Apart from quality and number of illustrations, there were also some differences in its content. While the warning at the end of the publication was still stern, the second edition played more on feelings of citizenship and patriotism: "Do not throw away this small book written about trachoma after reading and learning the advice by heart. Give it to other citizens advising them to read it. In this way, you will once again prove your patriotism".[132] Another Ministry of Health and Social Assistance publication on venereal diseases also reminded citizens of their responsibilities as well as the calamities which could befall their families if the warnings contained in the booklet were ignored:

> Do not tear and discard this paper, read it carefully and teach those who do not know [about it]; the disease, which catches you today, can catch your sibling tomorrow, your child the day after. Hand-in-hand and with common effort, let us expel this calamity from among us. The state can only reach this happy outcome if the people are on their guard. The state expects assistance from every citizen.[133]

The message contained in the small booklet published by the Kayseri Mıntıkası Sıtma Mücadele Heyeti (The Kayseri District Committee for the Fight against Malaria) and distributed free, was simple and to the point: "After reading, do not throw away, please give to another person!"[134]

Not all publications were free. Although their contents and presentation were similar, some were sold, at affordable prices, those of the General Inspectorate of Thrace (Trakya Umumi Müfettişliği) in 1937, for example, varying from 3.5 to 7.5 *kuruş*. Such publications were apparently popular among villagers. In an anonymous account of a tour of İzmir villages, the author notes that in the village of Zeytindağı, villagers liked "little books which were produced by the Village Bureau and which were useful for the villagers",[135] while in another İzmir village, Adagide, villagers were "very devoted" to such publications.[136] The İzmir Village Bureau produced 18 little books, the price of which varied

---

132 *Gözleri Kör Eden Trahom Hastalığı Hakkında Halka Nasihatler. İkinci Tabi* [Advice to the Public about the Disease of Trachoma which Blinds Eyes. The Second Edition] (Sıhhat ve İctimaî Muavenet Vekâleti Neşriyatından, No. 33) (Istanbul: Hüsnütabiat Matbaası, 1941), p. 8.
133 *Zührevî Hastalıklar Müptelalarına Öğütler ve Tavsiyeler*, p. 8.
134 *Sıtma* (Kayseri Mıntıkası Sıtma Mücadele Heyeti 2), back cover.
135 *Gezi Notları*, pp. 26–7.
136 *Gezi Notları*, p. 30.

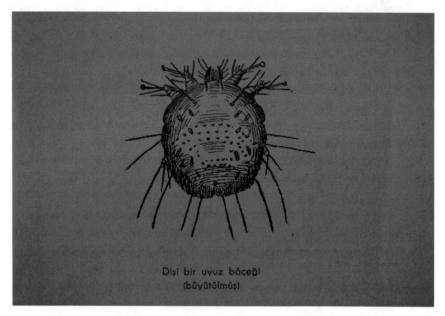

FIGURE 8.2   An itch mite on the cover of Uyuz, published in Ankara in 1941.

from one to ten *kuruş* and which included books on the health of villagers. All were written by experts and in a language easily understandable by the villagers who "read them with great pleasure and benefitted greatly from them".[137]

Written in "popular language",[138] simple, direct and blunt, and generally with a few illustrations, the main objective of these booklets was to inform people about diseases, their symptoms and treatment, how they were transmitted and what should be done in order not to contract or spread them. Although the content and style of booklets varied depending on the specific disease as well as on an individual publisher or author, the general tendency was to give such information concisely and clearly.

As an article in *Le Matin* in November 1918 on the impact of films about hygiene noted, "man is like a child, he believes what he has seen".[139] Turkish authorities certainly made much use of visual material in order to ram home the messages of their health publications. Illustrations of organisms, microbes and diseased internal organs, such as lungs destroyed by tuberculosis,[140] made the

137   *Gezi Notları*, pp. 26–7.
138   No Author, "Cumhuriyetin Sağlık, Bakım ve Yardım İşleri", p. 259.
139   Quoted in Lefebvre, Thierry, "Les films de propagande sanitaire de Lortac et O'Galop (1918–1919)", *1895- Mille huit cent quatre-vingt-quinze*, 59 (2009), p. 178.
140   Kutkam, *Verem*, p. 4; *Verem (Tüberküloz)* [Tuberculosis] (T.C. Sıhhat ve İçtimaî Muavenet Vekâleti Neşriyatından No. 60) (Ankara: Ankara Cezaevi Matbaası, 1938), p. 8.

invisible visible and thus believable. Publications carried graphic pictures of parasites and mites and descriptions of their activities. For instance, the front page of a 1941 publication on itch had a magnified image of a female itch mite (fig. 8.2),[141] demonstrating that itching in bed at night was not because of the warmness of the bed but because of the increasing activities of nocturnal itch mites.[142]

The possibility of harbouring such monstrous-looking organisms inside one's own body provided an incentive to do something about them and to avoid living in such a way that encouraged their presence. This was the reaction that the Ministry of Health and Social Assistance sought to produce with the illustration of a tapeworm (taenia) in its 1940 publication (fig. 8.3).[143] The reproduction of magnified images served to visualise these creatures as dangerous. This applied also in the case of malaria, where descriptions of anopheles, a type of mosquito which carried malaria parasites, as well of other types of mosquito were accompanied by magnified images of larvae, eggs and the insects themselves.

Many health publications explained how diseases were transmitted, sometimes through the use of illustrations. A Ministry of Health and Social Assistance publication from 1938, for example, gave a one page black and white illustration that showed how tuberculosis was spread.[144] Similarly, a colour illustration in a 1933 publication on trachoma showed the role of flies in carrying microbes from the eyes of an old man to a modern-looking young and healthy man. The caption read "The fly is the greatest enemy of your eye. It takes the disease of a person with trachoma with its feet and transmits it to your healthy eye. Do not allow the fly to live!" (fig. 8.4)

Having thus explained how flies carried trachoma, mosquitos transmitted malaria viruses, and the spittle of an infected person spread tuberculosis microbes to others, the next step was to engender changes in life style, social habits and hygiene, and to persuade people to adopt precautions such as washing their hands regularly, avoiding dust and dirt, not kissing children, not having contacts with diseased people, not allowing your children to be kissed, not using other people's personal belongings, avoiding communal use of glasses or cutlery, and drinking hygienic water and using mosquito nets.[145] The

---

141 *Uyuz* [Itch] (T.C. Sıhhat ve İçtimaî Muavenet Vekâleti Neşriyatından No. 73) (Ankara: Alâeddin Kıral Basımevi, 1941), the front page.
142 *Uyuz*, p. 2.
143 *Sağlığımıza Zarar Veren Barsak Kurtları* [Intestinal Parasites Harming Our Health] (T.C. Sıhhat ve İçtimaî Muavenet Vekâleti Neşriyatından No. 70) (Ankara: n.p., 1940), p. 6.
144 *Verem (Tüberküloz)*, p. 5.
145 See for example, *Şark Çıbanı*, p. 6.

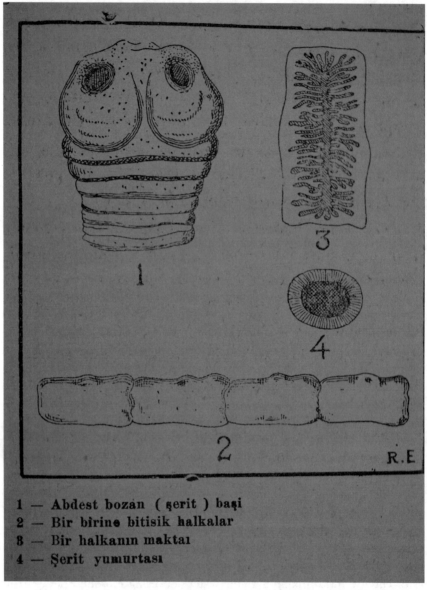

FIGURE 8.3   *Tapeworm from* Sağlığımıza Zarar Veren Barsak Kurtları (*Ankara, 1940*).

importance of persuasion is particularly evident in the material on diseases against which there were vaccines, for although such vaccines might be legally compulsory, brochures still sought to inform and persuade. While vaccination against smallpox was a legal requirement, what was emphasized in publicity was not its compulsory nature but its personal benefit: "People can only protect

TAKING HEALTH TO THE VILLAGE 193

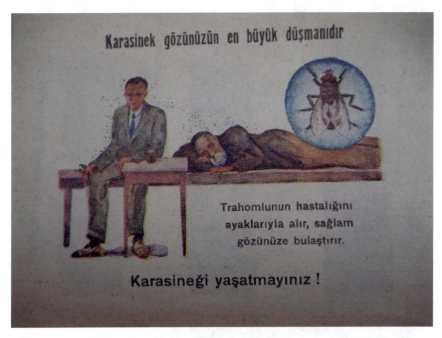

FIGURE 8.4 *"The fly is the greatest enemy of your eye", illustration from,* Gözleri Kör Eden Trahom Hastalığı Hakkında Halka Nasihatler *(1933).*

themselves from smallpox by being vaccinated. Get vaccinated. Especially vaccinate your children".[146] A brochure on scarlet fever makes a point not only about the necessity of vaccination for protecting children against scarlet fever but also reassures the population about the harmlessness of the vaccine: "To inoculate children against scarlet fever is, too, a means of protection. Therefore when the government is providing vaccination and when there is the danger of scarlet fever, it is necessary immediately to bring your children and have them inoculated. There is no danger or harm in vaccination".[147]

While generally advice on simple preventative measures was not accompanied by illustrations, some publications had informative pictures. For instance a 1933 publication and its 1941 edition had a picture of a man washing his hands with a generous amount of soap under running water. "Trachoma", the caption reads, "is quickly transmitted. The way to protect yourself is: wash your hands

---

146 *Çiçek Hastalığı Çok Tehlikelidir* [Smallpox is Very Dangerous] (T.C. Sıhhat ve İçtimai Muavenet Vekaleti Neşriyatından No 91) (Ankara: Ulusal Matbaa, 1943), p. 1.
147 *Kızıl Hastalığı ve Korunma Çareleri* [Scarlet Fever and Measures for Protection] (Türkiye Cumhuriyeti Sıhhat ve İçtimai Muavenet Vekâleti) (Ankara: Türk Ocakları Merkez Heyeti Matbaası, 1930), p. 4.

FIGURE 8.5   *"Trachoma is quickly transmitted", from* Gözleri Kör Eden Trahom Hastalığı Hakkında Halka Nasihatler *(1941).*

frequently with soap; do not touch your eyes with dirty hands; protect your eyes from dust and flies" (fig. 8.5).[148] The connection between germed hands and eyes was something which was repeated many times in trachoma related material. In a 1930 publication, the caption under an illustration of a man rubbing his eyes reads "Rubbing your eyes with your hands before washing them is dangerous".[149] Sometimes an image alone was sufficient. The cover of a 1939 publication by the Ministry of Health and Social Assistance on flu showed a

---

148   *Gözleri Kör Eden Trahom Hastalığı Hakkında Halka Nasihatler* (1933) and *Gözleri Kör Eden Trahom Hastalığı Hakkında Halka Nasihatler* (1941), p. 9.
149   Dr. Nuri Fehmi, *Trahom Halk Kitabı*, p. 10.

boy with watery eyes sneezing into his handkerchief to trap germs.[150] This image, and idea behind it, was similar to images produced for the famous "coughs and sneezes spread diseases. Trap your germs in a handkerchief" campaign of the 1940s in Britain.

Apart from providing information on diseases and how to avoid them, pamphlets also gave information on how to treat diseases once they had been contracted. Here pamphlets emphasized seeking medical advice and adhering strictly to doctors' orders. Medicine was to be taken according to the instructions, quinine, for example, the "main medicine for malaria" was "to be swallowed as prescribed".[151] Folk remedies, such as wearing a bracelet of cotton thread which had been prayed over or tying a cloth to the branches of a tree, as believed in by elders, were to be avoided, as was the misuse of medicines. Taking, for example, quinine sulphate mixed with vinegar or euphorbium did not protect people from malaria.[152]

It was one thing, however, to give easily comprehensible information, but another to ensure that the population absorbed it and put it into practice. The way to ensure this, adopted by the health propaganda literature, was to instil fear and guilt.

Pamphlets stressed the colossal devastation wreaked by diseases, the danger of malaria being such, according to a 1925 publication that "many villages were left without human habitation".[153] The widespread nature of disease also meant that the chances of contraction were extremely high. A 1933 educational booklet on trachoma underlined that 60 to 70 percent of the population in some towns carried it.[154]

When death was not immediate, diseases could result in pain and physical deformation, the diseased person condemned to endure a wretched life before ultimately expiring. Dr. Yılal did not mince his words in his booklet on malaria. "The end of a person with malaria", he explained, "is to die wretchedly in sickness, poverty and loneliness".[155] A 1938 pamphlet published by the Ministry of Health and Social Assistance was equally blunt in explaining the

---

150 *Grip* [Influenza] (T.C. Sıhhat ve İçtimaî Muavenet Vekaleti Neşriyatından No. 63) (Ankara: n.p., 1939), the cover page.
151 *Sıtma* (Kayseri Mıntıkası Sıtma Mücadele Heyeti 2), p. 6.
152 *Sıtma* (Kayseri Mıntıkası Sıtma Mücadele Heyeti 2), p. 6.
153 *Sıtmaya Tutulmamak İçin Öğüdler. Sıtmadan Korunmak Tutulunca Kurtulmakdan Kolaydır* [Advice on How not to Contract Malaria. To Protect Oneself from Malaria is Easier than to Save Oneself from It Once It has been Contracted] (Istanbul: Matbaa-i Ahmed İhsan ve Şürekası, 1341/1925), p. 2.
154 *Gözleri Kör Eden Trahom Hastalığı Hakkında Halka Nasihatler*, p. 2.
155 Yılal, *Sıtma Hakkında Köylüye Öğütler*, p. 6.

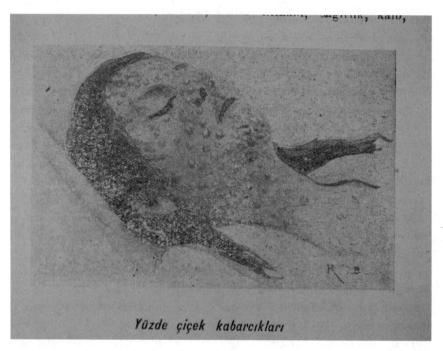

Yüzde çiçek kabarcıkları

FIGURE 8.6   *A young girl with smallpox boils, illustration from* Çiçek Hastalığı ve Çiçek Aşısı (*Ankara, 1938*).

damage that could be caused by smallpox. Those who survived suffered from pneumonia, blindness, ear infections, deafness, heart and kidney diseases and unsightly pox marks on their skin for life.[156] This scary prospect was reinforced by a picture of a young girl who carried smallpox boils on her face, physical blemishes which would damage her marriage prospects (fig. 8.6).[157] Pamphlets made use of illustrations of deformed bodies. A photograph of six naked boys with swollen stomachs appeared in a 1938 publication on malaria with the caption "frog bellied little ones".[158] The same photograph was used in two different publications, one of which was the Ministry of Health and Social Assistance's pamphlet on malaria, where the boys, this time provided with underwear, appeared with the caption "a group of children whose spleens were enlarged in a malaria-ridden village".[159]

---

156   *Çiçek Hastalığı ve Çiçek Aşısı*, p. 3. Repeated in *Çiçek Hastalığı Çok Tehlikelidir*, p. 3.
157   *Çiçek Hastalığı ve Çiçek Aşısı*, p. 3.
158   *Sıtma* (Kayseri Mıntıkası Sıtma Mücadele Heyeti 2), p. 2.
159   *Sıtma. Sıtmayı İnsanlara Geçiren Sivrisineklerdir*, p. 5; Duru, *Sağlık Bakımından Köy ve Köycülük*, p. 93.

Even the simple negligence of not looking after one's teeth could lead to pain, diseases and defects, and great emphasis was thus placed on dental health.[160] In 1927, Himaye-i Etfal Cemiyeti prepared a very well-illustrated booklet for children to inform them about why they had to look after their teeth and how to do so. Teeth should be cleaned, the pamphlet explained, "because if we do not keep our teeth clean, they will wither and decay. Food will be eaten with difficulty by withered teeth. Morsels cannot be chewed sufficiently by withered teeth. Therefore digestion will not be in order".[161] The outcome of neglect of dental hygiene was illustrated by a stereotypic image of a crying boy whose swollen jaw was enveloped in a handkerchief, and who admitted that "This happened because I did not take care of my teeth"[162] (fig. 8.7).

Fear of pain, death and physical deformation was reinforced by fear of alienation, of being shunned and excluded from society. This fear was particularly played on in publications on venereal diseases. Dr. İhsan Özgen, at the beginning of his booklet *Üç Bela. Frengi, Fuhuş, İçki* (Three Menaces. Syphilis, Prostitution and Alcohol), published by the Village Bureau of the Province of İzmir, addressed his "peasant brothers" and wrote: "Syphilis is a dreadful disease ... It cripples and disables and makes people childless. Syphilis makes a man mad and thrusts him into a lunatic asylum or a prison. Syphilis makes man into a beast and disgraces him".[163] In the publication of Bursa Halkevi, the connection between madness and syphilis was put forward as a matter of fact, for, it announced, "those with syphilis make up 60–70 per cent of the inhabitants of mental institutions".[164] For İsmail Hakkı Kutkam, an expert in internal medicine in the Edirne Memleket Hastanesi (the Edirne Provincial Hospital), who wrote a booklet on syphilis published by the Village Bureau of the General Inspectorate of Thrace in which he used the same visual material as that used by Özgen, syphilis was "the most dangerous of contagious diseases. Those who catch this disease cannot be easily saved. This disease is contracted

---

160 *Diş Sağlığı. Diş Temizliği* [Dental Health. Dental Hygiene] (T.C. Sıhhat ve İçtimaî Muavenet Vekâleti Neşriyatından No. 45) (Ankara: n.p., 1937), and reprinted in 1941, *Diş Sağlığı. Diş Temizliği* [Dental Health. Dental Hygiene] (T.C. Sıhhat ve İçtimaî Muavenet Vekâleti Neşriyatından No. 45) (Ankara: Alaeddin Kıral Basımevi, 1941).
161 Dr. Ali Vahid, *Dişlerimizi Niçin Temizleriz?* [Why do We Clean Our Teeth?] (Türkiye Himaye-i Etfal Cemiyeti Hıfz el-Sıhha ve Neşriyat Şubesi Numero 11) (Istanbul: Resimli Ay Matbaası-Türk Limited Şirketi, 1927), p. 5.
162 Dr. Ali Vahid, *Dişlerimizi Niçin Temizleriz?*, p. 7.
163 Dr. İhsan Özgen, *Üç Bela. Frengi, Fuhuş, İçki* [Three Menaces. Syphilis, Prostitution, Alcohol] (İzmir: Dereli Basımevi, 1935), p. 1.
164 *Zührevi Hastalıklar Nelerdir*, p. 7.

FIGURE 8.7   "This happened because I did not take care of my teeth", from Dişlerimizi Niçin Temizleriz? (*Istanbul, 1927*).

TAKING HEALTH TO THE VILLAGE 199

from pleasure-giving bad women".[165] As Özgen had pointed out in his booklet, infected prostitutes did not always bear visible signs of the disease but nevertheless "the poison of the disease flowed through their veins".[166] "Poison in the blood" was a popular metaphor used in relation to syphilis. Sara, Halide Edip Adıvar's main character in her novel *Mev'ud Hüküm* (Promised Sentence) first published in *Yeni Mecmua* in 1917–8, had asked how she could continue to live among people "with this terrible poison in her blood".[167] Kutkam's advice about how not to contract syphilis, whose victim was "doomed to death", whom "death alone could make clean" and "from whom all flee revolted",[168] was to avoid prostitutes and alcohol, for a drunkard "sees everything in rosy colours and for him every dirty woman is a beauty of the world".[169]

The importance attributed to visual material is evident in the advice given in a pamphlet on venereal diseases which urged its readers that if there was a hygiene museum in their area, they should go and visit it.[170] Although the pamphlets generally used cheaply produced black and white pictures, their impact on the reader was no less significant. The picture representing a syphilitic in the third phase of his disease left nothing to the imagination in its depiction of the destruction of the face and the skull by the disease.[171] The coloured version of this picture was first displayed in the Ankara Hıfzısıhha Müzesi and reproduced in colour in *Sıhhi Müze Atlası* published in 1926.[172] (fig. 8.8) Captions, when used, hammered home the message. Özgen, using this same image, added the caption "Look at that. Do you believe that this man is alive? Well in fact this unfortunate man lives. What kind of a life is this, you tell me".[173]

Similarly, another picture displaying the damage of syphilis on the skull and face of a third-phase syphilitic patient displayed in İstanbul Hıfzısıhha Müzesi was then reproduced in colour in *Sıhhi Müze Atlası* with the caption "the destruction of third-phase syphilis on the body and the skull"[174] (fig. 8.9A). This picture, too, became one of the popular illustrations used in booklets and

---

165 Kutkam, İsmail Hakkı, *Frengi* [Syphilis] (Istanbul: Halk Basımevi, 1937), p. 3.
166 Özgen, *Üç Bela. Frengi, Fuhuş, İçki*, p. 4.
167 Adıvar, Halide Edib, *Mev'ut Hüküm* [Promised Sentence] (İstanbul: Atlas Kitabevi, 1968), p. 58.
168 Kutkam, *Frengi*, pp. 11–12.
169 Kutkam, *Frengi*, p. 20.
170 *Zührevî Hastalıklar Müptelalarına Öğütler ve Tavsiyeler*, p. 4.
171 Kutkam, *Frengi*, p. 15.
172 *Sıhhi Müze Atlası*, plate 23, p. 21.
173 Özgen, *Üç Bela. Frengi, Fuhuş, İçki*, p. 26.
174 *Sıhhi Müze Atlası*, plate 22, p. 20.

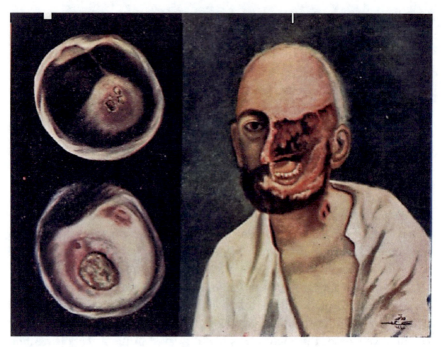

FIGURE 8.8   *A syphilitic in the third phase of his disease from* Sıhhi Müze Atlası *(1926).*

brochures on venereal diseases. In the Ministry of Health and Assitance's publication on venereal diseases, this man appeared with the caption "the outcome for a syphilitic man who did not receive regular treatment"[175] (fig. 8.9B). In Özgen's publication, the same man appeared described as "another example of those living dead". The text continued "stupidity brings a punishment like this. Before this, he was a clean citizen but inattention, lack of knowledge, brought him to this condition".[176]

The fear of being ridiculed or/and pitied was played on in the health pamphlets, particularly in the case of blindness. The cover of a pamphlet on smallpox used an image of a blind man with a stick in his hand to show what smallpox could do to somebody.[177] The caption under the picture of a blind man in Nuri Fehmi's book on trachoma read "a wretched man who was blinded because of trachoma".[178] A Ministry of Health and Social Assistance booklet, which used coloured illustrations, included a drawing of an old man with his

---

175   *Zührevî Hastalıklar Müptelalarına Öğütler ve Tavsiyeler*, p. 3.
176   Özgen, *Üç Bela. Frengi, Fuhuş, İçki*, p. 23.
177   The cover of *Çiçek Hastalığı ve Çiçek Aşısı*.
178   Dr. Nuri Fehmi, *Trahom Halk Kitabı*, p. 24.

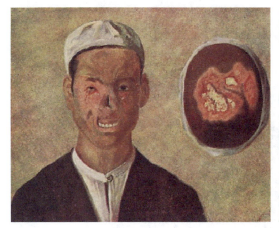 

FIGURES 8.9 A & B   *On the left "the destruction of third-phase syphilis on the body and the skull" from* Sıhhi Müze Atlası *(1926), and on the right "the outcome for a syphilitic man who did not receive regular treatment" from* Zührevî Hastalıklar Müptelalarına Öğütler ve Tavsiyeler *(Ankara, n.d.).*

son. The caption read "If trachoma is not treated, it blinds one. This old man was blinded by trachoma. His disease was also transmitted to his child. If his child is left untreated, he will be blinded like his father" (fig. 8.10). The picture in fact tells more than the written message, for it shows the old man needing assistance from a small boy and the couple look like beggars, an impression strengthened by the position of the boy's hand.[179]

Apart from the fear of the catastrophic consequences of disease or of being reduced to dependency or to being an object of pity, the literature also stressed the responsibilities of parents and portrayed the child as an innocent victim. Reşit Galip's short story in the *Dört Azgın Canavar* (Four Ferocious Monsters) on syphilis, gonorrhoea, tuberculosis and malaria, published by the Ministry of National Education in a book series, Books for People, recounted the story of Ahmet, a "green" young man who went from his village to İzmir for his military service. One day, on the invitation of his friend, Ahmet went drinking and womanizing and ended up in a brothel. Without knowing anything about syphilis and gonorrhoea, Ahmet, drunk, slept with a prostitute. A couple of days later, he felt pain while urinating and noticed a yellow greenish discharge on his underwear. When he talked to his friends, they told him pityingly that he had caught a disease from the prostitute. Ashamed, "ignorant" Ahmet, rather than going to see the battalion doctor, used some folk remedies

---

179   *Gözleri Kör Eden Trahom Hastalığı Hakkında Halka Nasihatler* (1933), and reproduced in 1941.

FIGURES 8.10   *"Trachoma, if not treated, blinds" from* Gözleri Kör Eden Trahom Hastalığı Hakkında Halka Nasihatler *(1941).*

suggested by his friends. After a while the symptoms of the disease became less visible and Ahmet interpreted this as meaning that his disease was cured. This was not, in fact, the case for the gonorrhoea had reached his internal organs and completely invaded his body. Some months later, Ahmet completed his military service, returned to his village and married Ayşe, who was "like an angel". Ahmet transmitted gonorrhoea to his wife, who did not understand the symptoms of this disease which inflicted her, and so "[the disease moved] from Ahmet to little Ayşe and from little Ayşe to Ahmet, refreshing itself and getting more and more out of control". After a while, Ayşe and Ahmet had a child. During the birth of the baby, the gonorrhoea microbes in Ayşe's genitalia passed to the baby's eyes. The couple did not speak to a doctor about their disease nor take the baby to a doctor, but instead tried to cure the baby's eyes using folk remedies. The outcome was that "the little one's eyes, which for weeks were full of pus, became blind without [ever] seeing the world".[180]

> The disease, passing to Ahmet's scrotum, to little Ayşe's womb and to her ovaries, made them sterile, their progeny was cut off, and they could not produce more children. They both became bedridden and they passed their lives in pain. Poverty and misery struck their home. On top of these, other diseases struck them. Strong Ahmet turned into a lifeless scarecrow. Little Ayşe shrivelled up like leaves which have encountered a premature winter. So this is the story of Ahmet who for a five-minute pleasure destroyed his own life and health, the health and life of blameless little Ayşe and the health and life of his innocent little child, who was the victim of ignorance.[181]

The danger of a "five-minute pleasure" was repeated in *Sıhhi Müze Rehberi*: "Do not have relations with bad women and do not put your life and the lives of your family and your children in danger for a few minutes of pleasure".[182] Demonstrating the consequences of such reckless actions became the basis of creating a feeling of guilt, and children, as innocent victims, were used to magnify this guilt. The caption under the picture of a young boy displaying syphilis boils exhibited in the Ankara Hıfzısıhha Müzesi, and then reproduced in the 1926 *Sıhhi Müze Atlası* read:

---

180   Dr. Reşit Galip, *Dört Azgın Canavar*, pp. 9–12.
181   Dr. Reşit Galip, *Dört Azgın Canavar*, pp. 11–12.
182   Dr. Hikmet Hamdi Bey, *Sıhhî Müze Rehberi* (1931), pp. 19–20.

One of our social disasters: the first syphilis wounds which pass by means of the kiss to an innocent and sinless child, who embraces his father, sharing in the joy produced among his family by the homecoming of a villager who went to the city with the aim of securing the prosperity and comfort of his family by earning money, but who, unable to control his desires, had relations with prostitutes and caught syphilis.[183]

Although the image of an irresponsible and weak father who surrendered to his base desires and brought disaster to his children was more related to venereal diseases, it was also used for other communicable diseases. Malaria, which "makes one weak, powerless and lifeless [and] renders one helpless", made people's offspring "lifeless, puny and useless".[184] Irresponsible or thoughtless disregard for hygiene by a parent could condemn a child, as underlined by a series of pictures in *Sıhhi Müze Atlası* which portrayed a father carrying tuberculosis germs into the house on the soles of his shoes and thus transferring tuberculosis to his small child, who, because of the "indifference of his father", was infected.[185]

The role parents played in the illnesses of their children and the responsibility they bore was a constantly reiterated theme. The 1930 *Zindelik Atlası* (The Atlas of Healthy Life), a translated excerpt from "a famous" work prepared for soldiers by the US government and sold for 50 *kuruş*, was a highly illustrated book giving advice to young men about healthy living. This book included a photograph of a group of small blind boys. The text under the picture read "These children became blind because of the gonorrhoea of their mothers. This disease is usually transmitted from their fathers to their mothers. Most blindness in children is the result of gonorrhoea" (fig. 8.11).[186] That parents were aware of their responsibility was highlighted in an illustration in a Ministry of Health and Social Assistance leaflet on venereal diseases, where a little blind girl was shown trying to find her way around with a stick while waving her other arm in air. Her parents, grief-stricken and ashamed, are not able to look at their little blind daughter. The caption reads as: "The catastrophe of those who get married before their gonorrhoea is treated: their children who are born blind" (fig. 8.12).[187]

---

183   *Sıhhi Müze Atlası*, p. 11.
184   *Sıtmaya Tutulmamak İçin Öğüdler*, p. 3.
185   *Sıhhi Müze Atlası*, p. 41.
186   *Zindelik Atlası*, p. 31.
187   *Zührevî Hastalıklar Müptelalarına Öğütler ve Tavsiyeler*, p. 5.

FIGURE 8.11   *A group of blind children from* Zindelik Atlası *(Istanbul, 1930)*.

Pamphlets ceaselessly emphasised the theme of responsibility. Those who, although ill, did not take the symptoms of their diseases seriously were not only responsible for themselves but also for others. If someone was married but did not seek treatment as soon as the first wounds and red marks of syphilis appeared, then the disease would without fail pass to the person's family, and this, regardless of whether it was done knowingly or unknowingly, was "a murder". It destroyed the family, caused children to be still born, and those who did survive either then died or, if they survived, did so "useless and a burden" on society.[188] If parents, and in particular mothers, did not follow the advice provided by the pamphlets on parenthood and childhood health, then they were condemned as having failed to perform their duties. In a 1926 publication, republished in the Latin script in 1929, parents were accused of being the reason

188   *Zührevî Hastalıklar Müptelalarına Öğütler ve Tavsiyeler*, pp. 3–4.

FIGURE 8.12   From Zührevî Hastalıklar Müptelalarına Öğütler ve Tavsiyeler (Ankara, n.d.).

for the deaths of 25,809 children, who, "victims of the neglect and ignorance of mothers and family heads", had died in 1924.[189] To make the point even clearer, a 1938 pamphlet on diarrhoea in children, the main reason for child deaths in the 1920s,[190] reproduced two pictures, one of a healthy, happy baby, described as "a normal healthy baby who suckles mother's milk" (fig. 8.13A), and one of a shrivelled, ill baby, "a neglected baby struck down by child diarrhoea"[191] (fig. 8.13B).

Illustrations of children, especially young children, were much used to demonstrate the devastating effects of diseases. Stylized illustrations based on images from hygiene museum exhibitions formed the basis for many images

189   Annelere Nasihat (1926), p. 2; Annelere Nasihat (1929), p. 3.
190   Annelere Nasihat (1926), p. 2; Annelere Nasihat (1929), p. 3.
191   Çocuk İshali [Diarrhoea in Children] (T.C. Sıhhat ve İctimaî Muavenet Vekâleti Neşriyatından, No. 55) (Ankara: n.p., 1938), pp. 3 and 4.

 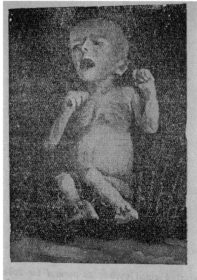

Ana sütü emen gürbüz ve normal bir bebek   *Çocuk ishaline tutulmuş bakımsız bebek*

FIGURES 8.13 A & B   *From* Çocuk İshali *(Ankara, 1938)*.

reproduced in health propaganda pamphlets, including those of the Ministry of Health and Social Assistance, even though the ministry employed its own artist in the 1930s.[192] Such illustrations could be used to represent more than one disease. One well-known image of a boy with a large swollen stomach was used in a 1925 publication to illustrate the effects of malaria with the caption "the end of a child with malaria who was not cured in time"[193] (fig. 8.14A). A slightly different coloured version of the same picture, with the same caption appeared, in the 1926 *Sıhhi Müze Atlası*.[194] Ten years later, another version of this image appeared in Özgen's booklet on syphilis, this time used to represent a child of a syphilitic woman and accompanied by the caption "a child with a huge stomach born from a syphilitic mother" (fig. 8.14B). What was required was not so much medical accuracy but a shocking image to reinforce the message of the text, here that "to contract syphilis can be an accident. [But] not to let oneself be examined, to transmit syphilis to one's wife and children is murder".[195]

---

192   *Vekâletin 10 Yıllık Mesaisi*, p. 7. In the late 1930s publications, the name of the artist who prepared the visual materials and whose name or initials appeared on them was given as Rüştü Ertuğ.
193   *Sıtmaya Tutulmamak İçin Öğüdler*, p. 2.
194   *Sıhhi Müze Atlası*, p. 3.
195   Özgen, *Üç Bela. Frengi, Fuhuş, İçki*, p. 15.

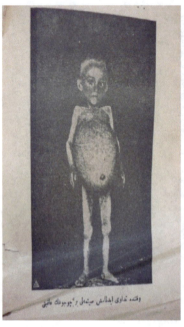 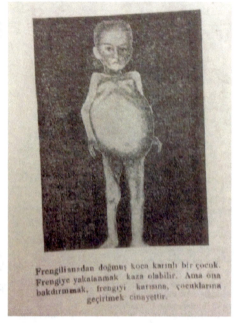

FIGURES 8.14 A & B   *The picture of a young boy used to illustrate, on the left, malaria, from* Sıtmaya Tutulmamak İçin Öğüdler (*Istanbul, 1925*), *and, on the right, syphilis, from* Üç Bela. Frengi, Fuhuş, İçki (*İzmir, 1935*).

Even when the image was used to demonstrate the effects of the same disease, the text could vary. In a Ministry of Health and Social Assistance publication on venereal diseases a picture of a baby whose body was covered with syphilis boils was reproduced, the caption reading "a still-born syphilitic child of a mother and father who were not treated properly". The illustration was in fact based on a picture from the İstanbul Hıfzısıhha Müzesi collection captioned "syphilis manifestations in a four-month old baby ill with the disease of syphilis transferred from its parents".[196] What mattered, then, was not correct representation but impact, an image which would produce a strong emotional reaction and lead the reader to take away the correct message.

The correct message, or at least one of them, was that individuals were responsible not only for their own health but also for that of others. Ignorance was no longer to be an excuse. Every mother had now to do what was necessary to protect her children from disease and had immediately to undertake the correct treatment as soon as the symptoms of diseases such as diarrhoea appeared, for in this way children would be kept safe and the population would

---

196   *Sıhhi Müze Atlası*, p. 23.

increase.[197] Similarly, fathers, the main bread winners, now had a responsibility both to take care of themselves and to avoid diseases such as syphilis and alcoholism in order not to endanger the health and well-being of their families. Inhabitants of a village or of a neighbourhood (*mahalle*) were to bear collective responsibility for the health of the people in their communities, an extension of the communal responsibilities such communities had carried for morality and social assistance.[198] Such responsibility was given religious weight: good believers sought cures for their illnesses, and respected and obeyed doctors' orders. Those who were infected had the responsibility of avoiding the 'sin' of spreading their diseases, as was explained in a Friday sermon published in 1928:

> The sin of those who escape from areas under quarantine and those who flee from battle are akin. Those who flee from a battlefield bring the enemy to their country, to their fatherland. Those who flee from quarantine bring contagious disease to the places they reach. Those who endure and do not flee from areas under quarantine resemble those who stand firm in the face of the enemy and bear every difficulty. What is the difference between a contagious disease and an enemy from the point of view of harm? Both are enemies. Whatever is necessary to stand against an enemy, is necessary too to stand against a disease.[199]

Those who were ill, even with mild illnesses, were not to go out but to stay in bed, "indispensible treatment both for their own health and that of the general public",[200] and those with flu had to take the right precautions so as not to spread the disease to others.[201] Those who failed to take such preventative measures were to be reported to the public health authorities.

To be a good citizen thus meant to be conscious of and responsible for one's own health, the health of one's family, of one's community and, by extension, one's country. Someone who "loved his family, his siblings, his nation" did not, for example, spit on the ground.[202] It was everyone's "national duty" not to

---

197 *Çocuk İshali*, p. 6.
198 Boyar, Ebru, "An imagined moral community: Ottoman female public presence, honour and marginality", in *Ottoman Women in Public Space*, ed. Ebru Boyar and Kate Fleet (Leiden and Boston: Brill, 2016), pp. 187–229.
199 "Hekim, İlaç, Hastalık" [Doctor, medicine and illness], in *Türkçe Hutbe*, pp. 211–12.
200 *Grip*, p. 4.
201 *Grip*, p. 6.
202 Kutkam, *Verem*, p. 10; Gönen, *Verem Nedir Nasıl Korunmalı?*, p. 8.

drink alcohol, to stop people drinking alcohol and to fight against alcohol.[203] As Dr. Arıkan explained to villagers in Thrace, "Your health is necessary for the state. When you are ill, you cannot work in the fields, when you are ill, you cannot pay your taxes, when you are ill you cannot be soldiers, in short when you remain ill you are of no use".[204] To be a useful citizen required not just attention to health, but a proactive engagement in sport, for "if you want to be an agile, brave, clever, healthy, and long-living citizen, a strong soldier, an able worker, do not neglect physical exercise".[205]

Health was incorporated into the construction of a sense of national and civic pride. Turks were healthy, disease was to be relegated to the realm of poor countries. Thus "the Turk loves cleanliness, she/he is clean".[206] It became an imperative matter of national pride to free the nation from trachoma, for trachoma was the disease of uncivilized countries with dirty and ignorant populations.[207] At a local level, health became an issue of civic pride. According to Dr. Yılal, the eradication of malaria from the province of Muğla would mean that "Gökabat [today Gökova], Dalaman, Köyceğiz and Milas, will no longer be known throughout the world for poisionous malaria, but Gökabat for its fish, Köyceğiz and Dalaman for their oranges and tangerines, Milas for its olives and Muğla for its tobacco".[208]

Although by 1938 the Ministry of Health and Social Assistance declared the victory of preventative medicine, at least in the case of diphtheria,[209] there was still a long way to go in order to change the general popular mind-set. Even in the late 1940s, Mahmut Makal wrote in frustration about the response of villagers, faced by an epidemic decimating small children, to the information from pamphlets read out to them by the health officer. One of the villagers commented:

> There's no sense in that ... As though any doctor could oppose the will of God! It is Allah who gives and He who takes away. We should be thankful

---

203   İspirtolu İçkilerin Sağlığa Zararları, p. 5.
204   Arıkan, Köylüler için Sıtma Hakkında Kısa Bilgiler, pp. 5–6.
205   Beden Terbiyesi ve Halk Sağlığı [Physical Exercise and Public Health] (T.C. Sıhhat ve İçtimaî Muavenet Vekâleti Neşriyatından No. 78) (Ankara: Alâeddin Kıral Basımevi, 1941), p. 13.
206   Kutkam, Verem, p. 13.
207   Dr. Nuri Fehmi, Trahom Halk Kitabı, p. 17.
208   Yılal, Sıtma Hakkında Köylüye Öğütler, p. 8.
209   Kuşpalazı (Difteri). Pek Tehlikeli Olan Bu Hastalıktan Çocuklarımızı Nasıl Koruyacağız [Diphtheria. How Will We Protect Our Children from This Very Dangerous Disease?] (T.C. Sıhhat ve İçtimai Muavenet Vekaleti Neşriyatından No 62) (Ankara: n.p, 1938), p. 6.

for the present day. We are alive, and what is the good of that? Day in, day out, it's our lot to curse our bad fortune – and that is a sin; as for these little innocents, leave them alone to join their mother angels in heaven![210]

Not all of the new citizens of the Turkish republic were, thus, persuaded by the health pamphlets and their often shocking illustrations. However, even if slow, the efforts of the early republican government and the constant campaign of health propaganda did contribute to the development of the concept of a healthy citizen, to a shift in attitudes to medicine and hygiene and to shaping a new, civic sense of responsibility for the well-being, both physical and moral, of the society of the new republic. Here, as in many other aspects of the building of the new nation, the efforts of the government were aimed at persuading and engaging the population in an environment where coercion was in essence not an option, and at bringing about a transformation of the human landscape of Anatolia.

---

210   Makal, *A Village in Anatolia*, p. 11; for Turkish original, see Makal, Mahmut, *Bizim Köy. Köy Öğretmeninin Notları* [Our Village. Notes of A Village Teacher], 5th print (Istanbul: Varlık Yayınları, 1952), p. 9.

CHAPTER 9

The Provision of Water to Istanbul from Terkos: Continuities and Change from Empire to Republic

Kate Fleet

In 1934 an article appeared in *Akşam*, a popular Istanbul daily newspaper, under the headline "Terrifying monster in Terkos Lake". Bemoaning the fact that, despite all efforts to persuade them, tourists were not coming to Turkey and noting the enormous drawing power of the Lochness monster, the author suggested a solution: articles in the British and American press about the discovery of a terrifying monster in the lake of Terkos outside Istanbul. Warming to his theme, the author described the monster as more than 50 metres long with teeth the size of the minarets of the Ayasofya mosque. Various eminent scholars regarded it as a survivor of the extinct species called "Hipotomyos Karphitos Phompos" which had lived in the period before the earth's crust had been formed, but, according to the theory of "Sir Klark", director of the London Nature and Geography Museum, it had entered the lake via an underwater passage that linked Terkos to the Mediterranean, of which the lake had in the distant geological past been part. This monster was, the author explained, the cause of the daily cuts in water supply that Istanbul experienced, for it inserted its head into the belly of the lake and cut off the city's water. Acknowledging that the visitors who would flock from America and all the cities of Europe would need to see an actual monster, the author suggested that this could be arranged by having very large people swim around the lake dressed in fur. Indeed, he announced, he would himself be willing to play monster for his country, just so long as the tourists came.[1]

Apart from poking fun at the gullibility of tourists and at the use of a British expert, the article demonstrates the importance of Terkos and its unreliable water supply for Istanbul. While the Terkos monster was mythical, the monstrous reputation of its water for the population of Istanbul was not. The lake of Terkos, north-west of Istanbul near the Black Sea coast, was a major source of water for the city in the late Ottoman and early republican periods. The provision of water from Terkos was from 1882 in the hands of the

---

1 Hikmet Feridun, in the column "Bir Çırpıda" [In One Breath], "Terkos Gölündeki Müthiş Canavar" [Terrifying monster in Terkos Lake], *Akşam*, 12 January 1934, p. 3.

Dersaadet, later the Istanbul Water Company, which was finally bought out by the government in 1933. The very troubled relationship between the state and this foreign company, the chronic failure of water provision and the undrinkable nature of the water that did emerge from the Istanbul taps continued from the late nineteenth century well into the twentieth and highlights both the continuities and the changes from Ottoman administration to that of the republican government.

For the leaders of the republic, celebrating the first decade of the state's existence in 1933, the contrast between the Ottoman and republican approach to public works and the provision of water was stark. In granting concessions the Ottoman government, swayed by political concerns and private interests, had given little thought to public benefit or the interests of the state and had concluded contracts that were "damaging to the state and the people". Such concessions were not considered "compatible with our national outlook today"[2] and in granting concessions the republican government gave the utmost importance to state and public benefit.[3] In relation to water provision, the Ottoman government, which had entirely neglected public health,[4] was more concerned with the pursuit of outside support and political influence than with the development of Anatolia and those to whom it granted concessions were "self-seeking and avaricious", men who knew well "how to benefit from the greed of the palace and from the capitulations". But now, the ministry announced triumphantly, water works in Turkey "are among the very successful and beneficial public works which will make the face of the nation light up in the future" and which owed their success to the founding of the republican government.[5]

But did the faces of the water-drinking Istanbul population reflect this apparent transformation? While the concession-granting policy adopted by the republic certainly did differ from that under the late Ottoman empire, as the British in particular were to find,[6] in the context of water provision was

---

2 T.C. Nafia Vekaleti, *On Senede Türkiye Nafiası 1923–1933* [Ten Years of Public Works in Turkey], 3 vols. (Istanbul: Matbaacılık ve Neşriyat Türk Anonim Şirketi, 1933), vol. III, pp. 5–6.
3 *On Senede Türkiye Nafiası 1923–1933*, III, p. 6.
4 *On Senede Türkiye Nafiası 1923–1933*, III, p. 57.
5 *On Senede Türkiye Nafiası 1923–1933*, III, pp. 57–8.
6 Fleet, Kate, "Geç Osmanlı Erken Türkiye Cumhuriyeti Döneminde Yabancılara Verilen Ekonomik İmtiyazlar" [Economic concessions given to foreigners in the late Ottoman and early Turkish republican period], *Kebikeç*, special issue *Uygur Kocabaşoğlu'na Armağan* [Festschrift for Uygur Koçabaşoğlu], ed. Onur Kınlı, 39 (2015), 343–62; Fleet, Kate, "Money and politics: the fate of British business in the new Turkish Republic", *Turkish Historical Review*, 2/1 (2011), 18–38.

there as stark a contrast between the position under the empire and that under the republic as republican rhetoric implied?

Seeking to answer this question contributes also to a more general understanding of the transition process from empire to republic and sheds light on the ways in which the new Turkish government sought strategies of legitimacy in its drive to incorporate its citizens into the new state with which they were to identify. One such strategy was the rhetoric of constant contrast between the past regime, its total disinterest in and lack of concern for the public good and its overall ineptitude, and the enlightened approach of the new, forward looking and successful republic.

The Little Frogs in Terkos: Providing Water to Istanbul in the Late Ottoman Empire

Provision of water to Istanbul had always been of major importance. Shortages of water were common and the populace often prayed for rain,[7] as they did, for example, in April 1576 when, Murad III conducted prayers at Eyüp.[8] One of Süleyman I's great acts of charity, according to Peçevi who expressed his hope that the sultan would receive God's blessings for it, was the construction of a waterway to bring water from Kırk Çeşme to the city, a work that cost as much as his great mosque complexes.[9] Evliya Çelebi described the knowledge of being able to locate water, construct waterways and bring water from the mountains to a city as "an incredible skill".[10]

In the later nineteenth century, as in the centuries before, Istanbul continued to suffer from periodic shortages of water, the summer of 1871, for example, seeing the people descending once more into "worries about water".[11] In 1873

---

7   Boyar, Ebru and Kate Fleet, *A Social History of Ottoman Istanbul* (Cambridge: Cambridge University Press, 2010), p. 66.
8   Gerlach, Stephan, *Türkiye Günlüğü 1573–1576* [Turkish Diary 1573–1576], 2 vols., trans. Türkis Noyan (Istanbul: Kitap Yayınevi, 2007), vol. I, p. 309.
9   İbrahim Peçevi, *Peçevî Tarihi* [Peçevi's History], 2 vols., ed. Murad Uraz (Istanbul: Neşriyat Yurdu, 1968), vol. I, p. 225.
10   Evliya Çelebi b. Derviş Muhammed Zıllı, *Evliya Çelebi Seyahatnamesi. Topkapı Sarayı Kütüphanesi Bağdat 304 Yazmanın Transkripsiyonu-Dizini* [Evliya Çelebi's Travel Account. Transcription-Index of the Baghdad 304 Manuscript in Topkapı Palace], vol. I, ed. Robert Dankoff, Seyit Ali Kahraman and Yücel Dağlı (Istanbul: Yapı Kredi Yayınları, 2006), p. 341.
11   Basiretçi Ali Efendi, *İstanbul Mektupları* [Istanbul Letters], ed. Nuri Sağlam (Istanbul: Kitabevi, 2001), from *Şehir Mektubu* no. 12, *Basiret*, no. 368, 29 Safer 1288/7 Mayıs 1287 (20 May 1871), pp. 2–3.

THE PROVISION OF WATER TO ISTANBUL FROM TERKOS   215

their backs were "splitting like cicadas from lack of water".[12] While Basiretçi Ali Efendi felt that the scarcity of water was not entirely due to the lack of rainfall, suspecting that the abuses of the water sellers and those responsible for the maintenance of the water conduits played a part, he nevertheless urged the religious teachers and their pupils to pray for rain.[13] By the late 1880s the issue was not merely one of water provision but involved also the providing of clean water.

It was in this climate, in a time when the empire was descending further and further into a morass of debt, that foreign concession hunters were in search of lucrative deals. One concession that was particularly attractive was the provision of water to the massive conurbation of Istanbul, and in the second half of the nineteenth century companies proposed various schemes in an attempt to secure contracts. The French company, Compagnie des Eaux pour l'Étranger, today Veolia Eau, sent officials to Istanbul during the reign of Abdülaziz to make proposals for the bringing of water to both shores of Istanbul from lakes and water sources surrounding the city. The company wanted the concession to bring water from the lake of Terkos first to Beyoğlu and then later to other parts of the city. Others also sought water concessions, including schemes to build a series of reservoirs in the valleys behind Bakırköy and bring water to the city from there, a scheme proposed by a French engineer Gavand (holder of the concession for Tünel) to pump water from Kağıthane to Beyoğlu and surrounding districts, a further project to bring water from Terkos to the city, put forward in 1864 by a construction engineer called Ritter, who was at the time working as advisor in the Ministry of Public Works, and one put forward by an Englishman (Oppenheim) to build a large dam at Alibeyköy and pump water from there using a steam machine.[14] There was thus a great deal of competition among western entrepreneurs for water projects.[15] Indeed it is even possible that there were concessionaire wars over obtaining water concessions, for later the holders of the Terkos concession, who had applied to the sultan for an extension of the concession period, complained in 1881 that "malicious rumours" claiming that the Ottoman government would not in fact grant the

12   Basiretçi Ali Efendi, *İstanbul Mektupları*, p. 163, from *Şehir Mektubu* no. 36, *Basiret*, no. 971, 9 Cemaziülevvel 1290/22 Haziran 1289 (5 July 1873), pp. 2–3. He uses the same phrase on p. 135.
13   Basiretçi Ali Efendi, *İstanbul Mektupları*, p. 329.
14   Öztürk, Ali İhsan, *Osmanlı'dan Cumhuriyet'e İmtiyaz Usulüyle Yürütülen İstanbul Belediye Hizmetleri (Yap-İşlet-Devret Ugulaması) (1852–1964)* [The Services of the Istanbul Municipality Carried out by Means of Concessions from the Ottomans to the Republic] (Istanbul: İstanbul Büyükşehir Belediyesi Kültür Yayınları, 2010), pp. 189–90.
15   Öztürk, *Osmanlı'dan Cumhuriyet'e İmtiyaz*, p. 189.

extension, had been spread against them in Paris, thus undermining their efforts to obtain the necessary capital for their company.[16]

While concessionaires were keen to obtain concessions, the government, accused by Basiretçi Ali Efendi of failing to deal with the problem of water provision,[17] was keen to grant them, but on certain conditions, one of which was that the concessionaires should provide a considerable quantity of free water to hospitals, schools and military barracks, as well as to the poor via free flowing public fountains. Apart from the clear financial advantages such an arrangement gave the government, this drive for free provision of water should also be seen within the context of the government's perceived public duty towards the population. Described by Basiretçi Ali Efendi as "the guarantor and constant protector of humanity and compassion and especially of our public repose",[18] the government clearly sought to present the granting of concessions as in the public interest and serving public needs. In their attempts to negotiate with the government, Otto Dingler, a German, and the Frenchman E. Didier, who obtained the Terkos concession in 1878, made frequent reference to the public benefit of the scheme, describing it in correspondence with the grand *vezir* as a "work of public utility of the first order",[19] "of the first necessity",[20] and one "of an incontestable utility".[21] The classifying of a concession as of public benefit was clearly important, for the phrase was also used in other concessions, such as in the 1890 *ferman* granting the concession for the Selanik-Manastır railway which referred to the enterprise as being "of public utility".[22] Hasan Fehmi Paşa, who presented a report in 1880 to Abdülhamid II on the economic conditions in Anatolia, referred to the need for the government to state that the public works it wished to see undertaken were for public benefit.[23]

---

16   Başbakanlık Osmanlı Arşivi, Istanbul (hereafter BOA), Y. A. Res. 13/3, letter from Luinet and Langierer to Said Paşa, 28 March/9 April 1881.
17   Basiretçi Ali Efendi, *İstanbul Mektupları*, from Şehir Mektubu no. 12, *Basiret*, no. 368, 29 Safer 1288/7 Mayıs 1287 (20 May 1871), pp. 2–3. See also pp. 95, 135, 432 and 471.
18   Basiretçi Ali Efendi, *İstanbul Mektupları*, from Şehir Mektubu no. 12, *Basiret*, no. 368, 29 Safer 1288/7 Mayıs 1287 (20 May 1871), pp. 2–3.
19   BOA, Y. A. Res. 13/3, letter from Luinet and Langierer to Said Paşa, 15/27 September 1880.
20   BOA, Y. A. Res. 13/3, letter from Luinet and Langierer to Said Paşa, 28 March/9 April 1881.
21   BOA, Y. A. Res. 13/3, letter from Luinet and Langierer to Said Paşa, 15/27 September 1880.
22   BOA, I. MMS. 121/5029, 13 Rebiülevvel 1308/15 Teşrin-i evvel 1306/27 October 1890, article 6.
23   Dinçer, Celal, "Osmanlı Vezirlerinden Hasan Fehmi Paşa'nın Anadolu'nun Bayındırlık İşlerine Dair Hazırladığı Lâyiha" [Memorandum prepared by Hasan Fehmi Paşa, one of the Ottoman *vezir*s, on Anatolian public works], *Belgeler*, 5–8/ 9–12 (1968–71), 26 Cemaziülahır 1297/24 Mayıs 1296 (5 June 1880), p. 164.

In its negotiations over the concession to provision Beyoğlu and surrounding areas from Terkos, the government thus imposed the provision of free water. Under the original concession of 1874, granted for 40 years to Kamil Bey, Master of Ceremonies in the Foreign Ministry[24] and Terno Bey,[25] reactivated after the Ottoman-Russian war and granted in 1878 to Didier and Dingler,[26] the concessionaires were to build, at their own expense and in locations selected by the municipality, 12 fountains for the public and to provide water daily to military barracks and military schools.[27] Under the 1878 agreement three further fountains were to be constructed. The government was also keen to ensure the provision of free water for fire-fighting, both the 1874 and the 1878 agreements stating that water for fire-fighting was to be provided free of charge.[28]

In 1887 the Terkos concession was extended to 70 years and the number of districts covered by the company increased.[29] Once again the agreement stipulated that the company was to provide free water to military schools, police stations, military hospitals, and to provision water reservoirs for fire-fighting. It was also to supply free water at a stipulated rate per day per bed to three hospitals, the municipal hospital in Tophane, the women's hospital in Haseki and the paupers' hospital in Yenibahçe.[30] Twenty small public fountains providing free water were to be built in Istanbul, again at the company's expense,[31] and the number of fire hydrants providing water free was

---

24 For biographical details of Kamil Bey, see Ergin, Osman Nuri, *Mecelle-i Umûr-ı Belediyye* [The Book of Municipal Affairs], 9 vols. (Istanbul: İstanbul Büyükşehir Belediyesi Kültür İşleri Daire Başkanlığı Yayınları, 1995), vol. III, pp. 1339–42.

25 "Terkos Su Şirketi Mukavelenamesi" [Terkos Water Company Agreement], 8 Receb 1291/9 Ağustos 1290 (21 August 1874), Ergin, *Mecelle-i Umûr-ı Belediyye*, V, pp. 2889–92.

26 BOA, Y. A. RES. 13/3, 10 Cemaziülahir 1295/30 Mayıs 1294 (11 June 1878), same date for both documents.

27 The daily figure was 40,000 *kıyye* (= 1 *okka*, c. 1,300 grams). If the company failed to carry out its concessions (that is for the İhsan Deresi reservoir, bringing water to Beyoğlu and surrounding areas and building water collection points), or if it was late in doing so, it would then provide 80,000 *kıyye* free.

28 Terkos Su Şirketi Mukavelenamesi, 8 Receb 1291/9 Ağustos 1290 (21 August 1874), Ergin, *Mecelle-i Umûr-ı Belediyye*, V, pp. 2889–90, clause 1; BOA, Y. A. RES. 13/3, 10 Cemaziülahir 1295/30 Mayıs 1294 (11 June 1878), clause 2 of the concession for the completion of İhsan Deresi and for the transportation of water, and clause 1 of the concession for the construction of water reserves.

29 BOA, I. MMS. 93/3929.

30 BOA, I. MMS. 93/3929, Mukavelename, clause 4. The rate was 40 *kıyye* daily per bed.

31 BOA, I. MMS. 93/3929, Mukavelename, with a note at bottom in French stating that it was accepted by the company and dated 17/23 July 1887, clause 3.

increased,[32] the company committing to build 173 new fire hydrants in Istanbul and an additional 130 fire hydrants in the Beyoğlu region.[33] Similar clauses were also included in the 1888 concession granted to the Üsküdar-Kadıköy Water Company.[34]

The government's drive to extract quantities of free water was clearly irritating to the company holding the Terkos concession, the Dersaadet Water Company,[35] which was not happy about the amounts involved which it regarded as excessive. In a letter sent to Münir Paşa, the Interior Minister and president of the commission on water, in August 1887, the director, Letall, protested about the Council of Ministers' desire to add yet further requirements for the provision of free water, namely three spouting fountains, to be built at the company's expense, as well as the provision of water free for three civil schools. Letall pointed out that the company already provided free water to various military and naval establishments representing an annual expense for the company of about 8,000 Turkish pounds.[36]

In granting concessions, the government thus wished to ensure the water supply of the city, perceived as part of its civic duty, and to secure as much of it for free as possible. There was a further aspect to water provision and that was the quality of the water provided. According to Alexander van Millingen, son of the Istanbul doctor Julius van Millingen, Turks were very fussy about the water they drank and had clear ideas about it. Good drinking water should come from rock, fall from a height, be lukewarm, flow fast and strong, be sweet, come from deserted plateaus, and should flow South-North, or East-West.[37]

---

32   BOA, I. MMS. 93/3929, Şartname, birinci fasıl, clause 7, 11/23 July 1887.

33   BOA, I. MMS. 93/3929, Mukavelename, with a note at bottom in French stating that it was accepted by the company and dated 17/23 July 1887, clause 3.

34   Elmalı (Üsküdar-Kadıköy) Su Şirketi Mukavelenamesi [Elmalı (Üsküdar-Kadıköy) Water Company Agreement], 23 Safer 1306/17 Teşrin-i evvel 1304 (29 October 1888), in Engin, *Mecelle-i Umûr-ı Belediyye*, V, p. 2919, clauses 4 and 5.

35   The Dersaadet Water Company was set up in 1882. For Dersaadet Osmanlı Anonim Şirketi Nizamname-i Dahiliyesi, see Ergin, *Mecelle-i Umûr-ı Belediyye*, V, pp. 2903-14, 5 Cemaziülahır 1299/12 Nisan 1298 (2 April 1882).

36   BOA, I. MMS. 93/3929, 20 August 1887, Letall, Directeur de exploitation, Compagnie des Eaux de Constantinople to Münir Paşa, Ministre de l'Interieur et Président de la Commission Supérieure des Eaux. The amount of water provided was 466,000 *ocques* (i.e. *kıyye*) per day. The company provided a list detailing all the places to which it provided free water and the amount of water provided, amounting to a total of 1,466 litres, BOA, I. MMS. 93/3929.

37   Van Millingen, Alexander, *Constantinople* (London: A. & C. Black, 1906), pp. 220-1.

According to Murad Efendi, originally from Vienna who served in the Ottoman army and then became an Ottoman diplomat in the mid-nineteenth century, the quality of water was as important to Ottomans as that of wine was to Westerners.[38]

Quality water, however, did not flow from the pipes in Beyoğlu bringing water from the lake of Terkos, a name which was to become synonymous with *musluk* or *şebeke suyu*, that is tap or piped water, which came to be referred to popularly as *Terkos suyu*. In the late nineteenth century Terkos was widely regarded as full of all kinds of carcasses.[39] It nevertheless provided water to such restaurants as the Sponik in Beyoğlu, described by the writer and journalist Ahmed Rasim as a pseudo-European restaurant popular with those with pretensions. Ahmed Rasim commented that if the water in the jugs on the tables at the Sponik stayed sitting there one more week, "the croaking of little yellow frogs, peculiar to Terkos will be heard. It is that clean!"[40]

By this period cholera microbes had appeared in the water of Terkos, and an Austrian expert was brought in to investigate,[41] giving rise to a satirical little poem written by a member of the staff of the prefect of the city who was clearly most unpopular at the time, as was the Austrian expert himself:[42]

> Monsieur Dr. Santimes was brought [to Istanbul]
> On the day he came he saw microbes in the water of Terkos
> The microbes escaped [the lake] and appeared in all the water of Taksim
> But with the Mayor we have, it is a waste of time to search for them.[43]

The cleanness of water was thus clearly an issue by the end of the nineteenth century. But it does not, interestingly, appear to have been one in either the

---

38 Murad Efendi, *Türkiye Manzaraları* [Views of Turkey], trans. Alev Sunata Kırım (Istanbul: Kitap Yayınevi, 2007), p. 56.
39 Mintzuri, Hagop, *İstanbul Anıları (1897–1940)* [Istanbul Memoirs (1897–1940)], trans. Silva Kuyumcuyan and ed. Necdet Sakaoğlu (Istanbul: Tarih Vakfı Yurt Yayınları, 1993), p. 103.
40 Ahmet Rasim, *Şehir Mektupları* [City Letters], ed. Nuri Akbayar (Istanbul: Oğlak Klasikleri, 2005), p. 206.
41 Sadri Sema, *Eski İstanbul Hatıraları* [Recollections of Old Istanbul], ed. Ali Şükrü Çoruk (Istanbul: Kitabevi, 2002), p. 31. This was during the cholera outbreak of 1893–94.
42 Many lampoons and satirical poems were written about him, Sadri Sema, *Eski İstanbul Hatıraları*, p. 33.
43 Yücel Eronat, Canan, *Ertuğrul Süvarisi Ali Bey'den Ayşe Hanım'a Mektuplar* [Letters from Ertuğrul Captain Ali Bey to Ayşe Hanım] (Istanbul: Türkiye İş Bankası Kültür Yayınları, 2006), pp. xv–xvi.

1874 Terkos concession agreement[44] or the 1878 Terkos agreements,[45] none of which contain clauses relating to the quality of water to be supplied. By 1887, however, when the concession was extended, this was not the case, for a clause was added to the agreement covering what should be done if the water of Terkos was found to be unclean and not suitable for drinking.[46] The fifth clause of the 1887 agreement stated that the water distributed was to be pure, without visible sediment and would not contain animal or vegetable matter of a level injurious to public health.[47] A very similar clause appeared in the 1888 concession granted to the Üsküdar-Kadıköy Water Company.[48]

Given that the concessions from the 1870s show no interest in water quality but those of the late 1880s do, one must assume that there was a shift between 1878 and 1887 in perceptions of public health and of the importance of clean water. Such a shift may be related to cholera which struck Istanbul regularly throughout the nineteenth century. A major outbreak occurred in 1865, referred to by Sadri Sema as "büyük kolera" (great cholera).[49] According to Sadri Sema, of eight or ten people going to a funeral for a victim of cholera in this "büyük kolera" outbreak, five or six would drop dead on the way and be buried together with the victim whose funeral they were attending.[50] This was an extremely serious epidemic which resulted in the government implementing various measures against the disease, including setting up a cholera hospital.[51] Further outbreaks of cholera occurred in Istanbul in 1870 in which 15,000 people died,[52] and in 1876 when 7,000 people perished.[53]

---

44 Terkos Su Şirketi Mukavelenamesi, 8 Receb 1291/9 Ağustos 1290 (21 August 1874), in Ergin, *Mecelle-i Umûr-ı Belediyye*, V, pp. 2889–92.

45 BOA, Y. A. RES. 13/3, 10 Cemaziülahır 1295/30 Mayıs 1294 (11 June 1878), same date for both documents.

46 BOA, I. MMS. 93/3929, Mukavelename, with a note at bottom in French stating that it was accepted by the company and dated 17/23 July 1887. Clause 2 says specifically that a new addendum was added. If the water from Terkos was bad, then water could be collected from a different designated catchment area.

47 BOA, I. MMS. 93/3929, Mukavelename, clause 4.

48 Elmalı (Üsküdar-Kadıköy) Su Şirketi Mukavelenamesi, 23 Safer 1306/17 Teşrin-i evvel 1304 (29 October 1888), in Engin, *Mecelle-i Umûr-ı Belediyye*, V, p. 2919, clause 6.

49 Ayar, Mesut, *Osmanlı Devletinde Kolera. İstanbul Örneği (1892–1895)* [Cholera in the Ottoman State. The Case of Istanbul (1892–1895)] (Istanbul: Kitabevi, 2007), p. 28. Figures for the numbers killed vary between a few thousand to 30,000, ibid, p. 29.

50 Sadri Sema, *Eski İstanbul Hatıraları*, p. 31.

51 Ayar, *Osmanlı Devletinde Kolera*, p. 29.

52 Ayar, *Osmanlı Devletinde Kolera*, p. 32.

53 Sadri Sema, *Eski İstanbul Hatıraları*, p. 31 and note 27. There was a further major outbreak between August 1893 and May 1894, killing 1,537 people, ibid, note 28. This was the one Sadri Sema lived through as a child and which he describes.

While there were thus major outbreaks before and during the 1870s, they did not apparently have an immediate impact on the provision of clean water. The major cholera pandemic, which broke out in 1881 and continued until to 1895,[54] however, may have been more influential. An outbreak of cholera in Edirne in December 1886 caused major panic in Istanbul. Sewers in Kasımpaşa, Hasköy, Pangaaltı and Tatavla were cleaned and unemployed provincials were expelled from the city and sent back to their home regions.[55] While it is possible that this cholera pandemic resulted in the inclusion of clauses concerning water quality in the 1887 Terkos agreement, there were also presumably other factors related to an increased understanding of the connection between clean water and cholera.

Concern about cholera, or more specifically, cholera reaching Europe, resulted in a series of international conferences on the disease, one of which was held in Istanbul in 1866.[56] The main view at this time was that the disease was spread by the movement of people and that therefore the best method of defence was to impose quarantine. Although the link between water and cholera was proposed at the 1874 international conference held in Vienna, and indeed had been demonstrated by the work of the British doctor John Snowden in the outbreak of cholera in Soho in 1854, quarantine continued to be the focus. The British authorities in India dismissed the work of Michael Cudmore Furnell, the sanitary commissioner for Madras, in the early 1880s who compared French water use and absence of cholera in Pondichery with the situation in British-ruled areas where there was no clean water and a great deal of cholera.[57] The actual organism which caused cholera was discovered in 1883. Ottoman awareness of the significance of clean water in the prevention of cholera seems to fit into this context and the setting up in 1885 of the public health commission is perhaps significant here.[58]

Although Ottoman governments from then on were aware of the need to ensure the quality of water, and although the companies were warned about

---

54 Ayar, *Osmanlı Devletinde Kolera*, p. 32.
55 Ayar, *Osmanlı Devletinde Kolera*, p. 34.
56 Huber, Valeska, "The unification of the globe by disease? The International Sanitary Conferences on Cholera, 1851–1894", *The Historical Journal*, 49/2 (2006), p. 462; Şehsuvaroğlu, Bedi N., *İstanbulda 500 Yıllık Sağlık Hayatımız* [Five Hundred Years of Our Health History in Istanbul] (Istanbul: Kemal Matbaası, 1953), p. 96.
57 Watts, Sheldon, "From rapid change to stasis: official responses to cholera in British-ruled India and Egypt: 1860 to c. 1921", *Journal of World History*, 12/2 (2001), pp. 327–8.
58 "Hıfzı Sıhhati Umumiye Komisyonunun Vezaifini Havi Talimat", [Instructions containing the duties of the Public Commission of Health Protection], *Düstur*, I. Tertib, vol. V (Ankara: Başvekalet Matbaası, 1937), pp. 349–52.

the quality of the water they supplied,[59] they proved unable to enforce the provision of clean water. On 8 March 1909, Zehrap Efendi, a deputy from Istanbul, complained in the Meclis-i Mebusan (Parliament) about the health conditions in the capital and, in particular, about the quality of water being delivered by the company from Terkos. "Public health in the capital", he noted, "is very defective". Concerned about the number of deaths from typhoid, averaging 16 a week since the beginning of the winter, he pointed out that the main, and indeed perhaps the sole, reason for the appearance of the disease was the existence of microbes in the drinking water. In Europe, he noted, where they paid attention to water quality, the disease had been almost eradicated. "The bad quality of the water of Terkos has been known for a long time". No measures had been taken against the Terkos Company (that is the Dersaadet Water Company) and Zehrap Efendi therefore demanded an explanation from the Ministry over the finding of a solution to the water problem which was "leaving public health exposed to a continuous danger".[60]

On 2 September 1909 the bacteriology laboratory, where water testing was conducted, presented a report on samples of water from Terkos and Elmalı. On water from Terkos taken from a tap in Nişantaşı, which was analysed on eight separate occasions over a 20-day period, in every cubic centimetre of water, they found numerous microbes, including e-coli and staphylococcus. The result of the testing was that the water was, in the words of the report, "impure".[61] A similar report was registered for the water of Elmalı which was also declared "impure and unsuitable for drinking".[62] The Meclis-i Mebusan discussed the issue in December 1909 and requested an investigation as to whether the conditions of the concession were or were not being adhered to.[63]

According to a report presented some years later, in August 1916, to the Ministry of Public Works about the Üsküdar-Kadıköy Water Company, the water in the reservoirs came from streams and from concrete channels that fed the run off from melting ice and snow from the forests and water from the rainy seasons into the reservoirs. The stream water was always very dirty and contaminated by organic matter while the reservoirs were polluted by animals which

---

59 Öztürk, *Osmanlı'dan Cumhuriyet'e İmtiyaz*, pp. 195–6.
60 *Meclisi Mebusan Zabıt Ceridesi* [Ottoman Parliamentary Records], İ:38, C:3, 23 Şubat 1324 (8 March 1909), p. 202.
61 Öztürk, *Osmanlı'dan Cumhuriyet'e İmtiyaz*, p. 211, facsimile of the report dated 10 Eylül 1325 (23 September 1909).
62 Öztürk, *Osmanlı'dan Cumhuriyet'e İmtiyaz*, p. 216.
63 Öztürk, *Osmanlı'dan Cumhuriyet'e İmtiyaz*, p. 196, note 999, 26 Teşrin-i sani 1325 (9 December 1909).

drank from them, entering the water and urinating in it. The fences put up by the company "in the name of public safety" had decayed and the watchmen, who had been placed there, had been withdrawn. The company's slowness is dealing with any of this was made clear in another report from July 1918.[64] In yet another report from December 1916 to the Interior Ministry on the reservoirs, conduits and drinkable water of Istanbul, it was noted that although the concession agreement with the company specified that the water should be hygienic and drinkable, this was not the case because the company did not concern itself with the issue and the water from the reservoirs was not being filtered. The report stated that this situation had to be ameliorated.[65]

It is thus clear that in relation to the provision of water, the Ottoman government, in granting concessions for water provision both to the Terkos Water Company and the Üsküdar-Kadıköy Water Company, expressed concern for public benefit and the quality of the water provided. Although fully aware of the dangers of dirty drinking water, concerned about the granting of concessions to foreigners and driven by a desire to ensure public benefit, the Ottomans, however, found themselves unable, despite the constant application of pressure, to force the foreign concession holders to fulfil their side of the contracts and to provide clean water in sufficient quantities.

The Little Frogs in a New Pond? Water Provision under the Republic

Such concerns continued under the republic, but what differed now was the government response. While the Ottomans, despite vociferous and frequent complaints about water quality, had been unable to force the company to provide drinkable water, the republic adopted a more robust approach which forced changes in provision, a renegotiation of the agreement[66] and ultimately led to the buyout of the company by the government in 1933. The original agreement drawn up between the Dersaadet Water Company and the "old government" was, in the eyes of the new republican administration, deeply flawed and had, as the Minister of Public Works Hilmi Bey put it in 1931, allowed the

---

64 Başbakanlık Cumhuriyet Arşivi, Ankara (hereafter BCA), 230 0 0 0 65 24 5, 15 Ağustos 1339 (15 August 1923), report date 25 Temmuz 1332 (7 August 1916) and 5 Temmuz 1334 (5 July 1918).
65 Engin, *Mecelle-i Umûr-ı Belediyye*, VIII, p. 4207, 23 Teşrin-i sani 1332 (6 December 1916).
66 Öztürk, *Osmanlı'dan Cumhuriyet'e İmtiyaz*, pp. 202–3, Ottoman facsimile and transcription dated 29 Mayıs 1339 (29 May 1923).

company to wriggle out of its obligations. This was, he said, a problem that the republican government would "sort out completely".[67]

The issue of water provision was to become part of the republican rhetoric against the "old government" and used as a shining example of how the new regime, with its concern for the public good and the material condition of its people, differed from that of the Ottomans. It also needed to be successful, for rhetoric alone in something as basic for the population as clean drinking water would not suffice, and for this rhetorical devise to carry any weight, talk had as much as possible to translate into reality. Such reality, however, was not easily attainable.

The success of water provision was not only a matter of infrastructure but also of education. The new republican government put considerable effort into educating its population about matters of health and hygiene, as Ebru Boyar's chapter in this volume shows.[68] One aspect of this was the emphasis on the importance of clean drinking water. While the Ottoman government had been perfectly aware of the dangers of polluted drinking water and had persistently run tests on the quality of the water arriving from Terkos, which invariably produced rather depressing results, now much more emphasis was placed on public education than had earlier been the case. Films dealing with health, for example, were distributed throughout the country covering, among other issues, clean water.[69] Articles were published about the effects of dirty water. An article by Dr. İbrahim Halil appeared in *Küçük Mecmua* in July 1922 in which he noted that it did not matter how good and clear water was if it became mixed with dirty water, something which happened with open water conduits into which the filth of the streets and sewage fell. The outcome was water which was no better than sewage. Thus when a cholera or typhus outbreak occurred in the city, it became an epidemic and many people died. The reason, he explained, for the spreading of typhus, paratyphus, cholera, dysentery, different diarrhoeas and intestinal worms was the water in the reservoirs. Water in the villages was, despite any belief that microbes could be sieved out, not drinkable.[70]

---

67   "Fırka Grupu İctimaında. Terkos Şirketi Su Şebekesinin Belediyeye Devri Takarrur Etti" [At the party group assembly. The turning over to the municipality of the Terkos Company's water network was decided], *Cumhuriyet*, 3 June 1931, front page.

68   See Ebru Boyar's chapter, "Taking health to the village: early Turkish republican health propaganda in the countryside", in this volume.

69   "Sıhhi ve İctimaî Sinema Filmleri" [Health and social cinema films], *Ülkü Halkevleri Mecmuası*, 9/2 (October 1933), pp. 253–9, here p. 259.

70   İbrahim Halil, "Şehrimiz Suları", *Küçük Mecmua*, 23 Temmuz 1338/29 Zilkade 1340 (23 July 1922), pp. 18–20.

Clean drinking water was something which the Terkos Water Company continued not to supply. In this, it was not alone. In December 1922 a report was presented to the Ministry of Public Works on the Üsküdar-Kadıköy Water Company. The report stated that in order to obtain drinkable water, the company had to improve the condition of its reservoirs. It further stated that water was being distributed without being filtered and that this was in contravention of the company's contract, and it concluded that the company must be required to implement filtering.[71] The 1922 report noted that from 1918 to the present, nothing had been done and it was clear that there had been no attempt to find ways of ameliorating the distribution problem. The water taken from the reservoirs remained in the same state as it had been before. In summing up, the report noted that the conditions of filtration requested as a result of the investigation conducted seven years before had not been achieved and concluded that it regarded it as unlikely that the water of Elmalı would in fact be made drinkable to the level required.[72] Several months later, in June 1923, the water of Terkos and Elmalı was once again described as undrinkable and the companies were again accused of not fulfilling their obligations. The water delivered contained microbes and these microbes would result in the appearance of deadly epidemics in the city.[73]

The republican response to this highly unsatisfactory state of the water provided was to insist that improvements had to be implemented before the renewal of the agreements with the two water companies, representatives of which were currently in Ankara. The companies were required to implement their obligations in full and according to scientific principles, repairs and renewals had to be made and the necessary measures undertaken to ensure the delivery of water to the city. The companies were required to analyse and check the water every day for microbes, in particular for e-coli, typhus and cholera, and if, after analysis, the quantity of e-coli bacteria was too high or there were typhus or cholera or other bacteria present or organic material was, through negligence, not at the agreed level, then the water was to be rejected and the company was to be held responsible for any delays. This was to be done "in the name of public health".[74] As a result of government pressure the Terkos Water Company was obliged to build the first purification plant at Kağıthane in 1926 to filter the water which was distributed.[75]

---

71 BCA, 230 0 0 0 65 24 5, 15 Ağustos 1339 (15 August 1923) report date 11 Kanun-u evvel 1338 (11 December 1922).
72 BCA, 230 0 0 0 65 24 5, 15 Ağustos 1339 (1923).
73 BCA, 230 0 0 0 65 24 5, 15 Ağustos 1339 (1923), report date 9 Haziran 1339 (9 June 1923).
74 BCA, 230 0 0 0 65 24 5, 15 Ağustos 1339 (1923).
75 Öztürk, Osmanlı'dan Cumhuriyet'e İmtiyaz, p. 204.

Despite any agreements or government pressure, however, the quality of the drinking water remained unacceptable. In 1930 the municipality reported that the water of Terkos was absolutely undrinkable and that the company did not employ a single bacteriologist.[76] Two years later the Terkos Water Company was under investigation by the Ministry of Health and Social Assistance over whether or not the water was drinkable, many feeling that it was not and that it was the cause of the majority of the illnesses in Istanbul.[77] An article in *Cumhuriyet*, a major Istanbul newspaper, towards the end of that year noted that although the company was bound under its agreement to bring water that was drinkable into the city, numerous reports showed that the water from Terkos was not potable and that the company's filter beds had failed to improve the situation.[78] In February 1931, the company requested yet another analysis of the water, Castelnau, the director of the Terkos Company, going to Ankara to discuss this. *Cumhuriyet* reported that such an analysis was unlikely to be agreed to because of the hundreds of analyses that had already been conducted, all of which had shown the water to be undrinkable.[79] In the following month the Ministry of Public Works warned the Terkos Company that reports showed that the water of Terkos was not potable and that if it was not drinkable within the next three months, the agreement with the company would be nullified.[80] An article in *Cumhuriyet* in April 1931, "Do We Still Believe It?", reported that the Terkos Company was in contact with the Ministry of Public Works and had informed it that it would undertake measures necessary to bring water into a drinkable condition, clearly something received with scepticism to judge by the title of the article.[81]

The company was harshly criticised in the press, being described by Yunus Nadi in *Cumhuriyet* in January 1929 as "traitorous" and "dishonourable".[82] The company was "a wound in every part of Istanbul" whose taps merely coughed into people's hands.[83] It was accused of spying for the Russians in the First

---

76 "Terkos İşi Şehir Meclisinde" [The Terkos issue in the City Council], *Cumhuriyet*, 21 November 1930, p. 4.
77 "Terkos Suyu İçilebilecek Bir Halde mi?" [Is Terkos water in a drinkable state?], *Cumhuriyet*, 30 December 1930, p. 2.
78 "Terkos. Tesisatın Mubayaası İçin 4 Ay Kaldı" [Terkos. Four months remaining until the purchase of the establishment], *Cumhuriyet*, 24 November 1930, p. 3.
79 "Hala mı Tahlil?" [Yet another analysis?], *Cumhuriyet*, 3 February 1931, p. 2.
80 "Terkos Şirketi. Nafia Vekâleti Cezrî Tedabir Alıyor" [The Terkos Company. The Ministry of Public Works takes radical measures], *Cumhuriyet*, 21 March 1931, p. 2.
81 "Hala İnanıyor mıyız?" [Do we still believe it?], *Cumhuriyet*, 20 April 1931, p. 3.
82 Yunus Nadi, "Terkos Mes'elesi" [The Terkos problem], *Cumhuriyet*, 31 January 1929, front page.
83 "Terkos İşi Şehir Meclisinde", *Cumhuriyet*, 21 November 1930, p. 4.

World War,[84] and of insisting on not employing Turkish officials,[85] and, in an article headed "The curse of Terkos", of selling air not water, as this was all that came out of their taps.[86] Those left without water or with a very poor supply complained to the Istanbul municipality against the Terkos Company[87] and unhappy customers took the company to court, one enraged customer stating during his case that "the company takes pleasure in torturing people".[88] Exasperated by yet another interruption in the supply of water from Terkos, an *Akşam* journalist exclaimed that an end had to be put to this situation.[89] It was said to be 1,000 times more difficult to get the Terkos Company to construct even the tiniest new plant than to "make a camel jump over a ditch".[90] The level of scepticism with which the company was regarded is summed up by the sarcasm of a piece in the *Cumhuriyet* column "Hem Nalına Hem Mıhına" (To Waver Between Two Sides), published under the heading "Ya Buna Ne Buyurulur Mösyöler?" ("What is this Monsieurs?"), in August 1931, which related to a fire in Fincancılar when there was said to be no water in the taps, something denied by the company. "Did the Terkos Company say there was water in the taps, it is my greatest principle absolutely not to believe it. Even if water gushes out of the taps, I still won't believe it, because it is my total conviction that the Terkos taps are a contrivance made not to give water but to take money".[91]

The failure of the company to provide either the quantity or the quality of water necessary and the mounting criticism of an unhappy Istanbul population led to demands for the company's concession to be annulled and for the company to be bought out. This was not in itself a new idea for in 1916 a report on water provision in the city argued that the failure of the company to provide sufficient water or water of the requisite quality was evidence enough to prove the need for such provision to be in the hands of the city administration. The government, therefore, should, the report argued, activate its right of

---

84 *Cumhuriyet*, 31 October 1932, p. 2.
85 *Cumhuriyet*, 14 February 1930, p. 4.
86 "Terkos Belâsı" [The curse of Terkos], *Cumhuriyet*, 16 January 1930, p. 3.
87 "Divanyolu'nda Su Yok" [No water on Divanyolu], *Cumhuriyet*, 2 January 1932, p. 2.
88 "Bir Su Davası" [A water case], *Cumhuriyet*, 2 October 1930, p. 4.
89 "Susuzluk. Dün İstanbul Ciheti Kerbelâya Döndü" [Drought. Yesterday a quarter of Istanbul turned into Karbala], *Akşam*, 30 August 1929, p. 2.
90 "İstanbulun Umumî Hizmetleri" [Istanbul public services], *Cumhuriyet*, 25 January 1939, p. 5.
91 "Ya Buna Ne Buyurulur Mösyöler?" [What is this Monsieurs?], *Cumhuriyet*, 7 August 1931, p. 2, in column "Hem Nalına Hem Mıhına" [To Waver between Two Sides]. A similar view was expressed the following year in the same column, *Cumhuriyet*, 5 April 1932, p. 3.

purchase in accordance with the agreement, buy the Terkos Water Company and hand it over to the Istanbul administration.[92]

From the point of view of the Istanbul municipality the situation was particularly pressing as under the Water Law of 1926, municipalities had been made responsible for the provision and distribution of clean water to their own regions. In an article on "Urban health work and the municipality" written by Dr. Asım Arar, the General Director of Hygiene in the Health Ministry, and published in 1935 in *Belediyeler Dergisi*, the monthly publication brought out by the Municipalities Association, the author noted that the administration of water in various areas had suffered "by being in many hands".[93] In the context of Istanbul, at the beginning of the War water being brought to Istanbul was under various administrations: the reservoirs and the water of Halkalı were administered by the Ministry of Pious Endowments, the water of Terkos by the Dersaadet Water Company and the spring water of Kağıthane by the municipality.[94] The law also stipulated that any municipal plans or projects concerning the provision of drinking water, an area very related to the health of the urban population, had to be approved by the Ministry of Health and Social Assistance.[95] The responsibilities of the municipalities over the provision of drinking water also appeared in the Public Hygiene Law of 1930 which stipulated that the municipality had to provide drinking water of a scientifically appropriate nature.[96] The Municipality Law of 1930 reiterated the duties of the municipality, one of which concerned the provision of drinking water in relation to public health and required the municipalities to provide water in accordance with the Water Law of 1926 and to keep their water clean and healthy.[97] As one speaker in the Istanbul city council put it in 1930, the new Municipality Law had thus "pushed the municipality into a responsible position over city water".[98]

---

92   Engin, *Mecelle-i Umûr-ı Belediyye*, VIII, pp. 4207–8.

93   Arar, Dr. Asım, "Şarın Sağlık İşleri ve Belediye" [Urban health work and the municipality], *Belediyeler*, 1 (1935), pp. 59–60.

94   Yurdakul, İbrahim, *Aziz Şehre Leziz Su. Dersaadet (İstanbul) Su Şirketi (1873–1933)* [Tasty Water to a Glorious City: the Dersaadet (Istanbul) Water Company (1873–1933)] (Istanbul: Kitabevi, 2010), p. 170.

95   http://www.mevzuat.gov.tr/MevzuatMetin/1.3.831.pdf, accessed 5 January 2017. See also *Belediyeler Dergisi*, 1/1 [1935], pp. 59ff.

96   *Resmi Gazete*, no. 1489, 6 May 1930, dördüncü fasıl, "Vilâyet Hususî İdareleri ve Belediyeler" [Special *Vilayet* Administrations and the Municipalities], clause 20, p. 8896.

97   "Belediye Kanunu" [Municipality Law], *Resmi Gazete*, no. 1471, 14 May 1930, ikinci fasıl, clause 15, no. 1, p. 8823 and no. 25, p. 8824.

98   "Terkos İşi Şehir Meclisinde", *Cumhuriyet*, 21 November 1930, p. 4.

Much of Istanbul's water came from Terkos,[99] which inevitably resulted in strained relations between the municipality and the Terkos Water Company, and discussions with the government in Ankara about finding a solution to the situation. In July 1932 *Akşam* reported that the municipality would be opening a court case on behalf of the city against the Terkos Company for leaving the population without water with no explanation.[100] In late 1928 the municipality met with the Ministry of Public Works about the Terkos Water Company.[101] Two years later, in November 1930, the Istanbul city council met to discuss the same issue and stated flatly that it wished "to be rescued from this evil". The company, which had "turned Istanbul into a ruin",[102] had done nothing that demonstrated any good intention towards the population or the municipality. Instead it alone was responsible for the fires which had reduced Istanbul to ruins, the failure of the Terkos fire hydrants to produce water having been documented numerous times by the police. The health of those who were in the unhappy position of drinking Terkos water was exposed to danger and the recently-constructed filter beds had no scientific value. It was thus essential to find a speedy solution to this "bitter affliction".[103] The solution that the municipality proposed was to dissolve or purchase the company as a matter of urgency.

Such a decision, however, was not in the hands of the municipality but of the government. In 1931 the Ministry of Public Works reported that as a result of investigations conducted into the possible annulment of the concession on the grounds that the company had for many years failed to fulfil its obligations, the only reason that was found which would be admissible for such an annulment was the quality of the water provided, which was not drinkable. This had prompted the company to investigate systems of canalisation and to employ a bacteriologist. However, the water provided still did not meet the necessary standards, due to the fact that the system used was "primitive", and there were still areas of dispute between the company and the government. It was therefore proposed that the company be purchased with an annual compensation

---

99 *Belediyeler* [Municipalities] (T.C. Dahiliye Vekâleti, Mahallî İdareler, Umum Müdürlüğü) (Istanbul: Holivut Matbaası, 1933), pp. 423–4, gives the annual consumption figures for Istanbul of water coming from Terkos. Terkos was the largest water source for the water needs of the people of Istanbul, and the Terkos Company's water network was the most important source of drinking water in the war years and earlier, Yurdakul, *Aziz Şehre*, pp. 170, 196–7.
100 "Terkostan Dava" [Case From Terkos], *Akşam*, 16 July 1932, p. 3.
101 "Terkos İşi Şehir Meclisinde", *Cumhuriyet*, 21 November 1930, p. 4.
102 "Terkos İşi Şehir Meclisinde", *Cumhuriyet*, 21 November 1930, p. 4.
103 "Terkos İşi Şehir Meclisinde", *Cumhuriyet*, 21 November 1930, p. 4.

being paid to the end of the period of the concession.[104] The decision to buy the company, because of the inefficiency of the network, the inability to satisfy the water needs of the city, the complaints which had been made against the company for years and the dissatisfaction of the population, was taken in September 1931.[105] Thus the Istanbul Terkos Water Company, whose concession was considered by the Ministry of Public Works to be incompatible with the new republican ethos, was finally bought out on 20 May 1933,[106] and, in the words of a headline in *Milliyet*, the people were rescued from Terkos.[107] The Istanbul Water Administration, under the control of the Istanbul municipality, was officially set up to deal with the water supply from Terkos at the beginning of June 1933. The Water Administration was to benefit from the rights and concessions which the Terkos Water Company had possessed.[108] At this point the water supply controlled by pious endowments was also handed over to the Istanbul Water Administration, so that all Istanbul water was under the control of one body.[109]

The endless struggles of the Turkish government and the Terkos Water Company mirrored those of the Ottoman administration. Both fought hard to wrench drinkable water from the concessionary company, something it was

---

104 BCA, 30 1 01 02 21 43 13, 17 June 1931.
105 BCA, 30 18 01 02 23 66 14, 21 September 1931.
106 *Düstur*, Dördüncü Tertib, vol. XIV (Ankara: Başvekalet Matbaası, 1933), pp. 646–50, 20 May, 1933. See also, *On Senede Türkiye Nafıası 1923–1933*, III, p. 15. Two companies, the Istanbul Terkos Water Company and the İzmir Jetty Company, whose concessions and the stipulations of their agreements were not seen as fitting with the present attitude, were bought out by the government, in accordance with the purchase clauses in their agreements, and their holdings became part of public property, *On Senede Türkiye Nafıası 1923–1933*, III, pp. 5–6. Under the sale agreement, the Istanbul municipality was to pay an annual sum of 1.5 million francs until the end of the concession, Thobie, Jacques, "Un contexte de crises: les relations économio-financières entre la Turquie et la France de 1929 à 1944", in *IIIrd Congress on the Social and Economic History of Turkey, Princeton University 24–6 August 1983*, ed. Heath W. Lowry and Ralph S. Hattox (Istanbul, Washington and Paris: The ISIS Press, 1990), p. 165, note 88. The "liberation" of the Terkos company was reported in *Oriente Moderno*, 13/1 (1933), p. 2, "Riscatto della Società 'Terkos' per il refornimento d'acqua di Costantinopoli".
107 Öztürk, *Osmanlı'dan Cumhuriyet'e İmtiyaz*, p. 210, note 1079, 29 December 1932.
108 *Resmi Gazete*, no. 2416, 1 June 1933, "İstanbul Belediyesine Bağlı (İstanbul Sular İdaresi) Teşkili Hakkında Kanun" [Law on the organisation (The Istanbul Water Administration) under the Istanbul Municipality], no. 2226, date accepted 27 May 1933, pp. 2589–90.
109 Yurdakul, *Aziz Şehre*, p. 223.

in fact bound to provide under its contractual agreements. What differed between the approach under the Ottomans and that of the new republican leaders, both in this particular instance and more generally, was, apart from the cancellation of the concession, not so much the drive for, or ignoring of, public benefit, as popular involvement and pressure through the press, and the government's determination to construct an economy free from foreign control.

Little Frogs Post Nationalisation: A New World of Water?

The issue of water provision and of clean drinking water continued to be a preoccupation for the government through the 1930s. In May 1934 the Law on the Organisations and Duties of the Ministry of Public Works was passed. One of the matters it covered was the organisation of water works. Under this new law a General Directorate of Water was established, the duties of which included overseeing projects related to bringing drinking water to villages, towns and cities and ensuring that they conformed to scientific requirements.[110] Under the Law for the Legal Expropriation to be Carried out by a Municipality passed on 9 June 1934, the municipalities were granted the right of legal expropriation if necessary of sources of water outside the borders of the city and the land between the source and the city.[111] The following year a directive was issued by the Ministry of Public Works dealing with how projects for drinking water were to be prepared and carried out. Chemical and bacteriological analyses were to be conducted on water for urban areas and the Ministry of Health and Social Assistance was to decide whether this water was or was not suitable for drinking upon the basis of these reports.[112]

The importance of clean water and the responsibility of the municipalities to provide it was regarded as paramount. "Today" wrote Dr. Asım Arar in 1935, "in the country and in the municipalities there is a responsibility the name of which was not even mentioned before: water responsibility".[113] Now the importance of this issue was understood by all, for "Today no one can be

---

[110] "Nafıa Vekâletinin Teşkilât ve Vazifelerine Dair Kanun" [Law on the organisation and duties of the Ministry of Public Works], *Resmi Gazete*, no. 2713, 29 May 1934, clause 10, "Sular Umum Müdürlüğü" [The General Directorate of Water], p. 3854.

[111] "Belediyece Yapılacak İstimlâk Hakkında Kanun" [Law for the legal expropriation to be carried out by a municipality], *Resmi Gazete*, no. 2722, 9 June 1934, p. 3956.

[112] "İçmesu Projelerinin Ne Suretle Hazırlanacağına Dair Talimatname" [Directive on how drinking water projects will be prepared], *Belediyeler Dergisi*, 1/4–5 (September-October 1935), p. 55.

[113] Arar, "Şarın Sağlık İşleri ve Belediye", p. 60.

found who does not understand the value of clean water".[114] For Halit Ziya, the engineering inspector for the land registry, writing in the same year, water provision was "the greatest need of the cities" and one which the municipalities had to tackle "immediately and root and branch". Qualified experts with previous experience should be employed and given strong financial support by the municipalities, who must ensure that such work did not fall into the hands of individuals who were amateurs with no experience and were out merely for profit, a clear allusion to the concessionary companies.[115] Clean water provision was regarded as being the number one health priority,[116] the link between typhus and water supply being noted.[117]

Much play was made of the difference between the old regime and the new. According to an article in *Belediyeler Dergisi* from March 1936 entitled "Temiz Su Meselesi" (The issue of clear water), "water works, which were ignored for hundreds of years, like all health issues in our country, were taken in hand by the municipalities under the directives of the republican laws and began to be worked on".[118] Writing in 1937 in an article which was published in *The Financial Times*, Ali Çetinkaya, the Minister of Public Works, stated that "In the old régime most of the public utilities were established with political aims and by foreign capital. They were uncontrolled and acted on their own will, while performing their duties and responsibilities. Besides, they aimed at making money rather than at giving full consideration to the needs of the public". With regard to concessionary companies whose agreements had been made under the Ottomans, he noted that the government required them to observe its aims and principles, "namely, to serve the public in the cheapest, but in the best way" and went on to state that "the Republican, unlike the Ottoman government was not willing to remain inert and negligent as regards the matters of public need, interest and safety". He also noted that "the drinking-water supply systems of the cities and towns are being given due attention".[119]

114   Arar, "Şarın Sağlık İşleri ve Belediye", p. 60.
115   Halit Ziya, "Şehirlerimizde Evler Nasıl Olmalı? Şehirlerin Sıhhî ve Ucuz Suyu Nasıl Temin Edilir. Hal Yapmalı mıyız ve Bu Nasıl Olmalı?" [How should our houses be in our cities? How can healthy and cheap water be secured? Should we build covered markets and how should they be?], *Belediyeler Dergisi*, 1/4–5 (September-October 1935), p. 34.
116   "Şehircilikte Egemen (Hakim) Olması Lâzım Gelen Fikirler" [Necessary ideas dominant in urban planning], *Belediyeler Dergisi*, 1/2 (July 1935), p. 13.
117   Rauf Ahmet, "Tifo ve Su Meselesi" [Typhus and the water problem], article published in *Kaynak*, 14 March 1936, reprinted in *Belediyeler Dergisi*, 1/9 (March 1936), p. 20.
118   Atamanoğlu, Dr. Şerafettin, "Temiz Su Meselesi" [The Problem of clean water], *Belediyeler Dergisi*, 1/9 (March 1936), p. 14.
119   Çetinkaya, Ali, "Achievements and future prospects of Turkish public works activity", *The Financial Times*, 1 February 1937, p. 29.

Despite such pronouncements, water provision throughout the country remained a massive problem for the authorities. In 1935 two studies of water quality in villages around Ankara were published in *Ülkü*.[120] The author's report was damning about the drinking water of one of the villages, Kutludüğün: "not just in our villages but even in the most primitive countries in the universe it would be impossible to see the surroundings of a source of water made so filthy with the filth of men and animals". Stating that "I have never seen villagers who are so unthinking about their health as the villagers of Kutludüğün", the author concluded that "this water is in every way a breeding ground for disease and microbes".[121]

Faced with such problems, the government put considerable efforts into educating the public about the importance of clean water. Dr. Zeki Nasır, writing in *Ülkü* in 1933, noted that "the most important health issue of a village is the water it possesses" and went on to explain that the rubbish of a village and the manure of animals should be collected together and deposited in a concrete cesspit to be constructed at a distance from the village. If this was not possible, then such material was to be tipped into and buried in a large pit.[122]

Such education continued into the 1940s. In 1940, the Ministry of Health and Social Assistance published a little booklet entitled *Sağlığımıza Zarar Veren Barsak Kurtları* (Intestinal Worms which Damage Our Health) in which one of the ways to guard against such parasites was not under any circumstances to drink water the cleanliness and nature of which was unknown.[123] In 1948 the Ministry of Health and Social Assistance produced a three-page pamphlet on *Su İjyeni* (Water Hygiene) which explained what type of water was drinkable, ways to ensure the cleanliness of spring and well water, what diseases where transmitted by dirty water, how to cleanse dirty water and how to kill microbes.[124] It also described how it was necessary to fence off an area of 20 to 25 metres around water sources to prevent animals and people entering, a

---

120 Çağlar, Kerim Ömer, "Ankara Köylerinde Bir Toprak ve Su Etüdü" [A soil and water study in villages of Ankara], *Ülkü Halkevleri Mecmuası*, 24/4 (February 1935), pp. 440-3; and Çağlar, Kerim Ömer, "Ankara Köylerinde Bir Toprak ve Su Etüdü" [A soil and water study in villages of Ankara], *Ülkü Halkevleri Mecmuası*, 25/5 (March 1935), pp. 40-6.
121 Çağlar, "Ankara Köylerinde Bir Toprak ve Su Etüdü", 25/5 (Mart 1935), p. 43.
122 Dr. Zeki Nasır, "Köylerimizin Sağlık İşleri" [The Health works of our villages], *Ülkü Halkevleri Mecmuası*, 7/2 (August 1933), p. 42.
123 *Sağlığımıza Zarar Veren Barsak Kurtları* [Intestinal Worms which Damage Our Health] (T.C. Sıhhat ve İctimaî Muavenet Vekâleti, no 70) (Ankara: n.p., 1940), p. 5.
124 *Su İjyeni* [Water Hygiene] (T.C. Sağlık ve Sosyal Yardım Bakanlığı, no. 137) (Ankara: Recep Ulusoğlu Basımevi, 1948).

requirement also stressed (but ignored) in the Ottoman government's dealing with the then Dersaadet Water Company.[125]

In Istanbul the municipality, after the sale of the Terkos Water Company and the establishment of the Istanbul Water Administration, continued to be plagued with problems of water provision. Officials looked abroad for inspiration. In December 1933 the deputy mayor Hamit Bey did a tour of the water establishments in Athens, and was "very impressed" by what he saw. In a period in which the water of Terkos was to be reformed the mayor Muhittin Bey thought it suitable to investigate closely the water organisation of Athens. Therefore the director of the municipal technical works, Ziya Bey, a water engineering professor from the school of engineering Burhanettin Bey and the director of the municipal water administration, İhsan Bey would be going to Athens in January 1934.[126] The municipality invested heavily in water infrastructure, claiming in 1938 to have spent two million lira since its takeover in 1933.[127] It imported equipment from England which would, it claimed, improve supplies so much that they would need to think about what to do with the excess.[128] It employed, or retained, foreign experts, such as the Viennese water engineer Monsieur Finer who conducted investigations at the lake of Terkos together with a municipal committee in 1933,[129] M. Marten, a specialist who had been retained with a monthly salary of 400 lira to work on preparations for the administration of the plant of the Istanbul Terkos Water Company and whose employment was extended in April 1933 for a further year,[130] and the English engineers Frank Mallinson and Leonard Tenent who came from England in 1937 to set up machinery and pumps which had been purchased for the Istanbul Terkos factory.[131] Much play was made, in line with the general rhetoric that drew a sharp distinction between the Ottoman and the republican administrations, of the contrast between the approach of the municipality and the company. When the municipality took over from the company it did not "inherit its bad character", because "it was not a foreign company whose only

---

125 *Su İjıyeni*, p. 2.
126 "Su Meselesi" [Water problem], *Akşam*, 5 December 1933, p. 3.
127 "İstanbulda Hakiki Bir Su Meselesi Var mıdır?" [Is there really a water problem in Istanbul?], *Cumhuriyet*, 18 January 1938, p. 5.
128 "İstanbulda Hakiki Bir Su Meselesi Var mıdır?", p. 5; "Belediyeye Devredildikten Sonra" [After the handover to the municipality], *Cumhuriyet*, 25 January 1939, p. 7; "Şehir, Hergün Sekiz Saat Susuzdur" [City without water for eight hours every day], *Cumhuriyet*, 5 February 1939, p. 2.
129 BCA, 30 18 1 2 35 32, 27 April 1933.
130 BCA, 30 18 1 2 35 23 12, 12 April 1933.
131 BCA, 30 18 1 2 80 95 17, 23 November 1937.

thought was money-making" but was "an institution of the people charged with service to the citizens of Istanbul".[132]

Despite such rhetoric and the municipality's claims that it had greatly increased the amount of water provided in comparison with the quantities delivered by the Terkos company, that it had made it much easier for people to have water in their houses and that it had reduced charges,[133] water provision in the city still remained a major problem. Areas of the city, such as Aksaray, remained without water[134] and Büyükada and Heybeliada were still without a water supply in 1938.[135] Some problems were blamed on the infrastructure of the old company, including the narrowness of the pipes which prevented the delivery of a sufficient volume of water for fire-fighting.[136]

Complaints about the inadequacy of the water supply continued and questions were posed about exactly what the difference was between the situation under the Terkos Water Company and now under the municipality. Ten days after the municipality had taken over, a journalist, together with a photographer, paid a visit one late afternoon to the new water administration. Passing through a narrow, badly lit doorway, they entered the building which had, until very recently, housed the Terkos Water Company. In a corner they noted a heap of signs which, they were told, were those which had hung up in front of the old company's headquarters and its branch offices. New ones were apparently being made. The stationary of the new water administration was, they found, that of the old company, the only change being that Municipal Terkos Water Administration was stamped on the paper headed Terkos Company. Not only was the stationary the same, but there had also been no change in personnel, apart from the director of municipal water administration, İhsan Bey, now having the position of assistant director of the administration of Terkos water added to his responsibilities. As they exited the building the reporter turned to the photographer and asked "what difference is there between the Terkos Company and the Istanbul Municipal Terkos Water Administration?" to which

---

132 "İstanbul Sularının Kurtuluşu" [Salvation of the waters of Istanbul], in the column "Hem Nalına Hem Mıhına", *Cumhuriyet*, 10 May 1938, p. 3.
133 "İstanbulda Hakiki Bir Su Meselesi Var mıdır?", p. 5, "Belediyeye Devredildikten Sonra", front page and p. 7.
134 "Halkın Şikayeti" [The complaint of the people], *Cumhuriyet*, 1 September 1938, p. 2.
135 *Cumhuriyet*, 20 August 1939, p. 2. The paper reported that water was to reach Büyükada that year and Heybeliada in the following year. The water, which was Terkos water, was to be shipped to the islands by tanker.
136 "Yangın Tahkikatı" [Fire investigation], *Cumhuriyet*, 29 June 1934.

the photographer replied without hesitation "Look at the names! One has water in it and the other doesn't".[137]

Stinging criticism was levelled again at the municipality in a 1935 article in *Cumhuriyet*. The departure of the Terkos Water Company had not, it stated, "rescued Istanbul from its water afflictions". Just as the handing over of the water plant to the municipality in Ankara had not solved the situation there, so too had the problems not been resolved in Istanbul. In fact, the article went on, "the inability of this country to deal with the water issue is astounding", a shining example being the situation in Istanbul.[138] Yunus Nadi, writing in 1939, noted that although the city of Istanbul had taken the administration of its water into its own hands, it had still not organised water provision. "The reason", he wrote, "is that Istanbul has still not reached the understanding that it is and will be master of its own affairs. Among the population the name of the Istanbul Water Administration is still the Terkos Company. But no, it is not like this, the water issue of Istanbul is the affair of the city of Istanbul itself and of the people of Istanbul personally".[139]

Conclusion

The Istanbul municipality might thus have been in charge of the provision of water from Terkos to the city, but its ability to do the job well was still very much under question seven years after the sale of the Istanbul Water Company. Despite the republican rhetoric contrasting the water provision of the Ottomans when, as the Cumhuriyet Halk Partisi (the governing Republican People's Party) put it in its 1938 publication, "drinking water was completely forgotten",[140] the Ottomans were neither indifferent to the water needs of the capital's population nor to the concept of public benefit. Ottoman authorities were also, at least by the 1880s, perfectly aware of the dangers of dirty water and put constant, but unsuccessful, pressure on the Dersaadet Water Company to ensure that the water it supplied was potable. Repeated analyses showed,

---

137 "İstanbul Su Meselesi. Terkos Şirketi İle Yeni İdarenin Farkı Nedir?" [The Istanbul water problem. What is the difference between the Terkos Company and the new administration?], *Cumhuriyet*, 13 January 1933, front page and p. 2.
138 "İstanbulun Su Derdi" [Istanbul's water affliction], *Cumhuriyet*, 25 April 1935, p. 1.
139 Yunus Nadi, "İstanbul Şehrinin İmari ve İdaresi" [The urban development and administration of Istanbul], *Cumhuriyet*, 17 January 1939, pp. 1 and 9, here p. 9.
140 Cumhuriyet Halk Partisi, *On Beşinci Yıl Kitabı* [The Fifteenth Year Book] (Istanbul: Cumhuriyet Matbaası, 1938), p. 265.

however, that, far from drinkable, the water was full of bacteria. What the Ottoman government thus failed to do was not to ignore public benefit or attempt to provide the Istanbul population with safe drinking water, but to force the concession-holding company to honour its obligations and to provide the quality and quantity of water it was contracted to deliver.

In the early years of the republic, the government continued to struggle with the company. However, its approach to concessions and to foreign capital was in marked contrast to that adopted previously by the Ottomans and its rhetoric of economic independence, while not new as it had also been employed in the late empire, was converted into practical policy as the new state sought to assert its independence in the dangerous waters of post-First World War international politics. The buy-out of the Istanbul Water Company was therefore only a matter of time, although it did not finally happen until a decade into the republic's existence.

The buy-out of the company and the hand-over of the administration of Terkos to the Istanbul municipality did not, however, lead to instant success or to a marked change in the delivery of water to the long-suffering inhabitants of the city which continued to suffer water shortages throughout the 1930s. The provision of water was of such a complexity and required such a significant investment in infrastructure that the municipality was inevitably faced with a herculean task and the water problems of the city continued well beyond the outbreak of the Second World War.

Examining the ways in which the issue of water provision was handled by the various governments, both Ottoman and republican, sheds light not merely on the mechanics of public works provision but also contributes to an understanding more generally of the period of transition from empire to republic and of the realities of the new Turkish regime. One aspect that becomes clear from this examination is the importance of anti-Ottoman rhetoric as a tool for legitimacy in the early republic. The Ottomans presented a constant foil for the leaders of the new state as they attempted to take the population with them along the road of progress. Advances, perceived or real, made by the new state were presented in terms of progress against the bench mark of Ottoman backwardness. The republican government's approach to the Terkos Company water concession, and to concessions more generally, highlights the reality of the drive for economic independence and the wariness of foreign concessions and foreign capital. Although anxious not to reject foreign investment out of hand, and although pragmatic statements were issued by the new government aimed at assuring potential investors that foreigners were by no means unwelcome, the underlying logic of much of Turkish economic policy was that of securing independence and avoiding any potentially dangerous reliance on an outside power. However, the gap between aspiration and performance was not an easy one to fill and the struggle with the Terkos Water Company contributes to a stark picture of the enormity of the task before the new state in the first decades of its existence, faced as it was by financial impoverishment, much foreign hostility, and the backlash against its own rhetoric of success and contrast with the Ottomans. While the British seethed with annoyance at the creation of the new state, and propagated a view of Turkish economic ineptitude, Geoffrey Knox, acting counsellor in Ankara in 1927, describing commerce and finance as being the spheres in which the Turks' "inexperience and native incompetence" were most marked,[141] the population was not always persuaded by the government's rhetoric and, in the case of water provision, proved highly capable of offering scathing criticism when confronted by rhetorical rather than real success.

---

141 The National Archives, London, FO 371/12320, p. 92b, 20 July 1927.

CHAPTER 10

Reforms or Restrictions? The Ottoman Muslim Family Law Code and Women's Marital Status in Mandate Palestine

Elizabeth Brownson

The world's first official Muslim family law code, the Ottoman Law of Family Rights (Hukuk-ı Aile Kararnamesi, hereafter OLFR) of 1917, would have an important impact beyond the empire, as it became the model for several states' family codes in the Middle East. But within the empire, there was little opportunity to implement the law because the Ottomans repealed it two years later, and in any case, Turkey's civil code eliminated all religious law in 1926. However, after the British occupied the Ottoman districts of Palestine (the *sancak*s of Jerusalem, Acre, and Nablus) during the First World War, they upheld the law for Muslims, instructing the shariʿa courts and the (British-invented) Supreme Muslim Council to apply it. Given this context of imperialism, it is perhaps not surprising that shariʿa court judges tended to observe classical Hanafi law more closely than the OLFR.[1] Indeed, the shariʿa court was the only institution that the British allowed Palestinians to control during the Mandate, which had the effect of strengthening the significance of family law as an element of Muslim identity, representing Palestinian cultural heritage untainted by colonial rule. Under these circumstances, Palestinians had little incentive to reform family law, and indeed opposing interference became a form of resistance to British rule and its support for Zionism.[2] Despite these realities, we will see how the

---

1   Brownson, Elizabeth, "Gender, Muslim Family Law, and Contesting Patriarchy in Mandate Palestine, 1925–1939", Ph.D. Dissertation, University of California, Santa Barbara, 2008, pp. 3–4, 139, 194–5.
2   Of course this trend emerged in other parts of the Middle East and beyond. For Algeria, see Lazreg, Marina, *The Eloquence of Silence: Algerian Women in Question* (New York: Routledge, 1994), pp. 80–8; for Egypt, see Badran, Margot, *Feminists, Islam, and Nation* (Princeton: Princeton University Press, 1995), pp. 124–5; for Syria, see Thompson, Elizabeth, *Colonial Citizens: Republican Rights, Paternal Privilege and Gender in French Syria and Lebanon* (New York: Columbia University Press, 2000), pp. 131–4, 148–54. Partha Chatterjee famously makes the same argument to explain Indians' resistance to British legislation and reforms concerning women in *The Nation and its Fragments: Colonial and Postcolonial Histories* (Princeton: Princeton University Press, 1993), pp. 116–34.

OLFR may have contributed to effecting changes in Palestinian Muslim society during the Mandate period.

In certain respects, the OLFR improved women's rights in marriage and divorce from their status in classical Hanafi law, the Ottoman's official school of shari'a law. The Hanafis were the most patriarchal of the orthodox Sunni schools in several ways, including the very narrow terms under which women could access judicial annulment and women's inability to sue for delinquent maintenance payments. However, the Hanafis did allow an adult woman to contract her marriage without a guardian. Each school of law had its own benefits and detriments for women, thus it was astute of the lawyers who constructed the Ottoman family code to use the classical principle of selection (*talfiq*), allowing them to select among the four schools. In some ways, they selected elements from the school that would improve women's status, but certainly not in all. Overall, the architects of the code had a general preference for Hanafi law; after all, it was the Ottoman's official school.[3]

Until recent decades, Western scholars have tended to hail the 1917 Ottoman code as an indicator of progress and social change.[4] This characterization contains a number of inaccuracies. First, the new code left the mother's restricted period of caretaking intact for child custody. Also, scholarship acclaiming the code has paid little heed to the law's application or the amount of change that it actually effected. In order to comprehensively assess a new law code, one must gauge the extent to which its laws are applied or their impact on social change, which we will examine throughout this chapter. Finally, it is important to be mindful that by condensing a large corpus of legal interpretations and practices into one code, the Ottoman law often limited litigants' options; that is, when judges chose to apply it. Thus, the code did not always translate into an improvement in women's legal status. Indeed, Judith Tucker argues that because the code limited the flexibility of interpretations of the law, "the overall result of codification was not a gain for women".[5]

I agree the Ottoman code was fairly conservative and in some respects restricted possibilities. However, I will show that it also included important

---

[3] Welchman, Lynn, *Beyond the Code: Muslim Family Law and the Shari'a Judiciary in the Palestinian West Bank* (New York: Springer, 2000), p. 44; also see Eisenman, Robert, *Islamic Law in Israel and Palestine* (Leiden: E.J. Brill, 1978), pp. 34–45.

[4] For example, see Anderson, J.N.D., *Law Reform in the Muslim World* (London: Athlone Press, 1976), pp. 48–50, or Coulson, Noel, *History of Islamic Law* (Edinburgh: Edinburgh University Press, 1964), pp. 184–6.

[5] Tucker, Judith, "Revisiting reform: women and the Ottoman Law of Family Rights, 1917", *The Arab Studies Journal*, 4/2 (1996), p. 16.

benefits for women, particularly in the long term, including raising the marriage age significantly, giving wives the option of living separately from their husbands' families, and explicitly allowing marriage contract stipulations preventing a husband from marrying additional wives. This chapter examines the ways in which the OLFR modified Hanafi law and attempted to change certain marriage practices via these three reforms, focusing on the code's impact in Mandate Palestine. More specifically, the chapter will explore indications that the average marriage age did rise among Palestinians during the Mandate. It will also examine examples suggesting that rural Palestinians, who were the vast majority of the population, likely did not follow the latter two reforms in the Ottoman family code widely during this period.

Gendered Marital Expectations and the Social Context

Marriage is a social and religious expectation of most Palestinian Muslims; those who are financially, physically, and mentally able are usually expected to marry. Historically, it was most common for the bride, particularly in rural Palestine, to leave her family home and live with her husband's family upon marriage. Urban Palestinians tended to live in nuclear households, but the oldest son's family often lived with his parents.[6] Despite its religious connotations, marriage is not a sacrament in Islam; rather, it is considered a contract with obligations that one should perform and rights that one can expect and claim in court if necessary. This is true for the husband and the wife, both of whom are responsible for fulfilling their gendered roles and duties. Both spouses also enjoy gendered privileges within the marriage. The husband is considered the provider for the family. He is required to support his wife, children, and any dependent family members with all the food, clothing, shelter, and any items they may need for daily life. Collectively, this support is called *nafaqa* and it is a wife's (and any dependent's) fundamental right in Muslim family law to receive it. A married woman is entitled to maintenance regardless of her personal finances; also, her husband is expected to provide for her in the manner to which she was accustomed before marriage. As for the wife's duties, she is responsible for maintaining the home, raising her children, and obeying her husband; she is constructed as the nurturer of the family. It is important to note that historically, obedience had several limitations and it was mostly used to determine a woman's right to receive maintenance. As Tucker

---

6 Farsoun, Samih K., *Culture and Customs of the Palestinians* (London: Greenwood Press, 2004), p. 27.

shows, Ottoman-period legal experts defined disobedience (*nushuz*) as leaving the home if forbidden and being sexually unavailable to one's husband.[7]

However, the husband must fulfill the sexual needs of his spouse as well. If there is one element of marriage that is equally obligatory on both the husband and the wife, it is the responsibility to provide sexual satisfaction for his or her partner. Either party may seek redress in court if his or her partner fails to meet those needs. In the Mandate period, if the husband was physically unable to perform sexually, my research indicates that a judge would require him to either financially compensate his wife or to consent to a divorce.[8] If a wife had refused to satisfy her husband sexually, a judge would have likely ordered her to obey her husband; a judge could have also permitted her husband to withhold maintenance. However, if these actions failed, the husband had little recourse beyond divorcing her or marrying an additional wife, neither of which were inexpensive options.

While the obligation of providing sexual partnership may appear to inherently pose a greater burden on the wife, my research suggests a more complicated picture. In two Jerusalem court cases from 1928 and 1936, the wife sued her husband for divorce because he was sexually incapable. In both cases, the husband ended up paying his wife compensation to persuade her to stay in the marriage.[9] However, there were no cases in which the husband sought permission to withhold maintenance due to his wife's inability or unwillingness to comply with his sexual needs. Perhaps it is unlikely that a husband would make such an emasculating claim in a public venue. In any case, he could always divorce her – if he could afford to pay her deferred dower, child support, maintenance during the waiting period, etc. Also, one should note that marital rape is not a concept in Muslim family law, as in much of the world. Consequently, we can probably assume that most wives were unlikely to contest their sexual duty. But it is important to emphasize that the sexual obligation in marriage was a mutual one. Indeed, a husband's inability to perform sexually was (and is) grounds for a woman to acquire a judicial divorce, which she could initiate unilaterally.

A perhaps more significant aspect to a couples' sexual relationship, particularly in rural areas, concerns the wife's status in her marriage. As anthropologist

---

7   Tucker, Judith, *Women, Family, and Gender in Islamic Law* (Cambridge: Cambridge University Press, 2008), pp. 53–4.
8   My dissertation examines *nafaqa* (maintenance), wife-initiated divorce, and child custody cases, approximately 370 cases in all, from 1925 to 1939.
9   Jerusalem Shari'a Court, box 99/sijillat 440–447, case 254, p. 464, 1928, and Jerusalem Shari'a Court, box 104/sijillat 473–479, case 58, p. 3, 1936.

Hilma Granqvist notes in her late 1920s study of marriage in Artas, a Muslim village south of Bethlehem, "the whole village knows whether a man has intercourse with his wife or not. Although a woman may be little inclined sexually, just this intercourse has great value and importance for her as the sign of the husband's favor and goodwill towards her personally and in public opinion; for she is in this way stamped as a 'beloved' or 'hated' wife".[10] Going to court could have been a way for a wife, especially from a rural area, to reclaim her social status by publically declaring there was a medical reason that she was not "beloved". It is worth noting that in both impotence cases discussed previously, each party was from a village.

In the context of interwar Palestine, as in much of the world, the first priority for selecting a marriage partner was meeting the family's needs and concerns. The cultural descriptions provided here will focus on Palestinian society in rural areas, where some 75 percent of Palestinians lived in the 1930s. For the Muslim community, the agrarian percentage of the population was even higher. Granqvist demonstrates that major considerations for rural families included keeping property within the family and obtaining affordable dowers for the groom's family.[11] The dower (*mahr*), sometimes called the bride's marriage gift, is the gold, cash or other gifts agreed upon in the marriage contract that the groom gives to the bride's father on her behalf. By the Mandate-era in Palestine, the dower was usually paid in cash, but it could also consist of some combination of land, olive trees, animals, other forms of property, or even service.[12] The amount of the dower depended on whether or not the bride's and groom's families were related; the closer the relationship, the smaller the dower. Other factors that affected dower negotiations included the families' social status, the bride's character, and her beauty.[13] Despite proverbs and villagers' assertions claiming that widows' dowers were worth half the amount of maidens, Granqvist found there was actually "no difference worth mentioning"

---

10   Granqvist, Hilma, *Marriage Conditions in a Palestinian Village II* (Helsingfors: Societas Scientiarum Fennica, 1935), p. 202.

11   Granqvist, Hilma, *Marriage Conditions in a Palestinian Village* (Helsingfors: Societas Scientiarum Fennica, 1931), pp. 78, 67.

12   Moors, Annelies, *Women, Property, and Islam* (Cambridge: Cambridge University Press, 1995), pp. 97–8, and Granqvist, *Marriage Conditions*, p. 119.

13   Granqvist, *Marriage Conditions*, pp. 69, 85, 121–3, and Baldensperger, P.J., "Birth, marriage and death among the fellahin of Palestine", in *Palestine Exploration Fund Quarterly Statement for 1894* (London: PEF Society, 1894), pp. 133–4. Wikisource, http://en.wikisource.org/w/index.php?title=Palestine_Exploration_Fund_-_Quarterly_Statement_for_1894/Birth,_Marriage,_and_Death_among_the_Fellahin_of_Palestine&oldid=5212400 (accessed January 26, 2016).

during this period, although the ceremonies were less elaborate.[14] The bride's parents usually spent part of the dower on gold and household items for their daughter. Annelies Moors's ethnographic and court record study of women's access to property in the Nablus region found that women typically received about a third of their dowers in this period.[15] Despite the Qur'an's declaration that the entire dower belongs to the bride, which was among its many new protections for women, the dower was often controlled by the bride's father in practice.

Because agrarian families wished to retain property and curb dower costs when selecting spouses for younger members, they preferred cousins who were the children of uncles on the father's side. Rural Palestinians favored cousins to the extent that a man had the "right" to his cousin, "even if she is already sitting on the bridal camel".[16] Preference for cousin marriages, followed by clan, and finally village marriages, was also because the bride's family was concerned about her well-being in her new home. Granqvist cites a common adage that fathers and brothers said to the bride as she left her family: "'We have not given [you] to any sort of people. We have given [you] to people upon whom we can depend'".[17] Also, if a woman married within her extended family, or at least within her village, it was a great deal easier for her family to ensure that she was well treated. Simply the wife's family's proximity would have likely encouraged her in-laws to treat her well. A man who married within the village was more likely to be considerate of his wife than one who married outside the village, knowing that his mother-in-law (and other in-laws) could descend at any time.[18] Also, it was critical for women to maintain strong relationships with their families in order to protect themselves in the event of difficulties with their in-laws, as we will see. Therefore, the bond with a woman's family could be upheld more easily if she married within the family or the village.[19] Interestingly, even though Artas residents preferred cousin marriages, marriages to "strangers", people from outside the village, were far more common. Granqvist explains that for grooms' families, there were simply not enough women within Artas to allow additional cousin marriages; the major factor affecting brides' families was that "stranger" wives received higher dowers.[20]

---

14 Granqvist, *Marriage Conditions*, pp. 121–2.
15 Moors, *Women*, p. 96.
16 Granqvist, *Marriage Conditions*, pp. 71–2.
17 Granqvist, *Marriage Conditions*, p. 53.
18 Granqvist, *Marriage Conditions*, p. 94.
19 Granqvist, *Marriage Conditions II*, p. 144.
20 Granqvist, *Marriage Conditions II*, pp. 85, 69.

Finally, families had greater options for a match when they looked beyond the village.

Marriage certainly was momentous for the two individuals concerned, but it was just as much about the bonding of two families. Granqvist illustrates the significance that rural Palestinians ascribed to the connection of two families in many respects. She explains that the common practice of villagers marrying several family members into another family simultaneously indicates "how anxious people are to bind families firmly together by marriage".[21] While it was certainly more cost-effective for families to hold more than one wedding at once, the bond created between families was also important and enduring. Granqvist cites the example of an Artas man who, after his engagement, began seeking his future in-laws socially and in everyday work; she also references two families who still worked together on both families' fields during the harvest, even though the marriage that connected them had taken place "long ago".[22] The village's practices of levirate and sororate were other means of strengthening the bonds of in-laws. Levirate, a pre-Islamic practice dating at least to the Hebrew Bible and forbidden in the Qur'an, is the term for a man marrying his deceased brother's widow. Granqvist describes levirate in Artas as "indeed a right but not a duty" but a somewhat rare practice, accounting for less than three per cent of marriages in the village.[23] Sororate refers to the custom when a woman dies and her husband requests a replacement bride from her family, usually a sister. Granqvist asserts that "such an appeal is not and scarcely can be rejected", indicating the importance of the two families' relationship.[24]

OLFR Marriage Reforms and Realities

The OLFR of 1917 preserved the patriarchal structure of marriage and its gendered rights and obligations, but it did improve women's legal status from classical Hanafi doctrines in several ways. Perhaps the code's most significant marriage reform was increasing the age of a girl's legal majority to 17 years. In classical Hanafi law, a girl could be married as young as nine years old. However, Ottoman muftis agreed marriage should not be consummated until the girl was sufficiently physically mature for a sexual relationship.[25] Hanafi

---

21 Granqvist, *Marriage Conditions*, pp. 86–7.
22 Granqvist, *Marriage Conditions*, p. 85.
23 Granqvist, *Marriage Conditions II*, pp. 208, 304.
24 Granqvist, *Marriage Conditions*, p. 86.
25 Tucker, *Women*, p. 61.

judges usually understood physical maturity to mean the development of the girl's body, as opposed to the beginning of menstruation.[26] The 1917 Ottoman code established both the ages of legal majority and competence to marry at 17 for girls and 18 for boys, but an underage adolescent (*murahiq*) could be allowed to marry if she (or he) had reached her physical maturity and her parents had obtained the court's permission.[27]

Granqvist maintains that the "marriageable age" for boys and girls was "shortly after puberty" in the Muslim village of Artas, and her research shows "very few unmarried males of marriageable age".[28] Rural families initiated marriages for adolescent members for a variety of reasons, often because they required an additional worker. Also, social expectations of marriage shortly after reaching puberty, the shortage of marriageable women in the village, and the strong preference for cousin and village marriages were significant reasons for early marriages.[29] These factors were closely connected. If a potential groom's family wanted a relative or another local bride, they had to seize the opportunity before she married another candidate. It is important to note that if a wedding took place before a girl had completed puberty, consummation of the marriage would usually occur after she started menstruating. Several years could transpire from the signing of the marriage contract, when one was considered "married", to consummation.

Granqvist emphasizes that while a man could have personal incentives for pursuing marriage or a particular woman's hand, it was just as likely that his family, particularly his mother, needed a female laborer.

> It may be that his [family] require[s] someone to carry out those duties which are specifically a woman's and cannot with propriety be done by a man, or there is not enough woman's help in the house; often it is a question of replacing a sister or a daughter who has [wed]; or the man's mother declares she can no longer manage the work and must have help ... One notices that, as soon as she has a daughter-in-law in the house, a woman no longer needs to grind the corn, which used to be one

---

[26] Tucker, Judith, *In the House of the Law: Gender and Islamic Law in Ottoman Syria and Palestine* (Berkeley: University of California Press, 1997), p. 44, and Eisenman, *Islamic Law*, pp. 38–9.

[27] Ottoman Law of Family Rights of 1917, Article 5, *Dustur* (Arabic translation), vol. 9, 1332 to 1333 and 1335 to 1336 (Istanbul: Evkaf Matbaası, 1928) p. 762. Also, see Layish, Aharon, *Women and Islamic Law in a Non-Muslim State* (Jerusalem: Israel Universities Press, 1975), pp. 16–17.

[28] Granqvist, *Marriage Conditions*, p. 38.

[29] Granqvist, *Marriage Conditions*, p. 38.

of the heaviest of the woman's tasks and necessitated their sitting at the mill for half the night. But the wives of her sons also fetch water, gather wood and manure, etc., so that a woman with daughter-in-laws is said to be a 'lady' who keeps servants, and a woman herself looks upon this position with job, as an ideal one.[30]

It is significant that a new wife's gender-specific labor duties eased the burden on her mother-in-law, and other women family members, considerably more than it reduced her husband's work load. As the passage above indicates, rural women's work was very labor-intensive in this period. In addition to the tasks mentioned of grinding corn, carrying water, and gathering firewood and manure, women were also responsible for caring for their children, tending and gathering grasses for the animals, baking bread, weeding the fields, planting certain crops, carrying crops to market, making *laban* (a thick yogurt) and cheese, mending clothes, and cleaning the home.[31] Also, during the harvest, women worked alongside the entire family to complete the harvesting chores, including threshing, sorting, and picking olives and fruit.[32] Men, women, and children performed most of the same harvesting jobs together, except ploughing, which Palestinians generally considered men's work. Thus, the need for additional workers was a significant reason for early marriage in rural Mandate Palestine.

However, there is little consensus on the average marriage ages for Palestinian Muslim women during the Mandate period. Granqvist cites a number of contemporary observers, whose estimates of marriage ages ranged from 12 to 17 for girls.[33] Moors's research on a village near Nablus indicates that many women who grew up during the Mandate period recalled they had married just after puberty, 30 per cent of whom were younger than 14.[34] On the other hand, the 1931 census claims the average marriage age for Muslim women was 20 years.[35] However, this estimate is likely unreliable. Not only did Palestinians detest British rule, but the British were attempting to crack down on child marriage. Thus Palestinians would have had little incentive to report accurate ages their on marriage contracts.

---

30 Granqvist, *Marriage Conditions II*, p. 149.
31 Granqvist, *Marriage Conditions II*, p. 293; Graham-Brown, Sarah, *Palestinians and their Society 1880–1946* (London: Quartet Books, 1980), p. 49, and Wilson, C.T., *Peasant Life in the Holy Land* (London: John Murray, 1906), pp. 117–28, 132–6.
32 Graham-Brown, *Palestinians*, p. 50.
33 Granqvist, *Marriage Conditions*, pp. 38–9, n. 1.
34 Moors, *Women*, p. 96.
35 Graham-Brown, *Palestinians*, p. 69.

Several other factors contribute to discrepancies on the average age of marriage during this period. Much of it arises from the great deal of ambiguity concerning peoples' ages in general. As C.T. Wilson, an English missionary and observer of rural Palestine noted in 1906, "people have but little idea of their children's ages, or, of their own ... if parents know, even approximately, their children's ages, it arises from ... their [birth occurring] in a year when some event of special interest took place".[36] Even among city folks in the Mandate era, remembering birth dates and years was not a common practice. Fadwa Tuqan, the famous poet from Nablus, recalls her mother's response when she inquired about her birth: "The day I was cooking *akkub* (globe thistle). That's the only birth certificate I have for you". Tuqan goes on to explain, "Like all our people Mother dated events by relating them to outstanding occurrences. She would say: 'That happened in the year of the grasshoppers, or the year of the earthquake', etc.".[37] Tuqan's mother eventually remembered her daughter's birth was in 1917 because her cousin died in the war the previous year.[38]

Moors points to another reason for the lack of consensus on marriage ages, which was the remarkable inconsistency between her oral histories and the shari'a court registers. Fifty-five per cent of her interviewees from the village of al-Balad said they had married under the age of 16, yet Moors found no marriage contracts in which the bride's age was younger than 17. She concludes that families must have either reported incorrect ages or waited until the girls were age 17 to register the marriages.[39] But if it was the former, did the courts knowingly record erroneous ages? It is impossible to say. Certainly, the Supreme Muslim Council was more progressive on minimum marriage ages than the Mandate government; the Council recommended 18 years for girls to the government, but British authorities chose 15 years as the minimum age for girls in the 1936 criminal code.[40] Perhaps some women had difficulty recalling their precise ages at marriage, but certainly Moors found a considerable discrepancy between 17 years in court records and shortly after menstruation in her interviews.

Despite the ambiguity of marriage ages, there are indications that Palestinian leaders were working and perhaps succeeding to promote older marriages in this period. Ruth Woodsmall, a YWCA researcher, reported in 1936 that the

---

36 Wilson, *Peasant Life*, p. 95.
37 Tuqan, Fadwa, *A Mountainous Journey: An Autobiography*, trans. Olive Kenny (Saint Paul: Graywolf Press, 1990), pp. 13–14.
38 Tuqan, *A Mountainous Journey*, p. 14.
39 Moors, *Women*, p. 96.
40 *Palestine Gazette*, Criminal Code Ordinance Articles 182–183, 28 September 1936, p. 1010.

Supreme Muslim Council actively encouraged its own minimum marriage age of 18 years for girls, which "was regarded by the common people as practically a law, and hence, was followed to a large degree".[41] She went on to describe "the Grand Mufti and SMC as an effective instrument for reform ... creating a public opinion against early marriage, and is, thus, effectively pushing up the marriage age".[42] Also, according to a Palestinian government doctor in 1923, shari'a court judges throughout Palestine were refusing to register marriages for girls who were younger than 16 years old.[43] Families could misrepresent a girl's age of course, but judges seemed to be trying to encourage change. Finally, Granqvist mentions a rural sheikh who refused to marry underage youth out of fear of the government's punishment.[44]

Another important marriage reform in the 1917 Ottoman code was a woman's right to live separately from her husband's family. According to classical Hanafi law, the only situations in which a wife could demand a discrete living space were a) if she were sharing accommodations with her husband's older children from another marriage, or b) with a co-wife. Otherwise, a wife could be compelled to live with members of her husband's family, including his younger children from another marriage, his concubine, and most significantly I would think, his mother.[45] However, the Ottoman code reformed this Hanafi interpretation, considerably improving the conditions under which a wife could be expected to live. The code specifies that a husband must obtain his wife's permission before housing her with any of his family members, with the exception of his younger children from another marriage.[46] Tucker notes this was a "clear advance" for women but also points out that "we may wonder whether many women were in a position to assert this right, but the potential advantages are manifest".[47] This new right was particularly important because under classical Hanafi law, a wife and her mother-in-law (and her husband ... and his concubine!) could be required to share a "house" that could amount to a lockable room with private toilet and cooking facilities.[48]

---

41 Woodsmall, Ruth, *Muslim Women Enter a New World* (New York: Roundtable Press, 1936), p. 100.
42 Woodsmall, *Muslim Women*, p. 101.
43 Report on polygamy, from Dr. Hamzeh, Medical Officer of Health, Ramallah, to Director of Health, Jerusalem, Israel State Archives, Record Group 10, 23 May 1923.
44 Granqvist, *Marriage Conditions*, p. 41.
45 Tucker, "Revisiting reform", p. 9.
46 Ottoman Law of Family Rights, Article 72, *Dustur*, vol. 9, p. 770.
47 Tucker, "Revisiting reform", p. 11.
48 Tucker, *In the House of the Law*, pp. 61–2.

There are indications that Palestinian villagers were aware of this improvement in women's legal status; however, it was common for wives to live with their husbands' relatives in village settings. Describing rural married life, Granqvist notes that after the wedding week "the husband is allotted only his little corner for his and his wife's bed ... In one single room live a man and his wife, his unmarried sons and daughters, but also his married sons with their wives and children".[49] She goes on to discuss the economic advantages of a family living together, and then explains that was why a woman in Artas "was blamed" when she "insisted on having a room for themselves and was not content to live with his relatives".[50] Also, it is worth noting that this woman had gained the support of her uncle and mother, which was central to obtaining her goal. Finally, her status as a "stranger" wife, from outside the village, likely did not help her reputation. Granqvist gives another example in which the woman's father welcomed her kindly when her husband sent her home, but

> not only due to love for her but chiefly because he wished ... to annoy her husband's relatives. They all live in the same place, a cave ... and he thought that it was the husband's relatives who were to blame ... and disturbed the harmony between her and her husband. So he reminded them that a wife has a legal right to a separate room.[51]

The woman ended up back with her husband's family, where she still had to perform hard labor; however she had done so in her father's house as well. In this anecdote the woman's father was likely using her as a pawn against his rivals, rather than endeavoring to improve his daughter's situation. Both of these accounts involved monogamous marriages, and therefore the demand for a separate room was in accordance with the 1917 Ottoman law. Also, both examples, along with Granqvist's accounts of married life, suggest that separate housing from the husband's relatives was a right that women, or their families, claimed rarely in rural Palestine. When they did so, it likely indicated a marital problem or a larger rivalry between families.

The last significant marriage reform in the 1917 Ottoman code was its explicit recognition of a woman's right to add stipulations to the marriage contract that would prohibit her husband from taking a second wife; of course, the groom had to agree to the terms.[52] If a husband contravened such a contract,

---

49 Granqvist, *Marriage Conditions II*, p. 141.
50 Granqvist, *Marriage Conditions II*, p. 141.
51 Granqvist, *Marriage Conditions II*, p. 238.
52 Ottoman Law of Family Rights of 1917, Article 38, *Dustur*, vol. 9, p. 766.

he would be forced to divorce one of his wives. This article was intended to encourage monogamous marriages. While indirectly giving women's families more control over their marriages was important, the article only included one type of marriage contract stipulation. This certainly did not nullify other sorts of stipulations; however, it also did not encourage them. Historically, marriage contract conditions could be on wide variety of issues, so long as they did not contravene shari'a. Hanbali legal experts wrote most extensively on appropriate stipulations in the medieval period. In addition to conditions allowing the wife to divorce if the husband married a second wife or acquired a concubine, Tucker shows that Hanbali muftis accepted stipulations requiring the couple to live in the wife's hometown and for the husband to accommodate and support his wife's children from a prior marriage.[53] Medieval Malikis and Hanafis allowed various stipulations as well, such as not harming the wife, providing particular clothing, and not asking her to perform hard labor.[54]

Mamluk courts (1250–1517) in Cairo and Damascus also saw a variety of marriage contract stipulations. Many were similar to the Hanbali conditions already discussed, including the wife's right to divorce if the husband married another wife and the husband's promise to house and support her other children; however, Yossef Rapoport demonstrates that Mamluk judges also allowed conditions that transformed part of the dower from a payment upon death or divorce into a 'payment on demand'.[55] This gave the wife considerable financial leverage over her husband within the marriage. This newly defined dower actually became "standard practice" in Damascus by the mid-fourteenth century.[56] It is logical to infer that changing the dower in this respect not only enhanced the wife's economic power, but it could also empower her in numerous other ways. For example, Rapoport argues that it facilitated the inclusion of additional advantageous conditions to the marriage contract and even enabled women to make new demands during their marriages because the new dower gave them increased financial leverage.[57]

Hanafi, Maliki, and Shafi'i law dominated different regions of Ottoman Egypt, and marriage contract conditions were common among all three schools. In fact, Nelly Hanna found stipulations in roughly a third of the seventeenth-century Cairo marriage documents that she examined, most often from those

---

53 Tucker, *Women*, p. 49.
54 Tucker, *Women*, p. 49.
55 Rapoport, Yossef, *Marriage, Money and Divorce in Medieval Islamic Society* (Cambridge: Cambridge University Press, 2005), pp. 69, 75, 56.
56 Rapoport, *Marriage*, p. 56.
57 Rapoport, *Marriage*, p. 58.

of merchants or artisans. Judges allowed conditions including the usual preventing of polygyny, the husband agreeing to a separate residence from his family, and guaranteeing divorce if the husband failed to provide maintenance.[58] As Hanna explains, a woman could have difficulty acquiring a divorce even if her husband was not providing maintenance. There was little agreement among the schools on the consequence for failing to provide; Hanafis were unwilling to allow wife-initiated divorce because of the husband's failure to provide, whereas other schools allowed these grounds.[59] But if a woman had such a condition in her contract, she could obtain a divorce without the risk of a legal hassle. In addition to the typical monogamy requirement and the husband's support of the wife's children, Abdal-Rehim demonstrates that the most common conditions used in marriage contracts throughout Ottoman Egypt included specifying the location of residence – usually to reside reasonably near the wife's family, the husband's promise not to harm his wife, and the husband's pledge not to be absent for a specified long period.[60] If any of these conditions were not fulfilled, the wife could obtain a judicial divorce in which she retained her financial rights.

In Ottoman Palestine and Syria, however, women appear to have had fewer legal protections in their marriages. Tucker's eighteenth-century research of marriage registers in Palestine and Syria indicates that conditions were added to marriage contracts rarely. This change in Syria is rather mystifying, given the frequent use of stipulations transforming the dower into a payment on demand in Damascus during Mamluk period. Because Ottoman Egypt, Palestine, and Syria all enjoyed a diversity of legal traditions and Sunni schools, she speculates that "local customs rather than doctrinal difference" explains the infrequency of including stipulations, compared to their commonplace use in Egypt.[61] Additional research is needed to provide a broader representation of marriages in Palestine and Syria during the Ottoman period.

Any discussion of the Ottoman code's recognition of marriage contract stipulations preventing additional wives should also recognize that there were various reasons for Palestinians to practice polygyny. Socially acceptable

---

58 Hanna, Nelly, "Marriage among merchant families in seventeenth-century Cairo", in *Women, the Family, and Divorce Laws in Islamic History*, ed. Amira el-Azhary Sonbol (Syracuse: Syracuse University Press, 1996), pp. 147–8.
59 Hanna, "Marriage", p. 148.
60 Abdal-Rehim, Abdal-Rehim Abdal-Rehman, "The family and gender laws in Egypt during the Ottoman period", in *Women, the Family, and Divorce Laws in Islamic History*, ed. Amira el-Azhary Sonbol (Syracuse: Syracuse University Press, 1996), pp. 110, 103.
61 Tucker, *Women*, p. 63.

reasons could include a first wife's inability to conceive, the high rate of child mortality, and a family's need for more workers. A man's personal reasons for marrying a second wife varied. His first wife could be older or not of his choosing; it could even be a punishment to his first wife.[62] In rural Palestine, a marriage becoming polygynous could actually be in response to the first wife's needs. Granqvist references two women's examples:

> One of them had a co-wife because the home required female labour and it is not the custom to keep women servants; another because in case of the husband's death his relatives would take possession of his home, and she would have to leave it because she had no son ... She had therefore, in order to insure her position, insisted on his marriage with another woman in spite of his first objections to the proposal.[63]

We can likely assume that these examples, particularly the latter one, occurred in urban areas as well. In her second book, Granqvist adds that in situations where it was the first wife requesting a co-wife, the new wife often "easily falls into the position of a servant to the first wife".[64] Clearly there were numerous motivations for a family to choose polygyny, which sometimes could enhance the first wife's quality of life by easing her workload.

Furthermore, polygyny was an indicator of enhanced social status because it was expensive for man and his a family to finance an additional dower. Another reason that polygyny was costly is because the Qur'an instructs men to provide separate households for each wife. Tucker shows that Ottoman-era legal experts interpreted this to mean a separate room with kitchen and bathroom accommodations for each wife.[65] However, it seems that rural Palestinians may have disregarded both the Qur'an's and the muftis' directions circa 1900. According to Baldensperger, a contemporary observer of rural Palestine, "... the parents of the wife also try their utmost to have a separate house, or at least room, for their daughter, but only in very rare cases have I known this to be done. They usually live in one room".[66] Unfortunately, Granqvist does not state whether or not this sort of living situation was common practice in agrarian areas during the Mandate. Her description of common living arrangements seems to suggest that families lived in one room, but she does not specify if

---

62   Granqvist, *Marriage Conditions II*, p. 208.
63   Granqvist, *Marriage Conditions*, p. 3.
64   Granqvist, *Marriage Conditions II*, p. 211.
65   Tucker, *In the House of the Law*, p. 62.
66   Baldensperger, "Birth, marriage and death", p. 131.

this happened in polygynous marriages.[67] Granqvist does discuss one polygynous marriage in which the first wife lived in the "front part of the house and the others in the back",[68] but it is not clear if she meant separate rooms. However, it is evident that when a sheikh or legal authority became involved in a family dispute, the co-wives received separate rooms.[69] In any case, the great expense of polygyny rendered it a relatively uncommon practice, especially in rural areas where Palestinians were unlikely to be able to afford an additional dower. Also, villages had fewer local women available for any type of marriage. Granqvist notes that for Artas, the polygyny rate was 10.7 per cent in 1935, down from 13 per cent when she included deceased men.[70] A few decades before the Mandate, Wilson mentions that polygyny was far less common in rural areas compared to towns.[71]

It appears that Palestinians employed marriage contract stipulations of any kind only on occasion during the Mandate era. Moors's research on women's access to property in the Nablus area found that including stipulations was "virtually done only in the city" during the Mandate period.[72] In these cases, stipulations most often guaranteed that a couple would live apart from the husband's family or required the husband to equip the household with certain items. Moors does not provide statistics for the Mandate era, but she estimates that only two percent of Nablus-area contracts in the 1970s to 1980s contained stipulations.[73] We can most likely assume the numbers were at best similar during the Mandate, given her observation about stipulations and that a small minority of Palestinians lived in cities. Today, however, women use marriage contract stipulation considerably more frequently in Palestine, particularly in educated, urban sectors of society.[74] Reaching this point has involved a learning curve, however. One woman who I interviewed in 2006, Jihad N., told me the following story about the importance of using stipulations:

---

67   Granqvist, *Marriage Conditions*, p. 141.
68   Granqvist, *Marriage Conditions II*, p. 214.
69   Granqvist, *Marriage Conditions II*, p. 191.
70   Granqvist, *Marriage Conditions II*, p. 205.
71   Wilson, *Peasant Life*, p. 104.
72   Moors, *Women*, p. 102.
73   Moors, *Women*, p. 246.
74   Qualitative interviews and surveys that I conducted among university students in Ramallah and at Birzeit University in 2014 indicate educated young people's considerable knowledge of women's rights in Muslim family law. Also, many women students asserted that women should take advantage of using marriage contract conditions in order to protect their interests.

> Women must always put conditions in the marriage contract. Yes, I knew about this right before my marriage. But it makes me sad to think about this because when my daughter Layla got married, her husband agreed to the condition that Layla could continue her studies to become a nurse, but we did not write it in the contract. Then later Layla's husband refused to let her continue, and it makes me so sad that I cry about it sometimes. Islam gives women a big opportunity to take their rights and connect them to her life, and I know so many women who must divorce because they did not include conditions in the contract.[75]

However, Jihad was in her mid-sixties at the time of the interview, and the current generation of educated Palestinian women appears to be learning from their mothers' experiences.[76]

Finally, other marriage reforms in the Ottoman family code included the requirement to register marriage contracts in court, the ban on forced marriages, and the emphasis on a woman's right to her dower. Before the twentieth century, unregistered marriages were not unusual, and marriages were conducted orally at times. Registering marriage contracts ensured that the terms of marriage were binding and more likely to follow the law; it also enabled judges to apply the prohibition on forced marriages. Regarding the dower, the Ottoman code prohibited parents from keeping any part of their daughter's dower, and it forbade them from compelling her to spend it on her trousseau and other items for her new life.[77] The bride's exclusive right to her dower had always been a woman's fundamental right in the Qur'an, but often this was ignored by local custom. Granqvist maintains that "the woman herself in many cases receives part of the [dower], at times the whole of it ... it is said in Palestine that only an avaricious father would not give the [dower] to his daughter or an outfit or other gifts bought with it".[78] Moors's research in al-Balad shows that women tended to receive about a third of the prompt dower in this period; however, it was not uncommon for women to sue in court when a guardian withheld part of the dower, if he was not her father.[79] It was quite rare for a woman to take her own father to court; his taking part of the dower was expected and a woman needed to maintain their relationship in the

---

75 Author's interview with Jihad N. (last name not used in order to protect her privacy), Jerusalem, June 29, 2006.
76 See note 74.
77 Ottoman Law of Family Rights, Article 90, *Dustur*, vol. 9, p. 772.
78 Granqvist, *Marriage Conditions*, p. 132.
79 Moors, *Women*, pp. 96–7.

event she encountered marital problems and wished to return home.[80] Granqvist makes the same point in explaining why women tended to let their kin keep their shares of the inheritance. She posed this question to a villager, who exclaimed, "But then she would have no more rights to her father's house!"[81] Thus not claiming her rights enabled a woman to reinforce the bond with her father or brothers, which gave her more protection from her in-laws. Similarly, when a brother was able to marry by means of a sister's dower in an exchange marriage, he felt more strongly in his duty to support her and to provide gifts throughout her life.[82] Thus, a woman who gave part or all of her dower to a male family member often did so for strategic reasons. Considering men's legal rights to marry additional wives and to unilaterally divorce, it made a great deal of sense for women to invest in protection for themselves vis-à-vis their close male relatives.

Social Practices Inconsistent with Family Law

Several Palestinian customs and mores during the Mandate period had no basis in Hanafi law or the Ottoman code, many of which departed from the patriarchal underpinnings of the law. First, a family's social standing was often a more important factor than gender in determining which party had more power in the marriage. The significance of marriage partners' social status is evident in Granqvist's account of a man who was duped by his in-laws when they switched his betrothed for the bride's aunt. There was very little he could do about it because he had already paid the dower and the father of his intended bride was the civil leader (*mukhtar*) of the village, whereas his own father was dead and his family impoverished.[83] Another important factor in determining a woman's status in the family was her assertiveness, which Baldensperger well describes:

> ... the [peasant]-woman is just as often – virtually – the head of the family, and differs in nothing from woman in the rest of Creation. She at least influences her husband, in most cases for all things, not only in the house, but in all matters affecting their common weal. She is interested in the agricultural business – looks after the herds and herdsmen, animals

---

80 Moors, *Women*, pp. 96–7.
81 Granqvist, *Marriage Conditions II*, p. 256.
82 Granqvist, *Marriage Conditions*, p. 139.
83 Granqvist, *Marriage Conditions*, pp. 49–50.

and servants. I have known many fellah-women to manage everything a good deal better than the husband, and even scolding him to some degree for any mismanagement, or teaching him what to say in the men's assembly. But, notwithstanding this, she did not escape a good flogging occasionally. Yet it does not follow that the [peasant]-woman is to be pitied in being considered an inferior being. She enjoys her life and liberty to a certain extent, at least in many instances.[84]

This account from circa 1900 was still accurate during the Mandate era. As observed here, rural women were critical to their families' livelihoods and participated extensively in agricultural and economic activities alongside their husbands. Baldensperger even notes that these women were "just as often virtually the head of family" and greatly influenced their husbands' political participation as well. Clearly, Palestinian women often had a great deal of agency in practice, which conflicted with their disadvantaged legal status in many ways.

But sometimes social practices contravened the law in ways that decreased women's status as well. As we have seen, the paternal extended family usually shared a single room, rather than providing separate rooms for sons and their families per the Ottoman code. Of course, this was not only a socially acceptable and conventional practice, but also an economic reality – rural Palestinians were unlikely to be able to afford such accommodations in this period.

Conclusion

This chapter has examined the complex social milieu in which rural Palestinian marriages were formed during the Mandate period and how this context could complicate family law reforms, namely those in the OLFR. It argues that although the OLFR indeed maintained the basic patriarchal structure of marriage, as others have noted, the code also contained important benefits for Muslim women. Also, the chapter shows how one of these reforms translated into social change during this period, while the others have percolated more gradually since the Mandate. First, the family law code increased the age of legal majority from nine years to 17 for girls. Despite a lack of consensus on marriage ages, it appears that the average age of marriage among Palestinians rose overall even though British authorities clearly did not prioritize curbing the

---

84 Baldensperger, "Birth, marriage and death", p. 133.

marriage of minors; in fact, the Mandate administration established 15 years as the minimum marriage age for girls. This trend of older marriages likely owes much to the efforts of judges, who reportedly refused to register underage marriages, and especially the Supreme Muslim Council. The SMC actively promoted 18 as the minimum marriage age, which was three years above what the British established in the 1936 Criminal Code. It is certainly feasible that the OLFR had some influence on both Muslim judges and religious scholars regarding this issue as well. Second, the OLFR gave women the right to live apart from their husbands' families, whereas classical Hanafi law compelled a woman to live in the same room with her husband's relatives if he wished (except for any co-wives and older children from another wife). Granqvist's research suggests that rural Palestinians were aware of this reform, although social norms and economic realities likely made it unrealistic for many women, or their families, to demand this right in rural Palestine during this period. Finally, the code explicitly recognized marriage contract conditions that restricted husbands to one wife. Although such stipulations were used only on occasion during the Mandate, they eventually became far more diverse and more widespread among educated classes of Palestinian society. The more common conditions in marriage contracts today include a guaranteed right for the wife to continue her education or work; they are also frequently used in regard to wedding arrangements. The OLFR well may have helped pave the way to the eventual use of stipulations among educated Palestinian women.

CHAPTER 11

Mapping Social Change through Matters of the Heart: Debates on Courtship, Marriage and Divorce in the Early Turkish Republican Era (1923–1950)

Nazan Çiçek

In this chapter I delve into the way marriage, both as an idea and an institution, was imagined, 'problematized', discussed and criticized in the early republican era in Turkey in a series of popular magazines published between 1923 and 1950. The debate on marriage in Turkey was intrinsically intertwined with the wider and highly complicated phenomenon of modernization/Westernization that had been going on in the Ottoman empire and later in the republic since the mid-nineteenth century. As the conventional and initial step to the formation of a family and parenthood (particularly motherhood), marriage was 'rediscovered' by the Turkish modernizing elites as an extremely potent vehicle to be used in their attempts to partly or wholly replace the former Islamic regulations of the body, home and social space. As part and parcel of nationalist projects almost everywhere, motherhood came to acquire a new and profound significance in the Turkish nation-building process whereby gendered demographic policies which were legitimized through the goals of development, population growth, progress and modernization were devised and vigorously put into practice. Accordingly, marriage and sexual life proved to be the main targets of state and social control mechanisms in ensuring the biological as well as ideological reproduction of the next generations.

By ascertaining how the definition and perception of marriage as a social construct figured in the cognitive map of the pro-modernization intelligentsia and decision-makers, and by sketching out the debate on courtship, marriage and divorce as perceived by and reflected in popular magazines in the early republican era I seek to contribute to our knowledge of the complex topography of bio-politics in Muslim Turkish society at a time when the legitimacy of traditional models appeared to have dissolved and yet the quest for new models was almost invariably accompanied by a general anxiety over losing cultural autonomy and national-self. In so doing, I examine in this chapter a large body of essays on the subject of marriage and divorce paying special attention to the discussions over the "merits" and "evils" of arranged marriage, love marriage and marriage based on companionship. The magazines under consideration are *Süs* (Ornament) (1923-24), *Resimli Ay* (Monthly Illustrated) (1924-28), *Asar-ı Nisvan* (Women's Stories) (1925-26), *Ülkü* (The Ideal) (1934-48), *Yedigün* (Seven Days) (1935-46) and *Ev-İş* (House-Work) (1942-50), which, with the exception of *Ülkü*, which was the official publication of Halkevleri (People's Houses), were all published by private publishers and more often than not targeted a literate yet intellectually/academically average female audience.[1] All the magazine articles canvassed in this study should be treated as part of a larger canon produced by the late Ottoman and early republican Turkish intelligentsia (the medical elite, the literati and politico-bureaucratic cadres) of the time who were only too cognizant of the importance of marriage as an institution in the processes of *habitus* changing, social engineering, modernization as well as nation-building. Despite the insistence of the republican regime on the so-called ontological rupture between itself and its predecessor, as far as the debate on marriage is concerned the continuum between the late Ottoman times and the early years of the Turkish nation state is unmistakable. An overview of a series of popular magazines that were published in the Second Constitutional era and targeted a Turkish speaking Muslim female readership provides innumerable examples whereby concerns about the 'archaic' and problematic nature of arranged marriage, discussions over the adverse effects of loveless marriages on spouses and children, the cautious approach to love match

---

1 These magazines were chosen with a view to analysing at least one publication from each decade between the 1920s and the 1940s. Each of them is assumed to be adequately representative because their publication span was long enough to testify to their popularity. Besides, their almost complete collections were available in various libraries in Turkey which enabled me to capture the main debates and trends of the era and also to make comparisons between decades and point out the patterns of continuity and breaks and discontinuities. Writers, editors and publishers of these magazines were overwhelmingly men which attests to Ayşe Durakbaşa's assertion that the woman issue in Ottoman/Turkish settings had been predominantly handled by men since the beginning of the modernization/Westernization process in the nineteenth century. See Durakbaşa, Ayşe, "Cumhuriyet Döneminde Modern Kadın ve Erkek Kimliklerinin Oluşumu: Kemalist Kadın Kimliği ve Münevver Erkekler" [The formation of identities of modern woman and modern man in the republican era: the identity of the Kemalist woman and enlightened men], in *75 Yılda Kadınlar ve Erkekler* [Women and Men in 75 Years], ed. Ayşe Berktay Hacımirzaoğlu (Istanbul: Tarih Vakfı Yayınları, 1998), pp. 29-50. Judging from the overwhelmingly male perspective that dominated the debates over the "woman question" as mirrored in the popular magazines under examination it would be fair to repeat Deniz Kandiyoti's witty remark that "men gave social birth to the new woman of the Republic". See Kandiyoti, Deniz, "Gendering the modern: on missing dimensions in the study of Turkish modernization", in *Rethinking Modernity and National Identity in Turkey*, ed. Sibel Bozdoğan and Reşat Kasaba (Seattle: University of Washington Press, 1997), p. 123.

due to its possible destructive impact on traditional Ottoman-Muslim family values, the hints at the taboo like nature of female virginity, the condemnation of staying unmarried for both sexes, the discouragement of divorce, the quest of young males to choose their own life companions, the advocacy for companionship as the backbone of marriage and the efforts to find a middle ground between conventional/Eastern and modern/Western types of marriage abound.[2] It seems that in the early republican era only a limited number of novelties that had been generated by the nation-building context were added to the already existing repertoire regarding marriage.

Marriage in Late Ottoman Times

In 1895, Richard Davey, the well-known contributor to the prominent and influential British political magazine the *Fortnightly Review* shared his customary Orientalist ideas with the readers on the conditions of Muslim women in the Ottoman empire. At some point in the article, Davey provided a vivid picture of how the "business of marriage" was conducted among Muslims inhabiting the Ottoman lands. Using a fictitious and stereotypical character he created and named Ahmed whom he believed represented the average middle-class Muslim male living in Istanbul, Davey explained that marriage in Turkey maintained its age-old Oriental texture and was still constructed on the lines of antiquated regulations. Despite a slight change that paid lip service to the prospective couples' right of choice, Ahmed was still at the mercy of his parents when it came to choosing the woman he would marry and spend his life with. Davey wrote:

> At last our young friend arrives at a marriageable age. In the good old times matters were considerably simplified. His mother would either have made up a match for him with some wealthy girl of her family or

---

2 See Çiçek, Nazan, The Report of the Project Titled "Geç Dönem Osmanlı ve Erken Dönem Cumhuriyette İnşa Edilen Toplumsal Cinsiyet Kategorilerinin Normallik/İdeallik ve Anormallik/Ötekilik Kategorileri Üzerinden Analizi" [The Analysis of Gender Categories in the Late Ottoman and Early Republican Era with a Special Reference to the Manifestations of Normality/Idealness and Abnormality/Otherization], code number 10B5260002, sponsored by Ankara University, Research Projects Office, 2010–2012; Keçeci Kurt, Songül, "II. Meşrutiyet Dönemi Osmanlı Kadın Dergilerinde Aile ve Evlilik Algısı" [The perception of marriage and family in Second Constitutional era women's magazines], *Belleten*, 79/286 (2015), 1073–97; Atamaz Hazar, Serpil, "'The Hands that Rock the Cradle will Rise', Women, Gender and Revolution in Ottoman Turkey (1908–1918)", Ph.D. Dissertation, University of Arizona, 2010.

acquaintance, or his father would have gone down to the slave market and purchased him the prettiest wench he could find. As for consulting Ahmed's wishes or taste in the matter, that would never have entered their head. Opinions have changed a little in Turkey, and Ahmed is allowed a voice in the matter. Still it is impossible for him to converse with his fiancée, or form for himself any idea of her character or appearance. He has to take all on maternal authority. Amongst the wealthier classes the marriage is always arranged between the mothers of the youth, with the approbation, of course, of their fathers. Several interviews take place in rapid succession between the two mothers, and preliminary matters are speedily arranged. Ahmed's family send the future bride as rich a present as their fortune will admit, and her father and mother, in return, make an equally rich present to young Ahmed. [...] At last, the great day comes – the marriage day. As the Koran does not consider marriage a religious necessity, an imam may or may not be invited to bless the couple. But recently, in imitation of the Europeans, the priest is usually present.[3]

Two decades earlier than Davey's mocking of Muslim marriage in *Fortnightly Review*, the Ottoman writer Şemseddin Sami (1850–1904) had skilfully narrated the Olympian tragedy of marriage that befell young Muslims in his famous novel *Taaşuk-ı Talat ve Fitnat* (Talat and Fitnat's Love) of 1875 in which he condemned the oppression of women in a male dominated society and criticised the practice of arranged marriage. Marriage, Sami believed, should be "a partnership, two individuals walking together on life's journey, in regular conversation with each other, an Ottoman version of soul mates".[4] Şemseddin Sami was not alone in his cry for an alteration in the foundation and workings of marriage. In fact, Turkish literature starting from the 1860s up until the 1920s was obsessed with the themes of love, marriage and inter-family conflict. The first *Tanzimat* intellectuals were all supporters of matrimonial love, and regarded conventional nuptial arrangements as backward and embarrassing. Largely through the French novels seeping into the Muslim Turkish psyche

---

3 Davey, Richard, "The present condition of Muhammedan women in Turkey", *Fortnightly Review*, 58/343 (1895), p. 58. Davey was wrong in assuming that the presence of an *imam* was a novelty caused by an attempt to emulate Europeans. Recent research shows that *kadıs* or *imams* witnessed marriage contracts from the early decades of the Ottoman state onwards. See Ercoşkun, Tülay, "Osmanlı İmparatorluğu'nda 19.Yüzyılda Evlilik ve Nikâha Dair Düzenlemeler" [Regulations Related to Marriage in the Nineteenth-Century Ottoman Empire], Ph.D. Dissertation, Ankara University, 2010, pp. 35–60.
4 Gawrych, George W., "Şemseddin Sami: women and social conscience in the late Ottoman empire", *Middle Eastern Studies*, 46/1(2010), p. 101.

many young men and women were looking to fall in love with their prospective spouse. The debate on marriage practices, in particular the evils of arranged and polygamous marriages, was part of the larger debate on women's visibility and participation in the public sphere, and occupied many members of the intelligentsia, overwhelmingly male, who broached the topic in their newspaper columns[5] and pamphlets and even discussed it in their "university lecture notes".[6] It is worth asking, however, whether this profuse interest in marriage was really about women's true emancipation. Could it be more about young males' increasing reluctance to bow to the wishes of their parents/older generations in a subject that profoundly concerned the domain of young males' sensual life (sexual indulgence and contentment being the essential part of it)? As Deniz Kandiyoti rightly remarks male reformers "found the plight of women a powerful vehicle for the expression of their own restiveness with social conventions ... [and] felt alienated from Ottoman patriarchal structures which curtailed their own freedom considerably, even though women were the most obvious victims of the system".[7] The late Ottoman and early republican modernist-minded males' ostensible combat against patriarchal structures appears mostly limited to the partial destruction of arranged marriage since, as we will see, neither their demands nor their suggestions vis-à-vis the process of re-constructing relations between the sexes embraced any genuine feminism. On the contrary, anti-feminism, frequently bordering on misogyny by today's standards, is omni-present in the majority of the texts in regard to the issues of the "woman question" and problems of arranged marriage so that it would be naive not to notice that young males eagerly instrumentalized women's cause in their own fight against the repressive dictates of traditional and age-related power relations. The Western-minded young male found the image of a silenced boy agreeing to marry a girl he had never laid his eyes on, let alone conversed with, upon the command of his parents or other elderly relatives emasculating. It was also deeply alienating because it left no room for free choice and individual fulfilment, two most obvious indices of modern Western existence.[8] As Niyazi Berkes argued, those intellectuals "aspired for the life

---

5 Davis, Fanny, *The Ottoman Lady: A Social History from 1718 to 1918* (Westport, Conn.: Greenwood Press, 1986), p. 94.
6 See Toprak, Zafer, "Muslihiddin Adil'in Görüşleri: Kadın ve Hukuk-ı Nisvan" [Opinions of Muslihiddin Adil: woman and women's rights], *Toplumsal Tarih*, 75 (2000), 14–17.
7 Kandiyoti, Deniz, "End of empire: Islam, nationalism and women in Turkey", in *Women, Islam and the State*, ed. Deniz Kandiyoti (London: MacMillan, 1991), p. 26.
8 See Raif Necdet, "Asri İzdivaç" [Contemporary Marriage], *İnci*, 1 Kanun-u sani 1335 [1919], pp. 9–11, where the author condemns arranged marriage as a "rotten and unnatural" practice, vows to destroy it and opines: "Obeying a parent who tyrannically exceeds his span of

of the European individual in which material comfort, scientific progress and individual liberty reigned. The individualists rebelled against everything that represented tradition, against everything irrational".[9] Thus, the literature on love and marriage, the rebellion against parental authority and state authority, and the political ideas of liberty went hand in hand for the intellectuals of late Ottoman society. The early republic only took out the part about "rebellion against state authority" from the equation and inherited the rest almost indiscriminately.

During the Second Constitutional era (1908–22) the debate on marriage maintained its status as a *topos* that was prominent in the late Ottoman intellectuals' cognitive map, and with the rise of the Ottoman feminist movement it took on new and diverse forms. This time female activists joined the polemic and embarked upon a discursive campaign against the patriarchal order demanding a more equal and inclusive society.

> Thousands of articles on marriage were written by intellectuals of different ideological origins. A considerable number of these articles were authored by women, who became key players in the debate, as the number of female publishers, writers, and readers increased and the press became a free and influential medium of expression after the 1908 Revolution.[10]

Most of the articles regarding marriage and divorce concluded that unless romantic love and companionship were introduced into the union between man and woman marital relationships would irrevocably deteriorate. Comparisons were frequently made between the marriage practices in Europe and the Ottoman empire and the former was favoured due to its approval of premarital courtship which supposedly decreased the possibility of divorce. The pages of the post-1908 Revolution era magazines were crammed with innumerable articles pleading for women's rights and pointing out the social problems caused by the prevailing gender regime. This "feminist rebellion" of the Unionist epoch would contribute enormously to the displacement of Islamic

---

authority and cannot comprehend the meaning of life and happiness through a European mentality, I believe, is a crime against society".

[9] Berkes, Niyazi, *The Development of Secularism in Turkey* (Montreal: McGill University Press, 1964), p. 295, quoted in Duben, Alan and Cem Behar, *Istanbul Households: Marriage, Family, and Fertility 1880–1940* (Cambridge: Cambridge University Press, 1991), p. 93.

[10] Atamaz Hazar, "'The Hands that Rock the Cradle will Rise': Women, Gender and Revolution in Ottoman Turkey (1908–1918)", p. 157. For a comprehensive work on women's magazines in the Second Constitutional era also See Çakır, Serpil, *Osmanlı Kadın Hareketi* [The Ottoman Woman's Movement] (Istanbul: Metis, 1996).

Weltanschaung and later lay the foundations of a number of social norms in the Turkish republic. Yet before long these modern European ideals would provoke an authoritarian response from the early republican elites for whom possible gender role reversals engendered by women's liberation would become a primary concern and indeed an anathema. The republic preferred a form of so-called "state feminism"[11] which in fact did not qualify as feminism since it had no intention of ending male domination over women and by no means negated woman's identity as defined by men, and as enshrined in the patriarchal family.[12] "The secular reformers were fighting against the religious authority that had formed the legal basis of the previous Ottoman state. The new 'rights' they granted to women carried a symbolic meaning in this fight".[13] The republic allowed and encouraged women to take part in the newly constructed nationalist and secularist public sphere through education and employment but vigorously reproduced traditional sexist stereotypes promoted by the patriarchal mentality. Instead of suggesting a radical transformation in the patriarchal order and providing an opportunity for the re-discovery of female identity for and in itself, Kemalists "strove to equip women with the education and skills that would improve their contributions to the republican patriarchy by making them better wives and mothers".[14] In Fatmagül Berktay's words "the absolute domination of father" was handed over "to the republic of brothers".[15]

---

11 Tekeli, Şirin, "The meaning and the limits of feminist ideology in Turkey", in *Women, Family and Social Change in Turkey*, ed. Ferhunde Özbay (Bangkok: UNESCO, 1990), pp. 145 and 152. Deniz Kandiyoti also uses the phrase state-sponsored 'feminism' in her "Patterns of patriarchy: notes for an analysis of male dominance in Turkish society", in *Women in Modern Turkish Society. A Reader*, ed. Şirin Tekeli (London: Zed Books, 1995), p. 314.

12 Mansbridge, Jane, "What is the feminist movement?", in *Feminist Organizations: Harvest of the Women's Movement*, ed. Myra Marx Ferree and Patricia Yancey Martin (Philadelphia: Temple University Press, 1995), pp. 27–34.

13 Tekeli, "The meaning and the limits of feminist ideology", p. 144.

14 Wyers, Mark David, "The New Republic's 'Other' Daughters: Legislating National Sex and Regulating Prostitution in Istanbul 1880–1933", M.A. Dissertation, The University of Arizona, 2008, p. 164.

15 Berktay, Fatmagül, *Tarihin Cinsiyeti* [The Gender of the History] (Istanbul: Metis Yayınevi, 2003), p. 105. I must mention at this point that in defining Kemalists as "not feminist" one should carefully avoid anachronism. When Kemalists were in power feminism as we know today, namely the social movement and the mentality that have been criticizing and deconstructing patriarchy, claiming that "the private is political" and struggling to end male domination over women in all areas of life were not fully developed and feminist demands and objections had not yet become a part of mainstream politics. In other words it would not be fair to blame the Kemalist cadres for not being ahead of their time or merely being the representatives of the time they lived in. The most progressive men of

Courtship, Marriage and Divorce in the Republican Era as Mirrored in the Popular Magazines

With the foundation of the Turkish republic, marriage turned into a site of struggle where the future of the nation and the nationalist regime were claimed to be at stake. In the official discourse marriage was fetishized.[16] It required constant intervention as well as close monitoring by the state. Addressing the Seventh National Turkish Medical Congress in 1939 Ali Esat Birol (1901–99), the doctor who founded the gynaecology and obstetrics clinics both in Ankara University and Gülhane Military Medicine Academy remarked that "to think of marriage as an abstract, personal, or need-based issue or a solution of a physiological need is very wrong ... this perspective is similar to benefiting only from the shade of a tree that was actually planted for its fruit. Since the family

---

their time went so far as to accept equal civil rights for women and that was what the Kemalists emulated and adopted. However, what would also be equally unfair is to treat the Kemalists' approach to the "woman question" as something more than it really was. Attributing ultra-feminist qualities to the Kemalist politics as if they were devised to destroy patriarchal hierarchies in the society is extremely misleading. Some feminist accounts severely censuring the Kemalist understanding of the "woman question" since the emergence of feminist movement in Turkey from the 1980s onwards seem to have fallen into the trap of anachronism to varying degrees. Nevertheless their frustration which seems to have largely contributed to their anachronistic attitude should also be forgiven to some extent because they were too busy with deconstructing the popular myth and the official rhetoric which was propagating that the Republic had rescued women from the practices of dark ages and had provided them with the rights fit for modern times, hence no further political efforts towards the betterment of women's lives in Turkey were needed. For a discussion on how "Westernization does not automatically bring about the liberation of women" and "how distinction between liberation and emancipation is crucial in order to avoid overenthusiastic assessments of the condition of women in Turkey" see Toprak, Binnaz, "Emancipated but unliberated women in Turkey: the impact of Islam", in *Women, Family and Social Change in Turkey*, ed. Ferhunde Özbay (Bangkok: UNESCO, 1990), pp. 39–49.

16 The Turkish republic's approach to the marriage question manifested itself in a crystallized form in the following words by Professor of Law Hüseyin Avni Göktürk in a lecture he gave in Ankara Halkevi (People's House) on 25 February 1939: "Marriage can be thought of as a national duty. All Turks who love their country and their nation must avoid staying single and marry. State intervention in this matter is an absolute necessity. In a country like Turkey where everything is in need of being re-constructed the state shall take the matter into its own hands and encourage marriage and support the families with a certain number of children". See Göktürk, Hüseyin Avni, *Evlenme Birliğinde Eşlerin Durumu* [The Footing of Each Spouse in Marriage], CHP Konferanslar Serisi, Kitap 4 (Ankara: Recep Ulusoğlu Basımevi, 1939), p. 24.

that consists of a man and a woman is the source of life and basis of the generations and state, there's no bigger mistake than leaving marriage to chance".[17] Popular magazines did their share of work in inciting, exhorting and educating the middle class reading public as to the merits of marriage and made sure that everyone without a spouse and children felt as if excommunicated.

The Swiss Civil Code was adopted in 1926. Monogamy became the rule and the processes of engagement, marriage and divorce were codified. Accordingly the husband was defined as the head of the household.[18] Five years later the government issued the Marriage Law (*Evlilik Kanunnamesi* of 1931) a new and wider version of similar regulations issued in late Ottoman times which demanded a health clearance report as a prerequisite to marriage with a view to prohibiting marriage among persons infected by contagious and venereal diseases, like tuberculosis and syphilis, as well as bearers of mental illness, and "infused legislation with racial health concerns underscored by an ethic of female virtue".[19] The new nation state's interest in the institution went far beyond merely structuring the normative domain and issuing the legal documents that would regulate the formation, maintenance and dissolution of marriage. As with so many other institutions, social constructs and values of the time, for the republican founding elite marriage came to be perceived in highly practical terms and assessed through its contribution to the consolidation of the new regime. A solid marriage was the first and necessary condition to produce well functioning family units which in turn would produce physically and mentally healthy children who would later grow into productive citizens.[20] Marriage, in other words, was the most potent vehicle in the young republic's population growth and human capital betterment policies which reflected a touch of eugenics rationale. As pointed out by a scholar of eugenics

---

17 Birol, Ali Esat, "Öjenik Tatbikatı: Yedinci Milli Türk Tıp Kurultayı" [The Application of Eugenics: The Seventh National Turkish Medical Congress] (Istanbul: Kader Basımevi, 1939), p. 5, quoted in Atabay, Efe, "Eugenics, Modernity and the Rationalization of Morality in Early Republican Turkey", M.A. Dissertation, Institute of Islamic Studies, McGill University, Montreal, 2009, p. 56.

18 For typical and representative accounts that fiercely condemn marriage practices and family law in Ottoman times and praise the novelties brought about by the republic, see Göktürk, *Evlenme Birliğinde Eşlerin Durumu*; Sevig, Vasfi Raşit, *Cumhuriyet Halk Partisi ve Aile* [The Republican People's Party and the Family], CHP Konferanslar Serisi, Kitap 10 (Ankara: Recep Ulusoğlu Basımevi, 1939).

19 Wyers, "The New Republic's 'Other' Daughters", p. 164.

20 It was reiterated that "the Kemalist regime's aim in the marriage issue was to create children" (Kemalci rejim evlenmede çocuk yaratmak gayesini takip eder). See Sevig, *Cumhuriyet Halk Partisi ve Aile*, pp. 9–10.

marriage was the most frequently examined issue in the eugenic literature produced by the Turkish medical elite in the 1930s.[21] The Turkish republic's interest in eugenics, however, mostly appears as part of its renowned aspiration for catching up with new scientific trends in the Western world and never turned into a systematically constructed and pursued state policy. There were believers of eugenics among the medical elite who worked in the higher echelons of the civil service and there were politicians and statesmen they influenced yet this did not mean that the Turkish state mechanism was guided by eugenics. Eugenics-inspired ideas voiced by several prominent figures from the strata of Turkish medical elite neither automatically translated into the Turkish legal realm nor dominated it. In the Turkish case, as Sanem Güvenç Salgırlı convincingly argues, eugenics was not "a reinforcing ideology of social engineering practised by the state".[22] Unlike other countries such as Germany or Italy eugenics was not practised by the Turkish state in instituting and strengthening its control over the population. "It was a social class, the new elite of the Republican Turkey and their culture which was comfortably conventionalized in the new scientific morality of the era that they called eugenics".[23]

> The eugenic view of reproduction and the demographic argument of preserving the strength of the nation (...) followed the logic that in a rational, secular state where science was the new religion, marriage was also supposed to be organized in accord with scientific principles. They encouraged people from the "valuable" classes to make more children and strove to convince their audience on the national imperative of this goal.[24]

"Daughters of sophisticated and advanced (*mütekâmil*) families should marry the valuable and potent sons of other sophisticated families" asserted Dr. Mahmud Şemsi, the chief assistant at Institute of Histology and Embryology in Ankara. He also complained that "sons and daughters of valuable families

---

21 Atabay, "Eugenics, Modernity and the Rationalization of Morality", p. 45. For projections and suggestions (especially regarding contraception, abortion, marriage) of a series of eugenist politicians, academics and scientists in 1930s Turkey to rehabilitate the Turkish human capital/"Turkish race" and accelerate population growth, see Öztan, G. Gürkan, "Türkiye'de Öjeni Düşüncesi ve Kadın" [The idea of eugenics and woman in Turkey], *Toplum ve Bilim*, 105 (2006), pp. 265–82.
22 Salgırlı, Sanem Güvenç, "Eugenics as Science of the Social: A Case from the 1930s Istanbul", Ph.D. Dissertation, Binghampton University, 2009, p. 1.
23 Salgırlı, "Eugenics as Science of the Social", p. 1.
24 Atabay, "Eugenics, Modernity and the Rationalization of Morality", p. 46.

either avoid or put off marriage and lead either childless marriages or content themselves with one child only".[25]

Bachelorhood as a Crime against the Nation

All the magazines examined for this study frowned upon a non-married status for both sexes. They repeatedly published articles that listed the advantages and joy of marriage and disadvantages and misery of staying single. Yet there was a tacit agreement that most unmarried women did not in fact choose spinsterhood, they were simply "left on the shelf" for various reasons some of which were their own fault.[26] As Mahmud Şemsi, one of the regular contributors to *Yedigün* asserted in a bold manner "obtaining a university degree and a profession prevented girls from marrying well or forced them into spinsterhood" because when they finally felt ready to marry after spending their most valuable years at school they found that their male counterparts either had been already married or wished to marry someone much younger:

> Girls with higher education usually put up with the consequences of a long term spinsterhood which can be likened to a gradual and extremely painful suicide, not because they lack sexual feelings or the instinct to reproduce but because they cannot find appropriate suitors. Normal men marry as soon as they begin earning their living. Most of those who remain single well into their old age are drunkards, sexually impotent, sufferers from tuberculosis and syphilis, namely those not good for marriage.[27]

In a similar vein Hüseyin Cahid Yalçın (1875–1957), the well-known journalist, writer and politician who was famous for his polemics and sharp-tongued criticism, was tried three times in the Independence Tribunals (İstiklal Mahkemeleri) for opposing the government and who would later become in 1948 the editor-in-chief of *Ulus*, the official newspaper of Cumhuriyet Halk Partisi

---

25 Mahmud Şemsi, "Mutlu Evliler: Aşk mı Firaset mi?" [Happily married couples: love or intellect?], *Yedigün*, no. 108, 3 April 1935, p. 17.

26 Girls with high education were accused of losing their feminine charm and competing with their male counterparts in intellectual and vocational matters, which frightened and put off eligible bachelors and caused them to become spinsters. See Nüzhet Abbas, "İyi Koca Kıtlığı" [The shortage of good husbands], *Yedigün*, no. 156, 4 March 1936, pp. 3–4.

27 Mahmud Şemsi, "Mutlu Evliler: Kadının Sosyal Yükselişi ve Evlilik" [Happily married couples: woman's social progress and marriage], *Yedigün*, no. 109, 10 April 1935, p. 16.

(The Republican People's Party), too put the blame on "the new type of girl" for the reluctance bachelors displayed towards marriage. "These new types of girls do not have the potential to encourage young men to marry" he complained nostalgically:

> In olden times the biggest attraction of the young girls came from the fact that they all were surrounded by a halo of mystery. Today they are stripped of that mystery and became largely available. The beaches look like huge exhibition areas where young girls are on display in a manner that leaves no room for imagination. A 15 minute conversation with them reveals that behind their latest fashion clothing and carefully painted finger nails lies a poor foundation of wisdom and soul. With these girls one can elegantly date, go on lovely picnics, build loyal friendships but cannot marry.[28]

Complaints from readers about the high expectations of girls at marriageable age overflowed the pages of magazines. "Even the poorest girls do not dream of living in humble conditions any more", cried out a reader of *Asar-ı Nisvan* in 1925 and the "majority of the young girls define happiness in materialistic terms which in turn discourage young men from proposing marriage".[29] Therefore self-induced bachelorhood among healthy youth was seen as predominantly a male issue that potentially threatened the dissolution of the family, and the exhortations for marriage usually targeted the male readership. "By bachelor we do not mean the ones who cannot or would not marry due to poverty or bad health", Ömer Rıza clarified in a piece titled "Bekârlar Niçin Evlenmez?"(Why do bachelors not marry?), "we mean the ones who choose not to marry because they think bachelorhood with the absolute freedom it allegedly provides is superior to marriage".[30] Many articles using a word play announced that the old Turkish saying of "bachelorhood is sultanate" was no longer valid, because in the new republican regime all sultanates including bachelorhood were abolished. Men "absolutely should and must marry" because "only after getting married could they grasp the sacred nature of womanhood and appreciate the real value of a woman as the most beautiful and

---

28 Hüseyin Cahid (Yalçın), "Evlenme Buhranı" [Marriage crisis], *Yedigün*, no. 118, 12 June 1935, p. 5.
29 C., "İzdivaçlar Niçin Azalıyor?" [Why do the number of marriages decrease?], *Asar-ı Nisvan*, no. 19, 1 Kanun-u sani 1342 [1926], p. 13.
30 Ömer Rıza, "Bekârlar Niçin Evlenmez?" [Why do the bachelors not marry?], *Yedigün*, no. 100, 6 February 1935, p. 3.

lovable being on earth".³¹ In many instances the effort made by the authors to counter the bachelôrs' reasoning of rejecting marriage and persuade them to settle down is couched in such hyperbolic language that the narrative frequently turned into a farce betraying the propagandist nature of the text.³² In *Resimli Ay* marriage was depicted as "the most intimate insurance for young men that guaranteed a healthy, wholesome and long life". Referring to some unauthenticated statistics from Europe and the USA, *Resimli Ay* asserted that convicts in prisons and lunatics in asylums were overwhelmingly bachelors.³³ As Madawi al-Rasheed remarks in her review of Hanan Khaloussy's work regarding the alleged "marriage crisis" in the Egyptian case, "shying away from marriage among urban men of [middle class] is guaranteed to create a cross-cultural, almost universal anxiety associated with elevating a personal choice into a political and national agenda that portends not only social ills and psychological turbulence but also communal disintegration and the withering of the nation as a whole".³⁴

The perceived threat posed by bachelorhood to the normative sexual and reproductive space regulated by marriage led the popular magazines to enlist the help of medical doctors in "scientifically" explaining the physiological and psychological merits of marriage. In line with the heavily medicalized nature of the bio-politics of republican Turkish modernization an ever burgeoning advice literature preaching on the "necessity of marriage for the human body and its functions in curing several health problems ranging from acne to epilepsy"³⁵ found its way into the popular magazines. In all articles marriage was presented as a panacea while bachelorhood was regarded as a negligence of one's duty towards the nation and society. Women, especially the educated ones, were admonished to lower their standards and stop looking for "a husband as handsome as Clark Gable, intelligent as Voronof and rich as Rockefeller's third son".³⁶ "Marriage is not a luxury that one can aspire to or avoid enjoying" wrote Nüzhet Abbas, "our women should realize that setting up a

---

31 Mahmud Şemsi, "Mutlu Evliler: Evlenmek ve Mesut Olmak Güç Bir İştir" [Happily married couples: marrying and being happy is a difficult task], *Yedigün*, no. 105, 13 March 1935, p. 11.

32 Ömer Rıza, "Bekârlar Niçin Evlenmez?", pp. 3–4.

33 No Author, "İzdivaç Dünyanın En Samimi Sigortasıdır" [Marriage is the most intimate insurance in the world], *Resimli Ay*, no. 16, Mayıs 1341 [1925], pp. 23–4.

34 al-Rasheed, Madawi, book review of Khaloussy, Hanan, *For Better, For Worse: the Marriage Crisis that Made Modern Egypt*, *Middle Eastern Studies*, 47/6 (2011), p. 964.

35 Ergene, Ömer Nuri, "Ev Doktoru Diyor ki: Evlenmek Bir İhtiyaçtır" [Home doctor says: marriage is a need], *Yedigün*, no. 350, 21 November 1939, p. 13.

36 Nüzhet Abbas, "İyi Koca Kıtlığı", p. 4.

happy nest is a debt they owe both to themselves and to the society".[37] Men too were encouraged to be assertive and persuade their fiancées into marrying without expensive wedding ceremonies.[38] The young Turkish nation state desperately in need of population growth could not afford bachelorhood and/ or childless marriages. Consequently all magazines stigmatized those who were unmarried, be they male or female, as abnormal reinforcing the idea that marriage rather than being a socially constructed institution was actually an integral and natural part of being human, the most fundamental indicator of leading a socially acceptable and meaningful life and the most visible proof of dutiful citizenship.

How to Marry?

The question of what would be the best method to marry remained as popular and complicated as in the late Ottoman times. What type of marriage would yield the greatest returns to the Turkish nation and the republican regime? Was it better if young and inexperienced people left such a momentous decision to their parents and elder relatives who could claim more experience and wisdom on the issue? Or perhaps it would be best if youngsters who were not yet tainted by the rotten, unscientific, Oriental and archaic notions of love and marriage were allowed to listen to their heart and mind? With the establishment of the republic a renewed frenzy about marriage choices flooded the magazines. Was a love match better than an arranged marriage? Numerous pieces devoted to the issue discussed the shortcomings of different types of marriage. The magazine *Süs* (Ornament), for example, published more than 50 articles between the years of 1923 and 1924 all discussing the various marriage methods (arranged, quasi-arranged, love), the meaning and value of marriage, the role of women in marriage, the proper conduct of a wife and a husband in marriage. Given that "the whole system of attribution and meaning that we call gender relies on and to a great extent derives from the structuring provided by marriage"[39] the emergence of such consuming preoccupation with the institution of marriage at a time when the validity of the traditional gender regime appeared to have disintegrated is not surprising. In June 1923, about

---

37 Nüzhet Abbas, "İyi Koca Kıtlığı", p. 4.
38 Çalapala, Rakım, "Bugün Nasıl Evlenilir?" [How to marry today?], *Yedigün*, no. 635, 6 May 1945, p. 11.
39 Cott, Nancy, *Public Vows: A History of Marriage and the Nation* (Cambridge: Harvard University Press, 2000), p. 3.

five months before the foundation of the Turkish republic was declared, *Süs* published a survey asking its readership's opinion with respect to the best marriage method. "Which one should you prefer", the survey asked, "arranged marriage [*görücülük*] or marriage based on prior acquaintance between couples [*görüşücülük*]?"[40] Apart from publishing a selection of the responses from the readers, *Süs* also consulted a group of well-known male and female public figures, mostly novelists and columnists, about the issue at hand and shared their answers. The answers given by those prominent figures such as Reşad Nuri (Güntekin), Hamdullah Suphi (Tanrıöver), Yakup Kadri (Karaosmanoğlu), Hüseyin Cahid (Yalçın), Falih Rıfkı (Atay), Mahmud Esat (Bozkurt) and Şükufe Nihal whose names would later become to be seen as almost identical with the intellectual, literary and political activities of the early republican era and whose work clearly reflected and reproduced the spirit of the time, indicated that the idea of arranged marriage, at least in discourse if not in practice, was rapidly becoming a *bête noire* and doomed to perish.[41] Accordingly, slowly yet decidedly a pattern to all articles in the magazines emerged. It became clear that the policy makers and pro-regime intelligentsia of the republic favoured love match marriage over the arranged marriage of previous times. Yet, what they meant by love was the key to understanding their highly pragmatist, practical notion of ideal marriage. Love by no means should be considered in "Oriental"[42] terms characterised by extreme passion, self-forgetfulness and pain that allegedly blinded the lover and presented the beloved in highly acclamatory light as a flawless meta-human creature.

---

40 Editorial, "Görücülük mü Görüşücülük mü?" [Arranged marriage or marriage following a Courtship?], *Süs*, no. 3, 30 Haziran 1339 [1923], p. 2.

41 Editorial, "Görücülük mü Görüşücülük mü?", *Süs*, no. 4, 7 Temmuz 1339 [1923], p. 3. Also See Editorial, "Görücülük mü Görüşücülük mü?", *Süs*, no. 5, 14 Temmuz 1339 [1923], p. 3.

42 As Aylin Özman remarks in her analysis of Vala Nureddin's writings on marriage, for example, "one can detect an overriding tension between passion/feelings and rationality as the cultural signifiers of the East and the West respectively. In marriage the contrast between the East and the West is presented as the tension between passionate love and friendship. Accordingly, while the Eastern man is said to go after his sexual desires the Western man prioritizes his intellectual satisfaction. Hence, according to Va-Nu the mental unity of couples is considered a prerequisite for a happy, life-long marriage in the West. On the other hand, the Eastern style of relationship is regarded as involving a useless emotional interaction between the partners that does not have any implications for a life-long marriage". Özman, Aylin, "The image of 'woman' in Turkish and social political thought: on the implications of social constructionism and biological essentialism", *Turkish Studies*, 11/3 (2010), p. 455.

> Passion is temporary. Love based on passion has no future. Real love has nothing to do with passion. Real love is immortal. It is constructive rather than destructive. Many men envy and aspire to be Don Juan without realizing that they will end up like Don Juan namely forgotten, deserted and lonely. Real love is a kind of love that leads you to marry and set up a happy home and rear children, promotes a fruitful career and nourishes a tranquil family life and makes you permanently happy. Passions that strike like lightening before rapidly disappearing into darkness bring only loss and disaster.[43]

This lightning-like love was immensely fragile and mostly fuelled by a strong yet temporary sexual attraction and lust. It could not offer the solid ground on which a long-lasting and fruitful marriage could be built. Therefore, the meaning, content and scope of love should be de-constructed and re-constructed so as to connote companionship, solidarity, sense of belonging and selflessness for the sake of family unit.

> There is no doubt that a marriage should be erected upon love [sevgi], yet we have to distinguish love from passion and lust [tutkunluk]. Passion is of a volatile nature, it may diminish easily due to simple reasons. Its existence does not necessarily generate companionship. In marriage, however, companionship is markedly more important than passion. Companionship requires two souls to be compatible and act in harmony. A solid, real and loyal love is a completely different thing from passion. Unlike passion, love does not prevent people from thoroughly comprehending, acknowledging and appreciating the virtues and vices of their prospective partner, it provides a better base upon which to build a union.[44]

If a marriage was to cultivate this new type of love, last long and produce joy and serenity along with healthy, robust children, then it was not to be based on the decision of parents and elders alone. In a piece titled "Kızımı Kiminle Evlendireyim" (Whom should I marry my daughter to?) İbrahim Alaettin Gövsa instructed fathers on the proper conduct in giving their daughters' hands:

> Because it is not you but your daughter who will be a life companion to one of those suitors then as a father you have to take her opinions

---

[43] Ömer Rıza, "Kadınların Tapındığı Erkekler" [Men worshipped by women], *Yedigün*, no. 95, 2 January 1935, p. 29.

[44] Mahmud Şemsi, "Mutlu Evliler: Aşk mı Firaset mi?", p. 17.

and feelings into consideration. Had your daughter already met some young men thanks to the opportunities provided by school or work life or befriended someone through her social life activities then it is a duty of immense importance for you to supervise that intercourse and make sure that it stays within the limits of formal and serious relationships. If you did not perform that duty properly then you need not worry yourself with the question of whom should I marry my daughter to. Good and solid marriage proposals are presented to the girls with a good reputation only.[45]

As the republican elites saw it, strictly practised arranged marriage was terribly outdated. Modern times had no room for such an ancient and dysfunctional institution which robbed the individuals of the possibility of choosing their life companions. Nevertheless as the general tenor of the articles under examination reveals women's free choice did not extend to every avenue of life in general and marriage life in particular. After either being duly consulted as to the suitors or allowed to marry someone of her own choosing, her free choice, individuality, equality and freedom almost ceased to exist and mostly became a thing of hollow rhetoric. Once she was married she would obediently retreat to her subservient position that she briefly left in her father's home. Her husband as the 'patriarch-elect' would take over the post of male domination while she "happily" carried out her heavily gendered national duty as a provider of logistic support (companion, mother, and housewife) in her matrimonial home. Hüseyin Rahmi (Gürpınar)'s play *Kadın Erkekleşince* (When a Woman Becomes Like a Man) of 1933 appears as the manifestation of monumental dread that seemed to have gripped the male community of the early republic. As Alan Duben and Cem Behar noted,

> the themes of the decline of authority and the growth of sexual immorality continue[d] to provide a central focus for writers and readers of novels and short stories into the 1930s. [...] The cultural world of gender relations and roles, the symbolic meanings underlying the basic conjugal and filial structures of Ottoman and early republican societies appeared to be shaken, and 'nature' to be reversed. As we have seen, however, domestic gender roles probably did not change very radically during the

---

45   Gövsa, İbrahim Alaettin, "Kızımı Kiminle Evlendireyim" [Whom should I marry my daughter to?], *Yedigün*, no. 375, 14 May 1940, p. 6.

period, even though many women appeared more modern and had begun to lead more liberated and freer ways of life in the public world.[46]

As Robert O. Blood asserts in *The Family*, "self-selection of one's spouse will reflect one's personal concerns; thus, the personal qualities and interpersonal compabilities of the potential spouse will be predominant factors in mate choice based on love. In contrast, the criteria for selection in kin-arranged marriage will reflect concerns with the impact of the prospective spouse on the total family unit".[47] Because the early republican political and intellectual elites were ultimately concerned about the durability and function of the new republican family they seem to have sought to reach a balance between love match and arranged marriage. By casting themselves in the role of *parens patriae* for the youth of the country they hoped to provide a new marriage model whereby the personal choice of love match would be grafted onto some reliable qualities of arranged marriage such as the concern with the socioeconomic status, health, strength, fertility and temperament of the prospective spouse.

Almost all participants in the survey in *Süs* referred to earlier were at pains to point out that the abandonment of arranged marriage should by no means usher in free love among young people. In fact, love was not the word used by many in talking about marriage.[48] The emphasis was on allowing limited contact between prospective bride and groom so that they could get to know each other's taste and choice in various matters under the supervision and close scrutiny of their family members.[49] Hüseyin Cahid Yalçın, after ridiculing segregation and arranged marriage as practised in Ottoman times proudly noted in *Yedigün* that nobody could accuse Turks of marrying blind-folded anymore, but flatly added that the handicaps of entering into marriage without any

---

[46] Duben and Behar, *Istanbul Households: Marriage, Family, and Fertility 1880–1940*, p. 199.

[47] Blood, Robert O., *The Family* (New York: Free Press, 1972), pp. 293–5, quoted in Fox, Greer Litton, "Love match and arranged marriage in a modernizing nation, mate selection in Ankara, Turkey", *Journal of Marriage and Family*, 31/1 (1975), p. 186.

[48] Derya Duman concludes that romanticism in the context of marital relations is virtually absent in the content of the early republican era women's magazines which in turn suggests a rather rational conceptualization of marriage. Lexemes referring to love are not overwhelmingly used. Instead of love there are perpetual references to physical, educational and social compatibility between couples. See Duman, Derya, "Gender politics in Turkey and the role of women's magazines: a critical outlook on the early republican era", *Hacettepe Üniversitesi Edebiyat Fakültesi Dergisi*, 28/1 (2011), pp. 87–9.

[49] Editorial, "Mehmed Emin Bey'in İstimzacımıza Cevabı" [Mehmed Emin Bey's answer to our survey], *Süs*, no. 4, 7 Temmuz 1339 [1923], p. 1.

genuine knowledge about the personality traits of the prospective spouse remained unchanged.

> Our latest revolution solved this problem radically and irrevocably. Today arranged marriage sounds like an exotic tale to us. We get to see girls with our own eyes and converse with them everywhere from tea parties to beaches. Our eyes have opened widely, perhaps a little too widely. Yet this new ease with the opposite sex does not allow us to infiltrate the mysteries of their character. We continue to marry people on the basis of their looks. Old practices do not vanish entirely without any trace, they simply morph into new practices and engender hybrid forms. Therefore we cannot say that we are completely free from the drawbacks of old marriage habits. Some girls and boys are being introduced to each other at a relative's or friend's house and have a brief conversation over tea or coffee. Is it enough to unite your life with someone? In short, despite the abandonment of arranged marriage young people continue to marry people whom they do not truly know.[50]

Any sort of sexual contact before marriage was absolutely unthinkable and loss of virginity, even the rumour of it, was almost equal to a symbolic death sentence for a girl. If a love match entailed a process of courtship that included sexual intercourse before marriage then love marriage was considered a threat to the women's chastity and honour, hence unwanted. As already mentioned by other scholars, the traditional sexual morality inherited from Ottoman times was "not ever radically questioned within the Kemalist ethic".[51] The old morality which perceived sexual virtue through the lenses of virginity of women before marriage was preserved and reproduced by Kemalist reformers. Indeed, concern over the protection of women's honour and chastity was a critical dimension of Kemalist understanding with respect to the woman question and frequently revealed itself during the debates over marriage. "The more a young girl remains romantic and devoid of any opportunity to grasp the [sexual] reality of marriage the more her bridal soul appears as a fire ground of strong excitements and anxieties" asserted İbrahim Alaettin Gövsa. "That ignorance, that oblivion is not only poetical but also a state of utmost importance for the institution of marriage and for the happiness of ensuing family

50   Hüseyin Cahid (Yalçın) "Evlenme Tarzları" [Methods of marriage], *Yedigün*, no. 147, 1 January 1936, p. 5.
51   Wyers, "The New Republic's 'Other' Daughters", p. 164.

life which concurrently affects the wellbeing of our country and society".[52] The opportunist and self-contradictory attitude the male community embraced in the early republican era vis-à-vis the virginity issue found its expression in a critical account by Rakım Çalapala in 1945 where he testily narrated the hypocrisy prevailing in the relationships with the opposite sex.

> Majority of us think like a Westerner in some areas and react like an Easterner in some others. This double-standard is best captured in sexual matters. Almost all men desire to fool around with their neighbours' daughters or wife, or sleep with any woman they come across. As long as they remain single they profess to be a European. They protest the notions of segregation, jealousy, honour, chastity and virginity. They keep reminding us that because one lives only once, life should be spent in having fun. When those very same men decide to marry they start looking for a virgin, a girl completely untouched. Do they ever recall that previously they violated the intimacy of numerous innocent girls through false promise of marriage?[53]

How to Behave in Marriage and Avoid Divorce?

Most of the articles examined for this chapter encompass various forms of antifeminism and misogyny,[54] and present an almost flawless blueprint of patriarchal gender hierarchies of the time. Women were constantly reminded that their first and utmost duty was to become a mother. The words mother and woman were frequently used interchangeably. A woman's mission in life was to support her husband and raise physically and mentally healthy children. Motherhood, often wrapped in the glittering package of jingoistic nationalist

---

52 Gövsa, İbrahim Alaettin, "Gelin Ruhu" [The soul of the bride], *Yedigün*, no. 135, 9 October 1935, p. 4.
53 Çalapala, Rakım, "Nasıl Koca Bulabilirsiniz?" [How to find a husband?], *Yedigün*, no. 645, 15 July 1945, p. 10.
54 Women were represented as childish, petulant, inconsistent, hysterical, flaccid, excessively possessive, having a weakness for money, worshipping power and having an inclination to be dominated. See Ömer Rıza, "Erkekleri Yiyen Kadınlar" [Women who eat men alive], *Yedigün*, no. 116, 29 May 1935, pp. 7–8 and 17. For a manifestation of this misogynistic approach, see Va-Nû, "Kadın Denen Meçhul" [The mystery called woman], *Yedigün*, no. 675, 10 February 1946, pp. 8–9 and 14 in which the author classifies woman types, one of which is "women who resemble bugs without any will" (iradesiz böceklere benzeyen kadınlar).

rhetoric,[55] was glorified and sacralised. In Rakım Çalapala's words in *Yedigün* "the value of woman is determined by her assignment in life which is indisputably motherhood. Let us remember that Atatürk too declared that motherhood comes first among the social and private duties of women".[56] Women seeking any kind of empowerment outside family life, be it higher education, holding a profession or devoting time to personal entertainment or fulfilment, were sneered at.

> Man is the true bread winner in the family. Women who acknowledge this fact readily devote their time and energy to housework whereas women who feel an urge to work outside of their home continue working even after they get married. Fortunately the latter is a minority among the female population. Mother Nature created woman exclusively for her husband, children and home. Those who believe that they can fulfil the needs of their soul and find happiness only outside of their house are not normal by birth. Only in marriages where man holds the power and is revered by woman can happiness and unison be sustained.[57]

As late as 1949, Hasip Ahmet Aytuna admitted in the official publication of Halkevleri, *Ülkü*, that womanhood could not be reduced to motherhood but insisted that women should nevertheless prioritize motherhood.

> The job of motherhood is much more valuable and important than whatever paid job she can do. The existence, independence and future of a nation depend on it. If working woman refuses to become a mother how can a nation survive? Women should be equal to men in terms of civil rights. Yet we prefer her to be a cultured housewife who is cognizant of her primary duties.[58]

---

55 See for example Fevziye Abdürreşid, "Valide" [Mother], *Asar-ı Nisvan*, no. 18, 15 Kanun-u evvel 1341 [1925], p. 4 where she writes "we need to raise mothers who can give birth to/create new victories like the ones we won in the Battles of Gallipoli and Dumlupınar". Also see No Author, "Türk Kadını ve Musul" [Turkish Woman and Mosul], *Asar-ı Nisvan*, no. 19, 1 Kanun-u sani 1342 [1926], pp. 2–4.

56 Çalapala, Rakım, "Kadın Nedir?" [What is a woman?], *Yedigün*, no. 632, 15 April 1945, p. 6.

57 Mahmud Şemsi, "Mutlu Evliler: Birlikte Kazanan Evli Kadın" [Happy couples: married woman who is a bread-winner], *Yedigün*, no. 114, 15 May 1935, p. 16.

58 Aytuna, Hasip Ahmet, "Ailenin ve Cemiyetin Temeli Kadın" [Woman as the foundation stone of family and society], *Ülkü*, 30 (September 1949), pp. 3–4. Also See Aytuna, Hasip, "Çok Çocuklu Ailelere Ne Gibi Yardımlar Yapılabilir?" [How can we help families with multiple children?], *Ülkü*, 30 (October 1949), pp. 3–4 and 13.

Men were told that after choosing a life companion they should focus on the well-being of their family and avoid disrupting the balance and tranquillity at home. Yet the main responsibility of preserving the marital union fell upon women. As Va-Nû (Vala Nureddin) (1901–67) argued "although she is inferior to her husband in intelligence a woman is nevertheless the centre and the guardian of the family thanks to her patience and fortitude".[59] Magazines prescribed the correct mode of behaviour for married women in minute detail while advice addressed to men mostly remained limited to a few abstract suggestions such as "try to be gentle and considerate towards your family" or "always display a trustworthy and honest attitude in relationships".[60] Women were expected to be in constant doubt of their self-worth, look presentable and rectify their mistakes so as to become more useful and desirable for their spouse. "If you replace useless visits to neighbours with excursions to exhibitions, theatres and cinemas you can keep fit and avoid being overweight"[61] wrote Mevhibe İclal in *Asar-ı Nisvan* in 1925. Sometimes they were invited to answer some questionnaires about the degree of affection and tolerance they experienced in their marriage in order to determine whether they were still loved by their husband.[62] As a scholar drawing on her content analysis of some Turkish women's magazines from the period of 1923 to 1950 suggested, all magazines were "devoid of feminist agenda" and women were "represented as the only source of dispute in the family, being selfish, rude, apathetic and not devoted".[63] In order to have peace in married life "man should be dominant without coercion and woman should be obedient without being coerced".[64] It was intimated that if divorce occurred it was probably the woman's fault[65] as she failed to keep

---

59 Va-Nû, "Kadın Denen Meçhul" [The Mystery called woman], *Yedigün*, no. 677, 24 February 1946, pp. 7–8 and Va-Nû, "Kadın Denen Meçhul" [The Mystery called woman], *Yedigün*, no. 678, 3 March, 1946, p. 9.

60 Nizamettin Nazif, "Erkekler Sevilmek mi İstiyorsunuz?" [Gentlemen do you wish to be loved?], *Yedigün*, no. 648, 5 August 1945, p. 6.

61 Mevhibe İclal, "Kadınlarda Faaliyet-i Fikriyyenin Mefkudiyyeti" [The lack of intellectual activities in women], *Asar-ı Nisvan*, no. 3, 26 Şubat 1341 [1925], p. 9.

62 No Author, "Kocanız Hâlâ Sizi Seviyor mu?" [Does your husband still love you?], *Yedigün*, no. 679, 10 March 1946, pp. 6 and 18. Some of the questions were as follows: Does he like to spend his spare time with you? Does he respect your opinion? Does he lose his temper? Does he cuddle and kiss you?

63 Duman, "Gender politics in Turkey and the role of women's magazines", pp. 90–1.

64 İ. A. G, "Kadın, Erkek, Para" [Woman, man, money], *Yedigün*, no. 387, 6 August 1940, p. 9.

65 Binbaşı İsmail Hakkı, "Dedikodu" [Gossip], *Süs*, no 38, 1 Mart 1340 [1924], p. 3 where the author boldly asserts that "divorced women have no one but themselves to blame for the divorce".

her husband happy and satisfied. Divorce was systematically discouraged and in harmony with the reasoning in the Civil Code of 1926 was regarded as the last resort only to be decided upon by a judge. "Divorce is unacceptable if the couple have children" argued Dr. Mahmud Şemsi in *Yedigün*. "Children need a home where both parents are present. Mothers and fathers who abandon their children due to an affair are despised everywhere in the world".[66] Divorce was allowed not because the policy makers of the early republic and their supporters among intelligentsia were feminists and liberals but because they were ardent champions of a well-functioning family unit. If there was an irretrievable breakdown in the relationship between the spouses and a marriage failed to contribute to the production and socialization of the next generations, then its continuation was worthless as it could no longer cater to the needs of the nation and the regime. In other words the practical terms that dominated the cognitive map of the Kemalist nationalists were also at play vis-à-vis the institution of divorce. As repeatedly expressed in agony aunt style advice columns in these magazines, because a strong bond of understanding, friendship and compassion were the main elements of a strong marriage, women were supposed to keep the first love alive and deepen the marital tie by constantly striving to please their husband.[67] In order to captivate their husband's tender loving care continuously women were to "combine the qualities of a child, a wife, a mother, a lover, and a companion in their personality and mobilize each of these qualities on demand".[68] Many lengthy pieces that were devoted to particular advice to married women crammed the pages of magazines year after year. "Do not ever search your husband's pockets"[69] women were admonished, "do not nag",[70] "be frugal",[71] "do not display excessive jealousy",[72]

---

66 Mahmud Şemsi, "Mutlu Evliler: Genç Evliler Ayrı Bir Yuva Açmalıdır" [Happy couples: newlyweds should have their own place], *Yedigün*, no. 130, 4 September 1935, p. 20.

67 Semiha Şekib, "Hanımlar İçtimaiyatı: Bir Aile Nasıl Mesud Olur?" [Sociology for women: how can a family be happy?], *Süs*, no. 30, 5 Kanun-u sani 1340 [1924], p. 2.

68 M. N., "Kadın Erkeği Nasıl Cezbedebilir?" [How can a woman allure a man?], *Resimli Ay*, no. 55, September 1928, pp. 22–3.

69 Mahmud Şemsi, "Mutlu Evliler: Kocanızın Ceplerini Karıştırmayınız" [Happy couples: do not search your husband's pockets], *Yedigün*, no. 127, 14 August 1935, p. 26.

70 Nermin Süreyya, "Kocalara Neleri Söylemeli?" [What should be kept from the husband?], *Resimli Ay*, no. 21, Teşrin-i evvel 1341 [1925], pp. 40–2.

71 No Author, "Karagün Dostu" [True friend], *Ev-İş*, September 1942, p. 87.

72 Mahmud Şemsi, "Mutlu Evliler: Kıskançlık II" [Happy couples: jealousy II], *Yedigün*, no. 122, 10 July 1935, p. 8.

"do not bother him with your trivial problems",[73] "try to ignore his infidelity",[74] "cook meals in the way he likes"[75] and in any case do not ever rock the boat. Women were supposed to get used to the quirkiness and habits of their husband, never complain about him to others, "keep their home in good order as a haven from a storm for the man of the house"[76] and become sufficiently informed to converse with him about his work and the world.[77] The ideal woman imagined by the early republican male elites was presentable and educated enough to accompany the new Turkish man in his modern life yet maintained the selfless, unchallenging, abstemious and docile heritage of her predecessors from Ottoman times.[78] As Gülsüm Baydar argued from an architectural perspective

> In the early years of the republic, discourses on the modern house and the modern Turkish woman are juxtaposed at a number of levels to aid the production of the masculine realm of nationhood. The modern house is seen as the microcosm of the space of the nation. (...) Both the modern house and the modern Turkish woman are desired to be highly visible with similar characteristics of beauty and elegance without extravagance. Woman is effectively stripped of her sexualised agency,

---

73 Mahmud Şemsi, "Mutlu Evliler: Erkeğin Akşam İstirahatı" [Happy couples: man's repose in the evening], *Yedigün*, no. 129, 28 August 1935, p. 4. Also see No Author, "Kocanızı İyi Karşılayınız!" [Welcome your husband with a smiling face], *Ev-İş*, October 1942, p. 97.

74 Mahmud Şemsi, "Mutlu Evliler: Kıskançlık" [Happy couples: jealousy], *Yedigün*, no. 118, 12 June 1935, p. 20. Also see Va-Nû, "Kadın Denen Meçhul" [The mystery called woman], *Yedigün*, no. 679, 10 March 1946, p. 8.

75 Mahmud Şemsi, "Mutlu Evliler: Ailede Mutfağın Ehemmiyeti" [Happy couples: the importance of the kitchen/cuisine in the family], *Yedigün*, no. 126, 7 August 1935, p. 17.

76 Mahmud Şemsi, "Mutlu Evliler: Erkeğin Mesleğindeki Üzüntüsü" [Happy couples: man's distress at work], *Yedigün*, no. 124, 24 July 1935, p. 9. Also see No Author, "Ev Kadınının 24 Saati" [Daily routine of a housewife], *Ev-İş*, October/November 1949, pp. 97 and 109.

77 Similarly, in her work on İsmail Hakkı Baltacıoğlu, one of the most influential intellectual figures of the early republican era, Aylin Özman shows that for Baltacıoğlu the major qualifications that a married woman should have were "to know what a child means; to be understanding with the caprices of man; to be cheerful; not to be jealous groundlessly; to economize; to be charming; to have good enough taste not to be victimized by fashion; not to be avaricious; to know how to prepare pickles, salad and marmalades; to be modest; to be able to withstand hunger", Baltacıoğlu, İsmail Hakkı, "Evli Kadının On iki Meziyeti [The Twelve Virtues of Married Woman]", *Yeni Adam*, 2 December 1937, p. 3, quoted in Özman, "The image of 'woman' in Turkish and social political thought", p. 454.

78 No Author, "Japon Kadınları" [Japanese women], *Süs*, no. 24, 24 Teşrin-i evvel 1339 [1923], p. 1.

which is always already in excess of the nationalist agenda of modern Turkey.[79]

The new Turkish woman with her European clothing, primary education and suffrage rights should look new only on the outside and preserve her old traditional maternal femininity on the inside. "There is much talk about modernization of Turkish womanhood" remarked Fevziye Abdürreşid, "but unfortunately our understanding of modernization consists in abandonment of sexual morality, wearing makeup, following latest fashions in clothing and spending time in theatres and recreation areas. Yet as desired and expressed by our Saviour [Mustafa Kemal] modernization has nothing to do with dolling up and putting on makeup".[80] According to Münire Handan from *Resimli Ay* neither did it have "anything to do with embracing free love [serbest aşk] and declaring marriage an archaic institution".[81] Some articles exhorted fathers not to allow their daughters to have higher education in order to preclude their possible spinsterhood. Passages that flew right in the face of the supposedly emancipating rhetoric of Kemalist "state feminism" were repeatedly written, and women's right of participation in public life was consistently sacrificed for the sake of motherhood. Citing the theories of so-called scientists and medical doctors İ. Şerif announced in 1945 that "working women with a profession could not possibly become good mothers" and that "we can rightfully describe their motherhood as half-way and defective".[82] Money and time invested in the education of girls beyond primary education were regarded as a total waste. Limited as it was, legal equality between sexes and the changing notion of marriage and family were blamed for the increase in divorce rates.[83] Women were frequently admonished not to be spoilt by the recently emerging potentiality of earning a life and living independently thanks to their newly found rights. 'Those are just for show or window dressing' the articles seemed to have been

---

79 Baydar, Gülsüm, "Tenuous boundaries: women, domesticity and nationhood in 1930s Turkey", *The Journal of Architecture*, 7/3 (2002), p. 240.
80 Fevziye Abdürreşid, "Türk Kadınlığı Asrileşmelidir" [Turkish womanhood should be modernized], *Asar-ı Nisvan*, no. 17, 15 Teşrin-i evvel 1341 [1925], p. 2. Also see Selami İzzet, "Süse ve Güzelliğe Dair" [On makeup and beauty], *Süs*, no. 2, 23 Haziran 1339 [1923], p. 1.
81 Münire Handan, "Meşru İzdivaç mı? Serbest Aşk mı?" [Legitimate marriage or free love?], *Resimli Ay*, no. 1, Şubat 1341 [1925], pp. 2–6.
82 İ. Şerif, "Kızlarımızı Ne Kadar Okutmalıyız?" [How much education is necessary for girls?], *Yedigün*, no. 665, 2 December 1945, pp. 5 and 7.
83 Yalçın, Hüseyin Cahid, "Niçin Ayrılıyorlar?" [Why do they get divorced?], *Yedigün*, no. 426, 5 May 1941, p. 4.

implying, 'you are still supposed to stick with your acrimonious and discontented husband for the good of your beloved country'.

Concluding Remarks

Owing to the fact that writing about marriage in Turkey in the first half of the twentieth century cuts across a number of inter-related/intermingling topics with vast literatures tagged onto them such as gender, women's rights, feminism, family, parenthood, childhood, re-organization of bio-politics, re-habituation of the society, modernization, nationalism, nation building, eugenics and population growth strategies etc., I have been ineluctably drawn in this chapter to present a colourful collage of the latest scholarly work in most of those areas and place the findings from the early republican era magazines against this backdrop. In other words, rather than discussing an utterly original and previously un-touched matter, I revisited in this study a much debated and well-researched domain and portrayed it through the filters of popular magazine articles consumed by the literate public of the era.[84] I also tried to accentuate that early republican society inherited an already well-established intellectual as well as popular discursive repertoire from the late Ottoman times regarding marriage, with the Second Constitutional era's "feminist" movement and the reactions it prompted having a decisive role in it. As for the early republican times, my findings and analysis verified and exemplified the main arguments of a previously produced body of scholarly work which concludes that the founding elites of the Turkish republic were "no feminists" and that their agenda of women's emancipation being mostly limited to legal terrain and civil rights did not accommodate any genuine intention of ending male domination over women.[85] As Celal Sahir put it in *Süs* in 1923 "feminism

---

84   All my findings about perception of and approach to marriage in the early republican era that were reflected in the mirror of popular magazines precisely overlap with the findings obtained from the analysis of romances written in the same decades. See for example Dede, Kadir, "Toplumsal Cinsiyet Rollerinin Yeniden Üretiminde Aşk Romanlarının Rolü: Muazzez Tahsin Berkand'la İzdivaç" [The role of romances in reproducing gender roles: Muazzez Tahsin Berkand and marriage], *Atatürk Üniversitesi İktisadi ve İdari Bilimler Dergisi*, 28/4 (2014), 193–212.

85   Arat, Yeşim, "The project of modernity and women in Turkey", in *Rethinking Modernity and National Identity in Turkey*, ed. Sibel Bozdoğan and Reşat Kasaba (Seattle: University of Washington Press, 1997), pp. 95–112. Feminist scholars repeatedly suggested that the woman question in the Ottoman/Turkish case had never been about women's rights and should be perceived as a "space for social critique or a battlefield between different social

at this moment should not mean something beyond equality before the law for women" because the "progress of women" was "a delicate matter that required treading with circumspection". "Running fast on that path causes exhaustion" he opined, "and leads to nowhere".[86] In Zehra Arat's words, "Kemalism ignored the notion of gender domination the same way it denied class conflicts".[87] The decision-making cadres perceiving women as agents of nationalist ideology rather than as autonomous subjects not only undermined the attempts for independent feminist organizations but also hegemonized women's movement as evidenced in the dissolution of *Türk Kadınlar Birliği* (Turkish Women's Association) in 1935.[88] Simten Coşar drawing on her analysis of the approach of three prominent thinkers from the early republican era (liberal-nationalist Ahmet Ağaoğlu, conservative Peyami Safa and leftist Zekeriya Sertel) to the woman issue, skilfully displays how feminist concerns hardly infiltrated rival ideologies, and professing different and contesting ideologies did not prevent these figures from operating through common assumptions such as the existence of a "universally valid woman nature", the inevitability of "masculinisation in the event of women's participation in the public sphere" and the fundamental importance of "motherhood as the significant feature of ideal womanhood".[89]

---

forms such as old and new", Durakbaşa, "Cumhuriyet Döneminde Modern Kadın ve Erkek Kimliklerinin Oluşumu", p. 37. Deniz Kandiyoti asserted that women were instrumentalized as "the object of political discourse", as "a pawn" of the Kemalist elite and "as vehicles for the symbolic representation of political intent" in the early years of the republic, Kandiyoti, Deniz, "Women and the Turkish state: political actors or symbolic pawns", in *Woman-Nation-State*, ed. Nira Yuval Davis and Floya Anthias (London: MacMillan, 1989), pp. 126–50. For an analysis of history of the feminist studies and their critic of the Kemalist politics see Fırat, Bilge, "Dissident, but Hegemonic: A Critical Review of Feminist Studies on Gendered Nationalism in Turkey", M.A. Dissertation, Binghamton University, 2006.

86 Editorial, "Türk Kadını: Celal Sahir Bey'in Mütalaatı" [Turkish woman: opinions of Celal Sahir Bey], *Süs*, no. 6, 21 Temmuz 1339 [1923], p. 1.

87 Arat, Zehra F., "Turkish women and the republican reconstruction of tradition", in *Reconstructing Gender in the Middle East*, ed. Fatma Müge Göçek and Shiva Balghi (New York: Columbia University Press, 1994), p. 59.

88 Coşar, Simten, "Women in Turkish political thought: between tradition and modernity", *Feminist Review*, 86 (2007), p. 117.

89 Coşar, "Women in Turkish political thought", p. 113. Likewise Aylin Özman in her analysis of the writing of Vala Nureddin and İsmail Hakkı Baltacıoğlu, two prominent intellectual figures of the early republican era, on the "women issue" also concludes that "both of the authors adopt a functionalist perspective emphasizing the reproductive function of women for men, family and the nation and approach the 'women issue' within borders of tradition-modernity continuum". See Özman, "The image of 'Woman' in Turkish and social political thought", p. 448. It should be mentioned that there were some cross currents

The early republican state had a modernization scheme that included promoting the child-centred conjugal family and companionate marriage[90] which were "thought to be the incubators of the nation's identity and 'modern' characteristics like individual initiative, responsibility and discipline".[91] The "Turkish woman today is neither a proper mother nor a proper wife because she lacks the necessary endowments for both" cried out *Resimli Ay* in 1924.[92]

> She has been denied the kind of education that is imperative to scientific child-rearing, and she has been treated as a slave without any rights in the house of autocratic Turkish family. Yet modern conception of wifehood construes wife as a life companion, someone much more than a mere toy or instrument for the pleasure and service of men.[93]

Considering gender serves as a tremendously important organizing principle of an entire worldview it was not surprising that the notions of maleness, femaleness and the regulation of their interaction in the form of marriage/family

---

in the intellectual fabric of the early republic that challenged, albeit feebly and unsystematically, the main stream anti-feminist attitude. Sabiha Zekeriya (Sertel)'s columns in the *Resimli Hafta* and *Resimli Ay* journals and in *Cumhuriyet* newspaper with feminist-leftist overtones were among them. See Shissler, Ada Holland, "'If you ask me': Sabiha Sertel's advice column, gender equity, and social engineering in the early Turkish republic", *Journal of Middle East Women's Studies*, 3/2 (2007), 1–30. There were also attempts made by some authors in the periodicals examined in this study openly to back women's right to obtain a profession and participate in public as opposed to absolute allocation of their energy and time to domestic space. See for example Ataç, Nurullah, "Kadın Erkek Müsavatı" [Equality between woman and man], *Yedigün*, no. 36, 15 November 1933, pp. 6–7 and Ömer Rıza, "İlmin Yeni Bir Davası: Kadın Erkekten Üstündür" [A new scientific hypothesis: woman is superior to man], *Yedigün*, no. 139, 6 November 1935, pp. 3–4.

90 *Resimli Ay*, true to the 'scientific' spirit of the time that fetishized numbers, calculations and taxonomies, claimed that in order to be able to pursue a happy, fulfilling married life couples needed at least 60 per cent compatibility in terms of their feelings and opinions. To gauge the percentage of their compatibility they should be given a chance to get to know each other's character and world view before marriage. See No Author, "İzdivaç Hayatında Kaç Türlü Aşk Vardır?" [How many types of love are involved in married life?], *Resimli Ay*, no. 48, February 1928, pp. 5–8.

91 Shissler, "'If you ask me': Sabiha Sertel's advice column", p. 23.

92 Editorial, "Türk Kadını: Niçin Anne Değildir? Niçin Vatandaş Değildir? Niçin Hayat Kadını Değildir?" [The Turkish woman: why is she not a mother, a citizen and a life companion?], *Resimli Ay*, no. 2, Nisan 1340 [1924], pp. 41–2.

93 Editorial, "Türk Kadını: Niçin Anne Değildir? Niçin Vatandaş Değildir? Niçin Hayat Kadını Değildir", p. 41.

attracted the utmost attention and profoundly occupied the intelligentsia at a time when Turkish society and polity underwent a significant transformation process that resulted in a regime change. In that, the Turkish republic was by no means alone. Writing on the New Culture Movement of China (1915–23) and the family reform it carried out, Susan L. Glosser instructively shows how radical Chinese intellectuals of the time intended to topple the traditional joint family system (*da jiating*) and "laid the blame for most of China's problems at the door of this patriarchal, hierarchical institution".[94] As in late Ottoman/early republican Turkish settings, in the Chinese case too traditional arranged marriage was deeply despised by the agents of the upcoming revolutionary shift. As expressed by Liao, one famous New Culture intellectual, "this kind of marriage in which a man and a woman who do not know each other are forced to live together" was "simply barbaric marriage, marriage as commerce, slave marriage".[95] What Glosser suggests vis-à-vis Chinese male intellectuals of the New Culture perfectly applies to the Western style educated male public of late Ottoman/early republican times: "Because it was so important to a man's identity as a modern, enlightened individual to make a freely chosen love marriage, the quality of his marriage and his wife became absolutely essential to his self-image".[96] Hence, many strikingly similar letters written by young Chinese or Ottoman/Turkish men presented a litany of misery caused by incompatible spouses, and relentlessly complained about the near impossibility of finding happiness in traditional marriage. The content of a letter from Jian Cheng printed in *Jiating Yanjiu* in 1921 for example largely coincided with a letter to the editor from Senih Müşir that was printed in *Resimli Ay* in 1340 [1924]. They both conveyed the feeling of helplessness and described prevailing marriage practices as suffering, torture, disaster, and catastrophe.[97]

In line with the pro-natalist paradigm of early republican bio-politics marriage and childbirth were regarded as the chief and essential duty of women not only towards their own biological needs but also towards the nation, society and the republican regime. Mustafa Kemal himself explicitly stated his vision of the ideal Turkish woman: "What should a Turkish woman be like?"

---

94   Glosser, Susan L., "'The truths I have learned': nationalism, family reform and male identity in China's New Culture Movement, 1915–1923", in *Chinese Femininities Chinese Masculinities A Reader*, ed. Susan Brownell and Jeffrey N. Wasserstrom (Berkeley and Los Angeles: University of California Press, 2002), p. 120.

95   Glosser, "'The truths I have learned'", p. 132.

96   Glosser, "'The truths I have learned'", p. 139.

97   Jian Cheng's letter was quoted in Glosser, "'The truths I have learned'", pp. 137–8. Senih Müşir's letter was published under the title of "Bizde Erkekler Nasıl Evlenirler?" [How do men get married in our society?], *Resimli Ay*, no. 7 Ağustos 1340 [1924], pp. 28–33.

he asked in a speech given on 14 October 1925 at İzmir Kız Eğitim Enstitüsü (Women's School of Education in İzmir). And replied as follows: "The Turkish woman should be the most enlightened the most virtuous and the most dignified woman in the world. The duty of the Turkish woman is to raise future generations with the necessary vigour to protect and defend the Turkish nation with intelligence, wisdom, strength and determination".[98] The popular magazines merely followed suit.

All Turkish citizens were thought to be born in debt to their newly established nation state. Men would do military service and women would give birth both running the risk of perishing in the process for the well-being of their country. Bachelors and spinsters were viewed with suspicion since they failed to conform to the codes of proper femininity and masculinity. Women who refused to marry on the basis of mere vanity and selfishness were wasting their life. Men who refused to marry because they were afraid of responsibility or reluctant to give up the pleasures of bachelorhood were destined to die in misery. The citizens of the early republican era Turkish state were exhorted to marry, and do it rather early (women were urged to have their first child before 20 and men before 25)[99] and preferably through a revised version of arranged marriage with some courtship added, a hybrid form of marriage that would serve to the exigencies of the young nation state. This was a partly liberalized form of arranged marriage infused with some elements of love match where women's docility, voluntary cooperation and logistical support would be better obtained in the republic's fight to build a modern nation state along Western lines.

Let us shift our gaze briefly to today. Judging from the proliferation of Islamic marriage websites,[100] the excessively popular matchmaking television

---

98   Mustafa Kemal, İzmir Kız Eğitim Enstitüsü'ndeki Konuşma, 14 Ekim 1925 [Speech given at Women's School of Education, 14 October 1925], in İnan, M. Rauf, *Atatürk ve Türk Kadını* [Atatürk and the Turkish Woman] (İstanbul: Arkın Kitabevi, 1991), pp. 54–5, quoted and translated in Baydar, "Tenuous boundaries: women, domesticity and nationhood in 1930s Turkey", p. 237.

99   Gövsa, İbrahim Alaettin, "Çoğalma Davası" [Population growth cause], *Yedigün*, no. 438, 28 July 1941, p. 11.

100 For the emergence of Islamic marriage websites and their role in transforming the marriage practices among adults with Islamic life style choices see Tütüncü, Fatma, "Güzel Ahlaklı Biriyle Hayırlı Bir İzdivaç İçin: İslami Evlilik Siteleri, Dönüşen Mahremiyetler ve Kadın Öznelliği" [For an auspicious marriage to a person of good moral character: Islamic marriage websites, intimacy transformations and woman's subjectivity], in *Yeni Medya Çalışmaları* [New Media Studies], ed. Mutlu Binark (Ankara: Dipnot Yayınları, 2007), pp. 281–305; Kaymas, Serhat, "İslami Sanal Kamusal Alanda Kolektif Kimlik: İslami Evlilik

programmes[101] and incessant plethora of statements offered by politicians as to the benefits of marrying young or the sacredness of motherhood, in millennial Turkish society the institution of heterosexual marriage with all its undisguised or tacit patriarchal rhetorics and practices seems to remain mostly free from the critical reception it has been meeting in Western habitus for decades, and appears to have preserved its early republican era popularity as a site of endless discursive struggle. The fact that in Turkey women and children have been increasingly prey to violence in nuclear family settings and that there are still a considerable number of children who have been sold or forced into marriage by their parents does not seem to have caused the institution to even slightly fall from grace. Neither does the rise of divorce rates seem to have tarnished the reputation of marriage or lessened its desirability. What causes Turkish society to fetishize marriage and approach it as almost the sole yardstick for a fulfilling existence through centuries deserves a series of comparative, extensive and in-depth scholarly research in a range of areas from psychoanalysis, sociology and anthropology to cultural studies and history. In this study by sketching out the debate on courtship, marriage and divorce as perceived by and reflected in popular magazines at a time of re-habituation, I attempted to enhance our repertoire in grasping the seemingly indomitable trust Turkish society has placed in marriage and family "for better and for worse".

Siteleri İçinden Kolektif Kimliği Okumak" [Collective identity in the virtual Islamic public sphere: reading collective identity through the Islamic marriage agencies], *Journal of Yaşar University*, 5/19 (2010), 3237–63.

101 For an instructive analysis of the matchmaking TV programmes and how they reinforce gender roles and reproduce arranged marriage in different forms despite the promise of emancipated partner choice and love marriage see Nüfusçu, Gözde Aytemur and Ayça Yılmaz, "Evlilik Pratiklerinin Dönüşüm/Yeniden Üretim Sürecinde Evlendirme Programları" [Marriage shows in process of transformation/reproduction of marriage practices], *Galatasaray Üniversitesi İletişim Dergisi*, 16 (2012), 23–48. For another article in a similar vein see Kaya, Tebrike, "Televizyonda Yayınlanan İzdivaç Programlarında Toplumsal Cinsiyetin Temsili" [Gender representations in marriage programmes on television], *Kadın Araştırmaları Dergisi*, 13/2 (2013), 81–110.

Bibliography

Primary

Archives

Archivio Centrale dello Stato-Presidenza del Consiglio dei Ministri (ACS-PCM), Rome.
Archivio Storico Ministero degli Affari Esteri (ASMAE), Ministero dell'Africa Italiana (MAI), Rome.
Başbakanlık Cumhuriyet Arşivi (BCA), Ankara.
Başbakanlık Osmanlı Arşivi (BOA), Istanbul.
The British Library (BL), India Office Records (IOR), London.
Gertrude Bell Archive Online (http://www.gerty.ncl.ac.uk/), Newcastle University, Newcastle.
Israel State Archives, Jerusalem.
Jerusalem Shari'a Court, Jerusalem.
League of Nations Archives (LON), Geneva.
Middle East Centre Archives (MEC), St. Antony's College, Oxford.
Ministère des Affaires étrangères (MAE), Centre des Archives diplomatiques de Nantes (CADN), Nantes.
The National Archives (TNA), London.
National Archives and Records Administration (NARA), USA.
Türk Tarih Kurumu (Turkish Historical Association) Library, Ankara.

Newspapers and Journals

L'Action du Peuple
L'Afrique française
al-Ahram
Akşam
Asar-ı Nisvan
al-Barq
Belediyeler Dergisi
The Bombay Chronicle
Bulletin économique du Maroc
Bulletin Official
Cumhuriyet
Ev-İş
Falastin/ Filastin
The Financial Times
Haftalık Mecmua
Hakimiyet-i Milliye
al-Hasna'
al-Hilal
İnci
al-Kashkul
Küçük Mecmua
Lisan al-Hal
al-Majallah al-Tibbiyya al-Misriyya
Majallat al-Jama'iya al-Tibbiyya al-'Arabiyya al-Falastiniyya
Majallat al-Maghrib

Majallat al-Ma'had al-Tibbi al-'Arabi
The Manchester Guardian
al-Ma'rad
al-Masrah
al-Mashreq
Le Matin
The Medical Society Gazette
al-Mu'ayyad
al-Musawwar
The New York Times
Palestine Gazette
Palestine Post
Resimli Ay
Ruz al-Yusuf
Sawt al-Hijaz
Sıhhiye Mecmuası
Süs
Tan
The Times
Ülkü Halkevleri Mecmuası
Umm al-Qura
Yedigün

Published

Official Documents

Düstur
Dustur
Meclis-i Mebusan Zabıt Cerideleri
http://www.mevzuat.gov.tr
T.C. Resmi Gazete
T.B.M.M. Zabıt Cerideleri

Books and Articles

Adıvar, Halide Edib, *Mev'ut Hüküm* (Istanbul: Atlas Kitabevi, 1968).

Aflalo, Moussa, *The Truth About Morocco: An Indictment of the Policy of the British Foreign Office with Regard to the Anglo-French Agreement* (London: John Lane, 1904).

Ahmet Rasim, *Şehir Mektupları*, ed. Nuri Akbayar (Istanbul: Oğlak Klasikleri, 2005).

Akrawi, Fathallah, "Etudes sur la peste en mesopotamie", Dissertation, Faculté de Médicine, Paris, 1928.

Ali Kami, *Musahabat-ı Ahlakiye ve Malumat-ı Vataniye* (Istanbul: Kitabhane-i Hilmi, 1927).

Doktor Ali Vahid, *Dişlerimizi Niçin Temizleriz?* (Türkiye Himaye-i Etfal Cemiyeti Hıfz el-Sıhha ve Neşriyat Şubesi Numero 11) (Istanbul: Resimli Ay Matbaası-Türk Limited Şirketi, 1927).

'Aluba, Muhammad 'Ali, "Ahmiyyat al-mu'tamarat al-'arabiyya fi nuhuud al-muslimin wa-l-'arab", *al-Hilal: 'Adad mumtaz al-'Arab wa-l-Islam fi-'asr al-hadith* (Cairo: Dar al-Hilal, 1939).

Amin Zaki, Saniha, *Memoirs of a Female Iraqi Doctor* (n.p.: n.p., 2014).

Annelere Nasihat (Türkiye Cumhuriyeti Sıhhiye ve Muavenet-i İçtimaiye Vekaleti Neşriyat Şubesi Numara 21) (Ankara: Sıhhiye ve Muavenet-i İçtimaiye Vekaleti Matbaası, 1926).

BIBLIOGRAPHY

Annelere Nasihat (Türkiye Cümhuriyeti Sıhhat ve İçtimaî Muavenet Vekâleti Neşriyatından No. 21) (Istanbul: Hilal Matbaası, 1929).

Annelere Öğütler (T.C. Sıhhat ve İçtimaî Muavenet Vekâleti Neşriyatından No. 51) (Ankara: Selen Matbaası, 1938).

Arda, Ramiz, *O Günler. Anılar (1928–1945)*, ed. Mustafa Özcan (Konya: Palet Yayınları, 2014).

Arıkan, Dr. İzzet, *Köylüler için Sıtma Hakkında Kısa Bilgiler* (T.C. Trakya Umumî Müfettişliği Köy Bürosu Yayını Sayısı 37) (Istanbul: Halk Basımevi, 1936).

Atay, C., *Köy Muhtarlarının Ödevleri* (T.C. Trakya Umumî Müfettişliği Köy Bürosu Yayım Sayısı 65) (Istanbul: Halk Basımevi, 1937).

Ayberk, Dr. Nuri, *Türkiyede Trahom Mücadelesi* (Istanbul: Kader Basımevi, 1936).

Azmi, Mahmud, *Khabaya Siyasiya* (Cairo: Jaridat al-Masri, 1939).

Balbo, Italo, "La politica sociale fascista verso gli arabi della Libia", *Convegno di scienze morali e storiche. 4–11 ottobre 1938-XVI. Tema: L'Africa. Vol. 1* (Rome: Reale Accademia d'Italia, 1939), pp. 733–49.

Baldensperger, P.J., "Birth, marriage and death among the fellahin of Palestine", in *Palestine Exploration Fund Quarterly Statement for 1894* (London: PEF Society, 1894), pp. 127–44.

Barbari, Mouslim [al-Wazzani, Mohammed Hassan], *Tempête sur le Maroc, où, les erreurs d'une "politique berbère"* (Paris: Éditions Rieder, 1931).

Basiretçi Ali Efendi, *İstanbul Mektupları*, ed. Nuri Sağlam (Istanbul: Kitabevi, 2001).

Beden Terbiyesi ve Halk Sağlığı (T.C. Sıhhat ve İçtimaî Muavenet Vekâleti Neşriyatından No. 78) (Ankara: Alâeddin Kıral Basımevi, 1941).

Belediyeler (T.C. Dahiliye Vekâleti Mahallî İdareler Umum Müdürlüğü) (Istanbul: Holivut Matbaası, 1933).

Dr. Besim Ömer (trans.), *Yüzyıl Yaşamak İçün «22» Emr-i Sıhhiyede Bütün Hıfz-ı Sıhhat* (Istanbul: Ahmed İhsan Matbaası, 1927).

"Da Bengasi a Tripoli in automobile. Come 38 macchine nel deserto annunciano che la Libia è unificata", *Giornale d'Oriente* (28 June 1931).

Bertarelli, L.V., *Guida d'Italia del TCI, possedimenti e colonie* (Milan: Tipografia Capriolo e Massimino, 1929).

Bit. İnsanlara Lekelihumma gibi Tehlikeli Hastalıkları Geçirir (T.C. Sıhhat ve İctimaî Muavenet Vekâleti Neşriyatından, No. 53) (Ankara: n.p., 1938).

Bousser, M., "Les transport au Maroc et leurs tarifs de l'origine à nos jours", *Bulletin économique du Maroc*, 3 (January 1934), 201–24.

Brûnel, René, *Essai sur la confrérie religieuse des 'Aîssâoûa au Maroc* (Paris: Librarie Orientaliste Paul Geuthner, 1926).

Brunelli, Claudio, "L'organizzazione turistica della Libia", *Rassegna Economica delle Colonie*, 25/3 (March 1937), 327–30.

Bruni, Giuseppe, "Il nuovo assetto politico-amministrativo della Libia", in *Viaggio del Duce in Libia per l'inaugurazione della litoranea. Anno XV. Orientamenti e note ad uso dei giornalisti* (Rome: Stabilmento Tipografico Il Lavoro Fascista, 1937), pp. 1–14.

C.H.P. *Denizli Köycüler Komitası Köylerde. Birinci Teşrin 1937* (Denizli: Yeni Basımevi, 1937).

Calzini, Raffaele, *Da Leptis Magna a Gadames* (Milan: Fratelli Treves Editori, 1926).

Çiçek Hastalığı ve Çiçek Aşısı (T.C. Sıhhat ve İçtimai Muavenet Vekaleti Neşriyatından No 59) (Ankara: n.p., 1938).

Çiçek Hastalığı Çok Tehlikelidir (T.C. Sıhhat ve İçtimai Muavenet Vekaleti Neşriyatından No 91) (Ankara: Ulusal Matbaa, 1943).

Çocuk İshali (T.C. Sıhhat ve İctimaî Muavenet Vekâleti Neşriyatından, No. 55) (Ankara: n.p., 1938).

Congres international de médicine tropicale et d'hygiène: comptes rendus (Cairo: Imprimerie Nationale, 1929).

Conker, Orhan, *Les chemins de fer en Turquie et la politique ferroviaire turque* (Paris: Librairie du Recueil Sirey, 1935).

Cumhuriyet Halk Partisi, *On Beşinci Yıl Kitabı* (Istanbul: Cumhuriyet Matbaası, 1938).

Dame, Louis P., "A Trip to Taif", *Neglected Arabia. Arabia Calling* 163 (October-December 1932), 7–15.

Davey, Richard, "The present condition of Muhammedan women in Turkey", *Fortnightly Review*, 58/343 (1895), 53–66.

Dinçer, Celal, "Osmanlı Vezirlerinden Hasan Fehmi Paşa'nın Anadolu'nun Bayındırlık İşlerine Dair Hazırladığı Lâyiha", *Belgeler*, 5–8/9–12 (1968–71), 153–233.

Diş Sağlığı. Diş Temizliği (T.C. Sıhhat ve İçtimaî Muavenet Vekâleti Neşriyatından No. 45) (Ankara: n.p., 1937).

Diş Sağlığı. Diş Temizliği (T.C. Sıhhat ve İçtimaî Muavenet Vekâleti Neşriyatından No. 45) (Ankara: Alaeddin Kıral Basımevi, 1941).

Duru, Dr. Muhittin Celal, *Sağlık Bakımından Köy ve Köycülük* (Cümhuriyet Halk Partisi Yayını, Klavuz Kitapları: VII) (Ankara: Sümer Matbaası, 1941).

Ente Nazionale Industrie Turistiche, *Annuario alberghi d'Italia, 1939* (Milano: Turati Lombardi E.C., 1939).

Ergin, Osman Nuri, *Mecelle-i Umûr-ı Belediyye*, 9 vols. (Istanbul: İstanbul Büyükşehir Belediyesi Kültür İşleri Daire Başkanlığı Yayınları, 1995).

Evliya Çelebi b. Derviş Muhammed Zıllı, *Evliya Çelebi Seyahatnamesi. Topkapı Sarayı Kütüphanesi Bağdat 304 Yazmanın Transkripsiyonu-Dizini*. vol. I, ed. Robert Dankoff, Seyit Ali Kahraman and Yücel Dağlı (Istanbul: Yapı Kredi Yayınları, 2006).

Fantoli, A., "Le strade della Tripolitania", *Le Vie d'Italia*, 40/4 (April 1934), 274–87.

Fehmi, Dr. Nuri, *İnsanı Kör Eden Hastalıklardan Trahom Halk Kitabı* (Istanbul: Kader Matbaası, 1930).

Frengi Mücadele Teşkilâtının Vazifelerini Gösterir Talimatname. Tasdik Tarihi: 22. XII. 1934 (T.C. Sıhhat ve İçtimaî Muavenet Vekâleti) (Ankara: n.p., 1935).

Gerlach, Stephan, *Türkiye Günlüğü 1573–1576*, 2 vols., trans. Türkis Noyan (Istanbul: Kitap Yayınevi, 2007).

Gezi Notları. Çanakkale-Bolayır, İzmir Köyleri, Orta Anadolu (Milli Türk Talebe Birliği Yayımlarından Bitik No. 2) (Istanbul: Asri Basımevi, 1935).

Girardière, E., "L'école coranique et la politique nationaliste au Maroc", *France méditerranéenne et africaine*, 1 (1938), 99–109.

Göktürk, Hüseyin Avni, *Evlenme Birliğinde Eşlerin Durumu*, CHP Konferanslar Serisi, Kitap 4 (Ankara: Recep Ulusoğlu Basımevi, 1939).

Gönen, Dr. Remzi, *Sıtma Nedir? Nasıl Korunulur?* (Mersin Halkevi Sağlık Öğütler Serisi Sayı: 1) (Mersin: Yeni Mersin Matbaası, 1934).

Gözleri Kör Eden Trahom Hastalığı Hakkında Halka Nasihatler (Sıhhat ve İctimaî Muavenet Vekâleti Neşriyatından, No. 33) (Istanbul: Kâatçılık ve Matbaacılık A.Ş., 1933).

Gözleri Kör Eden Trahom Hastalığı Hakkında Halka Nasihatler. İkinci Tabi (Sıhhat ve İctimaî Muavenet Vekâleti Neşriyatından, No. 33) (Istanbul: Hüsnütabiat Matbaası, 1941).

Granqvist, Hilma, *Marriage Conditions in a Palestinian Village* (Helsingfors: Societas Scientiarum Fennica, 1931).

Granqvist, Hilma, *Marriage Conditions in a Palestinian Village II* (Helsingfors: Societas Scientiarum Fennica, 1935).

Grip (T.C. Sıhhat ve İçtimaî Muavenet Vekaleti Neşriyatından No. 63) (Ankara: n.p., 1939).

Gündüz, Aka, *Köy Muallimi* (Ankara: Hakimiyet-i Milliye Matbaası, 1932).

Güntekin, Reşat Nuri, "Sinekler", in *Anadolu Notları*, II (Istanbul: İnkılâp ve Aka Kitabevleri, 1966), pp. 28–30.

Dr. Hasan Tahsin, *Sıvas Vilâyeti Sıhhî ve İçtimaî Coğrafyası 1931* (Istanbul: Hilâl Matbaası, 1932).

Hicaz Vilayeti Salnamesi: 1305 Sene-i Hicriye (Mekke-i Mükerreme: Vilayet Matbaası, 1305/1888).

Dr. Hikmet Hamdi Bey, *Sıhhi Müze Rehberi* (Sıhhiye ve Muavenet-i İçtimaiye Vekaleti) (Ankara: Vilayet Matbaası, 1340/1924).

Dr. Hikmet Hamdi Bey, *Sıhhî Müze Rehberi* (T.C. Sıhhat ve İçtimai Muavenet Vekâleti) (n.p.: n.p., 1931).

İbrahim Peçevi, *Peçevî Tarihi*, 2 vols., ed. Murad Uraz (Istanbul: Neşriyat Yurdu, 1968).

İspirtolu İçkilerin Sağlığa Zararları (T.C. Sıhhat ve İçtimaî Muavenet Vekâleti Neşriyatından No: 76) (Ankara: Alâeddin Kıral Basımevi, 1941).

İstanbul Verem Mücadelesi Cemiyeti Merkez Heyeti Raporu 1930–1931 (Istanbul: Kader Matbaası, n.d.).

İstanbul Verem Mücadelesi Cemiyeti Merkez Heyeti Raporu 1932 (Istanbul: Kader Matbaası, n.d.).

İstatistik Yıllığı, Üçüncü Cilt 1930 (Istanbul: Ahmet İhsan Matbaası Limited, 1930).

İstatistik Yıllığı, Dördüncü Cilt 1930/1931 (Ankara: Hüsnütabiat Matbaası, 1931).
İstatistik Yıllığı, Cilt 5 1931/32 (Ankara: Devlet Matbaası, n.d.).
İstatistik Yıllığı, Cilt 8 1935/36 (Ankara: Devlet Basımevi, n.d.).
İstiklal Harbi Sıhhi Raporu. 336-337-338 Mudanya Mütarekesine Kadar (Türkiye Cumhuriyeti Müdafaa-i Milliye Vekaleti Sıhhiye Dairesi) (Istanbul: Matbaa-i Askeriye, 1341/1925).
Kalbimizi Koruyalım (T.C. Sıhhat ve İçtimai Muavenet Vekâleti Neşriyatından No. 92) (n.p.: n.p., n.d.).
Karaosmanoğlu, Yakup Kadri, Bütün Eserleri I: Yaban (Istanbul: İletişim Yayınları, 2005).
al-Khuri, Shakir, Majma' al-Masarrat (Beirut: Matba'at al-Ijtihad, 1908).
Kızıl Hastalığı ve Korunma Çareleri (Türkiye Cumhuriyeti Sıhhat ve İçtimai Muavenet Vekâleti) (Ankara: Türk Ocakları Merkez Heyeti Matbaası, 1930).
Kuşpalazı (Difteri). Pek Tehlikeli Olan Bu Hastalıktan Çocuklarımızı Nasıl Koruyacağız (T.C. Sıhhat ve İçtimai Muavenet Vekaleti Neşriyatından No 62) (Ankara: n.p, 1938).
Kutkam, İsmail Hakkı, Frengi (Istanbul: Halk Basımevi, 1937).
Kutkam, İsmail Hakkı, Köylülere Öğütlerim Verem (T.C. Trakya Umumî Müfettişliği Köy Bürosu Yayım Sayısı 30) (Istanbul: Halk Basımevi, 1937).
Ladreit de Lacharrière, J., "A l'assaut du Maroc français", L'Afrique Française: Bulletin du Comité de l'Afrique Française, 42/9 (September 1932), 516–27.
Lekeli Humma. Bitten Korkunuz! Bitten Sakınınız! Bu Tehlikeli Hastalığı İnsana Yalnız Bit Bulaştırır (T.C. Sıhhat ve İctimaî Muavenet Vekâleti Neşriyatından, No. 93) (Ankara: n.p., 1943).
Linke, Lilo, Allah Dethroned. A Journey through Modern Turkey (London: Constable and Co., 1937).
Londres, Albert, Pêcheurs de perles (Paris: Albin Michel, 1931).
Luiggi, Luigi, "Le opere pubbliche a Tripoli", Nuova Antologia, 47/965 (1 March, 1912), 115–30.
Makal, Mahmut, Bizim Köy. Köy Öğretmeninin Notları, 5th print (Istanbul: Varlık Yayınları, 1952).
Makal, Mahmut, Köyümden (Istanbul: Varlık Yayınları, 1952).
Makal, Mahmut, A Village in Anatolia, trans. Sir Wyndam Deedes (London: Valentine, Mitchell & Co. Ltd. 1965).
van der Meulen, Daniël, Don't You Hear The Thunder: A Dutchman's Life Story (Leiden: Brill Academic Publishers, 1981).
van Millingen, Alexander, Constantinople (London: A. & C. Black, 1906).
Mintzuri, Hagop, İstanbul Anıları (1897–1940), trans. Silva Kuyumcuyan and ed. Necdet Sakaoğlu (Istanbul: Tarih Vakfı Yurt Yayınları, 1993).
Moshe, Behar and Benite Zvi Ben-Dor (eds.), Modern Middle Eastern Jewish Thought: Writings on Identity, Politics, and Culture, 1893–1958 (Waltham Massachusetts: Brandeis University Press, 2013).

Murad Efendi, *Türkiye Manzaraları*, trans. Alev Sunata Kırım (Istanbul: Kitap Yayınevi, 2007).

Nafıa Vekaleti, T.C., *On Senede Türkiye Nafıası 1923–1933*, 3 vols. (Istanbul: Matbaacılık ve Neşriyat Türk Anonim Şirketi, 1933).

Nahid Sırrı, *Anadoluda. Yol Notları* (Istanbul: Kanaat Kitabevi, 1939).

Nasif, Husayn Muhammad, *Madi al-Hijaz wa-hadiruhu* ([s.n.], 1349/1930).

Neşat Ömer, *Bitler. Bitlerin Ahval-i Hayatı ve Vesait-i İtlafıyesi. Lekeli Tifo ve Humma-i Racianın Bitler ile Sirayeti* (Jerusalem: Matbaa-i Darüleytam-ı Suriye, 1332/1916).

Nevuea-Lemaire, Endjun, "La bilharziose vésicale en Iraq", Dissertation, Faculté de Médicine, Paris, 1928.

Nicolson, Harold, *Peacemaking 1919* (London: Constable & Co. Ltd., 1933).

Ökçün, A. Gündüz, *Türkiye İktisat Kongresi 1923 İzmir. Haberler – Belgeler – Yorumlar* (Ankara: Ankara Üniversitesi Siyasal Bilgiler Fakültesi Yayınları, 1968).

Dr. Osman Şevki, *Bursada Verem Dispanseri* (Bursa: A. Refik Matbaası, 1932).

Özel, Sabahattin and Işıl Çakan Hacıibrahimoğlu (eds.), *Türk Devrimi Mülakatları* (Istanbul: Türkiye İş Bankası Yayınları, 2011).

Özgen, Dr. İhsan, *Üç Bela. Frengi, Fuhuş, İçki* (İzmir: Dereli Basımevi, 1935).

Pellegrineschi, A.V., "Le nuove strade della Libia", *Rivista delle Colonie Italiane*, 7/11 (November 1933), 882–90.

Piccioli, Angelo, "Le comunicazioni", in *Vigor di vita in Tripolitania (anno 1928-VI)* (Tripoli: Ufficio Studi e Propaganda del Governo della Tripolitania, 1928), pp. 75–85.

Piccioli, Angelo, *La nuova Italia d'oltremare l'opera del fascismo nelle colonie Italiane* (Milan: A. Mondadori Editore, 1933).

Piccioli, Angelo, "L'opera di S.E. Emilio De Bono in Tripolitania", in *Vigor di vita in Tripolitania (anno 1928-VI)* (Tripoli: Ufficio Studi e Propaganda del Governo della Tripolitania, 1928), pp. 17–22.

Piccioli, "La valorizzazione turistica", in *La nuova Italia d'oltremare l'opera del fascismo nelle colonie Italiane* (Milan: A. Mondadori Editore, 1933), pp. 1558–65.

Queirolo, Ernesto, "La politica delle comunicazioni", in *La rinascità della Tripolitania. Memorie e studi sui quattro anni di governo del Conte Giuseppe Volpi di Misurata* (Milan: Casa Editrice A. Mondadori, 1926), pp. 259–83.

La rinascità della Tripolitania. Memorie e studi sui quattro anni di governo del Conte Giuseppe Volpi di Misurata (Milan: Casa Editrice A. Mondadori, 1926).

Dr. Reşit Galip, *Dört Azgın Canavar* (Istanbul: Devlet Matbaası, 1929).

Dr. Reşit Galip, *Sıhat Koruma Bilgisi* (Maarif Vekâleti Halk Kitapları Serisi No 4) (Istanbul: Devlet Matbaası, 1929).

Rossi, Francesco M., "Le piccole industrie indigene", in *La rinascità della Tripolitania. Memorie e studi sui quattro anni di governo del Conte Giuseppe Volpi di Misurata* (Milan: Casa Editrice A. Mondadori, 1926), pp. 513–19.

Dr. Rüşdi Edhem (trans.), *Sineklerle Mücadele* (Istanbul: Hilal Matbaası, 1926).

Sadri Sema, *Eski İstanbul Hatıraları*, ed. Ali Şükrü Çoruk (Istanbul: Kitabevi, 2002).

Sağlığımıza Zarar Veren Barsak Kurtları (T.C. Sıhhat ve İçtimaî Muavenet Vekâleti Neşriyatından No. 70) (Ankara: n.p., 1940).

Şark Çıbanı (Yıl Çıbanı) (Sıhhat ve İçtimaî Muavenet Vekâleti Neşriyatından, No. 77) (Ankara: Uğur Basımevi, 1941).

Saylam, M., *Köylüler Arasında I* (Kırşehir: Kırşehir Basımevi, 1937).

Sevig, Vasfi Raşit, *Cumhuriyet Halk Partisi ve Aile*, CHP Konferanslar Serisi, Kitap 10 (Ankara: Recep Ulusoğlu Basımevi, 1939).

Shakir, Fa'iq, *Kitab al-Amrad al-Zahariyya* (Baghdad: Matba'at al-'Ahd, 1934).

Sıhhi Müze Atlası (Sıhhiye ve Muavenet-i İçtimaiye Vekaleti) (n.p.: n.p., 1926).

Sıtma (Kayseri Mıntıkası Sıtma Mücadele Heyeti 2) (Kayseri: Sümer Matbaası, 1938).

Sıtma. Sıtmayı İnsanlara Geçiren Sivrisineklerdir (TC. Sıhhat ve İçtimaî Muavenat Vekaleti Neşriyatından No. 65) (Ankara: n.p., 1939).

Sıtmaya Tutulmamak İçin Öğüdler. Sıtmadan Korunmak Tutulunca Kurtulmakdan Kolaydır (Istanbul: Matbaa-i Ahmed İhsan ve Şürekası, 1341/1925).

Sıtmadan Nasıl Korunacağız? (Sıhhiye ve İçtimai Muavenet Vekaletinden No. 86) (Ankara: n.p., 1943).

La strada litoranea della Libia (Verona: Officine Grafiche A. Mondadori, 1937).

Su İjiyeni (T.C. Sağlık ve Sosyal Yardım Bakanlığı, no. 137) (Ankara: Recep Ulusoğlu Basımevi, 1948).

Talimcıoğlu, Şükrü Kamil, *Belsoğukluğu, Zührevi Hastalıklar, Frengi* (Istanbul: Tefeyyüz Kitabevi, n.d.).

Tanpınar, Ahmet Hamdi, *Beş Şehir*, ed. M. Fatih Andı (Istanbul: Yapı Kredi Yayınları, 2001).

Trahom Hakkında Halka Nesayih (Sıhhiye ve Muavenet-i İçtimaiye Vekaleti Neşriyatından) (Dersaadet: Hilal Matbaası, 1340/1924).

Tülbentçi, Feridun Fazıl (ed.), *Türk Atasözleri ve Deyimleri* (Istanbul: İnkılâp ve Aka Kitabevleri, 1963).

Tuqan, Fadwa, *A Mountainous Journey: An Autobiography*, trans. Olive Kenny (Saint Paul: Graywolf Press, 1990).

Türkçe Hutbe. Diyanet İşleri Reisliği Tarafından Tertib Edilmiştir, second edition (Türkiye Cumhuriyeti Diyanet İşleri Reisliği Neşriyatından Aded 3) (Istanbul: Evkaf Matbaası, 1928/1346).

Uyuz (T.C. Sıhhat ve İçtimaî Muavenet Vekâleti Neşriyatından No. 73) (Ankara: Alâeddin Kıral Basımevi, 1941).

Validelere Nasihat (Türkiye Cumhuriyeti Sıhhıye ve Muavenet-i İctimaiye Vekaleti Şişli Etfal Hastahanesi 27) ([Istanbul]: Kader Matbaası, 1341/1925).

Verem (Tüberküloz) (T.C. Sıhhat ve İçtimaî Muavenet Vekâleti Neşriyatından No. 60) (Ankara: Ankara Cezaevi Matbaası, 1938).

Vicari, Eros, "L'Ente turistico ed alberghiero della Libia (E.T.A.L.)", *Gli Annali dell'Africa Italiana*, 5/4 (December 1942), 955–75.

al-Wazzani, Mohammed Hassan, *Dirasat wa ta'mulat, 2: Hurriyat al-fard wa sultat al-dawla* (Beirut and Fez: Dar al-Nahda al-'Arabiyya and Mu'asasat Mohamed Hassan al-Wazzani, 1987).

al-Wazzani, Mohammed Hassan, "Harakat al-nahda al-sharqiyya", in *Mudhakarat hayat wa jihad: Al-tarikh al-siyasi li-l-haraka al-wataniyya al-tahririyya al-maghribiyya, al-juz' al-awal* (Beirut and Fez: Dar al-Nahda al-'Arabiyya and Mu'asasat Mohamed Hassan al-Wazzani, 1982), pp. 313–51.

al-Wazzani, Mohammed Hassan, "Man huwa al-da'iya?", *Dirasat wa ta'mulat, 5: Al-Islam wa-l-mujtam' wa-l-madaniya* (Beirut and Fez: Dar al-Nahda al-'Arabiyya and Mu'asasat Mohamed Hassan al-Wazzani, 1987), p. 36.

Wilson, C.T., *Peasant Life in the Holy Land* (London: John Murray, 1906).

Woodsmall, Ruth, *Muslim Women Enter a New World* (New York: Roundtable Press, 1936).

Yılal, Dr. Mustafa Musa, *Sıtma Hakkında Köylüye Öğütler* (T.C. Muğla Vilâyeti Köy Bürosu Yayın Serisi: 10) (Muğla: Halk Basımevi, 1936).

Young, George, *Corps de droit ottoman: recueil des codes, lois, règlements, ordonnances et actes les plus importants du droit intérieur, et d'études sur le droit coutumier de l'empire ottoman*, 6 vols. (Oxford: Clarendon Press, 1905).

Yücel Eronat, Canan, *Ertuğrul Süvarisi Ali Bey'den Ayşe Hanım'a Mektuplar* (Istanbul: Türkiye İş Bankası Kültür Yayınları, 2006).

al-Zayani, Abu al-Qassim, *Al-Turjamana al-kubra fi akhbar al-ma'mur barran wa bahran*, ed. Abdelkarim al-Filali (Rabat: Dar Nashr al-Ma'rifa, 1991).

Zindelik Atlası. Çocuklar ve Delikanlılar için Zindelik Numuneleri (Istanbul: Muhit Neşriyat Limited Şirketi, 1930).

Zührevî Hastalıklar Müptelalarına Öğütler ve Tavsiyeler (T.C. Sıhhat ve İctimaî Muavenet Vekâleti Neşriyatından, No. 69) (Ankara: n.p., n.d.).

Zührevi Hastalıklar Nelerdir? (Bursa Halkevi Neşriyatı 9) (Bursa: Yeni Basımevi, 1937).

Secondary Sources

Abdal-Rehim, Abdal-Rehim Abdal-Rehman, "The family and gender laws in Egypt during the Ottoman period", in *Women, the Family, and Divorce Laws in Islamic History*, ed. Amira el-Azhary Sonbol (Syracuse: Syracuse University Press, 1996), pp. 96–110.

Abdulrazak, Fawzi, "The Kingdom of the Book: The History of Printing as an Agency of Change in Morocco between 1865 and 1912", Ph.D. Dissertation, Boston University, 1990.

Abécassis, Frédéric, "La mise en place du réseau routier au Maroc", *Aperçu historique* (2009) (https://halshs.archives-ouvertes.fr/halshs-00435869).

Abou-Hodeib, Toufoul, "Taste and class in late Ottoman Beirut", *International Journal of Middle East Studies*, 43/3 (2011), 475–92.

Abu-Lughod, Janet L., *Cairo: 1001 Years of the City Victorious* (Princeton: Princeton University Press, 1971).

Abugideiri, Hibba, *Gender and the Making of Modern Medicine in Colonial Egypt* (London: Ashgate, 2010).

Abugideiri, Hibba, "The scientisation of culture: colonial medicine's construction of Egyptian womanhood, 1893–1929", *Gender and History*, 16/1 (2004), 83–98.

Abun-Nasr, Jamil, "The Salafiyya movement in Morocco: the religious bases of Moroccan nationalist movement", *St. Anthony's Papers*, 16 (1963), 90–103.

Ahmida, Ali Abdullatif, *The Making of Modern Libya. State Formation, Colonization and Resistance, 1830–1932* (Albany: State University of New York Press, 1994).

Altan, Özlem, "The American Third World: Transnational Elite Networks in the Middle East", Ph.D. Dissertation, New York University, 2006.

Amin, Bakri Shaykh, *al-Haraka al-adabiyya fi 'l-mamlaka al-'arabiyya al-su'udiyya* (n.p., 1392/1972).

Amin, Cameron Michael, "Globalizing Iranian feminism, 1910–1950", *Journal of Middle East Women's Studies*, 4/1 (2008), 6–30.

Anderson, Benedict, *Imagined Communities*, rev. edition (London and New York: Verso, 2006).

Anderson, Benedict, "Nationalism, identity, and the logic of seriality", in Benedict Anderson, *The Spectre of Comparisons: Nationalism, Southeast Asia and the World* (London and New York: Verso, 1998), pp. 29–45.

Anderson, Betty S., *The American University of Beirut: Arab Nationalism and Liberal Education* (Austin: University of Texas Press, 2011).

Anderson, J.N.D., *Law Reform in the Muslim World* (London: Athlone Press, 1976).

Appadurai, Arjun, *Après le colonialisme. Les conséquences culturelles de la globalisation* (Lausanne: Payot, 2015).

Arat, Yeşim, "The project of modernity and women in Turkey", in *Rethinking Modernity and National Identity in Turkey*, ed. Sibel Bozdoğan and Reşat Kasaba (Seattle: University of Washington Press, 1997), pp. 95–112.

Arat, Zehra F., "Turkish women and the republican reconstruction of tradition", in *Reconstructing Gender in the Middle East*, ed. Fatma Müge Göçek and Shiva Balghi (New York: Columbia University Press, 1994), pp. 57–78.

Asad, Talal, "The Idea of an Anthropology of Islam" (Washington, DC: Georgetown University Center for Contemporary Arab Studies, Occasional Papers Series, 1986).

Atabay, Efe, "Eugenics, Modernity and the Rationalization of Morality in Early Republican Turkey", M.A. Dissertation, Institute of Islamic Studies, McGill University, Montreal, 2009.

Atamaz Hazar, Serpil, "'The Hands that Rock the Cradle will Rise', Women, Gender and Revolution in Ottoman Turkey (1908–1918)", Ph.D. Dissertation, University of Arizona, 2010.

Atiyeh, George N., *The Book in the Islamic World: The Written Word and Communication in the Middle East* (Albany and Washington, D.C.: State University of New York Press, 1995).

Atmaca, Nushin, "Saudische Lebensgeschichten: Die 'Generation des Aufbaus' im Spiegel zeitgenössischer Autobiographien", M.A. Dissertation, Freie Universität Berlin, 2012.

Avcı, Yasemin and Vincent Lemire, "De la modernité administrative à la modernisation urbaine: une réévaluation de la municipalité ottomane de Jérusalem (1867–1917)", in *Municipalités méditerranéennes: Les réformes urbaines ottomanes au miroir d'une histoire comparée*, ed. Nora Lafi (Berlin: Klaus Schwarz Verlag, 2005), pp. 73–138.

Ayalon, Ami, "Modern texts and their readers in late Ottoman Palestine", *Middle Eastern Studies*, 38/4 (2002), 17–40.

Ayalon, Ami, *Reading Palestine: Printing and Literacy, 1900–1948* (Austin: University of Texas Press, 2004).

Ayar, Mesut, *Osmanlı Devletinde Kolera. İstanbul Örneği (1892–1895)* (Istanbul: Kitabevi, 2007).

Badran, Margot, *Feminists, Islam, and Nation* (Princeton: Princeton University Press, 1995).

Baida, Jamaa, "Mohamed Salih Missa", in *Ma'lamat al-maghrib*, vol. 21 (Salé: Matbaʿ Sala, 2005), pp. 7343–4.

Barlas, Uğurol, *Safranbolu Halk Hekimliği* (Karabük: Özer Matbaası, n.d.).

Baron, Beth, *Egypt as a Woman: Nationalism, Gender, and Politics* (Berkeley: University of California Press, 2005).

Başar, Zeki, *Halk Hekimliğinde ve Tıp Tarihinde Yılan* (Ankara: Atatürk Üniversitesi Diş Hekimliği Fakültesi Yayınları, 1978).

Bashkin, Orit, "Representations of women in the writings of the intelligentsia in Hashemite Iraq, 1921–1958", *Journal of Middle East Women's Studies*, 4/1 (2008), 53–82.

Bashkin, Orit, *The Other Iraq: Pluralism and Culture in Hashemite Iraq* (Stanford: Stanford University Press, 2009).

Bashkin, Orit, "'When Muʿawiya entered the curriculum' – some comments on the Iraqi education system in the interwar period", *Comparative Education Review*, special issue *Islam and Education – Myths and Truths*, ed. Wadad Kadi and Victor Billeh, 50/3 (2006), 346–66.

Başustaoğlu, Ahmet, *Bir Nefes Sıhhat. Tevfik Sağlam'ın Yaşamı* (Istanbul: Türkiye İş Bankası Kültür Yayınları, 2012).

Baydar, Gülsüm, "Tenuous boundaries: women, domesticity and nationhood in 1930s Turkey", *The Journal of Architecture*, 7/3 (2002), 229–44.

Bazzaz, Sahar, *Forgotten Saints: History, Power, and Politics in the Making of Modern Morocco* (Cambridge, MA: Harvard University Press, 2010).

Bein, Amit, *Kemalist Turkey and the Middle East: International Relations in the Interwar Period* (Cambridge: Cambridge University Press, 2017).

Beinin, Joel, *Workers and Peasants in the Modern Middle East* (Cambridge and New York: Cambridge University Press, 2001).

Beinin, Joel and Frédéric Vairel (eds.), *Social Movements, Mobilization, and Contestation in the Middle East and North Africa*, 2nd ed. (Stanford: Stanford University Press, 2013).

Beinin, Joel and Zachary Lockman, "1919: labour upsurge and national revolution", in *The Modern Middle East: A Reader*, ed. Albert Hourani, Philip S. Khoury and Mary C. Wilson (London and New York: I.B. Tauris, 1993), pp. 395–428.

Bennison, Amira K., "The 'New Order' and Islamic order: The introduction of the Nizami army in the western Maghrib and its legitimation, 1830–73", *International Journal of Middle East Studies*, 36/4 (2004), 591–612.

Berktay, Fatmagül, *Tarihin Cinsiyeti* (Istanbul: Metis Yayınevi, 2003).

Berque, Jacques, "Cà et là dans les débuts du réformisme religieux au Maghreb", *Extrait des études d'orientalisme dédiées à la mémoire de Lévi-Provençal* (Paris: Maisonneuve et Larose, 1962), pp. 471–94.

Berque, Jacques, *French North Africa: The Maghrib between Two World Wars*, trans. Jean Stewart (New York: Praeger Publishers, 1967).

Blecher, Robert Ian, "The Medicalization of Sovereignty: Medicine, Public Health, and Political Authority in Syria, 1861–1936", Ph.D. Dissertation, Stanford University, 2002.

Bourdieu, Pierre, *Distinction: A Social Critique of the Judgment of Taste*, trans. Richard Nice (Cambridge, MA: Harvard University Press, 2002).

Bourdieu, Pierre, *The Field of Cultural Production: Essays on Art and Literature*, ed. Randal Johnson (New York: Columbia University Press, 1993).

Bourmaud, Philippe, "Ya doktor: Devenir médecin et exercer son art en 'Terre sainte', une expérience du pluralisme médical dans l'Empire ottoman finissant (1871–1918)", Ph.D. Dissertation, Université Aix-Marseille I, 2007.

Boyar, Ebru, "An imagined moral community: Ottoman female public presence, honour and marginality", in *Ottoman Women in Public Space*, ed. Ebru Boyar and Kate Fleet (Leiden: Brill, 2016), pp. 187–229.

Boyar, Ebru, "'An inconsequential boil' or a 'terrible disease'? Social perceptions of and state responses to syphilis in the late Ottoman empire", *Turkish Historical Review*, 2/2 (2011), 101–24.

Boyar, Ebru and Kate Fleet, "'Mak[ing] Turkey and the Turkish revolution known to foreign nations without any expense': propaganda films in the early Turkish Republic", *Oriente Moderno*, 24/1 (2005), 117–32.

Boyar, Ebru and Kate Fleet, *A Social History of Ottoman Istanbul* (Cambridge and New York: Cambridge University Press, 2010).

Boyar, Ebru and Kate Fleet, "A dangerous axis: the 'Bulgarian Müftü', the Turkish opposition and the Ankara government, 1928–1936", *Middle Eastern Studies*, 44/5 (2008), 775–89.

Brown, James A.O.C., "Morocco and Atlantic history", in *The Atlantic World*, ed. D'Maris Coffman, Adrian Leonard and William O'Reilly (London: Routledge, 2015), pp. 187–206.

Brown, Nathan J., *The Rule of Law in the Arab World* (New York: Cambridge University Press, 1997).

Brown, Kenneth, "The impact of the Dahir Berbere in Salé", in *Arabs and Berbers*, ed. Ernest Gellner and Charles Micaud (London: Duckworth, 1973), pp. 200–14.

Brownson, Elizabeth, "Gender, Muslim Family Law, and Contesting Patriarchy in Mandate Palestine, 1925–1939", Ph.D. Dissertation, University of California, Santa Barbara, 2008.

Burke, Edmund III, *The Ethnographic State: France and the Invention of Moroccan Islam* (Berkeley: University of California Press, 2014).

Burrage, Michael, Konrad Jarausch and Hannes Siegrist, "An actor-based framework for the study of the professions", in *Professions in Theory and History: Rethinking the Study of the Professions*, ed. Michael Burrage and Rolf Torstendahl (London: Sage Publications, 1990), 203–25.

Büssow, Johann, *Hamidian Palestine: Politics and Society in the District of Jerusalem 1872–1908* (Leiden and Boston: Brill, 2011).

Çakır, Serpil, *Osmanlı Kadın Hareketi* (Istanbul: Metis, 1996).

Chaoqun, Lian, "Language Planning and Language Policy of Arabic Language Academies in the Twentieth Century: A Study of Discourse", Ph.D. Dissertation, University of Cambridge, 2015.

Chatterjee, Partha, *The Nation and its Fragments: Colonial and Postcolonial Histories* (Princeton: Princeton University Press, 1993).

Chiffoleau, Sylvia, *Médecines et médecins en Egypte: construction d'une identité professionnelle et projet médical* (Paris: L'Harmattan, 1997).

Çınar, Alev, "The imagined community as urban reality: the making of Ankara", in *Urban Imaginaries: Locating the Modern City*, ed. Alev Çınar and Thomas Bender (Minneapolis: University of Minnesota Press, 2007), pp. 151–81.

Clark, Martin, *Modern Italy, 1871–1982* (London and New York: Longman Group Limited, 1984).

Collins, R., "Changing conceptions of the sociology of the professions", in *The Formation of Professions: Knowledge, State and Strategy*, ed. Rolf Torstendahl and Michael Burrage (London: Sage, 1990), pp. 11–23.

Cooper, Frederick, *Colonialism in Question: Theory, Knowledge, History* (Berkeley: University of California Press, 2005).

Cornell, Vincent J., *Realm of the Saint: Power and Authority in Moroccan Sufism* (Austin: University of Texas Press, 1998).

Coşar, Simten, "Women in Turkish political thought: between tradition and modernity", *Feminist Review*, 86 (2007), 113–31.

Cott, Nancy, *Public Vows: A History of Marriage and the Nation* (Cambridge: Harvard University Press, 2000).

Coulson, Noel, *History of Islamic Law* (Edinburgh: Edinburgh University Press, 1964).

Cresti, Federico, "Edilizia ed urbanistica nella colonizzazione agraria della Libia (1922–1940)", *Storia Urbana*, 11/40 (1987), 189–231.

Davie, May, *Beyrouth et ses faubourgs (1840–1940): une intégration inacheveé* (Beirut: CERMOC, 1996).

Davis, Fanny, *The Ottoman Lady: A Social History from 1718 to 1918* (Westport, Conn.: Greenwood Press, 1986).

Dede, Kadir, "Toplumsal Cinsiyet Rollerinin Yeniden Üretiminde Aşk Romanlarının Rolü: Muazzez Tahsin Berkand'la İzdivaç", *Atatürk Üniversitesi İktisadi ve İdari Bilimler Dergisi*, 28/4 (2014), 193–212.

Del Boca, Angelo, *Gli Italiani in Libia. Dal fascismo al Gheddafi* (Bari and Rome: Giuseppe Laterza e Figli, 1991).

Demirhan Erdemir, Ayşegül, "The importance of Ḥaydarpāshā Medical Faculty (the first Turkish medical faculty) (1903–1933) from the point of view of Turkish medical history and some original results", *Hamdard Islamicus*, 20 (1997), 61–75.

Dennis, Richard, *Cities in Modernity: Representations and Productions of Metropolitan Space, 1840–1930* (Cambridge and New York: Cambridge University Press, 2008).

Derrida, Jacques, "No apocalypse, not now (full speed ahead, seven missives, seven missiles)", *Diacritics*, special issue *Nuclear Criticism*, 14/2 (1984), 20–31.

Devos, Bianca, "Engineering a modern society? Adoptions of new technologies in early Pahlavi Iran", in *Culture and Cultural Politics under Reza Shah. The Pahlavi State, New Bourgeoisie and the Creation of a Modern Society in Iran*, ed. Bianca Devos and Christoph Werner (Abingdon, Oxon, and New York: Routledge, 2014), pp. 266–87.

Dewachi, Omar, *Ungovernable Life: Mandatory Medicine and Statecraft in Iraq* (Stanford: Stanford University Press, 2017).

Dodge, Toby, *Inventing Iraq. The Failure of Nation Building and a History Denied* (London: Hurst and Co., 2003).

Donzelot, Jacques, *L'Invention du social: essai sur le déclin des passions politiques* (Paris: Éditions du Seuil, 1994).

Duben, Alan and Cem Behar, *Istanbul Households: Marriage, Family, and Fertility 1880–1940* (Cambridge: Cambridge University Press, 1991).

Duman, Derya, "Gender politics in Turkey and the role of women's magazines: a critical outlook on the early republican era", *Hacettepe Üniversitesi Edebiyat Fakültesi Dergisi*, 28/1 (2011), 75–92.

Durakbaşa, Ayşe, "Cumhuriyet Döneminde Modern Kadın ve Erkek Kimliklerinin Oluşumu: Kemalist Kadın Kimliği ve Münevver Erkekler", in *75 Yılda Kadınlar ve Erkekler*, ed. Ayşe Berktay Hacımirzaoğlu (Istanbul: Tarih Vakfı Yayınları, 1998), pp. 29–50.

BIBLIOGRAPHY

During, Jean, "Question de gout, l'enjeu de la modernité dans les arts et les musiques de l'Islam", *Cahiers d'ethnomusicologie*, 7 (1994), 27–49.

Eddé, Carla, *Beyrouth, Naissance d'une capitale (1918–1924)* (Paris: Actes Sud, 2009).

Eddé, Carla, "La municipalité de Beyrouth (1920–1943): un difficile équilibre entre héritage ottoman et contraintes mandataires", in *Municipalités méditerranéennes: Les réformes urbaines ottomanes au miroir d'une histoire comparée*, ed. Nora Lafi (Berlin: Klaus Schwarz Verlag, 2005), pp. 255–300.

Eddé, Carla, Franck Friès, Marlène Ghorayeb and Jade Tabet, "Damas, Beyrouth, regards croisés", in *Damas: miroir brisé d'un Orient arabe*, ed. Anne-Marie Bianquis (Paris: Autrement, 1993), pp. 136–45.

Efrati, Noga, "The other 'awakening' in Iraq; the women's movement in the first half of the twentieth century", *British Journal of Middle East Studies*, 31/2 (2004), 153–73.

Eickelman, Dale, *Knowledge and Power in Morocco: The Education of a Twentieth-Century Notable* (Princeton: Princeton University Press, 1985).

Eickelman, Dale, "Mass higher education and the religious imagination in contemporary Arab societies", *American Ethnologist*, 19/4 (1992), 643–55.

Eickelman, Dale F. and Jon W. Anderson (eds.), *New Media in the Muslim World: The Emerging Public Sphere*, 2nd ed. (Bloomington: Indiana University Press, 2003).

Eppel, Michael, "The elite, the effendiyya, and the growth of nationalism and pan-Arabism in Hashemite Iraq 1921–1958", *International Journal of Middle East Studies*, 30/2 (1998), 227–50.

Ercoşkun, Tülay, "Osmanlı İmparatorluğu'nda 19. Yüzyılda Evlilik ve Nikâha Dair Düzenlemeler", Ph.D. Dissertation, Ankara University, 2010.

Evered, Emine Ö. and Kyle T. Evered, "Sex and the capital city: the political framing of syphilis and prostitution in early republican Ankara", *Journal of the History of Medicine and Allied Sciences*, 68/2 (2013), 266–99.

Fahmy, Ziad, "Media-capitalism: colloquial mass culture and nationalism in Egypt, 1908–18", *International Journal of Middle East Studies*, 42/1 (2010), 83–103.

Fahmy, Ziad, *Ordinary Egyptians: Creating the Modern Nation through Popular Culture* (Stanford: Stanford University Press, 2011).

Farsoun, Samih K., *Culture and Customs of the Palestinians* (London: Greenwood Press, 2004).

al-Fassi, *Al-Harakat al-istiqlaliyyah fi-l-maghrib al-'arabi* (Tangier: 'Abd al-Salam Jasus, 1948).

al-Fattal, Sa'ad, "Sir Harry Sinderson Pasha and Iraq's first medical school", *Journal of Medical Biography*, 21/3 (2013), 164–8.

Faulconbridge, James R. and Daneil Muzio, "Professions in a globalizing world: towards a transnational sociology of the professions", *International Sociology*, 27 (2011), 136–52.

Fawaz, Leila and Robert Ilbert, "Political relations between city and state in the colonial period", in *The Urban Social History of the Middle East, 1750–1950*, ed. Peter Sluglett (Syracuse: Syracuse University Press, 2011), pp. 141–53.

Fırat, Bilge, "Dissident, but Hegemonic: A Critical Review of Feminist Studies on Gendered Nationalism in Turkey", M.A. Thesis, Binghamton University, 2006.

Fleet, Kate, "Geç Osmanlı Erken Türkiye Cumhuriyeti Döneminde Yabancılara Verilen Ekonomik İmtiyazlar", *Kebikeç*, special issue *Uygur Kocabaşoğlu'na Armağan*, ed. Onur Kınlı, 39 (2015), 343–62.

Fleet, Kate, "Money and politics: the fate of British business in the new Turkish Republic", *Turkish Historical Review*, 2/1 (2011), 18–38.

Fleischmann, Ellen L., *The Nation and its "New" Women. The Palestinian Women's Movement 1920–1948* (Berkeley, Los Angeles and London: University of California Press, 2003).

Fleischmann, Ellen, "The other 'awakening': the emergence of women's movements in the modern Middle East, 1900–1940", in *Social History of Women and Gender in the Modern Middle East*, ed. Margaret L. Meriwether and Judith E. Tucker (Boulder, Colo.: Westview Press, 1999), pp. 89–140.

Foucault, Michel, *Security, Territory, Population: Lectures at the Collège de France 1977–1978*, ed. Michel Senellart, trans. Graham Burchell (New York: Picador, 2007).

Fox, Greer Litton, "Love match and arranged marriage in a modernizing nation, mate selection in Ankara, Turkey", *Journal of Marriage and Family*, 31/1 (1975), 180–93.

Freitag, Ulrike, "The Falah School in Jeddah: civic engagement for future generations?", *Jadaliyya* (http://www.jadaliyya.com/pages/index/21430/the-falah-school-in-jeddah_civic-engagement-for-fu).

Freitag, Ulrike, "When festivals turned violent in Jeddah, 1880s–1960s", in *Violence and the City in the Modern Middle East*, ed. Nelida Fuccaro (Stanford: Stanford University Press, 2016), pp. 63–74.

Fuccaro, Nelida, "Reading oil as urban violence: Kirkuk and its oil conurbation, 1927–58", in *Urban Violence in the Middle East: Changing Cityscapes in the Transformation from Empire to Nation State*, ed. Ulrike Freitag, Nelida Fuccaro, Claudia Ghrawi and Nora Lafi (New York and Oxford: Berghahn Books, 2015), pp. 222–42.

Ganz, Cheryl R., *The 1933 Chicago World's Fair: A Century of Progress* (Chicago: Illinois University Press, 2010).

Gawrych, George W., "Şemseddin Sami: women and social conscience in the late Ottoman empire", *Middle Eastern Studies*, 46/1(2010), 97–115.

Geertz, Clifford, *Islam Observed* (Chicago: University of Chicago Press, 1968).

Gelvin, James L., *Divided Loyalties. Nationalism and Mass Politics in Syria at the Close of Empire* (Berkeley: University of California Press, 1998).

Gelvin, James L., *The Modern Middle East: A History* (New York and Oxford: Oxford University Press, 2005).

BIBLIOGRAPHY

Gelvin, James L, "Was there a Mandate period?", in *The Routledge Handbook of the History of the Middle East,* ed. Cyrus Schayegh and Andrew Arsan (London and New York: Routledge, 2015).

Gelvin, James L., "Secularism and religion in the Arab Middle East: reinventing Islam in a world of nation-states", in *The Invention of Religion: Rethinking Belief in Politics and History,* ed. Derek R. Peterson and Darren R. Walhof (New Brunswick: Rutgers University Press, 2002), pp. 115–30.

Gelvin, James L. and Nile Green (eds.), *Global Muslims in the Age of Steam and Print* (Berkeley: University of California Press, 2013).

Gershoni, Israel, "Rethinking the formation of Arab nationalism in the Middle East, 1920–1945: old and new narratives", in *Rethinking Nationalism in the Arab Middle East,* ed. Israel Gershoni and James Jankowski (New York: Columbia University Press, 1997), pp. 3–25.

Gershoni, Israel and James Jankowski, *Redefining the Egyptian Nation, 1930–1945* (Cambridge: Cambridge University Press, 1995).

Ghazal, Amal N., "The other frontiers of Arab nationalism: Ibadis, Berbers, and the Arabist-Salafi press in the interwar period", *International Journal of Middle East Studies,* 42/1 (2010), 105–22.

Ghorayeb, Marlène, *Beyrouth sous mandat français: construction d'une ville moderne* (Paris: Éditions Karthala, 2014).

Ghoulaichi, Fatima, "Of Saints and Sharifian Kings in Morocco: Three Examples of the Politics of Reimagining History through Reinventing King/Saint Relationship", M.A. Dissertation, College Park, MD, University of Maryland, 2005.

Glosser, Susan L., "'The truths I have learned': nationalism, family reform and male identity in China's New Culture Movement, 1915–1923", in *Chinese Femininities Chinese Masculinities A Reader,* ed. Susan Brownell and Jeffrey N. Wasserstrom (Berkeley and Los Angeles: University of California Press, 2002), pp. 120–44.

Graham-Brown, Sarah, *Palestinians and their Society 1880–1946* (London: Quartet Books, 1980).

Grallert, Till, "To Whom Belong the Streets? Property, Propriety, and Appropriation: The Production of Public Space in Late Ottoman Damascus, 1875–1914", Ph.D. Dissertation, Freie Universität Berlin, 2014.

Gül, Murat, *The Emergence of Modern Istanbul: Transformation and Modernisation of a City* (London and New York: Tauris Academic Studies, 2009).

Habermas, Jürgen, *Die Moderne, ein unvollendetes Projekt: Philosophisch-politische Aufsätze, 1977–1990,* 1st ed. (Leipzig: Reclam, 1990).

Halstead, John, "The changing character of Moroccan reformism 1921–1934", *Journal of African History,* 5/3 (1964), 435–47.

Halstead, John, *Rebirth of a Nation: The Origins and Rise of Moroccan Nationalism, 1912–1944* (Cambridge, MA: Harvard University Press, 1967).

Hanna, Nelly, "Marriage among merchant families in seventeenth-century Cairo", in *Women, the Family, and Divorce Laws in Islamic History*, ed. Amira el-Azhary Sonbol (Syracuse: Syracuse University Press, 1996).

Hannoum, Abdelmajid, "The historiographic state: how Algeria once became French", *History and Anthropology*, 19/2 (2008), 91–114.

Hanssen, Jens, *Fin de Siècle Beirut: The Making of an Ottoman Provincial Capital* (Oxford: Oxford University Press, 2005).

al-Harbi, Dalal bte Mukhlid, "al-Awda' al-dakhiliyya fi Jidda fi fatrat al-hisar 1343-144 h./1925 m. min khilal sahifat 'Barid al-Hijaz'", *al-Dar'iyya*, 47–48 (2010), 123–84.

al-Hashimi, Hashim Makki, *Tarikh wa-muhattat: Sira dhatiyya tu'arrakh li-kulliyyat al-Tibb al-'iraqiyya* (Beirut: al-Mu'assasah al-'Arabiyah lil-Dirasat wa-al-Nashr, 2009).

Heilbron, Johan, Nicolas Guilhot and Laurent Jeanpierre, "Toward transnational history of the social sciences", *Journal of the History of the Behavioral Sciences*, 44/2 (2008), 146–60.

Herzstein, Rafael, *Université Saint Joseph de Beyrouth: fondation et fonctionnement de 1875 à 1914* (Brussels: Le Cri Edition, 2008).

Heynickx, Rajesh and Tom Avermaete, "Community as a prism", in *Making a New World: Architecture and Communities in Interwar Europe*, ed. Rajesh Heynickx and Tom Avermaete (Leuven: Leuven University Press, 2012), pp. 9–26.

Hirschkind, Charles, *The Ethical Soundscape: Cassette Sermons and Islamic Counterpublics* (New York: Columbia University Press, 2006).

Hirschkind, Charles, "Experiments in devotion online: the YouTube Khutba", *International Journal of Middle East Studies*, 44/1 (2012), 5–21.

Huber, Valeska, "The unification of the globe by disease? The International Sanitary Conferences on Cholera, 1851–1894", *The Historical Journal*, 49/2 (2006), 453–76.

Hobsbawm, Eric, *On History* (London: Abacus, 1997).

Holston, James, *Insurgent Citizenship: Disjunctions of Democracy and Modernity in Brazil* (Princeton: Princeton University Press, 2008).

Houston, Christopher, "Ankara, Tehran, Baghdad: three varieties of Kemalist urbanism", *Thesis Eleven*, 121/1 (2014), 57–75.

Hunter, F. Robert, "Promoting empire: the Hachette tourist in French Morocco, 1919–36", *Middle Eastern Studies*, 43/4 (2007), 579–91.

İhsanoğlu, Ekmeleddin, *Al-Mu'assasat al-sihhiyya al-'uthmaniyya al-haditha fi Suriya: al-mustashfayat wa-kulliyyat Tibb al-Sham* (Amman: Lajnat tarikh bilad al-Sham, al-Jami'a al-urdunniyya, 2002).

Jacob, Wilson Chaco, *Working Out Egypt* (Durham, NC: Duke University Press, 2011).

Johnson, Amy J., *Reconstructing Rural Egypt. Ahmed Hussein and the History of Egyptian Development* (Syracuse: Syracuse Univesity Press, 2004).

Johnson, Christopher, "'French' cybernetics", *French Studies*, 69/1 (2015), 60–78.

Joubin, Rebecca, "Creating the modern professional housewife: scientifically based advice extended to middle- and upper-class Egyptian women, 1920s–1930s", *The Arab Studies Journal*, 4/2 (1996), 19–45.

Kaçar, Duygu, "Ankara, a small town, transformed to a nation's capital", *Journal of Planning History*, 9/1 (2010), 43–65.

Kalisman, Hilary Falb, "Bursary scholars at the American University of Beirut: living and practising Arab unity", *British Journal of Middle Eastern Studies*, 42/4 (2015), 599–617.

Kandiyoti, Deniz, "End of empire: Islam, nationalism and women in Turkey", in *Women, Islam and the State*, ed. Deniz Kandiyoti (London: MacMillan, 1991), pp. 22–47.

Kandiyoti, Deniz, "Gendering the modern: on missing dimensions in the study of Turkish modernization", in *Rethinking Modernity and National Identity in Turkey*, ed. Sibel Bozdoğan and Reşat Kasaba (Seattle: University of Washington Press, 1997), pp. 113–32.

Kandiyoti, Deniz, "Patterns of patriarchy: notes for an analysis of male dominance in Turkish society", in *Women in Modern Turkish Society. A Reader*, ed. Şirin Tekeli (London: Zed Books, 1995), pp. 306–18.

Kandiyoti, Deniz, "Women and the Turkish state: political actors or symbolic pawns", in *Woman-Nation-State*, ed. Nira Yuval Davis and Floya Anthias (London: MacMillan, 1989), pp. 126–50.

Kaya, Tebrike, "Televizyonda Yayınlanan İzdivaç Programlarında Toplumsal Cinsiyetin Temsili", *Kadın Araştırmaları Dergisi*, 13/2 (2013), 81–110.

Kayali, Zeina Saleh, *La vie musicale au Liban de la fin du 19ème siècle à nos jours* (Paris: Geuthner, 2015).

Kaymas, Serhat, "İslami Sanal Kamusal Alanda Kolektif Kimlik: İslami Evlilik Siteleri İçinden Kolektif Kimliği Okumak", *Journal of Yaşar University*, 5/19 (2010), 3237–63.

Keçeci Kurt, Songül, "II. Meşrutiyet Dönemi Osmanlı Kadın Dergilerinde Aile ve Evlilik Algısı", *Belleten*, 79/286 (2015), 1073–97.

Khater, Ahram, *Inventing Home: Emigration, Gender, and the Middle Class in Lebanon, 1870–1920* (Berkeley and Los Angeles: University of California Press, 2001).

Khoury, Philip S., "The paradoxical in Arab nationalism: interwar Syria revisited", in *Rethinking Nationalism in the Arab Middle East*, ed. Israel Gershoni and James Jankowski (New York: Columbia University Press, 1997), pp. 273–88.

Khoury, Philip S., *Syria and the French Mandate: The Politics of Arab Nationalism, 1920–1945*, 1st ed. (Princeton: Princeton University Press, 1987).

King, Anthony D., *Colonial Urban Development: Culture, Social Power, and Environment* (London and Boston: Routledge and Kegan Paul, 1976).

King, Anthony D., "Writing transnational planning histories", in *Urbanism: Imported or Exported?*, ed. Joe, Nasr and Mercedes, Volait (Chichester, UK and Hoboken: Wiley-Academy, 2003), pp. 1–14.

Kostiner, Joseph, *The Making of Saudi Arabia, 1916–1936: From Chieftaincy to Monarchical State* (New York: Oxford University Press, 1993).

al-Khutabi, Arwa, "The Financial Policies of the Yemeni Imams (1918–1962)", Ph.D. Dissertation, Freie Universität Berlin, 2014.

Kugle, Scott, *Rebel between Spirit and Law: Ahmad Zarruq, Sainthood, and Authority in Islam* (Bloomington: Indiana University Press, 2006).

Lafuente, Gilles, *La Politique berbère de la France et le nationalisme marocain* (Paris: L'Harmattan, 1999).

Lagrange, Frédéric, "Musiciens et poètes en Égypte au temps de la Nahda", Ph.D. Dissertation, Paris VIII University, 1994.

Laroui, Abdallah, *Les origins sociales et culturelle du nationalism marocain, 1830–1912* (Paris: Maspero, 1977).

Layish, Aharon, *Women and Islamic Law in a Non-Muslim State* (Jerusalem: Israel Universities Press, 1975).

Lawrence, Adria, "Rethinking Moroccan nationalism, 1930–44", *Journal of North African Studies*, 17/3 (2012), 475–90.

Lazreg, Marina, *The Eloquence of Silence: Algerian Women in Question* (New York: Routledge, 1994).

Lefebvre, Thierry, "Les films de propagande sanitaire de Lortac et O'Galop (1918–1919)", *1895- Mille huit cent quatre-vingt-quinze*, 59 (2009), 171–83.

Lerner, Daniel, *The Passing of Traditional Society: Modernizing the Middle East*, 5th ed. (New York: Free Press, 1964).

Lévy-Aksu, Noémy, *Ordre et désordres dans l'Istanbul ottomane (1879–1909)* (Paris: Éditions Karthala, 2013).

Lewis, Bernard, "Baladiyya", in *The Encyclopaedia of Islam*, 2nd ed., ed. Peri J. Bearman et al. (Leiden: E.J. Brill, 1954–2009), vol. 1., pp. 972–5.

Libal, Kathryn R., "Staging Turkish women's emancipation: Istanbul, 1935", *Journal of Middle East Women's Studies*, 4/1 (2008), 31–52.

Low, Michael C., "Ottoman infrastructures of the Saudi hydro-state: the technopolitics of pilgrimage and potable water in the Hijaz", *Comparative Studies in Society and History*, 57/4 (2015), 942–74.

Makdisi, Ussama, "Rethinking Ottoman imperialism: modernity, violence and the cultural logic of Ottoman reform", in *The Empire in the City, Arab Provincial Capitals in the Late Ottoman Empire*, ed. Jens Hanssen, Thomas Philipp and Stefan Weber (Beirut: Orient-Institut, 2002), pp. 29–48.

Man, Fuat, "The perception of the relationship between trade unions and politics in Turkey: a tracking on the related acts", *Mediterranean Journal of Social Sciences*, 4/9 (2013), 212–19.

Mansbridge, Jane, "What is the feminist movement?", in *Feminist Organizations: Harvest of the Women's Movement*, ed. Myra Marx Ferree and Patricia Yancey Martin (Philadelphia: Temple University Press, 1995), pp. 27–34.

El-Mansour, Mohamed, *Morocco in the Reign of Mawlay Sulayman* (Wisbech, UK: Middle East and North African Studies Press, 1990).

Al-Manuni, Mohammed, *Madhahir yaqdhat al-maghrib al-hadith*, 2 vols. (Dar al-Bayda': Sharikat al-Nashr wa-l-Tawzi' al-Madaris, 1985).

Masarih Bayrut wa tawarikhiha (Beirut: Dar al-tafahum lil tiba'a wal nashr wal-tawzi', 2006).

Mattelart, Armand, *The Invention of Communication*, trans. Susan Emanuel (Minneapolis, Minn.: University of Minnesota Press, 1996).

Mazower, Mark, *Salonica City of Ghosts, Christians, Muslims and Jews 1430–1950* (London and New York: Harper Perennial, 2005).

Mazza, Roberto, "Transforming the Holy City: from communal clashes to urban violence, the Nebi Musa riots in 1920", in *Urban Violence in the Middle East: Changing Cityscapes in the Transformation from Empire to Nation State*, ed. Ulrike Freitag, Nelida Fuccaro, Claudia Ghrawi and Nora Lafi (New York and Oxford: Berghahn Books, 2015), pp. 179–96.

McDougall, James, *History and the Culture of Nationalism in Algeria* (Cambridge: Cambridge University Press, 2009).

McLuhan, Marshall, *The Gutenberg Galaxy: The Making of Typographic Man*, new edition (Toronto: University of Toronto Press, 2011).

McLuhan, Marshall, *Understanding Media: The Extensions of Man*, critical edition W. Terrence Gordon (New York: Gingko Press, 2003).

Messick, Brinkley, *The Calligraphic State: Textual Domination and History in a Muslim Society* (Berkeley: University of California Press, 1993).

Messick, Brinkley, "On the question of lithography", *Culture and History* (Copenhagen, Denmark: Museum Tusculanum Press), 16 (1997), 158–76.

al-Messiri-Nadim, Nawal, "The concept of the Hara: a historical and sociological study of al-Sukkariyya", *Annales Islamologiques*, 15 (1979), 323–48.

Mishaqah, Mikha'il, and W M. Thackston, *Murder, Mayhem, Pillage and Plunder: The History of Lebanon in the 18th and 19th Centuries* (Albany: State University of New York Press, 1988).

Moors, Annelies, *Women, Property, and Islam* (Cambridge: Cambridge University Press, 1995).

Morton, Patricia A., "National and colonial: the Musée des colonies at the Colonial Exposition, Paris, 1931", *The Art Bulletin*, 80/2 (1998), 357–77.

Najmabadi, Afsaneh, *Women with Mustaches and Men without Beards. Gender and Sexual Anxieties of Iranian Modernity* (Berkeley, Los Angeles and London: University of California Press, 2005).

Neep, Daniel, *Occupying Syria under the French Mandate: Insurgency, Space and State Formation* (Cambridge: Cambridge University Press, 2012).

Neill, Deborah J., *Networks in Tropical Medicine: Internationalism, Colonialism, and the Rise of a Medical Specialty, 1890–1930* (Stanford: Stanford University Press, 2012).

Nelson, Cynthia, *Doria Shafik, Egyptian Feminist: A Woman Apart* (Gainseville: University of Florida Press, 1996).

Noga, Efrati, "Colonial gender discourse in Iraq. Constructing noncitizens", in *The Routledge Handbook of the History of the Middle East*, ed. Cyrus Schayegh and Andrew Arsan (London and New York: Routledge, 2015), pp. 157–69.

Nüfusçu, Gözde Aytemur and Yılmaz, Ayça, "Evlilik Pratiklerinin Dönüşüm/Yeniden Üretim Sürecinde Evlendirme Programları", *Galatasaray Üniversitesi İletişim Dergisi*, 16 (2012), 23–48.

Ofer, Pinhas, "A scheme for the establishment of a British university in Jerusalem in the late 1920s", *Middle Eastern Studies*, 22/2 (1986), 274–85.

Onaran, Alim Şerif, *Muhsin Ertuğrul'un Sineması* (Ankara: Kültür Bakanlığı Yayınları, 1981).

Örnek, Sedat Veyis, *Sıvas ve Çevresinde Hayatın Çeşitli Safhaları ile İlgili Bâtıl İnançların ve Büyüsel İşlemlerin Etnolojik Tetkiki* (Ankara: Ankara Üniversitesi Basımevi, 1966).

Ortaylı, İlber, *Tanzimat Devrinde Osmanlı Mahallî İdareleri, 1840–1880* (Ankara: Türk Tarih Kurumu Basımevi, 2000).

Oruç, Yener, *Atatürk'ün "Fikir Fedaisi" Dr. Reşit Galip. Günümüz Gözüyle* (Istanbul: Gürer Yayınları, 2007).

van Os, Nicole A.N.M., "Ottoman Muslim and Turkish women in an international context", *European Review*, 13/3 (2005), 459–79.

Osmanoğlu, Ahmed E., "Hicaz Eyaletinin Teşekkülü (1841–1864)", M.A. Dissertation, Marmara University, 2004.

Osterhammel, Jürgen, *Die Verwandlung der Welt: Eine Geschichte des 19. Jahrhunderts* (Munich: Beck, 2009).

Özervarlı, M. Sait, "Intellectual foundations and transformations in an imperial city: Istanbul from the late Ottoman to the early republican periods", *The Muslim World*, 103 (2013), 518–34.

Özman, Aylin, "The image of 'woman' in Turkish and social political thought: on the implications of social constructionism and biological essentialism", *Turkish Studies*, 11/3 (2010), 445–64.

Öztan, G. Gürkan, "Türkiye'de Öjeni Düşüncesi ve Kadın", *Toplum ve Bilim*, 105 (2006), pp. 265–82.

Öztürk, Ali İhsan, *Osmanlı'dan Cumhuriyet'e İmtiyaz Usulüyle Yürütülen İstanbul Belediye Hizmetleri (Yap-İşlet-Devret Ugulaması) (1852–1964)* (Istanbul: İstanbul Büyükşehir Belediyesi Kültür Yayınları, 2010).

Panzac, Daniel, "Les docteurs orientaux de la faculté de médecine de Paris au XIXe siècle", *Revue du monde musulman et de la Méditerranée*, 75/76 (1995), 295–303.

Panzac, Daniel, "Médicine révolutionnaire et révolution de la médicine dans l'Égypte de Muhammad Ali: le Dr. Clot-Bey", *Revue des mondes musulmans et de la Méditerranée: les Arabes, les Turcs et la révolution française*, 52/53 (1989), 95–110.

BIBLIOGRAPHY

Parusheva, Dobrinka, "Europe imagined and performed: the impact of Western Europe's modernity on Southeast European urban space", in *Städte im europäischen Raum: Verkehr, Kommunikation und Urbanität im 19. und 20. Jahrhundert*, ed. Ralf Roth (Stuttgart: Steiner, 2009), pp. 187–204.

Penrose, Stephen B.L., *That They May Have Life: The Story of the American University of Beirut, 1866–1941* (Beirut: American University of Beirut Press, 1970).

Pétriat, Philippe, "For pilgrims and for trade: merchants and public works in Ottoman Jeddah", *Turkish Historical Review*, 5/2 (2014), 200–20.

Poché, Christian, "Vers une musique libanaise", *Les cahiers de l'Oronte*, 5 (1965), 115–36.

Podeh, Elie, *The Politics of National Celebrations in the Arab Middle East* (Cambridge: Cambridge University Press, 2011).

Pollard, Lisa, "The family politics of colonizing and liberating Egypt, 1882–1919", *Social Politics*, 7/1 (2000), 47–79.

Prestel, Joseph B., "Feeling Urban Change: Debates on Emotions in Berlin and Cairo, 1860–1910", Ph.D. Dissertation, Freie Universität Berlin, 2014.

Provence, Michael, "Ottoman modernity, colonialism, and insurgency in the interwar Arab East", *International Journal of Middle East Studies*, 43/2 (2011), 205–25.

al-Racy, Salam, *Li'alla tadi'* (Beirut: Dar Nawfal, 1995).

al-Racy, Ali-Jihad, "Music in contemporary Cairo: a comparative overview", *Asian Music*, 13/1 (1981), 4–26.

al-Racy, Ali-Jihad, "Musical Change and Commercial Recording in Egypt, 1904–1932", Ph.D. Dissertation, University of Illinois at Urbana-Champaign, 1977.

Ramadan, Dina, "The Aesthetics of the Modern: Art, Education, and Taste in Egypt 1903–1952", Ph.D. Dissertation, Columbia University, 2013.

Rapoport, Yossef, *Marriage, Money and Divorce in Medieval Islamic Society* (Cambridge: Cambridge University Press, 2005).

al-Rasheed, Madawi, book review of Khaloussy, Hanan, *For Better, For Worse: the Marriage Crisis that Made Modern Egypt*, *Middle Eastern Studies*, 47 /6 (2011), 964–6.

al-Rasheed, Madawi, *A History of Saudi Arabia* (New York: Cambridge University Press, 2002).

Reiss, Nira, *The Health Care of Arabs in Israel* (Boulder: Westview Press, 1991).

Reynolds, Nancy Y., *A City Consumed. Urban Commerce, the Cairo Fire, and the Politics of Decolonization in Egypt* (Stanford: Stanford University Press, 2012).

Robinson, Francis, "Technology and religious change: Islam and the impact of print", *Modern Asian Studies*, 27/1 (1993), 229–51.

Romano, Sergio, *Giuseppe Volpi. Industria e finanza tra Giolitti e Mussolini* (Milan: Bompiani, 1979).

Russell, Mona, *Creating the New Egyptian Woman: Consumerism, Education, and National Identity, 1863–1922* (New York: Palgrave Macmillan, 2004).

Ryzova, Lucie, "Egyptianizing modernity through the 'New Effendiya': social and cultural constructions of the middle class in Egypt under the monarchy", in *Re-Envisioning Egypt: 1919–1952*, ed. Arthur Goldschmidt, Amy J. Johnson and Barak A. Salmoni (Cairo and New York: The American University in Cairo Press, 2005), pp. 124–63.

Sabban, Suhayl, *Nusus 'uthmaniyya 'an al-awda' al-thaqafiyya fi 'l-Hijaz: al-Awqaf, al-madaris, al-maktabat* (Riyadh: Maktabat al-Malik 'Abd al-'Aziz al-'amma, 1422/2001).

Sabban, Suhayl, "Jidda fi watha'iq al-arshif al-'uthmani" (unpublished manuscript, prepared as part of project of *Encyclopedia of Jeddah*, n.d. (2005?)).

Salami, Gholamreza and Afsaneh Najmabadi, *Nahzat-e Nisvan-e Sharq* (Tehran: Shirazeh, 2005).

Salgırlı, Sanem Güvenç, "Eugenics as Science of the Social: A Case from the 1930s Istanbul", Ph.D. Dissertation, Binghampton University, 2009.

Saliba, Robert, "Looking East, looking West: provincial ecclecticism and cultural dualism in the architecture of French Mandate Beirut", in *The British and French Mandates in Comparative Perspectives/ Les Mandates français et anglais dans une perspective comparative*, ed. Nadine Méouchy and Peter Suglett (Leiden and Boston: Brill, 2004), pp. 201–15.

Saßmannshausen, Christian, "Reform in Translation: Family, Distinction, and Social Mediation in Late Ottoman Tripoli", Ph.D. Dissertation, Freie Universität Berlin, 2012.

al-Sayyid Marsot, Afaf Lutfi, *Egypt's Liberal Experiment, 1922–1936* (Berkeley: University of California Press, 1977).

Schayegh, Cyrus, "The many worlds of 'Abu Yasin: or what narcotics trafficking in the interwar Middle East can tell us about territorialization", *The American Historical Review*, 116/2 (2011), 273–306.

Schivelbusch, Wolfgang, *The Railway Journey: The Industrialization of Time and Space*, rev. edition (Berkeley: University of California Press, 2014).

Schulz, Dorothea Elisabeth, *Muslims and New Media in West Africa: Pathways to God* (Bloomington: Indiana University Press, 2012).

Scognamillo, Giovanni, *Türk Sinema Tarihi* (Istanbul: Kabalcı Yayınevi, 2003).

Sehnaoui, Nada, *L'occidentalisation de la vie quotidienne a` Beyrouth, 1860–1914* (Beirut: Dar an-Nahar, 2002).

Şehsuvaroğlu, Bedi N., *İstanbulda 500 Yıllık Sağlık Hayatımız* (Istanbul: Kemal Matbaası, 1953).

Segrè, Claudio, *Fourth Shore. The Italian Colonization of Libya* (Chicago: The University of Chicago Press, 1974).

Seikaly, May, *Haifa: Transformation of a Palestinian Arab Society, 1918–1939* (London and New York: I.B. Tauris, 1995).

Shechter, Relli, *Smoking, Culture and Economy in the Middle East: the Egyptian Tobacco Market, 1850–2000* (London: I.B. Tauris, 2006).

Sheehi, Stephen, *Foundations of Modern Arab Identity* (Gainesville: University Press of Florida, 2004).

Shissler, Ada Holland, "'If you ask me': Sabiha Sertel's advice column, gender equity, and social engineering in the early Turkish republic", *Journal of Middle East Women's Studies*, 3/2 (2007), 1–30.

Siegel, James, *Fetish, Recognition, Revolution* (Princeton: Princeton University Press, 1997).

Siegel, James T., *The Rope of God*, rev. edition (Ann Arbor: University of Michigan Press, 2000).

Şimşir, Bilal N., *Doğu'nun Kahramanı Atatürk* (Ankara: Bilgi Yayınevi, 1999).

Sluggett, Peter, "Les mandats/the mandates: some reflections on the nature of the British presence in Iraq (1914–1932) and the French presence in Syria", in *The British and French Mandates in Comparative Perspectives/ Les Mandats français et anglais dans une perspective comparative*, ed. Nadine Méouchy and Peter Suglett (Leiden and Boston: Brill, 2004), pp. 103–27.

Smith, Valene (ed.), *Hosts and Guests: The Anthropology of Tourism* (Philadelphia: University of Pennsylvania Press, 1977).

Sonbol, Amira el-Azhary, *The Creation of a Medical Profession in Egypt, 1800–1922* (Syracuse: Syracuse University Press, 1991).

Souami, Taoufik, "Émergences des professionnels locaux de l'urbanisme", in *Concevoir et gérer les villes: milieux d'urbanistes du sud de la Méditerranée*, ed. Taoufik Souami and Éric Verdeil (Paris: Économica/Anthropos, 2006), pp. 13–63.

Souami, Taoufik and Éric Verdeil, "Introduction", in *Concevoir et gérer les villes: milieux d'urbanistes du sud de la Méditerranée*, ed. Taoufik Souami and Éric Verdeil (Paris: Économica/Anthropos, 2006), pp. 1–12.

Souriau-Hoebrechts, Christine, *La Presse Maghrebine: Libye - Tunisie - Maroc - Algérie: évolution historique, situation en 1965, organisation et problèmes actuels* (Paris: Editions du CNRS, 1975).

Spadola, Emilio, *The Calls of Islam: Sufis, Islamists, and Mass Mediation in Urban Morocco* (Bloomington: Indiana University Press, 2014).

Starks, Tricia, *The Body Soviet: Propaganda, Hygiene and the Revolutionary State* (Madison: University of Wisconsin Press, 2008).

Steinberg, Guido, *Religion und Staat in Saudi-Arabien: Die wahhabitischen Gelehrten 1902–1953* (Würzburg: Ergon, 2002).

Stephen, Daniel Mark, "'The white man's grave': British West Africa and the British Empire Exhibition of 1924–1925", *Journal of British Studies*, 48/1 (2009), 102–28.

Stetkevych, Jaroslav, *The Modern Arabic Literary Language: Lexical and Stylistic Developments* (Publications of the Center for Middle Eastern Studies. vol. 6) (Chicago: University of Chicago Press, 1970).

Tanyu, Hikmet, *Türklerde Taşla İlgili İnançlar* (Ankara Üniversitesi İlâhiyat Fakültesi Yayınları: LXXXI) (Ankara: Ankara Üniversitesi Basımevi, 1968).

Tarde, Gabriel, "The public and the crowd", in *On Communication and Social Influence: Selected Papers*, ed. Terry N. Clark (Chicago: University of Chicago Press, 2010), pp. 277–94.

Tekeli, Şirin, "The meaning and the limits of feminist ideology in Turkey", in *Women, Family and Social Change in Turkey*, ed. Ferhunde Özbay (Bangkok: UNESCO, 1990), pp. 139–59.

Terem, Etty, *Old Texts, New Practices: Islamic Reform in Modern Morocco* (Stanford: Stanford University Press, 2014).

Tevfikoğlu, Muhtar, *Âkil Muhtar Özden* (Ankara: Türk Kültürünü Araştırma Enstitüsü, 1996).

Thobie, Jacques, "Un contexte de crises: les relations économio-financières entre la Turquie et la France de 1929 à 1944", in *IIIrd Congress on the Social and Economic History of Turkey, Princeton University 24-6 August 1983*, ed. Heath W. Lowry and Ralph S. Hattox (Istanbul, Washington and Paris: The ISIS Press, 1990), pp. 146–87.

Thompson, Elizabeth, *Colonial Citizens, Republican Rights, Paternal Privilege, and Gender in French Syria and Lebanon* (New York: Columbia University Press, 2000).

Toprak, Binnaz, "Emancipated but unliberated women in Turkey: the impact of Islam", in *Women, Family and Social Change in Turkey*, ed. Ferhunde Özbay (Bangkok: UNESCO, 1990), pp. 39–49.

Toprak, Zafer, "Muslihiddin Adil'in Görüşleri: Kadın ve Hukuk-ı Nisvan", *Toplumsal Tarih*, 75 (2000), 14–17.

Trabulsi, Muhammad Yusuf Muhammad Hasan, *Jidda: Hikayat madina* 2nd ed. (Riyadh: al-Madina al-Munawwara li-l-tibaʻa wa-l-nashr, 1429/2008).

Tucker, Judith, *In the House of the Law: Gender and Islamic Law in Ottoman Syria and Palestine* (Berkeley: University of California Press, 1997).

Tucker, Judith, "Revisiting reform: women and the Ottoman Law of Family Rights, 1917", *The Arab Studies Journal*, 4/2 (1996), 4–17.

Tucker, Judith, *Women, Family, and Gender in Islamic Law* (Cambridge: Cambridge University Press, 2008).

Turhanoğlu, F. Ayşın Koçak, "Spatial production of Ankara as capital city of republican Turkey", *Journal of Interdisciplinary Social Sciences*, 5/5 (2010), 309–18.

Tütüncü, Fatma, "Güzel Ahlaklı Biriyle Hayırlı Bir İzdivaç İçin: İslami Evlilik Siteleri, Dönüşen Mahremiyetler ve Kadın Öznelliği", in *Yeni Medya Çalışmaları*, ed. Mutlu Binark (Ankara: Dipnot Yayınları, 2007), pp. 281–305.

Urry, John, *Mobilities* (Cambridge, UK and Malden, MA: Polity Press, 2007).

BIBLIOGRAPHY

Vassiliev, Alexei, *The History of Saudi-Arabia* (London: Saqi, 2000).

Vejdani, Farzin, *Making History in Iran: Education, Nationalism, and Print Culture* (Stanford: Stanford University Press, 2014).

Verdeil, Chantal, "L'empire, les communautés, la France: les réseaux des médecins ottomans à la fin du XIXe siècle", in *Hommes de l'entre-deux: parcours individuels et portraits de groupes sur la frontière de la Méditerranée XVIe–XXe siècle*, ed. Bernard Heyberger and Chantal Verdeil (Paris: Les Indes Savantes, 2009), pp. 133–50.

Verdeil, Chantal, "Naissance d'une nouvelle élite ottomane. Formation et trajectoires de médecins diplômés de Beyrouth à la fin du XIXe siècle", *Revue du mondes musulman et de la Méditerranée*, 121–122 (2008), 217–37.

Virilio, Paul, *Speed and Politics*, new edition, trans. Mark Polizzotti (Cambridge, MA: MIT Press, 2006).

Warner, Michael, *Publics and Counterpublics* (New York: Zone Books, 2005).

Watenpaugh, Heghnar Zeitlian, "An uneasy historiography: the legacy of Ottoman architecture in the former Arab provinces", *Muqarnas, History and Ideology: Architectural Heritage of the "Lands of Rum"*, 24 (2007), 27–43.

Watenpaugh, Keith, *Being Modern in the Middle East: Revolution, Nationalism, Colonialism, and the Arab Middle Class* (Princeton and Oxford: Princeton University Press, 2006).

Watenpaugh, Keith D., "Middle-class modernity and the persistence of the politics of notables in inter-war Syria", *International Journal of Middle East Studies*, 35/2 (2003), 257–86.

Watts, Sheldon, "From rapid change to stasis: official responses to cholera in British-ruled India and Egypt: 1860 to c. 1921", *Journal of World History*, 12/2 (2001), 321–74.

Weber, Charlotte, "Between nationalism and feminism: the Eastern Women's Congresses of 1930 and 1932", *Journal of Middle East Women's Studies*, 4/1 (2008), 83–106.

Welchman, Lynn, *Beyond the Code: Muslim Family Law and the Shari'a Judiciary in the Palestinian West Bank* (New York: Springer, 2000).

White, Jenny B., *Islamist Mobilization in Turkey: A Study in Vernacular Politics* (Seattle: University of Washington Press, 2002).

Wickham, Carrie Rosefsky, *Mobilizing Islam: Religion, Activism, and Political Change in Egypt* (New York: Columbia University Press, 2002).

Wien, Peter, *Iraqi Arab Nationalism: Authoritarian, Totalitarian and Pro-Fascist Inclinations, 1932–1941* (London and New York: Routledge, 2006).

Wiener, Norbert, *Cybernetics; or, Control and Communication in the Animal and the Machine*, 2nd ed. (New York: MIT Press, 1965).

Wyers, Mark David, "The New Republic's 'Other' Daughters: Legislating National Sex and Regulating Prostitution in Istanbul 1880–1933", M.A. Dissertation, The University of Arizona, 2008.

Wyrtzen, Jonathan, "Colonial state-building and the negotiation of Arab and Berber identity in Protectorate Morocco", *International Journal of Middle East Studies*, special issue, *Relocating Arab Nationalism*, 43/2 (2011), 227–49.

Wyrtzen, Jonathan, *Making Morocco: Colonial Intervention and the Politics of Identity* (Ithaca: Cornell University Press, 2015).

Yamani, Mai, "Evading the habits of a life time: the adaptation of Hejazi dress to the New Social Order", in *Languages of Dress in the Middle East*, ed. Nancy Lindisfarne-Tapper and Bruce Ingham (Richmond, Surrey: Curzon, 1997), pp. 55–66.

Yurdakul, İbrahim, *Aziz Şehre Leziz Su. Dersaadet (İstanbul) Su Şirketi (1873–1933)* (Istanbul: Kitabevi, 2010).

Zürcher, Erik Jan, *Turkey: A Modern History*, 3rd ed. (London: I.B. Tauris, 2004).

Index

Abaza, Fikri 151
Abbas Hilmi II 159, 160
'Abd al-'Aziz 102n15
'Abd al-Hafidh 102
'Abduh, Muhammad 101, 102, 107n37
Abdullah, King of Jordan 17
al-'Abed, Fatima Sharifa 12, 14
al-'Abed, Muhammad 'Ali 12
Abu al-Yaqzan, Ibrahim 8
Abu Za'bal 128
Acre 239
Adana 9, 174
Aden 41, 44
Adıvar, Halide Edip 199
al-Afghani 101
Afghanistan 10, 11, 13, 41
Aftimos, Yusuf 58
Ağaoğlu, Ahmet 285
Agedabia 74n25
Ahmed Sayf al-Din, Prince 158, 159
Ahmed Şerif 170
'Ajami, Mary 14
Aka Gündüz 175
'Akrawi, Fathallah 129
'Alawi dynasty 100, 101, 101n11, 108
Alba (al-Fager) 89, 90
Aleppo 14, 18, 19, 46, 138, 140, 143
Alexandria 27, 41, 48, 147, 151, 161
Algeria 8, 11, 16, 25, 41, 86, 103, 239n2
Algiers 81
'Aluba, Muhammad 'Ali 123
American University of Beirut *See* Syrian Protestant College
Amin Zaki, Saniha 23, 25
Amir, Aziza 9
Amman 24n
Anatolia 2, 24, 130, 154, 157, 158, 164, 165n4, 167, 169, 170, 172, 173, 180, 182, 188, 211, 213, 216
Anglo-Egyptian Treaty (1936) 163
Ankara 7, 13, 25, 29, 31, 45, 45n73, 145, 149, 155, 156, 157, 158, 159, 160, 161, 166, 180, 182, 225, 226, 229, 233, 236, 238, 266n16, 268
Ankara Museum of Hygiene 177, 199, 203

Apollonia 90
Arab 8, 10, 11, 14, 16, 17, 22, 24, 29, 30, 34, 40, 49, 65, 72, 86, 95, 97, 122, 123, 126, 127, 130, 131, 135, 136, 138, 139, 142, 143, 145
Arab historiography 22, 127
Arab music 4, 54, 58, 61, 67, 69, 70, 71, 92, 93
Arab nationalism 24, 40, 64, 123, 124, 126, 127, 128, 131, 143, 160, 163
Arab press 67, 114, 134, 142, 144
Arab Café (in Suq al-Mushir, Tripoli) 4, 92, 93, 95–6
Arab Medical School 128, 133
Arabia 11, 101n10
Arabian peninsula 28
Arabic language 6, 8, 23, 24n, 65, 103n19, 107n37, 114, 118n68, 127, 128, 129, 130, 131, 133, 134, 135, 136, 137, 138, 139, 140, 141, 143, 148, 155
Arar, Asım 228, 231
Ardahan 167, 175
Arıkan, İzzet 183, 210
Arqatnaji, Yusuf 139
arsenobenzol 173
Arslan, Shakib 109, 114
Artas 243, 244, 245, 246, 250, 254
'Asir 44
Astfan, Yusuf 130
Astor, Lady 13
Aswan 138
Atatürk, Mustafa Kemal 3, 11, 13, 14, 15, 19, 24, 25, 41, 42, 144, 155, 156, 157, 160, 176, 279, 283, 287
Atay, C. 183, 184
Atay, Falih Rıfkı 29, 273
atebrine 168
Atfiyyash, Ibrahim 8
Athens 234
Australia 13
Austrian 31, 57, 219
Aytuna, Hasip Ahmet 279
Azerbaijan 11

Babini, Valentino 78, 96
Badoglio, Pietro 7, 83, 84, 85
Badr, Salim 57

Baghdad   10, 44, 45, 46, 130, 131, 132, 134, 138, 140, 141, 143
Baida, Farjallah   76
al-Balad   248, 255
Balbo, Italo   86, 87, 88, 89, 90, 90n45, 92, 93, 95
Baldensperger, P.J.   253, 256, 257
Balkan Wars   180
Balkans   9, 129, 130
Baltacıoğlu, İsmail Hakkı   282n77, 285n89
Bardia   95
Basiretçi Ali Efendi   215, 216
Bayda, Elia   64
Ba'yun, Muhyeddine   76
Bedouin   32, 51
Beirut   2, 5, 6, 10, 11, 15, 27, 28, 36, 41, 45, 46, 47n85, 48, 54, 54n3, 55, 56, 57, 58, 59, 60, 61, 62, 63, 64, 65, 65n35, 66, 67, 68, 69, 70n53, 71, 72, 73, 74, 76, 124, 126, 128, 130, 132, 134, 135, 136, 138, 139, 141, 143
Belgium   144
Bell, Gertrude   11, 15, 19, 23, 24n
Benghazi   83, 87, 88, 89, 90, 91
Berber   95, 112
Berber dahir   112, 113, 113n52, 114
Bethlehem   243
Beyoğlu   215, 217, 218, 219
bilharzia   129
Birol, Ali Esat   266
bismuth   173
Black Sea   212
Bolshevik propaganda   11
Bolshevik Revolution   58
Bolshevism   11
De Bono, Emilio   81
Bozkurt, Mahmud Esat   273
Britain   4, 129, 158, 159, 195, 234, 238
British   2, 3, 4, 6, 11, 13, 17, 18, 28, 37–8, 39, 43, 44, 46, 49, 50, 51, 80, 95, 101n11, 102n15, 131, 135, 137, 140, 141, 142, 159, 160, 161, 212, 213, 221, 239, 239n2, 248, 257, 258
British rule   2, 17, 25, 136, 156, 247
British Anti-Suffrage League   15
Buenos Aires   8
Bulgaria   7
Burhanettin Bey   234
Bursa   170, 185, 197
al-Bustani, Karam   69, 70, 71, 72

Cairo   2, 10, 11, 12, 27, 41, 46, 47, 81, 113, 124, 126, 128, 129, 134, 138, 140, 141, 142, 143, 145, 146, 147, 148, 155, 156, 157, 159, 161, 251
de Caix, Robert   18, 19, 20
Çalapala, Rakım   278, 279
Caliphate   3, 8, 17, 26, 163
Calzini, Raffaele   78
Celal Sahir   284
Çetinkaya, Ali   232
Chicago World Fair (1933)   146
child diarrhoea   182, 206, 208
China   13, 287
cholera   48, 182, 219n41, 220, 220n53, 221, 224, 225
Circassian   154, 158
Clemenceau, Georges Benjamin   2n3
Clot, Antoine Bartholomey   130
Colonial Exhibitions   3, 4
Conservatoire, Beirut   59, 60
Corbet Ashby, Mrs   13
Cumhuriyet Halk Partisi   8, 42, 186, 236, 269–70
Cyprus   131
Cyrenaica   7, 83, 85, 86
Cyrene   84n25, 90

Daccache, Laure   64
Dalgır, Recep   186
Damascus   10, 11, 13, 14, 15, 24, 35, 44, 46, 47n85, 120n74, 126, 128, 134, 136, 138, 139, 140, 141, 143, 160, 251, 252
Damascus Faculty of Medicine   135
Dannevig, Mlle   20
Davey, Richard   261, 262
Denizli   186
Denmark   157
Derna   87, 89
Dimashqiya, Julia   15
diphtheria   210
Dirik, Kazım   187, 187n127
Diyarbakır   170
Al-Duqqali, Abu Sha'ib   102
Duru, Muhittin Celal   170, 176
dysentery   182, 224

Eastern Women's Congress   10, 13, 150
Edirne   197, 221

INDEX

Egypt   6, 8, 9, 10, 14, 22, 24, 28, 39, 43, 49,
    52, 53, 56, 62, 63, 70n53, 71, 87, 88, 103,
    117n64, 124, 127, 129, 130, 136, 137, 138,
    140, 144, 145, 146, 147, 148, 149, 150, 151,
    152, 153, 154, 155, 156, 156n27, 157, 158,
    159, 161, 162, 163, 239n2, 251, 252
Egyptian   4, 14, 23, 49, 57, 59, 66, 70, 127,
    128–9, 135, 136, 138, 139, 140, 142, 145, 146,
    147, 148, 151, 152, 154, 155, 156, 157, 158,
    159, 160, 162, 163, 271
Egyptian music   61, 63, 71, 76
Egyptian press   8, 9, 12, 67, 107n37, 127, 147,
    148, 153, 156, 162
Egyptian Feminist Union   4, 147, 148, 150, 151,
    152, 153
Egyptian Association for Social Studies   5
Egyptian eye disease See trachoma
Egyptian Medical Association   10, 136, 137,
    138
Egyptian Revolution (1919)   137
Egyptian women   8, 12, 149, 150, 152, 153
Elazığ   170
Elmalı   222, 225
Ertuğ, Rüştü   207n192
erysipelas   171, 172, 173
Ethiopia   162
Europe   5, 12, 14, 20, 29, 31, 48, 54, 56, 57, 58,
    59, 60, 61, 63, 64, 65, 67, 68, 70, 73, 74,
    75, 76, 77, 81, 100n6, 101, 101n11, 103n19,
    105, 105n28, 109, 113, 117n66, 124, 126,
    129, 130, 135, 137, 144, 146, 151, 157, 159,
    161, 212, 221, 222, 262n3, 264, 264n8, 265,
    271, 278, 283
Evliya Çelebi   214

al-Fadl, Shaykh ʿAbdallah b. Muhammad   37
Faisal, King   24n, 64, 65, 120n74, 128, 160
Farkas, Nikolas   9
Al-Fassi, ʿAllal   103
Fehmi, Dr.   174, 175
Fevziye Abdürreşid   283
Fez   102n15, 103, 113, 114, 115, 118, 120
Fez Incident (1932)   155–7, 161, 162
Fezzan   79
Fiat   7
Flayfel brothers   62, 63, 64
France   59, 106, 107, 129, 159, 160, 187n123
Franco-Syrian War (1920)   64

French   2, 3, 5, 6, 8, 13, 16, 17, 18, 20, 25, 28,
    45, 46, 47n85, 59, 63, 65, 80, 106, 114, 118,
    118n69, 121, 130, 132, 133, 135, 139, 141, 160,
    182, 218n32, 221, 262
French rule   2, 11, 17, 18, 25, 36, 58, 59, 61, 72,
    86, 101, 101n11, 103n19, 105, 112, 112n50,
    113, 114, 114n56, 118, 119, 120, 121
Fuad, King   137, 148, 157, 158, 159, 160, 163

Gandhi   12
Gavrilides   9
Gaziantep   11, 170
Geneva   12, 18, 109, 129
George V   3
German   23, 31, 95, 96, 135, 216, 135
Germany   129, 268
Ghadames   78, 78n3, 79, 82, 83, 84n25, 91,
    93, 94
Gökçeli   9
Göktürk, Hüseyin Avni   266n16
gonorrhoea   171, 201, 203, 204
Gövsa, İbrahim Alaettin   274, 277
Granqvist, Hilma   243, 245, 246, 247, 249,
    250, 253, 254, 255, 256, 258
Graziani, Rodolfo   78, 79, 81, 82, 83, 95
Greece   7, 9, 14, 131, 157, 158
Green Crescent   184, 186
Güngör, Selahaddin   179
Güntekin, Reşat Nuri   164, 165, 180, 273
Gürpınar, Hüseyin Rahmi   275

Haifa   28, 36, 46
Halit Ziya   232
Halkalı   228
Halkevi (People's House)   165, 170, 179, 185,
    186, 188, 197, 260, 266n16, 279
Hall, J.H.   21
Hamada, Nur   10, 13, 150
Hamit Bey   234
Hamouda, Ibrahim   149
Hashemite   36, 38, 48, 49, 64
Hasan Fehmi Paşa   216
Hassan II   112n48
Hassar, Mohammad   120
Hatay   166
Haydarpaşa Medical College   129
Haydarpaşa Military College   23
Haykal, Muhammad Husayn   149

Hebrew press 142
Herz, George 114
Hijaz 8, 10, 32, 35, 36, 37, 38, 39, 40, 42, 43, 44, 48, 50
Hilmi Bey 223, 223
al-Hizb al-Watani 43, 44
Homs 84n25, 89
Hulusi, Behçet 187
Hüseyin Remzi 148
al-Husri, Sati' 23
Hussein, King of Hijaz 11, 17, 43

İ. Şerif 283
ibn Saud 36, 39, 40, 43, 44, 52
Ibrahim, 'Ali Basha 139
İbrahim Halil 224
İhsan Bey 234, 235
India 12, 13, 221
Indian 11, 12, 239n2
Indonesia 98n3, 109n40
İnebolu 7
İnönü, İsmet 160
International Alliance for Women for Suffrage and Equal Citizenship Conference 12, 13, 14
International Congress of Tropical Medicine 12
International Organisation of Female Doctors 12
Iran 7, 9, 40, 41, 130
Iranian 5, 7, 9, 10, 15
Iraq 2, 3, 8, 10, 15, 17, 23, 25, 124, 127, 129, 130, 131, 138, 160
Iraqi 2, 8, 10, 13, 14, 17, 127, 129, 130, 135, 136, 142n58
Iraqi Medical School 128, 130, 131
Ismail, Khedive 47
Istanbul 2, 13, 14, 23, 24, 24n, 27, 41, 45, 48, 124, 128, 129, 134, 136, 146, 147, 158, 159, 161, 166, 176, 179, 212, 213, 214, 215, 216, 217, 218, 220, 221, 222, 223, 226, 227, 228, 229, 229n99, 230, 235, 236, 237, 261
Istanbul Hygiene Museum 186, 199, 208
Istanbul Society for the Fight Against Tuberculosis 177
Istanbul (Dersaadet) Water Company 213, 218, 218n35, 222, 223, 225, 226, 227, 228, 229, 229n99, 230, 230n106, 234, 235, 236, 237, 238

Istanbul Terkos Water Company
    See Istanbul (Dersaadet) Water Company
Istiqlal 112n50
İstanbul Sokaklarında 9
Italian 5, 7, 79, 80, 85, 86, 89n, 91, 95, 96, 146
Italian rule 3, 4, 7, 78, 80, 80n8, 81, 83, 85, 86, 91, 92, 95, 96, 158
Italian Touring Club 82
Italy 11, 74, 79, 81, 86, 87, 87n34, 91, 92, 95, 96, 146, 157, 159, 162, 268
itch 190, 191
İzmir 27, 161, 166, 187, 189, 197, 201, 288

Japan 13, 138
Java 13, 44
Jazira 46
Jebel Akhdar 85
Jeddah 27, 28, 30, 32, 34, 35, 36, 37, 38, 39, 41, 44, 46, 47, 49, 50, 51, 53
Jefren 82, 84n25, 91
Jerusalem 10, 29, 46, 134, 138, 139, 141, 142, 239, 242, 255n75
Jewish 28, 43, 138, 142, 142n58
Jordan 10, 20, 21, 131, 136, 138, 160
Jufra 81

Kamil Bey 217
al-Kattani, Muhammad 102n15
al-Khattabi, 'Abd al-Karim 11
Karaosmanoğlu, Yakup Kadri 2, 273
Kastamonu 170
Kayseri 189
al-Kayyali, Sami 14
Kemalism 8, 14, 144, 145, 146, 148, 153, 162, 163, 265, 265–6n15, 277, 281, 283, 285, 285n85
Keriman Halis 9, 24, 144, 145, 146, 147, 148, 149, 150, 151, 152, 153, 154, 155, 156, 158, 161, 162, 163
Khuri, Ilias 130, 139
al-Khuri, Shakir 130
Kırklareli 183
Kırşehir 167
Kız Kulesi 6
Knox, Geoffrey 238
Kraydiya, Salim Agha 57
Kutkam, İsmail Hakkı 177, 197, 199

INDEX

al-Ladhqani, Alexi 61, 70, 70n53
Lausanne 129
League of Nations 11, 13, 18, 20, 25
Lebanon 8, 10, 25, 59, 61, 64, 71, 124, 138, 141
Lebanese 10, 14, 28, 55, 61, 127, 135, 140, 142
Lebanese Medical Association 139
Lebanese press 55, 66, 127
Lenin 179
Leptis Magna 90
Lessona, Alessandro 83
Levant 1, 8, 43, 57, 59, 71, 102, 127, 130, 134
Liberal Constitutionalist Party, Egypt 149
Libya 3, 4, 7, 78, 79, 80, 83, 84, 86, 87, 87n34, 88, 89, 90, 91, 92, 95
Libyan 4, 5, 7, 80, 85, 86, 88, 90, 91, 92, 93, 95, 96
Libyan Tourism and Hotel Association (ETAL) 91, 92, 93, 95
Linke, Lilo 9, 174
Lloyd George, David 2n3
London 12, 80, 156, 212, 221
Longuet, Jean-Robert 114
Lugard, Lord 20, 21
Luiggi, Luigi 80, 81
Luxor 138
Lyon 12, 129

MacDonald, Ramsay 3
Madrasat al-Falah 51
Mahfuz, Naguib 107n37
Mahmud Şemsi, Dr. 268, 269, 281
Makal, Mahmut 171, 188, 210
malaria 10, 139, 166, 168, 170, 171, 172, 173, 174, 175, 176, 182, 183, 187, 189, 191, 195, 196, 201, 204, 207, 208
Malatya 170
Mandate 19, 25, 28, 31, 36, 39, 54, 55, 56, 59, 61, 62, 63, 68, 73, 76, 129, 137, 139, 142, 239, 240, 241, 242, 243, 247, 248, 253, 254, 256, 257, 258
Mandate powers 16, 17, 18, 19, 20, 21, 22, 24, 29, 45, 129, 139
Mandates Commission 18, 19, 20, 21
Mansoura 155
Maraş 170
Marcel, Olivier 4
Mardin 7, 170
Marrakesch 103, 120
Marsa Brega 84, 85

Marseilles 13
Masabni, Badi'a 149
Mawlay Sulayman 101, 101n10
Mecca 35, 36, 39, 48, 50
Medina 37
Mediterranean 82, 90, 157, 212
Mehmed Ali (Muhammad 'Ali) Paşa 130, 134, 138, 158
Meknes 117, 119
mercury 173, 173n41
Mevhibe İclal 280
Mishaqa, Michel 134
Misratah 83, 84n25, 87, 89
missionaries 54, 61, 130
Mohammed V (Sidi Mohammed) 112n48, 114, 120, 121
Mohammed bin 'Isa 117
Montpellier 129
Morocco 3, 6, 7, 8, 16, 86, 97, 98, 98n3, 99, 100, 100n8, 101, 102, 103, 104, 105n28, 106, 108, 113, 114, 115, 117, 118n69, 119, 120
Moroccan 98, 100n8, 102, 103n16, 104, 105, 112n48, 112n50, 113, 114, 115, 116, 117, 118, 118n67, 118n69, 120
Moroccan nationalism 11, 100n6, 102, 109, 112, 112n50, 119, 120
Moroccan press 114, 121
Moroccan reformists 104, 109, 112
Mosul 23
Moulay Idriss II 115
Mount Lebanon 130
Moyal, Esther Azhari 68, 69
Muğla 184, 210
Muhammad Hilmi 'Isa Paşa 149
Muhittin Bey 234
Muhsin Ertuğrul 9
al-Mukhtar, 'Umar 86
Münir Paşa 218
Münire Handan 283
al-Murr, Mitri 59, 62, 63, 64, 65
Mussolini, Benito 85, 87, 88
Mustafa Kemal *See* Atatürk

Nabarawi, Saiza 148
Nablus 239, 244, 247, 248, 254
Naciri, Mekki 113
Nahda 54, 55, 60, 68, 70, 72, 75
Najd 37, 38, 39, 40
Nalut 82, 91, 93, 94

National Turkish Students Association   168, 186
neosalvarsan   168, 173
Neşet Ömer   179
Nevuea-Lemaire, Endjun   129
Nevzad, Dr.   182
Nicolson, Harold   2n3
Nuri Fehmi, Dr.   181, 186, 200
Nüzhet Abbas   271

Ömer Rıza   270
oriental sore   170
Örik, Nahid Sırrı   180
Ottoman   2, 5, 9, 17, 18, 20, 21, 22, 23, 25, 26, 27, 30, 32, 34, 34n25, 50, 57, 65, 128, 129, 131, 132, 134, 157, 178, 213, 215, 219, 221, 223, 224, 230, 231, 232, 234, 236, 237, 238, 239, 240, 260, 260n, 261, 262, 262n3, 263, 264, 275, 284n85, 287
Ottoman empire   6, 16, 17, 18, 22, 36, 39, 40, 42, 53, 61, 80n8, 100, 101n11, 124, 129, 131, 132, 174, 175n50, 214, 215, 259, 264, 265
Ottoman Law of Family Rights (Hukuk-ı Aile Karanamesi) (1917)   20, 21, 239, 240, 241, 245, 246, 249, 250, 252, 255, 256, 257, 258
Ottoman Medical School of Damascus   128, 130, 133
Ottoman past   1, 16, 17, 18, 20, 22, 23, 24, 25, 27, 28, 29, 32, 34, 35, 36, 38, 48, 51, 52, 53, 145, 157, 158, 185, 212, 242, 251, 252, 253, 260, 261, 267, 267n18, 272, 277, 282, 284, 287
Ottoman rule   16, 17, 18, 21, 33, 61, 100, 132, 133, 170, 175
Ottoman Second Constitutional Era   260, 264, 284
Özgen, İhsan   197, 199, 200, 207

Palacios   21
Palestine   8, 10, 13, 19, 20, 21, 43, 52, 124, 127, 130, 131, 132, 134, 136, 138, 141, 142, 143, 160, 239, 240, 241, 244, 245, 247, 248, 249, 250, 252, 253, 254, 255, 256, 257, 258
Palestinian Medical Association   136
Pan-Islamism   11–12, 101, 117n64, 124, 127
Paris   9, 57, 59, 80, 114, 129, 136, 144, 216
Peyami Safa   285
Piccioli, Angelo   85

Piraeus   161
Poland   9
Pyramids   6, 139

Qamishli   46
Qarawiyyin   102, 103
Qasr al 'Aini   129, 130, 132, 134, 136
quarantine   48, 49, 209, 221
quinine   168, 175, 184, 195

Rabat   103, 113, 114, 118, 120
Rabbat, Edmond   14
al-Racy, Salam   54
Ramallah   254n74
Rappard   19
Red Crescent   186
Red Sea   48
relapsing fever   179, 180
Republican People's Party See Cumhuriyet Halk Partisi
Reşit Galip   172, 176n53, 179, 181, 201
Reza Shah   9
Riyadh   46
de Robeck   11
Rome   12, 85
Rommel   95
Russian   57, 58, 226

Sa'adi dynasty   100, 100n8
Sabra, Wadi'   59, 60, 61, 62, 63, 70, 70n53
Sabrata   90
Sadri Sema   220, 220n53
Safranbolu   172
Sagiati, Marguerite   18, 19
Sahara   78, 84, 90, 93, 94
St. Joseph   128, 130
Salafi   8, 11, 22, 102, 103, 104, 109, 117
Salé   103, 113, 118, 120
al-Salih Missa, Mohammed   114
Samsun   7
al-Sanussi, 'Abdallah   102
São Paulo   8
Saudia Arabia   10, 28, 36, 38, 39, 40, 41, 44, 47, 48, 49, 50, 51, 52, 53, 138
al-Sawi Muhammad, Ahmad   152
Saydam, Refik   167, 169, 186
Saylam, M.   167
Sayyah, Fatimih   15
Sbihi, Abdellatif   113

INDEX

scarlet fever 193
Şemseddin Sami 262
Senih Müşir 287, 287n97
Senussi 85
Sertel, Sabiha Zekeriya 286n89
Sertel, Zekeriya 285
Shafik, Doria 152
Shakir, Fa'iq 142
Shalfoun, Iskandar 70n53
Shallash, Ramadan 24
al-Sha'rawi, Huda 14, 147, 148, 150, 151, 152
al-Shaykh, 'Abd al-Malik b. Ibrahim 39
Shumayl, Shibly 134
al-Sidawi, Sami 64
Sidi Muhammad 104
Siirt 170
Sinop 173
Sirt 82, 84n25, 85
Sivas 7, 172, 187
smallpox 175n50, 176, 192, 193, 196, 200
Society for the Protection of Youth 186, 197
solusalvarsan 173
Spain 101, 157
al-Sqalli, Mohammed 117
Suakin 43
al-Suda, Chikri Afandi 59
Sudan 10, 131, 138
Suez Canal 12
Şükufe Nihal 273
Sulayman, 'Abdallah 38
Sururi, Ahmad 136
Switzerland 31, 159, 267
syphilis 142, 166, 169, 170, 173, 174, 186n115, 187, 197, 199, 201, 203, 204, 205, 207, 208, 209, 267, 269
Syria 2, 8, 9, 10, 13, 18, 19, 21, 31, 46, 49, 52, 53, 64, 65, 71, 106n32, 124, 127, 133, 135, 138, 141, 143, 144, 160, 161, 239n2, 252
Syrian Protestant College 128, 130, 131, 132, 141

Tabet, Jacques 58
Tabriz 7
Ta'if 43, 44, 48
Taj, Youssef 76
Talaat, Harb 47
Talat Bey 167, 175
al-Tamimi, Rushdi 143
Tanpınar, Ahmet Hamdi 5
Tanrıöver, Hamdullah Suphi 273
Tanzimat 34n25, 54, 262
Tarcan, Selim Sırrı 187
Tehran 10, 13, 45, 150
Terakkiperver Cumhuriyet Fırkası 42
Terkos 212, 214, 215, 216, 217, 218, 219, 220, 220n46, 221, 222, 224, 225, 226, 227, 229, 229n99, 230, 234, 236, 237
Terkos Water Company See Istanbul (Dersaadet) Water Company
Tevfik Fikret 23
Theodoli, Marquis 19, 21
Thrace 183, 189, 197, 210
Tobruk 87, 88, 90, 95
Topuzlu, Cemil 187
Trabzon 7
trachoma 142, 164, 166, 170, 181, 182, 186n115, 188, 189, 191, 193, 194, 195, 200, 201, 202, 210
Transjordan See Jordan
Treaty of Fez (1912) 113
Tripoli 3, 4, 8, 35, 78, 79, 80, 81, 82, 83, 87, 88, 89, 90, 91, 92, 93
Tripolitania 7, 78, 80n8, 81n12, 83, 86
tuberculosis 170, 171, 172, 177, 182, 183, 186, 187, 190, 191, 201, 204, 267, 269
Tunisia 8, 86, 87, 88
Tuqan, Fadwa 248
Turk 11, 14, 17, 23, 24, 49, 154, 158, 159, 181, 268n21, 275, 276, 282, 286, 288, 289
Turkey 1, 2, 6, 7, 8, 9, 10, 11, 12, 13, 14, 15, 16, 17, 19, 21, 22, 23, 24, 25, 26, 28, 29, 31, 36, 39, 40, 41, 42, 45, 49, 52, 74, 144, 145, 146, 147, 148, 149, 150, 152, 153, 154, 155, 156, 157, 158, 159, 160, 161, 162, 163, 164, 165, 166, 167, 169, 170, 173, 174, 175, 185, 187, 190, 211, 212, 213, 214, 223, 224, 227, 229, 230, 231, 232, 234, 237, 239, 259, 260, 260n, 261, 262, 263, 264, 265, 265, 266n15, 266n16, 267, 267n18, 268, 268n21, 270, 271, 272, 273, 275, 276, 276n48, 277, 281, 282, 282n77, 283, 284, 284n84, 284n85, 285n85, 285n89, 286, 287, 288, 289
Turkish Benevolent Society, Cairo 148
Turkish language 6, 23, 33, 34, 143, 148, 155, 187, 260, 270
Turkish National Liberation War 166, 178, 182
Turkish press 9, 13, 148, 153, 154, 155, 156

Turkish propoganda 7–8, 150, 164
Turkish women 14, 15, 24, 144, 155, 162, 280, 283, 286, 287, 288, 289
Turkish Women's Union 42, 285
typhus 178, 180, 181, 182, 224, 225, 232
typhoid 222

Uludağ, Osman Şevki 177
Umm Kulthum 149
United States 12, 15, 49, 50, 68, 129, 146, 148, 153, 187, 204, 212, 271
Urfa 170
Üsküdar-Kadıköy Water Company 218, 220, 222, 223, 225

Vala Nureddin 273n42, 280, 285n89
venereal diseases 184, 185, 189, 197, 199, 200, 204, 208, 267
Vienna 80, 219, 221, 234
Volpi, Giuseppe 78, 79, 81, 85, 93

ibn 'Abd al-Wahhab 101, 101n10
Wahhabi 39, 51, 52
Washington 13
Wassef, Charlotte 152
al-Wazzani, Mohammed Hassan 109, 110, 111, 112, 112n50, 114, 118
Wilson, C.T. 248, 254
Wilson, Woodrow 2n3, 11
Wissa, Esther 4
Women's Arabic Assembly 10
Women's International League for Peace and Freedom 12

Women's Party (Iran) 15
Woodsmall, Ruth 248
World War I 1, 6, 12, 15, 17, 24, 36, 41, 46, 54, 57, 68, 100n8, 102, 106, 137, 159, 178, 180, 226–7, 228, 239
World War II 1, 28, 42, 47, 53, 95, 120n74, 163, 168, 180, 237

Yalçın, Hüseyin Cahid 269, 273, 276
Yasami, Rashid 16
al-Yaziji, Ibrahim 134
al-Yaziji, Sheikh Nasif 54
Yemen 28, 32, 33, 39, 138
Yifran 93, 94
Yılal, Mustafa Musa 195
Young, M.A. 21
Young Moroccans 103, 104, 113
Young Ottomans 41
Young Turks 41, 103
Young Turk Revolution (1908) 41
Yunus Nadi 226, 236

Zaghloul, Safiyya 150, 150n15
al-Zayani, Abu al-Qassim 101n10
Zehrap Efendi 222
Zeki Nasır 165, 169, 233
al-Z'inni, 'Umar 59, 62, 63, 64, 71, 72
Zionism 131, 142, 143, 239
Ziraat Bankası 168
Ziya Bey 234
Zuwarah 83, 84n25, 88, 90

Printed in the United States
By Bookmasters